THE RISE OF MODERN RELIGIOUS IDEAS IN AMERICA

– Editorial Director –

SYDNEY E. AHLSTROM, American Studies Program, Yale University

EDWARD HITCHCOCK, D.D., LL.D.

The Religion of Geology
and Its Connected Sciences

BS
657
. H53
1975

Reprint Edition
with a New Introduction

THE REGINA PRESS

Reprint Edition 1975

THE REGINA PRESS
7 Midland Avenue
Hicksville, New York 11801

New Introduction © 1975 by The Regina Press

Library of Congress Catalog Number: 74-78277
International Standard Book Number: 0-88271-014-1

Manufactured in the United States of America.

NEW INTRODUCTION TO THE REPRINT EDITION
by Conrad Wright,
Harvard Divinity School

EDWARD HITCHCOCK (1793-1864) lived at a time when the dividing lines between the professions were less sharply marked than now, and it was perhaps easier to make one's mark in more than one of them. He was a clergyman, who served for a time as the Congregational minister in Conway, Massachusetts; he was a scientist, responsible for official geological surveys of Massachusetts (1833) and Vermont (1861); and he was an educator, teaching scientific subjects, especially geology, at Amherst College, of which he was President from 1845 to 1854.

He is best remembered today for his scientific work. As a field geologist, he prepared the first scientific reports on the dinosaur tracks in the red sandstone of the Connecticut valley, and he explored extensively the problem of the surface deposits, or "drift," which Agassiz attributed to a continental ice sheet. As a leader of the nascent scientific community, he was the first chairman of the Association of American Geologists which later developed into the American Association for the Advancement of Science.

But in his own mind, he was a minister first of all, and his educational and scientific work fell into place around the ministry as his primary career. Amherst College had a strongly evangelical religious tradition. As President, Hitchcock was concerned for the religious well-being of the students, and fostered revivals among them with conspicuous success. His scientific work he regarded as ancillary to a greater objective, the glorification of God by means of a reverent understanding of his Creation. The term "natural theology" is the traditional one used to identify precisely this concern; and so the title of Hitchcock's chair from 1845 on quite properly was: Professor of Natural Theology and Geology.

Hitchcock dreamed of preparing a complete treatise on Natural Theology, "in which all its great principles should be stated and fully illustrated by modern science." His administrative duties interfered, however, and he regarded *The Religion of Geology* and various articles in periodicals as but "insulated fragments" of a larger grand design. *The Religion of Geology* nevertheless reveals sufficiently well his methods and assumptions, and points to two kinds of problems for the "natural theologian" to grapple with.

3m

In the first place, if God reveals himself both through his Creation and through the particular revelation of Scripture, there cannot be any real contradiction between the two. Apparent contradictions must be reconciled in such a way as to respect the claims of both. In an earlier century, this problem was confronted in terms of astronomy, when Copernicus insisted that the earth was not the fixed point around which the heavens revolved. For the generation following Hitchcock, the problem would be confronted in terms of biology, with the Darwinian theory of the origin of species. But in Hitchcock's day, the question at issue was a geological one, the age of the earth. Was the world created in six days, perhaps in the year 4004 B. C.? Or must long periods of geologic time be postulated, if we are to explain the thick layers of sediments and the evidences of crumpled rocks in the earth's crust. As a geologist, Hitchcock was committed to the latter view, and he reconciled it with the Book of Genesis by accepting the argument that the "six days of creation" were not the creation of the world *ab initio*, but rather its subsequent preparation to be the habitation of mankind. The long periods of geologic time were accepted; the age of the earth was as great as any geological evidence might require; but the Bible concerns itself only with that part of geologic time that is relevant to human life and the salvation of human souls.

In the second place, if God's Creation is necessarily an expression of his will, his attributes may be discovered in it, as well as in the Bible. Hence *The Religion of Geology* devotes chapters to the support given by geological science to such theological concepts as divine benevolence, providence, and the unity of God's plan.

It was a matter of prime consequence that among religious leaders there should have been some who, like Hitchcock, did not fear modern science, but insisted that religious truths must be in harmony with it. In the short run, the way was opened for the development of Progressive Orthodoxy later in the century and Modernism therafter. But it was ironical that the particular arguments used by Hitchcock to accommodate Genesis and geology should have rested to the extent they did on the concept of a purposive adaptation by God between organisms and their environments. It was precisely this kind of adaptation that Darwinism cast into question, giving encouragement in the long run to a purely naturalistic world-view. Consider a characteristic argument by Hitchcock in proof of the divine benevolence, based on the distribution of water on the earth's surface: "We should expect that on so uneven a surface as the earth presents, that this element . . . must be very unequally distributed, and fail entirely in many places; and yet we find it in almost every spot where man erects his habitation." This argument was persuasive to one of the foremost scientific minds in America in 1851! Little wonder that many religious people, deeply committed to this kind of argument for the existence of God and proof of his benevolence, were distressed when it was undercut by the publication of *The Origin of Species* in 1859. And little wonder that *The Religon of Geology*, which was issued in a second and enlarged edition that very same year was not reprinted again.

Bibliographical suggestions: For Hitchcock in relationship to his American contemporaries, see Conrad Wright, "The Religion of Geology," *New England Quarterly*, 14 (1941): 335-358. For parallel developments in Great Britain, with which Hitchcock was in touch, see Charles C. Gillispie, *Genesis and Geology* (Cambridge, Mass.: Harvard University Press, 1951). Hitchcock's scientific achievement is placed in the context of the history of science in America in Dirk J. Struik, *Yankee Science in the Making* (Boston: Little, Brown and Co., 1948).

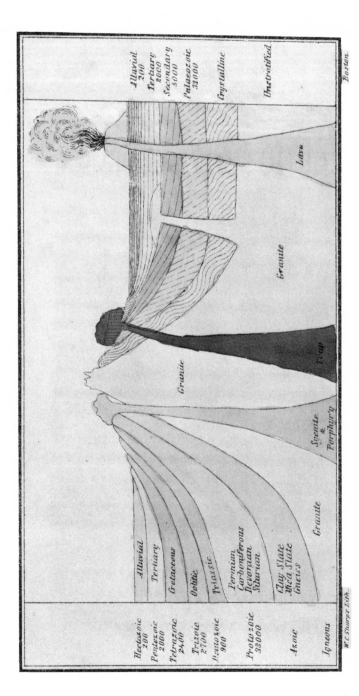

SECTION OF THE EARTH'S CRUST.

W.C. Sharpe Lith.

Boston.

THE

L. C. Boynton

RELIGION OF GEOLOGY

AND ITS

CONNECTED SCIENCES.

BY

EDWARD HITCHCOCK, D. D., LL. D.,

PRESIDENT OF AMHERST COLLEGE, AND PROFESSOR OF NATURAL THEOLOGY
AND GEOLOGY.

"Science has a foundation, and so has religion; let them unite their foundations, and the basis will be broader, and they will be two compartments of one great fabric reared to the glory of God. Let the one be the outer and the other the inner court. In the one, let all look, and admire, and adore; and in the other, let those who have faith kneel, and pray, and praise. Let the one be the sanctuary where human learning may present its richest incense as an offering to God; and the other the holiest of all, separated from it by a veil now rent in twain, and in which, on a blood-sprinkled mercy seat, we pour out the love of a reconciled heart, and hear the oracles of the living God." — *M'Cosh.*

BOSTON:

PHILLIPS, SAMPSON, AND COMPANY.

1852.

STEREOTYPED AT THE
BOSTON STEREOTYPE FOUNDRY.

TO MY BELOVED WIFE.

BOTH gratitude and affection prompt me to dedicate these lectures to you. To your kindness and self-denying labors I have been mainly indebted for the ability and leisure to give any successful attention to scientific pursuits. Early should I have sunk under the pressure of feeble health, nervous despondency, poverty, and blighted hopes, had not your sympathies and cheering counsels sustained me. And during the last thirty years of professional labors, how little could I have done in the cause of science, had you not, in a great measure, relieved me of the cares of a numerous family! Furthermore, while I have described scientific facts with the pen only, how much more vividly have they been portrayed by your pencil! And it is peculiarly appropriate that your name should be associated with mine in any literary effort where the theme is geology; since your artistic skill has done more than my voice to render that science attractive to the young men whom I have instructed. I love especially to connect your name with an effort to

defend and illustrate that religion which I am sure is
dearer to you than every thing else. I know that you
would forbid this public allusion to your labors and sacrifices, did I not send it forth to the world before it
meets your eye. But I am unwilling to lose this opportunity of bearing a testimony which both justice and
affection urge me to give. In a world where much is
said of female deception and inconstancy, I desire to
testify that one man at least has placed implicit confidence in woman, and has not been disappointed. Through
many checkered scenes have we passed together, both
on the land and the sea, at home and in foreign countries;
and now the voyage of life is almost ended. The ties
of earthly affection, which have so long united us in
uninterrupted harmony and happiness, will soon be sun-
dered. But there are ties which death cannot break;
and we indulge the hope that by them we shall be
linked together and to the throne of God through
eternal ages.

In life and in death I abide

Your affectionate husband,

EDWARD HITCHCOCK.

PREFACE.

Most of the following lectures were written as much as eight or ten years ago, though additions and alterations have been made, from time to time, to adapt them to the progress of science. They were undertaken at the suggestion of my friend, Rev. Henry Neill, then of Hatfield, now of Lenox. I had no definite intention as to the use to be made of the lectures; but having for many years turned my attention to the bearings of science, and especially of geology, upon religion, I felt a desire to put upon paper the final results of my examinations. I threw them into the lecture form, that I might, if best, deliver them to the geological classes which I should instruct in the college with which I am connected. This I have done for many years, and also have used them in various places before lyceums. They are at length published, from a conviction that something of the kind, from some quarter, is needed. Many of the thoughts, indeed, which, at the time they were put upon paper, were original, have since been brought out by other writers. Yet enough of this description probably remain to expose me to severe criticism. I beg the intelligent Christian, however, before he condemns my views, to settle it in his mind what he can substitute for them that will be more honorable to religion. It is much easier to find fault with a mode of defending the truth than to invent a

a *

better method. We may not be pleased with certain views in
vindication of religion, and yet the alternative of rejecting
them may be so much worse as to lead us at least to be silent.
Would that Christian critics had always kept this fact in mind
when writing upon the views of geologists! They would
find often that they are straining at a gnat and must swallow
a camel.

If my views are erroneous, as exhibited in these lectures, I
cannot plead that they have been hastily adopted. Most of
them, indeed, have been the subjects of thought occasionally
for thirty years. I hope, however, that all my suggestions
will not be thought of equal importance in my own estima-
tion; since some of them are merely hypothetical hints
thrown out for the consideration of abler minds.

This work does not exhibit quite so much of logical exactness
as I could wish. But my leading object has been fully carried
out, viz., to exhibit all the religious bearings of geology.
Several of the lectures, however, have been written as if independent of all the rest; and, therefore, the reader will find
some leading thoughts repeated, but always in different
connections.

After acknowledging that more than a quarter of a century
has elapsed since this subject first engaged my attention, it
may be useless for me to ask any indulgence from criticism.
But really, I feel less prepared to write upon it than I did
during the first five years in which I studied it. I have learnt
that it is a most difficult subject. It requires, in order to master it, an acquaintance with three distinct branches of knowledge, not apt to go together. First, an acquaintance with
geology in all its details, and with the general principles of
zoölogy, botany, and comparative anatomy ; secondly, a
knowledge of sacred hermeneutics, or the principles of inter-

preting the Scriptures; thirdly, a clear conception of the principles of natural and revealed religion.

As examples of efforts made by men who were deficient in a knowledge of some of these branches, I am compelled to quote a large proportion of the works which, within the last thirty or forty years, have been written on the religion of geology; especially on its connection with revealed religion. I am happy to except such writers as Dr. J. Pye Smith, Dr. Chalmers, Dr. Harris, Dr. Buckland, Professor Sedgwick, Professor Whewell, Dr. King, Dr. Anderson, and Hugh Miller; for they, to a greater or less extent, acquainted themselves with all the subjects named above, before they undertook to write. But a still larger number of authors, although men of talents, and familiar, it may be, with the Bible and theology, had no accurate knowledge of geology. The results have been, first, that, by resorting to denunciation and charges of infidelity, to answer arguments from geology which they did not understand, they have excited unreasonable prejudices and alarm among common Christians respecting that science and its cultivators; secondly, they have awakened disgust, and even contempt, among scientific men, especially those of sceptical tendencies, who have inferred that a cause which resorts to such defences must be very weak. They have felt very much as a good Greek scholar would, who should read a severe critique upon the style of Isocrates, or Demosthenes, and, before he had finished the review, should discover internal evidence that the writer had never learnt the Greek alphabet.

On the other hand, prejudices and disgust equally strong have been produced in the mind of many a man well versed in theology and biblical exegesis by some productions of scientific men upon the religious bearings of geology, because

they advanced principles which the merest tyro in divinity
would know to be false and fatal to religion, and which they
advocated only because they had never studied the Bible or
theology.

And here I would remark that it does not follow, because a
man is eminent in geology, that his opinion is of any value
upon the religion of geology. For the two subjects are quite
distinct. And a man may be a Coryphæus in the principles
of geology, who is an ignoramus in its religious applications.
Indeed, many of the ablest writers upon geology take the
ground that its religious bearings do not belong to the science.

These statements, instead of pleading my apology for the
following work, may only show my temerity and vanity. Nevertheless, they afford me an opportunity of calling the attention
of the religious public to the great inadequacy of the means now
possessed of acquiring a knowledge of the different branches
of natural science. I refer especially to comparative anatomy, zoölogy, botany, and geology, in our literary and theological seminaries. The latter, so far as I know, do not pretend to give any instruction in these branches. And in our
colleges that instruction is confined almost entirely to a few
brief courses of lectures ; often so few that the students
scarcely find out how ignorant they are of the subjects ; and
hence those who are expecting to enter the sacred ministry
vainly imagine that, at almost any period of their future
course, they can, in a few weeks, become sufficiently acquainted with physical science to meet and refute the sceptic.
In all our seminaries, however, abundant provision is made,
as it ought to be, for the study of intellectual philosophy and
biblical interpretation.

So well satisfied are two of the most enlightened and efficient Christian denominations in Great Britain — the Congre-

gationalists and the Scottish Free Church — of the need of more extensive acquaintance with the natural sciences in ministers of the gospel, that they have attached a professorship of natural history to their theological seminaries. That in the New College in Edinburgh is filled by the venerable Dr. Fleming; that in the New College in London by Dr. Lankester. From a syllabus of Dr. Fleming's course of lectures, which he put into my hands last summer, I perceive that it differs little from the instruction in natural science in the colleges of our country. This being the case, it strikes me that this is not exactly the professorship that is needed in the theological seminaries of our country. But they do need, it seems to me, professorships of natural theology, to be filled by men who are practically familiar with the natural sciences. If any such chairs exist in these seminaries, I do not know it. They are amply provided with instruction in the metaphysics of theology, hermeneutics, and ecclesiastical history; and I should be sorry to see these departments less amply provided for. But here is the wide field of natural theology, large enough for several professorships, which finds no place, save a nook in the chair of dogmatics. This might have answered well enough when the battle-field with scepticism lay in the region of metaphysics, or history, or biblical interpretation. But the enemy have, within a few years past, intrenched themselves within the dominions of natural science; and there, for a long time to come, must be the tug of the war. And since they have substituted skeletons, and trees, and stones, as weapons, in the place of abstractions, so must Christians do, if they would not be defeated. Let me refer to a few examples to show how inadequately furnished the minister must be for such a contest, who has used only the means of instruction provided in our existing seminaries, literary and theological.

Take the leading points discussed in the following lectures.
How can a man who has heard only a brief and hurried
course of thirty lectures on chemistry, twenty on anatomy
and physiology, fifteen upon zoölogy, ten upon botany, ten
upon mineralogy, and twenty upon geology, at the college,
with no additional instruction at the theological seminary, —
how can he judge correctly of points and reasoning difficult
to be mastered by adepts in these sciences ? How certain to
be worsted in an argument with an accomplished naturalist
who is a sceptic !

Suppose the sceptic takes the ground advocated by Oken
and the author of the " Vestiges." Let the clergyman, whom
I have supposed, read the works of Miller and Sedgwick in
reply to the development hypothesis, and see whether he can
even understand their arguments without a more careful study
of the sciences on which they rest.

A subject of no small importance in its religious bearings
has recently excited a good deal of sharp discussion in this
country. I refer to the questions of the specific unity and
unity of origin of the human race. To a person who has
never studied the subject, it seems a matter easy to settle ;
yet, in fact, it demands extensive research even to understand.
And we have seen one of the most accomplished zoölogists
and anatomists of the present age take ground on these points
in opposition to the almost universal opinion. The result has
been that not a few talented replies to his arguments have
appeared, mostly, I believe, from ministers. I have not seen
them all. But in respect to those which I have read it has
seemed to me, without having the least sympathy with the
views of Professor Agassiz, that the authors have not the most
remote conception of the principal arguments on which he
relies, derived from zoölogy and comparative anatomy ; nor

do I believe that they can understand and appreciate them until they have studied those sciences.*

Although I fear that theologians are not aware of the fact, yet probably the doctrines of materialism are more widely embraced at this day than almost any other religious error. But in which of our schools, save the medical, is there any instruction given in physiology and zoölogy, that will prepare a man to make the least headway against such delusions? The arguments by which materialism is defended are among the most subtle in the whole range of theology and natural science; and without a knowledge of the latter they can neither be appreciated nor refuted. The mere metaphysical abstractions by which they are usually met excite only the contempt of the acute physiologist who is a materialist.

I might refer, in this connection, to the whole subject of pantheism, in its chameleon forms. The rhapsodies of spiritual pantheism must, indeed, be met by metaphysics equally transcendental. But, after all, it is from biology that the pantheist derives his choicest weapons. He appeals, also, to astronomy, zoölogy, and geology; nor is it the superficial naturalist that can show how hollow is the foundation on which he rests.

These are only a few examples of the points of physical science on which scepticism at this moment has batteries erected with which to assail spiritual religion. Will the minister but slightly familiar with the ground chosen by the enemy be able not only to silence his guns, but, as every able defender of the truth ought to do, to turn them against its foes?

* I ought surely to except the work of Professor Bachman, which I have not read, but which was certainly written by an able naturalist.

Surely it needs a professor of natural theology in our theological seminaries, (and if such chairs existed in our colleges they would be serviceable,) to teach those who expect to be officers in the sacramental host how to carry on the holy war. I do not see how much more time can be given to the natural sciences in our colleges than is usually done, without encroaching upon other indispensable branches. If, therefore, provision be not made for studying the religious bearings of these sciences in our theological seminaries, our youthful evangelists must go forth to their work without the ability to vindicate the cause of religion against the assaults of the sceptical naturalist. Would not, then, those wealthy and benevolent individuals be great public benefactors, who should endow professorships of natural religion in our schools of the prophets?

But I must not pursue this subject farther. I commit my work to the public with no raised expectations of its welcome reception. I have a high opinion of the enlightened candor of the educated classes of our country, especially those in the ministry. Yet I know that many prejudices exist against science in its connections with religion. And, therefore, my only hope of any measure of success in this effort rests upon the divine blessing. But if the work be not pleasing to Infinite Wisdom and Benevolence, why should I desire for it an ephemeral success among men?

AMHERST COLLEGE, May 1, 1851.

EXPLANATION OF THE FRONTISPIECE.

THIS section of the earth's crust is intended to bring under the eye the leading features of geology.

1. *The relative Position of the Stratified and the Unstratified Rocks.*

The unstratified rocks, viz., granite, sienite, porphyry, trap, and lava, are represented as lying beneath the stratified class, for the most part, yet piercing through them in the centre of the section, and by several dikes or veins, through which masses have been protruded to the surface. The unstratified class are all colored red, to indicate their igneous origin. Granite seems to have been first melted and protruded, and it continued to be pushed upward till the close of the secondary period of the stratified rocks, as is shown by the vein of granite on the section. Sienite and porphyry seem to have been next thrust up, from below the granite; next, the varieties of trap were protruded from beneath the porphyry; and last, the lava, which still continues to be poured out upon the surface from beneath all the rest.

2. *The Stratified Rocks.*

The stratified rocks represented on both flanks of the granite peak in the section, appear to have been deposited from water, and subsequently more or less lifted up, fractured, and bent. An attempt is made, on the right hand side of the section, to exhibit the foldings and inclination of the strata. The lowest are bent the most, and their dip is the greatest; and, as a general fact, there is a gradual approach to horizontality as we rise on the scale.

3. *The right hand side of the Section.*

The strata on the right hand are divided into five classes: first and lowest, *the crystalline*, or *primary*, destitute of organic remains, and probably metamorphosed from a sedimentary to a crystalline state, by the action of subjacent heat. 2. *The palæozoic class*, or those containing the earliest types of animals and plants, and of vast thickness, mostly deposited in the ocean. 3. *The secondary class*, reaching from the top of the lower new red or Permian system, to the top of the chalk. 4. *The tertiary strata*, partially consolidated, and differing entirely from the rocks below by their organic contents. 5. *Alluvium*, or strata now in a course of deposition. This classification is sometimes convenient, and frequently used by geologists.

4. *The left hand Side.*

On the left hand side of the section the strata are so divided as to correspond to the six great groups of animals and plants that have appeared on the globe. The names attached to the groups are derived from ζωὸς, (*vivus*, living,) with the Greek numerals prefixed. The lowest group, being destitute of organic remains, is called *azoic*, (from α privitive and ζωὸς,) that is, wanting in the traces of life ; and corresponds to the crystalline group on the other side of the section, embracing gneiss, mica slate, limestone, and clay slate, of unknown thickness. The *protozoic group* corresponds to the palæozoic of the right hand side, and embraces lower and upper Silurian, Devonian, or old red sandstone, the carboniferous group, and the Permian, or lower new red ; the whole in Great Britain not less than thirty-three thousand feet thick. The *deutozoic group* consists only of the triassic, or upper new red sandstone, and is only nine hundred feet thick, but marks a distinct period of life. The *tritozoic* embraces the lias and oölite, with the Wealden, and is three thousand six hundred feet thick. The *tetrazoic* consists of the chalk and green sand, one thousand five hundred feet thick. The *pentezoic* embraces the tertiary strata of the thickness of two thousand feet. The *hectozoic* is confined to the modern deposits, only a few hundred feet thick, but entombing all the existing species of animals.

5. *Characteristic Organic Remains.*

Had space permitted, I should have put upon the section a reference to the most characteristic and peculiar mineral, animal, or plant, in the different groups. Thus the azoic group is *crystalliferous*, or crystal-bearing. The lower or Silurian part of the protozoic group is *brachiopodiferous, trilobiferous, polypiferous*, and *cephalopodiferous ;* that is, abounding in brachiopod and cephalopod shells ; in polypifers, or corals ; and in trilobites, a family of crustaceans. The middle part, or the Devonian, is *thaumichthiferous*, or containing remarkable fish. The upper part, or the coal measures, is *carboniferous ;* that is, abounding in coal. The *deutozoic group* is *ichniferous*, or track-bearing, from the multitude of its fossil footmarks. The *tritozoic group* is *reptiliferous*, or reptile-bearing, from the extraordinary lizards which abound in it. The *tetrazoic* is *foraminiferous*, from the abundance of coral animalcula, called foraminifera, or polythalmia, which it contains. The *pentezoic* is *mammaliferous*, because it contains the remains of mammalia, or quadrupeds. The *hectozoic* is *homoniferous*, or man-bearing, because it embraces human remains.

There is no one place on earth where all the facts exhibited on this section are presented before us together. Yet all the facts occur somewhere, and this section merely brings them into systematic arrangement.

CONTENTS.

THE

RELIGION OF GEOLOGY.

LECTURE I.

REVELATION ILLUSTRATED BY SCIENCE.

THE leading object, which I propose in the course of lectures which I now commence, is to develop the relations between geology and religion. This cannot be done fully and fairly, however, without exhibiting also many of the religious bearings of several other sciences. I shall, therefore, feel justified in drawing illustrations and arguments from any department of human knowledge which may afford them. I place geology first and most conspicuous on the list, because I know of no other branch of physical science so prolific in its religious applications.

In treating of this subject, I shall first exhibit the relations between science and revealed religion, and afterwards between science and natural religion; though in a few cases these two great branches cannot be kept entirely distinct.

Geology is usually regarded as having only an unfavorable bearing upon revealed religion; and writers are generally satisfied if they can reconcile apparent discrepancies. But I regard this as an unfair representation; for if geology, or any

1

other science, proves to us that we have not fairly understood the meaning of any passage of Scripture, it merely illustrates, but does not oppose, revelation.

A fundamental principle of Protestant Christianity is, that the Scriptures of the Old and New Testaments are the only infallible standard of religious truth ; and I desire to hold up this principle prominently at the outset, as one to which I cordially subscribe. The mass of evidence in favor of the divine inspiration of the Bible is too great to be set aside by any thing short of scientific demonstration. Were the Scriptures to teach that the whole is not equal to its parts, the mind could not, indeed, believe it. But if it taught a truth which was only contrary to the probable deductions of science, science, I say, must yield to Scripture ; for it would be more reasonable to doubt the probabilities of a single science, than the various and most satisfactory evidence on which revelation rests. I do not believe that even the probabilities of any science are in collision with Scripture. But the supposition is made to show how strong are my convictions of the evidence and paramount authority of the Bible.

But does it follow, from these positions, that science can throw no light upon the truths of Scripture ? By no means ; and it will be my leading object, in this lecture, to show how this may be done by science in general, and by geology in particular.

In discussing this subject, we ought to bear in mind the object of science, and the object of revelation. And by the term *science* I refer mainly to physical science. Its grand aim is, by an induction from facts, to discover the laws by which the material universe is governed. Those laws do, indeed, lead the mind almost necessarily to their divine Author. But this is rather the incidental than the direct result of scientific investigations, and belongs rather to natural theology than to natural science.

On the other hand, the exclusive object of revelation is of a moral character. It is a development of the divine character and the divine government; especially that part of it which discloses a plan for the reconciliation of a lost and wicked world to the favor of God by the death of his Son. Every other subject mentioned in Scripture is incidental, and would not have been noticed had it not some connection with the plan of salvation. The creation of the world and the Noachian deluge, for instance, are intimately related to the divine character and government, and therefore they are described; and the same is true of the various phenomena of nature which are touched upon in the Bible.

If these positions be correct, it follows, that as we ought not to expect to find the doctrines of religion in treatises on science, so it is unreasonable to look for the principles of philosophy in the Bible. Nay, we ought not to expect to find the terms used by the sacred writers employed in their strict scientific sense, but in their popular acceptation. Indeed, as the Scriptures were generally addressed to men in the earliest and most simple states of society, with very limited views of the extent of creation, we ought to suppose that, in all cases where no new fact is revealed, the language was adapted to the narrow ideas which then prevailed. When, for instance, the sacred writers speak of the rising and setting of the sun, we cannot suppose they used language with astronomical correctness, but only according to appearances. Hence we ought not to be very confident, that when they employ the term *earth*, they meant that spherical, vast globe which astronomy proves the earth to be, but rather that part of it which was inhabited, which was all the idea that entered into the mind of a Jew. God might, indeed, have revealed new scientific as well as religious truth. But there is no evidence that in this way he has anticipated a single modern discovery. This would have been turning aside from the much more important object he had in view, viz., to teach the world religious truth. Such being the case, the language employed to describe natural phenomena must have been adapted to the state of knowledge among the people to whom the Scriptures were addressed.

Another inference from these premises is, that there may be an apparent contradiction between the statements of science and revelation. Revelation may describe phenomena according to apparent truth, as when it speaks of the rising and setting of the sun, and the immobility of the earth.; but science describes the same according to the actual truth, as when it gives a real motion to the earth, and only an apparent motion to the heavens. Had the language of revelation been scientifically accurate, it would have defeated the object for which the Scriptures were given ; for it must have anticipated scientific discovery, and therefore have been unintelligible to those ignorant of such discoveries. Or if these had been explained by inspiration, the Bible would have become a text-book in natural science, rather than a guide to eternal life.

The final conclusion from these principles is, that since science and revelation treat of the same subjects only incidentally, we ought only to expect that the facts of science, rightly understood, should not contradict the statements of revelation, correctly interpreted. Apparent discrepancies there may be ; and it would not be strange, if for a time they should seem to be real ; either because science has not fully and accurately disclosed the facts, or the Bible is not correctly interpreted ; but if both records are from God, there can be no real contradiction between them. But, on the other hand, we have no reason to expect any remarkable coincidences, because the general subject and object of the two records are so unlike. Should such coincidences occur, however, they will render it less probable that any apparent disagreement is real.

If the positions taken in these preliminary remarks be correct, it will follow, that in judging of the agreement or disagreement between revelation and science, it is important, in the first place, that we rightly understand the Bible ; and, in the second place, that we carefully ascertain what are the settled and demonstrated principles of science. An examination of these points will constitute the remainder of this lecture.

The meaning of the Scriptures is to be determined in the same way as the meaning of any other book written in similar circumstances. Its inspiration puts no bar in the way of the most rigid application of the rules of criticism, nor renders it unnecessary to seek for light in whatever quarter it can be obtained. The rules of grammatical and rhetorical construction, the study of contemporary writers, a knowledge of the history, customs, opinions, and prejudices of the times, and other circumstances that need not be mentioned, become important means of attaining the true *usus loquendi*, or principle of interpretation. But I pass by all these on the present occasion, because no one doubts their importance in rightly understanding the Bible. I maintain that scientific discoveries furnish us with another means of its correct interpretation, where it describes natural phenomena. And in this position we shall not probably find an entire unanimity of opinion. Let us, therefore, proceed to examine its truth.

1 *

It will not be denied that modern science has corrected the opinions of men in regard to very many natural phenomena. The same term that conveyed one idea to an ancient reader, or hearer, of the Bible, often conveys an opposite meaning to a modern ear. And yet that term may be very proper to use in modern times, if understood to express only apparent, and not real truth. The Jew understood it to mean the latter; and it would seem as if we might employ modern scientific discovery to enable us to decide in which sense the Bible did use the term. For if we admit the Jew to have been correct in his interpretation, then we bring revelation into direct collision with the demonstrations of physics.

But facts are vastly more satisfactory in deciding this question than reasoning, and I shall now proceed to adduce some examples in which modern scientific discovery has thrown light upon the meaning of the Bible.

For one or two examples I appeal to chemistry. In the book of Proverbs, (chap. 25, v. 20,) we find it said, that *as vinegar upon nitre, so is he that singeth songs to a heavy heart.* We should expect from this statement that when we put vinegar upon what we call nitre, it would produce some commotion analogous to the excitement of song-singing. But we should try the experiment in vain; for no effect whatever would be produced. Again, it is said by the prophet Jeremiah, (chap. 2, v. 22,) *Though thou wash thee with nitre, and take thee much soap, yet thine iniquity is marked before me, saith the Lord.* Here, too, we should expect that the use of the nitre would increase the purifying power of the soap; but the experiment would prove rather the reverse. The chemist, however, informs us that there is a substance, viz., the *carbonate of soda*, which, if substituted for the nitre, would effervesce with vinegar, and aid the purifying power of soap, and thus strikingly illustrate the thought both of Solomon and Jeremiah. And on recurring to the original, we find that נהר (nether, *nitrum*, *natrum*) does not necessarily mean the salt which we call nitre, but rather a fossil alkali, the *natron* of the ancients, and the carbonate of soda of the moderns.

It is probably the prevailing opinion among intelligent Christians at this time, and has been the opinion of many commentators, that when Peter describes the future destruction of the world, he means that its solid substance, and indeed that of the whole material universe, will be utterly consumed or annihilated by fire. This opinion rests upon the common belief that such is the effect of combustion. But chemistry informs us, that no case of combustion, how fiercely soever the fire may rage, annihilates the least particle of matter; and that fire only changes the form of substances. Nay, there is no reason whatever to suppose that one particle of matter has been annihilated since the world began. The chemist moreover asserts that all the solid parts of the globe have already undergone combustion, and that although heat may melt them, it cannot burn them. Nor is there any thing upon or within the earth capable of combustion, but vegetables, and animals, and a few gases. Has Peter, then, made a mistake because he did not understand modern chemistry? We have only to examine his language carefully, as it seems to me, in order to be satisfied that he means only, that whatsoever upon, or within, the earth, is combustible, will be burned up at the final conflagration; and that the whole globe, the *elements*, *will melt with fervent heat.* He nowhere asserts, or implies, that one particle of matter will be annihilated by that catastrophe. Thus science, instead of proving his statements to be erroneous, only enables us more correctly to understand them.

Scarcely any truth seems more clearly taught in the Bible than the future resurrection of the body. Yet this doctrine has always been met by a most formidable objection. It is said that the body laid in the grave is ere long decomposed into its elements, which are scattered over the face of the earth, and enter into new combinations, even forming a part of other human bodies. Hence not even Omnipotence can raise from the grave the identical body laid there, because the particles may enter successively into a multitude of other human bodies. I am not aware that any successful reply has ever been given to this objection, until chemistry and natural history taught us the true nature of bodily identity; and until recently the objector has felt sure that he had triumphed. But these sciences teach us that the identity of the body consists, not in a sameness of particles, but in the same kinds of elementary matter, combined in the same proportion, and having the same form and structure. Hence it is not necessary that the resurrection body should contain a single particle of the matter laid in the grave, in order to be the same body; which it will be if it consist of the same kinds of matter combined in the same proportions, and has the same form and structure. For the particles of our bodies are often totally changed during our lives; yet no one imagines that the old man has not the same body as in infancy.* What but the principles

* I am not aware that this reply to the objection was ever advanced, till the publication, by myself, last year, of a sermon on the Resurrections of Spring, in a small volume of sermons, entitled Religious Lectures on some peculiar Phenomena in the Four Seasons. I may be mistaken; but I cannot see why this reply does not completely meet the difficulty, and free an important doctrine from an incubus under which it has long lain half smothered.

of science could have thus vindicated a precious doctrine of revelation?

In the description which Paul gives of the spiritual body, a naturalist, — and I fancy no one but a naturalist, — will discover its specific identity. By this I mean that it will possess peculiarities that distinguish it from every thing else, but which are so closely related to the characteristics of the natural body in this world, from which it was derived, that one acquainted with the latter would recognize the former. Hence the Christian's friends in another world may be recognized by him from their external characters, just as we identify the plants and animals of spring with those that seemed to perish in the preceding autumn. There is neither time nor room for the proof of this exegesis, which is founded chiefly upon the principles of natural history; but for their elucidation, I must refer to another place.*

I take my next example from meteorology. It was the opinion of the ancients that the earth, at a certain height, was surrounded by a transparent hollow sphere of solid matter, which they called the firmament. When rain descended, they supposed it was through windows, or holes, made in this crystalline curtain suspended in mid heaven. To these notions the language of the Bible is frequently conformed. In the account of the creation, in Genesis, we have a description of the formation of this firmament, and how it divided the waters below it, viz., the ocean, lakes, and rivers, from the waters above it, viz., the clouds. Again, in the account of the deluge, the windows of heaven are said to have been opened.

---

* I hope it is not vanity to say that this subject, also, was first suggested in the sermon referred to in the preceding note. If correct, it opens an animating prospect to the afflicted Christian.

But it is hardly necessary to say, that meteorology has shown that no such solid firmament exists over our heads ; that, in fact, nothing but one homogeneous, transparent atmosphere encloses the earth, in which the clouds float at different altitudes at different times. Are we, then, to suppose that the sacred writers meant to teach as certain truth, the fiction of a solid firmament ; or that on this subject they conformed their language to the prevailing belief, because it was not their object to teach philosophy, meaning neither to assert nor to deny the existence of a solid firmament, but using language that was optically, although not physically, correct, and which, therefore, conformed to the general belief ? It is doubtful whether any thing but scientific discovery could enable us to decide this question. But since it is certain that the solid firmament does not exist, we must admit that the Bible did not intend to teach its existence, or allow it to teach a falsehood ; and since we know that it does often speak, in natural things, according to apparent, and not real truth, it is most reasonable to give such a construction to its language in the present instance.

δ But the most decisive example I have to give on this subject is derived from astronomy. Until the time of Copernicus, no opinion respecting natural phenomena was thought more firmly established, than that the earth is fixed immovably in the centre of the universe, and that the heavenly bodies move diurnally around it. To sustain this view, the most decided language of Scripture could be quoted. God is there said to have *established the foundations of the earth, so that they could not be removed forever ;* and the sacred writers expressly declare that the sun and other heavenly bodies *arise and set,* and nowhere allude to any proper motion in the earth. And those statements corresponded exactly to the testimony of the senses. Men felt the earth to be immovably firm under

their feet, and when they looked up, they saw the heavenly
bodies in motion. What bold impiety, therefore, did it seem,
even to men of liberal and enlightened minds, for any one to
rise up and assert that all this testimony of the Bible and of
the senses was to be set aside ! It is easy to conceive with
what strong jealousy the friends of the Bible would look upon
the new science which was thus arraying itself in bold defiance of inspiration, and how its votaries would be branded as
infidels in disguise. We need not resort to Catholic intolerance to explain how it was, that the new doctrine of the earth's
motion should be denounced as the most fatal heresy, as alike
contrary to Scripture and sound philosophy, and that even the
venerable Galileo should be forced to recant it upon his knees.
What though the astronomer stood ready with his diagrams
and formulas to demonstrate the motion of the earth ; who
would calmly and impartially examine the claims of a scientific discovery, which, by its very announcement, threw
discredit upon the Bible and the senses, and contradicted the
unanimous opinion of the wise and good, — of all mankind,
indeed, — through all past centuries ? Rather would the distinguished theologians of the day set their ingenuity at work
to frame an argument in opposition to the dangerous neology,
that should fall upon it like an avalanche, and grind it to powder. And to show you how firm and irresistible such an argument would seem, we need no longer tax the imagination ;
for Francis Turretin, a distinguished Protestant professor of
theology, whose writings have even to the present day sustained no mean reputation, has left us an argument on the
subject, compacted and arranged according to the nicest rules
of logic, and which he supposed would stand unrefuted as
long as the authority of the Bible should be regarded among
men. He propounds the inquiry, " Do the sun and moon

move in the heavens and revolve around the earth, while the
earth remains at rest?" This he affirms, "in opposition to
certain philosophers," and sustains his position by the following arguments: " First. The sun is said [in Scripture] to
move in the heavens, and to rise and set. (Ps. 19, v. 5.)
The sun is *as a bridegroom coming out of his chamber, and
rejoiceth as a strong man to run a race.* (Ps. 104, v. 19.)
The sun knoweth his going down. (Eccles. 1, v. 5.) *The
sun also ariseth, and the sun goeth down.* Secondly. The
sun, by a miracle, stood still in the time of Joshua. (Joshua,
ch. 10, v. 12, 13, 14,) and by a miracle it went back in the
time of Hezekiah. (Isa. ch. 38, v. 8.) Thirdly. The earth is
said to be *fixed immovably.* (Ps. 93, v. 1.) *The world also is
established, that it cannot be moved.* (Ps. 104, v. 5.) *Who
laid the foundations of the earth, that it should not be removed
forever.* (Ps. 119, v. 90, 91.) *Thou hast established the
earth, and it abideth. They continue this day according to
thine ordinances.* Fourthly. Neither could birds, which often
fly off through an hour's circuit, be able to return to their
nests ; for in the mean time the earth would move four hundred and fifty of our miles. Fifthly. Whatever flies or is
suspended in the air ought [by this theory] to move from west
to east ; but this is proved not to be true from birds, arrows
shot forth, atoms made manifest in the sun, and down floating
in the atmosphere."

If it be replied to this reasoning that the Scripture, in natural things, speaks according to the common opinion, Turretin
answers, " First, that the spirit of God best understands nat
ural things ; secondly, that, in giving instruction in religion, he
meant these things should be used, not abused ; thirdly, that
he is not the author of any error ; fourthly, neither is he to
be corrected on this pretence by our blind reason."

If it be replied that birds, the air, and all things are moved with the earth, he answers, " First, that this is a mere fiction, since air is a fluid body ; and secondly, if so, by what force would birds be able to go from east to west." — *Compendium Theologicæ Didactico-Elencticæ*, (Amsterdam, **1695.**)

In the present state of knowledge we may smile at some of these arguments ; but to men who had been taught to believe, as in a self-evident principle, that the earth was immovable and the heavenly bodies in motion, the most of them must have been entirely satisfactory ; and especially must the Scriptures have seemed in *point blank* opposition to the astronomical heresy. What, then, has so completely annihilated this argument, that now the merest schoolboy would be ashamed to advocate it ? The clear demonstrations of science have done it. Not only has the motion of the earth been established, but it has been made equally obvious that this truth is in entire harmony with the language of Scripture ; so that neither the infidel nor the Christian ever suspect, on this ground, any collision between the two records. So soon as the philologist perceived that there was no escape from the astronomical demonstration, he was led to reëxamine his interpretation of Scripture, and found that the whole difficulty lay in his assuming that the sacred writers intended to teach scientific instead of popular truth. Only admitting that they spoke of astronomical phenomena, according to appearances and in conformity to common opinion, and their language became perfectly proper. It conveyed no error, and is in fact as well adapted now as ever to the common intercourse of life. Yet, in consequence of the scientific discovery, that language conveys quite a different meaning to our minds from what it did to those who supposed it to teach a scientific truth.

2

Hence it strikingly illustrates the value of scientific discovery in enabling us rightly to understand the Bible.

Is it necessary to quote any more examples to establish the principle that scientific discovery is one of the means which the philologist should employ in the interpretation of Scripture ? And if the principle has been found of service in chemistry, meteorology, and astronomy, why should it be neglected in the case of geology ? Why should not this science also, which has probably more important religious bearings than any other, be appealed to in illustration of the meaning of Scripture, when phenomena are described of which geology takes cognizance ? I know that some will reply, that the principles of geology are yet too unsettled to be allowed to modify the interpretation of the Bible. This brings me to the second part of my subject, in which I am to inquire whether the principles of physical science, and of geology in particular, are so far settled that we can feel ourselves upon firm ground as we compare them with the principles of revelation.

Before proceeding to this part of the subject, however, I must pause a moment, in order to point out another mode, in which science may contribute to elucidate Scripture. In the way just described, it may enable the interpreter more correctly to understand the language, but it may also give a fuller illustration to the sentiments of the Bible. Revelation, for instance, represents God as benevolent. Now, if we can derive from the records of geology striking and hitherto unthought-of manifestations of this attribute, we shall make the doctrine of Scripture more impressive ; or, if we appeal to the numerous changes which the earth has undergone, and the vast periods which they have occupied, we find that the unsearchableness of divine wisdom, and the vastness of the divine plans, are brought more vividly before the mind, and task its power of comprehension more than illustrations from any other quarter. In short, the principles of religion that derive important elucidation from science, and especially from geology, are very numerous, as I hope to show in subsequent lectures. But I now return to the inquiry, whether the principles of science, and especially of geology, are so well settled that we can employ them in this manner.

As to the more mathematical sciences, there will be no one to doubt but some of their principles must be admitted as infallible truth ; for our minds are so constituted that they are incapable of resisting a fair presentation of mathematical demonstration. Now, there is scarcely any physical science that is not based more or less upon mathematical truth ; and as to the facts in those sciences, some of them are so multiplied, and speak so uniformly the same language, that we doubt them no more than we do a mathematical demonstration. Other classes of facts are less decided ; and in some cases they are so insulated as to be regarded as anomalies, to be set aside until better understood. The same grades of certainty exist in respect to inferences from the facts of science. Some theories are scarcely less doubtful than mathematics ; others are as strong as probable reasoning can make them ; and others are merely plausible. Hypotheses are still less to be trusted, though sometimes extremely probable.

Now, most of the physical sciences embrace facts, theories, and hypotheses, that range widely along the scale of probability, from decided demonstration to ingenious conjecture. It is easy, however, in general, to distinguish the demonstrated and the permanent from the conjectural and the fanciful ; and when we bring the principles of any science into comparison with religion, it is chiefly the former that should be considered, although scientific hypothesis may sometimes be made to illustrate religious hypothesis. But, passing by all other sciences, it is my desire to present before you, on this occasion, the claims of geology, as having fundamental principles so well settled that they claim attention from the interpreter of the Bible. I ought, however, to remark, that there exists a strange jealousy of this science even among intelligent men ; a suspicion that its votaries have jumped at strange and dangerous conclusions through the influence of hypothesis, and that in fact the whole science is little else but hypothesis, and that there is almost no agreement even among its ablest cultivators. It is indeed a comparatively recent science, and its remarkable developments have succeeded one another so rapidly, as to leave men in doubt whether it would not prove a dazzling meteor, instead of a steady and permanent luminary. When the men who are now in the full maturity of judgment and reason, (and whose favorable opinion I am, therefore, anxious above that of all others to secure,) when these were young, geology did not constitute a branch of finished education ; and amid the pressure of the cares and duties of middle life, how few find the leisure, to say nothing of the disposition, carefully to investigate a new and extensive science ! Even though younger men should be found standing forth as the advocates of geology, yet how natural for those more advanced to impute this to the ardor and love of novelty, characteristic of youth !

There is another difficulty, in relation to this subject, that embarrasses me. It is not even yet generally understood that geology is a branch of knowledge which requires long and careful study fully to understand ; that a previous knowledge of many other sciences is indispensable in order to comprehend its reasonings ; that its reasonings are in fact, for the most part, to be mastered only by long and patient consideration ; and finally, and more especially, that they will appear inconclusive and feeble, unless a man has become somewhat familiar with specimens of rocks and fossils, and has examined strata as they lie in the earth. How very imperfect must be the most intelligent man's knowledge of botany, who had never examined any plants ; or of chemistry, who had not seen any of the simple substances, nor experiments upon them in the laboratory ; or of crystallography, whose eyes had perhaps never rested upon a crystal. No less important is it that he, who would reason correctly about rocks and their organic contents, should have studied rocks. But upon such an amount of knowledge it is no disparagement to say we have no right to presume in all, even of publicly educated men. Before such a state of preparation can exist, it is necessary that practical geology, at least, should be introduced into our schools of every grade, as it might be with great success.

It ought to be mentioned, in this connection, that, within a few years past, geology has experienced several severe attacks of a peculiar character. Men of respectable ability, and decided friends of revelation, having got fully impressed with the belief that the views of geologists are hostile to the Bible, have set themselves to an examination of their writings, not so much with a view of understanding the subject, as of finding contradictions and untenable positions. The next step has been to write a book against geology, abounding, as we might expect from men of warm temperament, of such prejudices, and without a practical knowledge of geology, with striking misapprehensions of facts and opinions, with positive and dogmatic assertions, with severe personal insinuations, great ignorance of correct reasoning in geology, and the substitution of wild and extravagant hypotheses for geological theories.

2 *

Hence English literature has been prolific of such works as
" A Comparative Estimate of the Mineral and Mosaic Geolo-
gies," by Granville Penn ; the " Geology of Scripture," by
Fairholme ; " Scriptural Geology," by Dr. Young ; " Popular
Geology subversive of Divine Revelation," by Rev. Henry
Cole ; " Strictures on Geology and Astronomy," by Rev. R.
Wilson ; " Scripture Evidences of Creation, and Geology, and
Scripture Cosmogony," by anonymous authors ; and many
other similar productions that might be named. The warm
zeal displayed, and doubtless felt, by these writers for the
Bible ; their familiar reference to eminent geological authors,
as if they understood them ; the skill in philology, which they
frequently exhibit ; and the want of a wide-spread and accurate knowledge of geology in the community, — have given to
these works a far more extensive circulation than those works
have had, which view geology as illustrating and not opposing
revelation. Foremost among these is the lectures of the venerable and learned Dr. John Pye Smith, late principal of the
Homerton Divinity College, London, " On the Relations between the Holy Scriptures and some Parts of Geological
Science." * This work, the result of long and patient research, and emanating from a man of eminent piety as well
as learning, affords a full refutation of all the works that have
been named, and in the kindness and candor of its spirit exhibits a fine contrast to their intolerance and dogmatism. In
the profound works of Dr. Harris, entitled " The Pre-Adamite
Earth," and " Man Primeval," the connections of geology
and revelation are briefly but ably treated, and also its connection with natural religion. Quite recently, a small and

* The first edition of this work was republished in this country.
In England it has reached the fifth edition, much enlarged.

more popular work on this subject has been published by Rev. David King, LL. D., of Glasgow, well worthy of attention. "The Course of Creation," by Rev. John Anderson, D. D. of recent publication, displays much learning and candor. But the causes that have been mentioned have secured a much wider circulation for the class of works first named, than for the latter, among the religious community generally. The consequence is, that the public mind is possessed of many prejudices unfavorable to the religious bearings of geology, and unfavorable to an impartial examination of its claims.

Under these circumstances, all that I can do is to state definitely what I apprehend to be the established principles of the science that have a bearing upon religious truth, and refer my hearers to standard works on the subject for the proof that they are true. If any will not take the trouble to examine the proofs, I trust they will have candor and impartiality enough not to deny my positions.

The first important conclusion, to which every careful observer will come, is, that the rocks of all sorts, which compose the present crust of the globe, so far as it has been explored, at least to the depth of several miles, appear to have been the result of second causes; that is, they are now in a different state from that in which they were originally created.

It is indeed a favorite idea with some, that all the rocks and their contents were created just as we now meet them, in a moment of time; that the supposed remains of animals and plants, which many of them contain, and which occur in all states, from an animal or plant little changed, to a complete conversion into stone, were never real animals and plants, but only resemblances; and that the marks of fusion and of the wearing of water, exhibited by the rocks, are not to be taken as evidences that they have undergone such processes, but

only that it has pleased God to give them that appearance
and that in fact it was as easy for God to create them just as
they now are as in any other form.

It is a presumption against such a supposition, that no men,
who have carefully examined rocks and organic remains, are
its advocates. Not that they doubt the power of God to produce such effects, but they deny the probability that He has
exerted it in this manner ; for throughout nature, wherever
they have an opportunity to witness her operations, they find
that when substances appear to have undergone changes, by
means of secondary agencies, they have in fact undergone
them ; and, therefore, the whole analogy of nature goes to
prove that the rocks have experienced great changes since
their deposition. If rocks are an exception to the rest of
nature, — that is, if they are the effect of miraculous agency,
— there is no proof of it ; and to admit it without proof is to
destroy all grounds of analogical reasoning in natural operations ; in other words, it is to remove the entire basis of reasoning in physical science. Every reasonable man, therefore,
who has examined rocks, will admit that they have undergone
important changes since their original formation.

In the second place, the same general laws appear to have
always prevailed on the globe, and to have controlled the
changes which have taken place upon and within it. We
come to no spot, in the history of the rocks, in which a system
different from that which now prevails appears to have existed. Great peculiarities in the structure of animals and
plants do indeed occur, as well as changes on a scale of
magnitude unknown at present ; but this was only a wise
adaptation to peculiar circumstances, and not an infringement
of the general laws.

In the third place, the geological changes which the earth

has undergone, and is now undergoing, appear to have been the result of the same agencies, viz., heat and water.

Fourthly. It is demonstrated that the present continents of the globe, with perhaps the exception of some of their highest mountains, have for a long period constituted the bottom of the ocean, and have been subsequently either elevated into their present position, or the waters have been drained off from their surface. This is probably the most important principle in geology ; and though regarded with much scepticism by many, it is as satisfactorily proved as any principle of physical science not resting on mathematical demonstration.

Fifthly. The internal parts of the earth are found to possess a very high temperature ; nor can it be doubted that at least oceans of melted matter exist beneath the crust, and perhaps even all the deep-seated interior is in a state of fusion.

Sixthly. The fossiliferous rocks, or such as contain animals and plants, are not less than six or seven miles in perpendicular thickness, and are composed of hundreds of alternating layers of different kinds, all of which appear to have been deposited, just as rocks are now forming, at the bottom of lakes and seas ; and hence their deposition must have occupied an immense period of time. Even if we admit that this deposition went on in particular places much faster than at present, a variety of facts forbids the supposition that this was the general mode of their formation.

Seventhly. The remains of animals and plants found in the earth are not mingled confusedly together, but are found arranged, for the most part, in as much order as the drawers of a well-regulated cabinet. In general, they appear to have lived and died on or near the spots where they are now found ; and as countless millions of these remains are often found piled together, so as to form almost entire mountains, the periods requisite for their formation must have been immensely long, as was taught in the preceding proposition.

Eighthly. Still further confirmation of the same important principle is found in the well-established fact, that there have been upon the globe, previous to the existing races, not less than five distinct periods of organized existence; that is, five great groups of animals and plants, so completely independent that no species whatever is found in more than one of them, have lived and successively passed away before the creation of the races that now occupy the surface. Other standard writers make the number of these periods of existence as many as twelve. Comparative anatomy testifies that so unlike in structure were these different groups, that they could not have coexisted in the same climate and other external circumstances.

Ninthly. In the earliest times in which animals and plants lived, the climate over the whole globe appears to have been as warm as, or even warmer than, it is now between the tropics. And the slow change from warmer to colder appears to have been the chief cause of the successive destruction of the different races; and new ones were created, better adapted to the altered condition of the globe; and yet each group seems to have occupied the globe through a period of great length, so that we have here another evidence of the vast cycles of duration that must have rolled away even since the earth became a habitable globe.

Tenthly. There is no small reason to suppose that the globe underwent numerous changes previous to the time when animals were placed upon it; that, in fact, the time was when the whole matter of the earth was in a melted state, and not improbably also even in a gaseous state. These points, indeed, are not as well established as the others that have been mentioned; but, if admitted, they give to the globe an incalculable antiquity.

Eleventhly. It appears that the present condition of the earth's crust and surface was of comparatively recent commencement; otherwise the steep flanks of mountains would have ceased to crumble down, and wide oceans would have been filled with alluvial deposits.

Twelfthly. Among the thirty thousand species of animals and plants found in the rocks,* very few living species have been detected; and even these few occur in the most recent rocks, while in the secondary group, not less than six miles thick, not a single species now on the globe has been discovered. Hence the present races did not exist till after those in the secondary rocks had died. No human remains have been found below those alluvial deposits which are now forming by rivers, lakes, and the ocean. Hence geology infers that man was one of the latest animals that was placed on the globe.

Thirteenthly. The surface of the earth has undergone an enormous amount of erosion by the action of the ocean, the rivers, and the atmosphere. The ocean has worn away the solid rock, in some parts of the world, not less than ten thousand feet in depth, and rivers have cut channels through the hardest strata, hundreds of feet deep and several miles long; both of which effects demand periods inconceivably long.

Fourteenthly. At a comparatively recent date, northern and southern regions have been swept over and worn down by the joint action of ice and water, the force in general

* Two or three years since Professor Bronn described twenty-six thousand six hundred and seventy-eight species; and, upon an average, one thousand species are discovered every year. M. Alcide D'Orbigny, in 1850, stated the number of mollusks and radiated animals alone at seventeen thousand nine hundred and forty-seven species.

having been directed towards the equator. This is called the *drift* period.

Fifteenthly. Since the drift period, the ocean has stood some thousands of feet above its present level in many countries.

Sixteenthly. There is evidence, in regard to some parts of the world, that the continents are now experiencing slow vertical movements — some places sinking, and others rising. And hence a presumption is derived that, in early times, such changes may have been often repeated, and on a great scale.

Seventeenthly. Every successive change of importance on the earth's surface appears to have been an improvement of its condition, adapting it to beings of a higher organization, and to man at last, the most perfect of all.

Finally. The present races of animals and plants on the globe are for the most part disposed in groups, occupying particular districts, beyond whose limits the species peculiar to those provinces usually droop and die. The same is true, to some extent, as to the animals and plants found in the rocks ; though the much greater uniformity of climate, that prevailed in early times, permitted organized beings to take a much wider range than at present; so that the zoölogical and botanical districts were then probably much wider. But the general conclusion, in respect to living and extinct animals, is, that there must have been several centres of creation, from which they emigrated as far as their natures would allow them to range.

It would be easy to state more principles of geology of considerable importance ; but I have now named the principal ones that bear upon the subject of religion. A brief statement of the leading truths of theology, whether natural or revealed, which these principles affect, and on which they cast light, will give an idea of the subjects which I propose to discuss in these lectures.

The first point relates to the age of the world. For while it has been the usual interpretation of the Mosaic account, that the world was brought into existence nearly at the same time with man and the other existing animals, geology throws back its creation to a period indefinitely but immeasurably remote. The question is not whether man has existed on the globe longer than the common interpretation of Genesis requires,— for here geology and the Bible speak the same language,— but whether the globe itself did not exist long before his creation; that is, long before the six days' work, so definitely described in the Mosaic account? In other words, is not this a case in which the discoveries of science enable us more accurately to understand the Scriptures?

The introduction of death into the world, and the specific character of that death described in Scripture as the consequence of sin, are the next points where geology touches the subject of religion. Here, too, the general interpretation of Scripture is at variance with the facts of geology, which distinctly testify to the occurrence of death among animals long before the existence of man. Shall geology here, also, be permitted to modify our exposition of the Bible?

The subject of deluges, and especially that of Noah, will next claim our attention. For though it is now generally agreed that geology cannot detect traces of such a deluge as the Scriptures describe, yet upon some other bearings of that subject it does cast light; and so remarkable is the history of opinions concerning the Noachian deluge, that it could not on that account alone be properly passed in silence.

It is well known that the philosophy of antiquity, almost without exception, regarded matter as eternal; and in modern

3

times, metaphysical theology has done its utmost to refute the supposed dangerous dogma. Geology affords us some new views of the subject; and although it does not directly refute the doctrine, it brings before us facts of such a nature as to show, that, so far as religion is concerned, such a refutation is of little importance. This will furnish another theme of discussion.

It may be thought extravagant, but I hazard the assertion, that no science is so prolific of direct testimony to the benevolence of the Deity as geology; and some of its facts bear strongly upon the objections to this doctrine. So important a subject will, therefore, occupy at least one or two lectures.

In all ages, philosophers have, in one form or another, endeavored to explain the origin and the phenomena of creation by a power inherent in nature, independent of a personal Deity, usually denominated *natural law.* And in modern times this hypothesis has assumed a popular form and a plausible dress. Not less than one lecture is demanded for its examination, especially as its advocates appeal with special confidence to geology for its support.

In existing nature, no one fact stands out more prominently than unity of design; and it is an interesting inquiry, whether the same general system prevailed through the vast periods of geological history as that which now adorns our globe. This question I shall endeavor to answer in the affirmative, by appealing to a multitude of facts.

Another question of deep interest in theology is, whether the Deity exercises over the world any special providence; whether he ever interferes with the usual order of things by introducing change; or whether he has committed nature to the control of unalterable laws, without any direct efficiency. Light is thrown on these points by the researches of geology, if I mistake not; and I shall not fail to attempt its development.

This science also discloses to us many new views of the vast plans of the Deity, and thus enlarges our conceptions of his wisdom and knowledge. In this field we must allow ourselves to wander in search of the golden fruit.

In the course of the discussion, we shall direct our attention to the new heavens and the new earth described in the Bible, and inquire whether geology does not cast a glimpse of light upon that difficult subject.

In approaching the close of our subject, we shall introduce a few lectures having a wider range, and deriving less elucidation from geology than from other sciences. One is a consideration of the physical effects of human actions upon the universe. And in conclusion of the whole subject, we shall endeavor to show that the bearings of all science, when rightly understood, are eminently favorable to religion, both in this world and the next.

With a few miscellaneous inferences from the principles advanced, I shall close this lecture.

In the first place, we see that the points of connection between geology and religion are numerous and important. A few years since, geology, instead of being appealed to for the illustration of religious truth, was regarded with great jealousy, as a repository of views favorable to infidelity, and even to atheism. But if the summary which I have exhibited of its religious relations be correct, from what other science can we obtain so many illustrations of natural and revealed religion? Distinguished Christian writers are beginning to gather fruit in this new field, and the clusters already presented us by such men as Dr. Chalmers, Dr. Pye Smith, Dr. Buckland, Dr. Harris, and Dr. King, are an earnest of an abundant

harvest. I hazard the prediction that the time is not far distant when it will be said of this, as of another noble science,
" The undevout *geologist* is mad."

Secondly. I would bespeak the candid attention of those
sceptical minds, that are ever ready to imagine discrepancies
between science and religion, to the views which I am about
to present. The number of such is indeed comparatively
small ; yet there are still some prepared to seize upon every new
scientific fact, before it is fully developed, that can be made to
assume the appearance of opposition to religion. It is strange
that they should not ere this time despair of making any serious
impression upon the citadel of Christianity. For of all the
numerous assaults of this kind that have been made, not one
has destroyed even an outpost of religion. Just so soon as
the subject was fully understood, every one of them has been
abandoned ; and even the most violent unbeliever never thinks,
at the present day, of arraying them against the Bible. One
needs no prophetic inspiration to be confident that every geological objection to Christianity, which perhaps now and then
an unbeliever of limited knowledge still employs, will pass
into the same limbo of forgetfulness.

Finally. I would throw out a caution to those friends of
religion who are very fearful that the discoveries of science
will prove injurious to Christianity. Why should the enlightened Christian, who has a correct idea of the firm foundation
on which the Bible rests, fear that any disclosures of the
arcana of nature should shake its authority or weaken its
influence ? Is not the God of revelation the God of nature
also ? and must not his varied works tend to sustain and elucidate, instead of weakening and darkening, one another ?
Has Christianity suffered because the Copernican system of
astronomy has proved true, or because chemistry has demon-

strated that the earth is already for the most part oxidized, and
therefore cannot literally be burned hereafter ?   Just as much
as gold suffers by passing through the furnace.   Yet how many
fears agitated the hearts of pious men when these scientific
truths were first announced!   The very men who felt so
strong a conviction of the truth of the Bible, that they were
ready to go to the stake in its defence, have trembled and
uttered loud notes of warning when the votaries of science
have brought out some new fact, that seemed perhaps at first,
or when partially understood, to contravene some statement
of revelation.   The effect has been to make sceptical minds
look with suspicion, and sometimes with contempt, upon Christianity itself.   It has built up a wall of separation between
science and religion, which is yet hardly broken down.   For
notwithstanding the instructive history of the past on this subject, although every supposed discrepancy between philosophy
and religion has vanished as soon as both were thoroughly
understood, yet so soon as geology began to develop her marvellous truths, the cry of danger to religion became again
the watchword, and the precursor of a more extended and
severe attack upon that science than any other has ever experienced, and the prelude, I am sorry to say, of severe personal
charges of infidelity against many an honest friend of religion.

In contrast to the contracted views and groundless fears
that have been described, it is refreshing to meet with such
sentiments as the following, from men eminent for learning,
and some of them veterans in theological science.   With
these I close this lecture.

"Those rocks which stand forth in the order of their formation," says Dr. Chalmers, "and are each imprinted with their
own peculiar fossil remains, have been termed the archives of
nature, where she hath recorded the changes that have taken

3*

place in the history of the globe. They are made to serve the purpose of scrolls or inscriptions, on which we might read of those great steps and successions by which the earth has been brought into its present state ; and should these archives of nature be but truly deciphered, we are not afraid of their being openly confronted with the archives of revelation. It is unmanly to blink the approach of light, from whatever quarter of observation it may fall upon us ; and those are not the best friends of Christianity, who feel either dislike or alarm when the torch of science, or the torch of history, is held up to the Bible. For ourselves, we are not afraid when the eye of an intrepid, if it be only a sound philosophy, scrutinizes, however jealously, all its pages. We have no dread of any apprehended conflict between the doctrines of Scripture and the discoveries of science, persuaded, as we are, that whatever story the geologists of our day shall find engraven on the volume of nature, it will only accredit that story which is graven on the volume of revelation." — *Chalmers's Works,* vol. ii. p. 227.

" For our own part," says Rev. Henry Melville, " we have no fears that any discoveries of science will really militate against the disclosures of Scripture. We remember how, in darker days, ecclesiastics set themselves against philosophers who were investigating the motions of the heavenly bodies, apprehensive that the new theories were at variance with the Bible, and therefore resolved to denounce them as heresies, and stop their spread by persecution. But truth triumphed ; bigotry and ignorance could not long prevail to the hiding from the world the harmonious walkings of stars and planets ; and ever since, the philosophy which laid open the wonders of the universe hath proved herself the handmaid of revelation, which divulged secrets far beyond her gaze. And thus,

we are persuaded, shall it always be ; science may scale new
heights and explore new depths, but she shall bring back
nothing from her daring and successful excursions which will
not, when rightly understood, yield a fresh tribute of testimony
to the Bible. Infidelity may watch her progress with eager-
ness, exulting in the thought that she is furnishing facts with
which the Christian system may be strongly assailed ; but the
champions of revelation may confidently attend her in every
march, assured that she will find nothing which contradicts,
if it do not actually confirm, the word which they know to be
divine." — *Sermons*, 2*d Am. edit.* vol. ii. p. 298.

" Shall it then any longer be said," says Dr. Buckland,
" that a science, which unfolds such abundant evidence of the
being and attributes of God, can reasonably be viewed in any
other light than as the efficient auxiliary and handmaid of
religion ? Some few there still may be, whom timidity, or
prejudice, or want of opportunity, allow not to examine its
evidence ; who are alarmed by the novelty, or surprised by
the extent and magnitude, of the views which geology forces
on their attention, and who would rather have kept closed the
volume of witness, which has been sealed up for ages, beneath
the surface of the earth, than impose upon the student in natural theology the duty of studying its contents ; — a duty in
which, for lack of experience, they may anticipate a hazardous
or a laborious task, but which, by those engaged in it, is found
to afford a rational, and righteous, and delightful exercise of
their highest faculties, in multiplying the evidences of the
existence, and attributes, and providence of God."

" It follows then," says Dr. J. Pye Smith, " as a universal
truth, that the Bible, faithfully interpreted, erects no bar
against the most free and extensive investigation, the most
comprehensive and searching induction. Let but the investi-

gation be sufficient, and the induction honest ; let observation take its farthest flight ; let experiment penetrate into all the recesses of nature ; let the veil of ages be lifted up from all that has been hitherto unknown, — if such a course were possible, religion need not fear ; Christianity is secure, and true science will always pay homage to the divine Creator and Sovereign, *of whom, and through whom, and to whom are all things ; and unto whom be glory forever.*" — *Lectures on Scripture and Geology,* 4*th London edit.* p. **223.**

LECTURE II.

THE EPOCH OF THE EARTH'S CREATION UNREVEALED.

THE Mosaic account of the creation of the universe has always been celebrated for its sublime simplicity. Though the subject be one of unparalleled grandeur, the writer makes not the slightest effort at rhetorical embellishment, but employs language which a mere child cannot misapprehend. How different, in this respect, is this inspired record from all uninspired efforts that have been made to describe the origin of the world!

But notwithstanding the great simplicity and clearness of this description, its precise meaning has occasioned as much discussion as almost any passage of Scripture. This results chiefly from its great brevity. Men with different views of inspiration, cosmogony, and philosophy, engage in its examination, not so much to ascertain its meaning, as to find out whether it teaches their favorite speculative views; and because it says nothing about them, they attempt to fasten those views upon it, and thus make it teach a great deal more than the mind of the Spirit. My simple object, at this time, is to ascertain whether the Bible fixes the time when the universe was created out of nothing.

The prevalent opinion, until recently, has been, that we are there taught that the world began to exist on the first of the six days of creation, or about six thousand years ago. Geologists, however, with one voice, declare that their science indicates the earth to have been of far higher antiquity. The question becomes, therefore, of deep interest, whether the common interpretation of the Mosaic record is correct.

Let us, in the first place, examine carefully the terms of that record, without reference to any of the conclusions of science.

A preliminary inquiry, however, will here demand attention, to which I have already given some thoughts in the first lecture. The inquiry relates to the mode in which the sacred writers describe natural phenomena.

Do they adapt their descriptions to the views and feelings of philosophers, or even the common people, in the nineteenth century, or to the state of knowledge and the prevalent opinions of a people but slightly removed from barbarism?

Do they write as if they meant to correct the notions of men on natural subjects, when they knew them to be wrong; or as if they did not mean to decide whether the popular opinion were true or false? These points have been examined with great skill and candor by a venerable clergyman of England, whose praise is in all the American churches, and whose skill in sacred philology, and profound acquaintance with the Bible, none will question, any more than they will his deep-toned piety and enlarged and liberal views of men and things. I refer to Dr. J. Pye Smith, lately at the head of the Homerton Divinity College, near London.*

* The news has just reached us that this venerable man is no more. I was present last summer at Homerton, when he resigned the charge of that beloved institution. From his addresses and his prayers, so redolent of the spirit of heaven, I might have known that he was pluming his wings for his upward flight. I am thankful that I was permitted to see the man, whom, of all others in Europe, I most desired to see. But Dr. Buckland I did not meet; for he was in an

He first examines the style in which the Old Testament describes the character and operations of Jehovah, and shows that it is done " in language borrowed from the bodily and mental constitution of man, and from those opinions concerning the works of God in the natural world, which were generally received by the people to whom the blessings of revelation were granted." Constant reference is made to material images, and to human feelings and conduct, as if the people addressed were almost incapable of spiritual and abstract ideas. This, of course, gives a notion of God infinitely beneath the glories of his character ; but to uncultivated minds it was the only representation of his character that would give them any idea of it. Nay, even in this enlightened age, such descriptions are far more impressive than any other upon the mass of mankind; while those, whose minds are more enlightened, find no difficulty in inculcating the pure truth respecting God from these comparatively gross descriptions.

Now, if, upon a point of such vast importance as the divine character, revelation thus condescends to human weakness and ignorance, much more might we expect it, in regard to the less important subject of natural phenomena. We find, accordingly, that they are described as they appear to the common eye, and not in their real nature ; or, in the language of Rosenmuller, the Scriptures speak " according to optical, and not physical truth." They make no effort to

---

insane hospital, with no prospect of recovery. Alas ! how sad to think of such Christian philosophers, so soon removed from the world, or from all concern in it ! Could I dare to hope that I shall meet them and kindred spirits before the throne of our common Redeemer, how should I exclaim with Cicero, " *O preclarum diem, quum in illud animorum concilium cœlumque proficiscar, ut quum ex hac turba et colluvione discedam !*

correct even the grossest errors, on these subjects, that then prevailed.

The earth, as we have seen on a former occasion, is described as immovable, in the centre of the universe, and the heavenly bodies as revolving round it diurnally. The firmament over us is represented as a solid, extended substance, sustaining an ocean above it, with openings, or windows, through which the waters may descend. In respect to the human system, the Scriptures refer intellectual operations to the reins, or the region of the kidneys, and pain to the bones. In short, the descriptions of natural things are adapted to the very erroneous notions which prevailed in the earliest ages of society and among the common people. But it is as easy to interpret such descriptions in conformity to the present state of physical science, as it is to divest the scriptural representations of the Deity of their material dress, and make them conform to the spiritual views that now prevail. No one regards it as any objection to the Old Testament, that it gives a description of the divine character so much less spiritual than the views adopted by the theologians of the nineteenth century; why then should they regard it as derogatory to inspiration to adopt the same method as to natural objects?

These considerations will afford us some assistance in rightly interpreting the description of the creation, in the first chapter of Genesis, to which we will now turn our attention.

In the beginning God created the heavens and the earth. And the earth was without form and void. And darkness was upon the face of the deep. And the Spirit of God moved upon the face of the waters. And God said, Let there be light, and there was light. And God saw the light that it was good. And God divided the light from the darkness, and the light

he called day, and the darkness he called night. And the
evening and the morning were the first day.

The first question that arises, on reading this passage, is,
whether the creation here described was a creation out of
nothing, or out of preëxisting materials. The latter opinion
has been maintained by some able, and generally judicious
commentators and theologians, such as Doederlin and Dathe
in Germany, Milton in England, and Bush and Schmucker in
this country. They do not deny that the Bible, in other
places, teaches distinctly the creation of the universe out
of nothing. But they contend that the word translated *to*
create, in the first verse of Genesis, teaches only a renovation, or remodelling, of the universe from matter already in
existence.

That there is a degree of ambiguity in all languages, in
the words that signify to *create*, to *make*, to *form*, and the like,
cannot be doubted; that is, these words may be properly used
to describe the production of a substance out of matter already
in existence, as well as out of nothing; and, therefore, we
must resort to the context, or the nature of the subject, to ascertain in which of those senses such words are used. The
same word, for instance, (*bawraw*,) that is used in the first
verse of Genesis, to describe the creation of the universe, is
employed in the 27th verse of the same chapter, to describe
the formation of man out of the dust of the earth. There was,
however, no peculiar ambiguity in the use of the Hebrew words
bawraw and *awsaw*, which correspond to our words *create* and
make; and, therefore, it is not necessary to be an adept in
Hebrew literature to judge of the question under consideration. We have only to determine whether the translation of
the Mosaic account of the creation most reasonably teaches a
production of the matter of the universe from nothing, or only

4

its renovation, and we have decided what is taught in the original.

Now, there can hardly be a doubt but Moses intended to teach, in this passage, that the universe owed its origin to Jehovah, and not to the idols of the heathen; and since all acknowledge that other parts of Scripture teach, that, when the world was made, it was produced out of nothing, why should we not conclude that the same truth is taught in this passage? The language certainly will bear that meaning; indeed, it is almost as strong as language can be to express such a meaning; and does not the passage look like a distinct avowal of this great truth, at the very commencement of the inspired record, in order to refute the opinion, so prevalent in early times, that the world is eternal?

The next inquiry concerning the passage relates to the phrase *the heavens and the earth*. Does it comprehend the universe? So it must have been understood by the Jews; for their language could not furnish a more comprehensive phrase to designate the universe. True, these words, like those already considered, are used sometimes in a limited sense. But in this place their broadest signification is in perfect accordance with the scope of the passage and with the whole tenor of the Scripture. We may, therefore, conclude with much certainty, that God intended in this place to declare the great truth, that there was a time in past eternity when the whole material universe came into existence at his irresistible fiat : — a truth eminently proper to stand at the head of a divine revelation.

But when did this stupendous event occur? Does the phrase *in the beginning* show us when? Surely not; for no language can be more indefinite as to time. Whenever it is used in the Bible, it merely designates the commencement of the series of events, or the periods of time, that are described. *In the beginning was the word ;* that is, at the commencement of things the word was in existence ; consequently was from eternity. But in Genesis the act of creation is represented by this phrase simply as the commencement of the material universe, at a certain point of time in past eternity, which is not chronologically fixed. The first verse merely informs us, that the first act of the Deity in relation to the universe was the creation of the heavens and the earth out of nothing.

It is contended, however, that the first verse is so connected with the six days' work of creation, related in the subsequent verse, that we must understand the phrase *in the beginning* as the commencement of the first day. This is the main point to be examined in relation to the passage, and therefore deserves a careful consideration.

If the first verse must be understood as a summary account of the six days' work which follows in detail, then *the beginning* was the commencement of the first day, and of course only about six thousand years ago. But if it may be understood as an announcement of the act of creation at some indefinite point in past duration, then a period may have intervened between that first creative act and the subsequent six days' work. I contend that the passage admits of either interpretation, without any violence to the language or the narration.

The first of these interpretations is the one usually received, and, therefore, it will be hardly necessary to attempt to show that it is admissible. The second has had fewer advocates, and will, therefore, need to be examined.

The particle *and*, which is used in our translation of this passage to connect the successive sentences, furnishes an argument to the English reader against this second mode of

interpretation, which has far less force with one acquainted
with the original Hebrew. The particle thus translated is
the general connecting particle of the Hebrew language, and
" may be copulative, or disjunctive, or adversative; or it may
express a mere annexation to a former topic of discourse, —
the connection being only that of the subject matter, or the
continuation of the composition. This continuative use forms
one of the most marked peculiarities of the Hebrew idiom,
and it comprehends every variety of mode in which one train
of sentiment may be appended to another." — J. Pye Smith,
Scrip. and Geol. p. 195, 4th edit.

In the English Bible this particle is usually rendered by the
copulative conjunction *and;* in the Septuagint, and in Josephus, however, it sometimes has the sense of *but.* And some
able commentators are of opinion that it admits of a similar
translation in the passage under consideration. The elder
Rosenmuller says we might read it thus : "*In the beginning
God created the heavens and the earth. Afterwards the earth
was desolate,*" &c. Or the particle *afterwards* may be placed
at the beginning of any of the succeeding verses. Thus, In
the beginning God created the heavens and the earth, and the
earth was desolate, and darkness was upon the face of the
waters. *Afterwards* the Spirit of God moved upon the face
of the waters. Dr. Dathe, who has been styled, by good authority, (Dr. Smith,) " a cautious and judicious critic," renders
the first two verses in this manner : " In the beginning God
created the heavens and the earth ; but afterwards the earth
became waste and desolate." If such translations as these be
admissible, the passage not only allows, but expressly teaches,
that a period intervened between the first act of creation and
the six days' work. And if such an interval be allowed, it is
all that geology requires to reconcile its facts to revelation.

For during that time, all the changes of mineral constitution and organic life, which that science teaches to have taken place on the globe, previous to the existence of man, may have occurred.

It is a presumption in favor of such an interpretation that the second verse describes the state of the globe after its creation and before the creation of light. For if there were no interval between the fiat that called matter into existence, and that which said, *Let there be light*, why should such a description of the earth's waste and desolate condition be given?

But if there had been such an intervening period, it is perfectly natural that such a description should precede the history of successive creative acts, by which the world was adorned with light and beauty, and filled with inhabitants.

But, after all, would such an interpretation have ever been thought of, had not the discoveries of geology seemed to demand it?

This can be answered by inquiring whether any of the writers on the Bible, who lived before geology existed, or had laid claims for a longer period previous to man's creation, whether any of these adopted such an interpretation. We have abundant evidence that they did. Many of the early fathers of the church were very explicit on this subject. Augustin, Theodoret, and others, supposed that the first verse of Genesis describes the creation of matter distinct from, and prior to, the work of six days. Justin Martyr and Gregory Nazianzen believed in an indefinite period between the creation of matter and the subsequent arrangement of all things. Still more explicit are Basil, Cæsarius, and Origen. It would be easy to quote similar opinions from more modern writers, who lived previous to the developments of geology. But I

4 *

will give a paragraph from Bishop Patrick only, who wrote one hundred and fifty years ago.

" How long," says he, " all things continued in mere confusion after the chaos was created, before light was extracted from it, we are not told. It might have been, for any thing that is here revealed, a great while ; and all that time the mighty Spirit was making such motions in it, as prepared, disposed, and ripened every part of it for such productions as were to appear successively in such spaces of time as are here afterwards mentioned by Moses, who informs us, that after things were digested and made ready (by long fermentation perhaps) to be wrought into form, God produced every day, for six days together, some creature or other, till all was finished, of which light was the very first." — *Commentary, in loco.*

Such evidence as this is very satisfactory. For at the present day one cannot but fear that the discoveries of geology may too much influence him insensibly to put a meaning upon Scripture which would never have been thought of, if not suggested by those discoveries, and which the language cannot bear. But those fathers of the church cannot be supposed under the influence of any such bias ; and, therefore, we may suppose the passage in itself to admit of the existence of a long period between the beginning and the first demiurgic day.

Against these views philologists have urged several objections not to be despised. One is, that light did not exist till the first day, and the sun and other luminaries not till the fourth day ; whereas the animals and plants dug from the rocks could not have existed without light. They could not, therefore, have lived in the supposed long period previous to the six days.

If it be indeed true, that light was not called into existence till the first day, nor the sun till the fourth, this objection is probably insuperable. But it would be easy to cite the opinions of many distinguished and most judicious expounders of the Bible, showing that the words of the Hebrew original do not signify a literal creation of the sun, moon, and stars, on the fourth day, but only constituting or appointing them, at that time, to be luminaries, and to furnish standards for the division of time and other purposes.

The word used is not the same as that employed in the first verse to describe the creation of the world; and the passage, rightly understood, implies the previous existence of the heavenly bodies. " The words מְאֹרֹת רְהַר are not to be separated from the rest," says Rosenmuller, " or to be rendered *fiant luminaria*, let there be light; i. e., *let light be made;* but rather, *let lights be;* that is, serve, in the expanse of heaven, for distinguishing between day and night; and let them be, or serve, for signs," &c. " The historian speaks (v. 16, end) of the determination of the stars to certain uses, which they were to render to the earth, and not of their first formation." In like manner we may suppose that the production of light was only rendering it visible to the earth, over which darkness hitherto brooded; not because no light was in existence, but because it did not shine upon the earth.

Another objection to this interpretation is, that the fourth commandment of the decalogue expressly declares, that *in six days the Lord made heaven and earth, the sea, and all that in them is,* &c., and thus cuts off the idea of a long period intervening between the *beginning* and the six days. I acknowledge that this argument carries upon the face of it a good deal of strength; but there are some considerations that seem to me to show it to be not entirely demonstrative.

In the first place, it is a correct principle of interpreting language, that when a writer describes an event in more than one place, the briefer statement is to be explained by the more extended one. Thus, in the second chapter of Genesis, we have this brief account of the creation : *These are the generations of the heavens and of the earth, when they were created, in the day that the Lord God made the earth and the heavens.*

Now, if this were the only description of the work of creation on record, the inference would be very fair that it was all completed in a single day.

Yet when we turn to the first chapter, we find the work prolonged through six days. The two statements are not contradictory ; but the briefer one would not be understood without the more detailed. In like manner, if we should find it distinctly stated in the particular account of the creation of the universe, in the first chapter of Genesis, that a long period actually intervened between the beginning and the six days, who would suppose the statement a contradiction to the fourth commandment ? It is true, we do not find such a fact distinctly announced in the Mosaic account of the creation. But suppose we first learn that it did exist from geology ; why should we not be as ready to admit it as if stated in Genesis, provided it does not contradict any thing therein recorded ? For illustration : let us refer to the account given in Exodus of the parents of Moses and their family. *And there went a man of the name of Levi, and took to wife a daughter of Levi. And the woman conceived and bare a son,* (that is, Moses,) *and when she saw that he was a goodly child, she hid him three months.* (Ex. ii. 12.) Suppose, now, that no other account existed in the Bible of the family of this Levite ; we could not surely have suspected that Moses had an elder brother and sister. But imagine the Bible silent on the subject, and that the fact was first brought to light in deciphering Egyptian hieroglyphics in the nineteenth century ; who could

hesitate to admit its truth because omitted in the Pentateuch ?
or who would regard it in opposition to the sacred record ?
With equal propriety may we admit, on proper geological
evidence, the intercalation of a long period between the beginning and the six days, if satisfied that it does not contradict
the Mosaic account. Hence all that is necessary, in this connection, for me to show, is, that such contradictions would not
be made out by such a discovery.

Once more : if this long period had existed, we should hardly
have expected an allusion to it in the fourth commandment,
if the views we have taken are correct as to the manner in
which the Old Testament treats of natural events. It is literally true, that all which the Jews understood by the heavens
and the earth, was made, (*awsaw,*) that is, renovated, arranged,
and constituted, — for so the word often means, — in six literal days. Had the sacred writer alluded to the earth while
without form and void, or to the heavenly bodies as any thing
more than shining points in the firmament, placed there on the
fourth day, he could not have been understood by the Hebrews,
without going into a detailed description, and thus violating
what seems to have been settled principles in writing the
Bible, viz., not to treat of natural phenomena with scientific
accuracy, nor to anticipate any scientific discovery.

I wish it to be distinctly understood, that I am endeavoring
to show, only, that the language of Scripture will admit of an
indefinite interval between the first creation of matter and the
six demiurgic days. I am willing to admit, at least for the
sake of argument, that the common interpretation, which
makes matter only six thousand years old, is the most natural.
But I contend that no violence is done to the language by
admitting the other interpretation. And in further proof of
this position, I appeal to the testimony of distinguished modern

theologians and philologists, as I have to several of the ancients. This point cannot, indeed, be settled by the authority of names. But I cannot believe that any will suppose such men as I shall mention were led to adopt this view simply because geologists asked for it, while their judgments told them that the language of the Bible would not bear such a meaning. When such men, therefore, avow their acquiescence in such an interpretation, it cannot but strengthen our confidence in its correctness.

" The interval," says Bishop Horsley, " between the production of the matter of the chaos and the formation of light, is undescribed and unknown."

" Were we to concede to naturalists," says Baumgarten Crusius, " all the reasonings which they advance in favor of the earth's early existence, the conclusion would only be, that the earth itself has existed much more than six thousand years, and that it had then already suffered many great and important revolutions. But if this were so, would the relation of Moses thereby become false and untenable ? I cannot think so."

" By the phrase *in the beginning*," says Doederlin, " the time is declared when something began to be. But when God produced this remarkable work, Moses does not precisely define."

" We do not know," says Sharon Turner, " and we have no means of knowing, at what point of the ever-flowing eternity of that which is alone eternal, — the divine subsistence, — the creation of our earth, or any part of the universe, began." " All that we can learn explicitly from revelation is, that nearly six thousand years have passed since our first parents began to be."

" The words in the text," says Dr. Wiseman, " do not merely express a momentary pause between the first fiat of creation and the production of light ; for the participial form of the verb, whereby the Spirit of God, the creative energy, is represented as brooding over the abyss, and communicating to it the productive virtue, naturally expresses a continuous, and not a passing action."

" I am strongly inclined to believe," says Bishop Gleig, " that the matter of the corporeal universe was all created at once ; though different portions of it may have been reduced to form at very different periods. When the universe was created, or how long the solar system remained in a chaotic state, are vain inquiries, to which no answer can be given."

" The detailed history of creation in the first chapter of Genesis," says Dr. Chalmers, " begins at the middle of the second verse ; and what precedes might be understood as an introductory sentence, by which we are most appositely told, both that God created all things at the first, and that afterwards — by what interval of time it is not specified — the earth lapsed into a chaos, from the darkness and disorder of which the present system or economy of things was made to arise. Between the initial act and the details of Genesis, the world, for aught we know, might have been the theatre of many revolutions, the traces of which geology may still investigate," &c.

" A philological survey of the initial sections of the Bible, (Gen. i. 1 to ii. 3,) " says Dr. Pye Smith, " brings out the result ; "

1. " That the first sentence is a simple, independent, all-comprehending axiom, to this effect, — that *matter*, elementary or combined, aggregated only or organized, and *dependent*, *sentient, and intellectual beings* have not existed from eternity, either in self-continuity or succession, but had a beginning ; that their beginning took place by the all-powerful will of one

Being, the self-existent, independent and infinite in all perfection ; and that the date of that beginning is not made known."

2. " That at a recent epoch, our planet was brought into a state of disorganization, detritus, or ruin, (perhaps we have no perfectly appropriate term,) from a former condition.

3. " That it pleased the Almighty, wise and benevolent Supreme, out of that state of ruin to adjust the surface of the earth to its now existing condition, — the whole extending through the period of six natural days."

" I am forming," continues Dr. Smith, " no hypotheses in geology ; I only plead that *the ground is clear*, and that the dictates of the Scripture *interpose no bar* to observation and reasoning upon the mineralogical constitution of the earth, and the remains of organized creatures which its strata disclose. If those investigations should lead us to attribute to the earth and to the other planets and astral spheres an antiquity which millions or ten thousand millions of years might fail to represent, *the divine records forbid not their deduction.*" — *Script. and Geol.* p. 502.

Says Dr. Bedford, " We ought to understand Moses as saying, *indefinitely far back, and concealed from us in the mystery of eternal ages, prior to the first moment of mundane time,* God created the heavens and the earth." — Smith, *Script. and Geol.* 4th edit.

" My firm persuasion is," says Dr. Harris, " that the first verse of Genesis was designed, by the divine Spirit, to announce the absolute origination of the material universe by the Almighty Creator ; and that it is so understood in the other parts of holy writ ; that, passing by an indefinite interval, the second verse describes the state of our planet immediately prior to the Adamic creation, and that the third verse begins the account of the six days' work."

"If I am reminded, in a tone of animadversion, that I am making science, in this instance, the interpreter of Scripture, my reply is, that I am simply making the works of God illustrate his word in a department in which they speak with a distinct and authoritative voice; that "it is all the same whether our geological or theological investigations have been prior, if we have not forced the one into accordance with the other." — (Davidson, *Sacred Hermeneutics.*) "And that it might be deserving consideration, whether or not the conduct of those is not open to just animadversion, who first undertake to pronounce on the meaning of a passage of Scripture, irrespective of all the appropriate evidence, and who then, when that evidence is explored and produced, insist on their *a priori* interpretation as the only true one." — *Pre-Adamite Earth,* p. 280.

"Our best expositors of Scripture," says Dr. Daniel King, of Glasgow, "seem to be now pretty generally agreed, that the opening verse in Genesis has no necessary connection with the verses which follow. They think it may be understood as making a separate and independent statement regarding the creation proper, and that the phrase 'in the beginning' may be expressive of an indefinitely remote antiquity. On this principle the Bible recognizes, in the first instance, the great age of the earth, and then tells us of the changes it underwent at a period long subsequent, in order to render it a fit abode for the family of man. The work of the six days was not, according to this view, a creation in the strict sense of the term, but a renovation, a remodelling of preëxisting materials." — *Principles of Geology explained,* &c. p. 40, 1st edit.

"Whether the Mosaic creation," says Dr. Schmucker, of the Lutheran church in this country, "refers to the present

5

organization of matter, or to the formation of its primary elements, it is not easy to decide. The question is certainly not
determined by the usage of the original words, עָשָׂה‎, בָּרָא‎, אָ‎,
which are frequently employed to designate mediate formation. Should the future investigations of physical science
bring to light any facts, indisputably proving the anterior
existence of the matter of this earth, such facts would not
militate against the Christian Scriptures."

" That a very long period," says Dr. Pond, — " how long no
being but God can tell, — intervened between the creation of
the world and the commencement of the six days' work recorded in the following verses of the first chapter of Genesis,
there can, I think, be no reasonable doubt."

But I need not adduce any more advocates of the interpretation of Genesis, for which I contend. Men more respected
and confided in by the Christian world I could not quote, though
I might enlarge the number ; but I trust it is unnecessary.
I trust that all who hear me are satisfied that the Mosaic history of the creation of the world does fairly admit of an interpretation which leaves an undefined interval between the
creation of matter and the six days' work. Let it be recollected that I do not maintain that this is the most natural
interpretation, but only that the passage will fairly admit it
by the strict rules of exegesis. The question still remains to
be considered, whether there is sufficient reason to adopt it as
the true interpretation. To show that there is, I now make
my appeal to geology. This is a case, it seems to me, in
which we may call in the aid of science to ascertain the true
meaning of Scripture. The question is, Does geology teach,
distinctly and uncontrovertibly, that the world must have
existed during a long period prior to the existence of the races
of organized beings that now occupy its surface ?

To give a popular view of the evidence sustaining the affirmative of this question is no easy task. It needs a full and
accurate acquaintance with the multiplied facts of geology,
and, what is still more rare, a familiarity with geological reasoning, in order to feel the full force of the arguments that
prove the high antiquity of the globe. Yet I know that I have
a right to presume upon a high degree of scientific knowledge,
and an accurate acquaintance with geology, among those
whom I address.

In the first place, I must recur to a principle already briefly
stated in a former lecture, viz., that a careful examination of
the rocks presents irresistible evidence, that, in their present
condition, they are all the result of second causes ; in other
words, they are not now in the condition in which they were
originally created. Some of them have been melted and re-
consolidated, and crowded in between others, or spread over
them. Others have been worn down into mud, sand, and
gravel, by water and other agents, and again cemented together, after having enveloped multitudes of animals and
plants, which are now imbedded as organic remains. In short,
all known rocks appear to have been brought into their present
state by chemical or mechanical agencies. It is indeed easy
to say that these appearances are deceptive, and that these
rocks may, with perfect ease, have been created just as we
now find them. But it is not easy to retain this opinion, after
having carefully examined them. For the evidence that they
are of secondary origin is nearly as strong, and of the same
kind too, as it is that the remains of edifices lately discovered
in Central America are the work of man, and were not created in their present condition.

In the second place, processes are going on by which rocks
are formed on a small scale, of the same character as those

which constitute the great mass of the earth.   Hence it is fair
to infer, that all the rocks were formed in a similar manner.
Beds of gravel, for instance, are sometimes cemented together
by heat, or iron, or lime, so as to resemble exactly the con-
glomerates found in mountain masses among the ancient
rocks.   Clay is sometimes converted into slate by heat, as is
soft marl into limestone, by the same cause.   In fact, we find
causes now in operation that produce all the varieties of known
rocks, except some of the oldest, which seem to need only a
greater intensity in some of the causes now at work to produce them.   By ascertaining the rate at which rocks are now
forming, therefore, we can form some opinion as to the time
requisite to produce those constituting the crust of the globe.
If, for instance, we can determine how fast ponds, lakes, and
oceans are filling up with mud, sand, and gravel, conveyed to
their bottoms, we can judge of the period necessary to produce those rocks which appear to have been formed in a similar manner ; and if there is any evidence that the process
was more rapid in early times, we can make due allowance.

In the third place, all the stratified rocks appear to have
been formed out of the fragments of other rocks, worn down
by the action of water and atmospheric agencies.   This is
particularly true of that large proportion of these rocks which
contain the remains of animals and plants.   The mud, sand,
and gravel of which these are mostly composed, must have
been worn from rocks previously existing, and have been
transported into lakes, and the ocean, as the same process is
now going on.   There the animals and plants, which died in
the waters, and were transported thither by rivers, must have
been buried ; next, the rocks must have been hardened into
stone, by admixture with lime, or iron, or by internal heat ; and,
finally, have been raised above the waters, so as to become

dry land. Beds of limestone are interstratified with those of shale, sandstone, and conglomerate; but these form only a small proportion of the whole, and, besides, were mostly formed in an analogous manner, though by agencies more decidedly chemical.

Now, for the most part, this process of forming rocks by the accumulation of mud, sand, and gravel is very slow. In general, such accumulations, at the bottom of lakes and the ocean, do not increase more than a few inches in a century. During violent floods, indeed, and in a few limited spots, the accumulation is much more rapid; as in the Lake of Geneva, through which the Rhone, loaded with detritus from the Alps, passes, where a delta has been formed two miles long and nine hundred feet thick, within eight hundred years.* And occasionally such rapid depositions probably took place while the older rocks were in the course of formation. But in general, the work seems to have gone on as slowly as it usually does at present.

Yet, in the fourth place, there must have been time enough

* This had always seemed to me a very strong case, as I had seen it described. But a recent visit to the spot (September, 1850) did not make so strong an impression upon me as I expected. In the first place, I found the head of Lake Lehman, where the Rhone enters, to be so narrow, that the detritus brought down by the river cannot spread itself out very far laterally. Secondly, I found, on ascending the Rhone, that it is every where a very rapid stream; and, on account of the origination of its branches from glaciers, it is always loaded with mud. So that the process of deposition must be going on continually. This cannot be the case in one in ten of other rivers, whose waters, for most of the year, are clear. This case, then, is only a quite unusual exception, and cannot be regarded as a standard by which to judge of the rate of deposition at present, or in past times.

5 *

since the creation to deposit at least ten miles of rocks in perpendicular thickness, in the manner that has been described. For the stratified rocks are at least of that thickness in Europe, and in this country much thicker ; or, if we regard only the fossiliferous strata as thus deposited, (since some geologists might hesitate to admit that the non-fossiliferous rocks were thus produced,) these are six and a half miles thick in Europe, and still thicker in this country. How immense a period was requisite for such a work ! Some do, indeed, contend that the work, in all cases, as we have allowed it in a few, may have been vastly more rapid than at the present day. But the manner in which the materials are arranged, and especially the preservation of the most delicate parts of the organic remains, often in the very position in which the animals died, show the quiet and slow manner in which the process went on.

In the fifth place, it is certain that, since man existed on the globe, materials for the production of rocks have not accumulated to the average thickness of more than one hundred or two hundred feet ; although in particular places, as already mentioned, the accumulations are thicker. The evidence of this position is, that neither the works nor the remains of man have been found any deeper in the earth than in the upper part of that superficial deposit called *alluvium*. But had man existed while the other deposits were going on, no possible reason can be given why his bones and the fruits of his labors should not be found mixed with those of other animals, so abundant in the rocks, to the depth of six or seven miles. In the last six thousand years, then, only one five hundredth part of the stratified rocks has been accumulated. I mention this fact, not as by any means an exact, but only an approximate, measure of the time in which the older rocks were deposited ;

for the precise age of the world is probably a problem which science never can solve. All the means of comparison within our reach enable us to say, only, that its duration must have been immense.

In the sixth place, during the deposition of the stratified rocks, a great number of changes must have occurred in the matter of which they are composed. Hundreds of such changes can be easily counted, and they often imply great changes in the waters holding the materials in solution or suspension; such changes, indeed, as must have required different oceans over the same spot. Such events could not have taken place without extensive elevations and subsidences of the earth's crust; nor could such vertical movements have happened without much intervening time, as many facts, too technical to be here detailed, show. Here, then, we have another evidence of vast periods of time occupied in the secondary production and arrangements of the earth's crust.

In the seventh place, numerous races of animals and plants must have occupied the globe previous to those which now inhabit it, and have successively passed away, as catastrophes occurred, or the climate became unfit for their residence. Not less than thirty thousand species have already been dug out of the rocks; and excepting a few hundred species, mostly of sea shells, occurring in the uppermost rocks, none of them correspond to those now living on the globe. In Europe, they are found to the depth of about six and a half miles; and in this country, deeper; and no living species is found more than one twelfth of this depth. All the rest are specifically and often generically unlike living species; and the conclusion seems irresistible, that they must have lived and died before the creation of the present species. Indeed, so different was the climate in those early times, — it having been much

warmer than at present in most parts of the world, — that but
few of the present races could have lived then. Still further:
it appears that, during the whole period since organized beings
first appeared on the globe, not less than four, or five, and
probably more — some think as many as ten or twelve — entire
races have passed away, and been succeeded by recent ones;
so that the globe has actually changed all its inhabitants
half a dozen times. Yet each of the successive groups occupied it long enough to leave immense quantities of their
remains, which sometimes constitute almost entire mountains.
And in general, these groups became extinct in consequence
of a change of climate; which, if imputed to any known
cause, must have been an extremely slow process.

Now, these results are no longer to be regarded as the
dreams of fancy, but the legitimate deductions from long and
careful observation of facts. And can any reasonable man
conceive how such changes can have taken place since the
six days of creation, or within the last six thousand years?
In order to reconcile them with such a supposition, we must
admit of hypotheses and absurdities more wild and extravagant
than have ever been charged upon geology. But admit of a
long period between the first creative act and the six days, and
all difficulties vanish.

In the eighth place, the denudations and erosions that have
taken place on the earth's surface indicate a far higher antiquity to the globe, even since it assumed essentially its present condition, than the common interpretation of Genesis
admits. The geologist can prove that in many cases the rocks
have been worn away, by the slow action of the ocean, more
than two miles in depth in some regions, and those very wide;
as in South Wales, in England. As the continents rose from
the ocean, the slow drainage by the rivers has excavated

numerous long and deep gorges, requiring periods incalculably extended.

I do not wonder that, when the sceptic stands upon the banks of Niagara River, and sees how obviously the splendid cataract has worn out the deep gorge extending to Lake Ontario, he should feel that there is a standing proof that the common opinion, as to the age of the world, cannot be true; and hence be led to discard the Bible, if he supposes that to be a true interpretation.

But the Niagara gorge is only one among a multitude of examples of erosion that might be quoted; and some of them far more striking to a geologist. On Oak Orchard Creek, and the Genesee River, between Rochester and Lake Ontario, are similar erosions, seven miles long. On the latter river, south of Rochester, we find a cut from Mount Morris to Portage, sometimes four hundred feet deep. On many of our southwestern rivers we have what are called *canons*, or gorges, often two hundred and fifty feet deep, and several miles long. Near the source of Missouri River are what are called the Gates of the Rocky Mountains, where there is a gorge six miles long and twelve hundred feet deep. Similar cuts occur on the Columbia River, hundreds of feet deep, through the hard trap rock, for hundreds of miles, between the American Falls and the Dalles. At St. Anthony's Falls, on the Mississippi, that river has worn a passage in limestone seven miles long, which distance the cataract has receded. On the Potomac, ten miles west of Washington, the Great Falls have worn back a passage sixty to sixty-five feet deep, four miles, continuously — a greater work, considering the nature of the rock, than has been done by the Niagara. The passage for the Hudson, through the highlands, is probably an example of river erosion; as is also that of the Connecticut at Brattleboro' and

Bellows Falls.   In these places, it can be proved that the river was once at least seven hundred feet above its present bed. On the Deerfield River, a tributary of the Connecticut, we have a gulf called the *Ghor*, eight miles long and several hundred feet deep, cut crosswise through the mica slate and gneiss by the stream.

On the eastern continent I might quote a multitude of analogous cases.   There is, for instance, the Wady el Jeib, in soft limestone, within the Wady Arabah, south of the Dead Sea. The defile is one hundred and fifty feet deep, half a mile wide, and forty miles long.   In Mount Lebanon, several remarkable chasms in limestone have been described by American missionaries, as that on Dog River, (Lycus of the ancients,) six miles long, seventy or eighty feet deep, and from one hundred and twenty to one hundred and sixty feet wide; also, Wady Barida, whose walls are six hundred to eight hundred feet high.   On the River Ravendoor, in Kurdistan, is a gorge, described in a letter from Dr. Perkins, one thousand feet deep. Another on the Euphrates, near Diadeen, is seventy feet deep, and is spanned by a natural bridge one hundred feet long. On the River Terek, in the Dariel Caucasus, is a pass one hundred and twenty miles long, whose walls rise from one thousand to three thousand feet high.   In Africa, the River Zaire has cut a passage, forty miles long, through mica slate, quartz, and syenite; and in New South Wales, Cox River passes through a gorge twenty-two hundred yards wide and eight hundred feet high.

Ninthly. Since the geological period now passing commenced, called the *alluvial*, or pleistocene period, certain changes have been going on, which indicate a very great antiquity to the drift period, which was the commencement of the alluvial period, and has been considered among the

most recent of geological events. I refer to the formation
of deltas and of terraces.

Of the deltas I will mention but a single example, to which,
however, many others correspond. The Mississippi carries
down to its mouth 28,188,803,892 cubic feet of sediment
yearly, which it deposits; or one cubic mile in five years and
eighty-one days. Now, as the whole delta contains twenty-
seven hundred and twenty cubic miles, it must have required
fourteen thousand two hundred and four years to form it in
this manner.

Terraces occur along some of the rivers of our country from
four hundred to five hundred feet above their present beds,
and around our lakes to the height of nearly one thousand feet.
They are composed of gravel, sand, clay, and loam, that have
been comminuted, and sorted, and deposited, by water chiefly.
At a height two or three times greater, on the same rivers
and lakes, we find what seem to be ancient sea beaches, of
the same materials, deposited earlier, and less comminuted.
The same facts also occur in Europe, and probably in Asia.

Now, it seems quite certain, that these beaches and terraces
were formed as the continents were being drained of the waters
of the ocean, and the rivers were cutting down their beds;
which last process has been going on in many places to the
present day. Yet scarcely nowhere, since the memory of
man, have even the lowest of these terraces and beaches been
formed, save on a very limited scale, and of a few feet in
height. The lowest of them have been the sites of towns and
cities, ever since the settlement of our country, and on the
eastern continent much longer. Yet we see the processes by
which they have been formed now in operation; but they
have scarcely made any progress during the period of human
history. How vast the period, then, since the work was first

commenced! Yet even its commencement seems to have been no farther back than the drift epoch, since that deposit lies beneath the terraces. But the drift period was comparatively a very recent one on the geological scale. How do such facts impress us with the vast duration of the globe since the first series of changes commenced!

Finally. There is no little reason to believe that, previous to the formation of the stratified rocks, the earth passed through changes that required vast periods of time, by which it was gradually brought into a habitable state. It is even believed that one of its earliest conditions was that of vapor; that, gradually condensing, it became a melted globe of fire, and then, as it gradually cooled, a crust formed over its surface; and so at last it became habitable. All this is indeed hypothesis; and, therefore, I do not place it in the same rank as the other proofs of the earth's antiquity, already adduced. Still this hypothesis has so much evidence in its favor, that not a few of the ablest and most cautious philosophers of the present day have adopted it. And if it be indeed true, it throws back the creation of the universe to a period remote beyond calculation or conception.

Now, let this imperfect summary of evidence in favor of the earth's high antiquity be candidly weighed, and can any one think it strange that every man, who has carefully and extensively examined the rocks in their native beds, is entirely convinced of its validity? Men of all professions, and of diverse opinions concerning the Bible, have been geologists; but on this point they are unanimous, however they may differ as to other points in the science. Must we not, then, regard this fact as one of the settled principles of science? If so, who will hesitate to say that it ought to settle the interpretation of the first verse of Genesis, in favor of that meaning which allows an intervening period between the creation of matter and the creation of light? This is the grand point which I have aimed to establish; and, in conclusion, I beg leave to make a few remarks by way of inference.

First. This interpretation of Genesis is entirely sufficient to remove all apparent collision between geology and revelation. It gives the geologist full scope for his largest speculations concerning the age of the world. It permits him to maintain that its first condition was as unlike to the present as possible, and allows him time enough for all the changes of mineral constitution and organic life which its strata reveal. It supposes that all these are passed over in silence by the sacred writers, because irrelevant to the object of revelation, but full of interest and instruction to the men of science, who should afterwards take pleasure in exploring the works of God.

It supposes the six days' work of creation to have been confined entirely to the fitting up the world in its present condition, and furnishing it with its present inhabitants. Thus, while it gives the widest scope to the geologist, it does not encroach upon the literalities of the Bible; and hence it is not strange that it should be almost universally adopted by geologists as well as by many eminent divines.

I would not forget to notice in this connection, however, a recent proposed extension of this interpretation by Dr. John Pye Smith, founded on the principle already illustrated, that the sacred writers adapted their language to the state of knowledge among the Jews. By the term *earth*, in Genesis, he supposes, was designed not the whole terraqueous globe, but "the part of our world which God was adapting for the dwelling-place of man and animals connected with him." And the narrative of the six days' work is a description

6

adapted to the ideas and capacities of mankind in the earliest
ages, of a series of operations, by which the Being of omnipo-
tent wisdom and goodness adjusted and furnished, not the earth
generally, but, as the particular subject under consideration
here, a PORTION of its surface for most glorious purposes.
This portion of the earth he conceives to have been a large
part of Asia, lying between the Caucasian ridge, the Caspian Sea and Tartary on the north, the Persian and Indian
Seas on the south, and the high mountain ridges which run
at considerable distance on their eastern and western flanks.
This region was first, by atmospheric and geological causes
of previous operation, under the will of the Almighty, brought
into a condition of superficial ruin, or some kind of general
disorder, probably by volcanic agency ; it was submerged,
covered with fogs and clouds, and subsequently elevated, and
the atmosphere, by the fourth day, rendered pellucid.—
Script. and Geol. p. 275, 2d edit.

Without professing to adopt fully this view of my learned
and venerable friend, I cannot but remark, that it explains one
or two difficulties on this subject, which I shall more fully
explain farther on. One is, the difficulty of conceiving how
the inferior animals could have been distributed to their present
places of residence from a single centre of creation without a
miracle. Certain it is, that, as the climate and position of
land and water now are, they could not thus migrate without
certain destruction to many of them. But by this theory they
might have been created within the districts which they now
occupy.

Another difficulty solved by this theory is, that several
hundred species of animals, that were created long before
man, as their remains found in the tertiary strata show, still
survive, and there is no evidence that they ever became

extinct; nor need they have been destroyed and recreated, if Dr. Smith's theory be true. Nevertheless, it does not appear to me essential to a satisfactory reconciliation of geology and revelation, that we should adopt it. But coming from such high authority, and sustained as it is by powerful arguments, it commends itself to our candid examination.

Secondly. I remark, that it is not necessary that we should be perfectly sure that the method which has been described, or any other, of bringing geology into harmony with the Bible, is infallibly true. It is only necessary that it should be sustained by probable evidence; that it should fairly meet the geological difficulty on the one hand, and do no violence to the language or spirit of the Bible on the other. This is sufficient, surely, to satisfy every philosophical mind, that there is no collision between geology and revelation. But should it appear hereafter, either from the discoveries of the geologist or the philologist, that our views must be somewhat modified, it would not show that the previous views had been insufficient to harmonize the two subjects; but only that here, as in every other department of human knowledge, perfection is not attained, except by long-continued efforts.

I make these remarks, because it is well known that other modes, besides that which I have defended, have been proposed to accomplish the same object; and it is probable that, even to this day, one or two of these modes may be defended, although the general opinion of geologists is in favor of that which I have exhibited.

Some, for instance, have supposed that the fossiliferous strata may all have been deposited in the sixteen hundred years between the creation and the deluge, and by that catastrophe have been lifted out of the ocean. Others have imagined them all produced by that event. But the most plausible theory regards the six days of creation as periods of great, though indefinite length, during which all the changes exhibited by the strata of rocks took place. The arguments in defence of this view are the following : 1. The word *day* is often used in Scripture to express a period of indefinite length. (Luke xvii. 24. John viii. 56. Job xiv. 6.) 2. The sun, moon, and stars were not created till the fourth day ; so that the revolution of the earth on its axis, in twenty-four hours, may not have existed previously, and the light and darkness that alternated may have had reference to some other standard. 3. The Sabbath, or seventh day, in which God rested from his work, has not yet terminated ; and there is reason to suppose the demiurgic days may have been at least of equal length. 4. This interpretation corresponds remarkably with the traditional cosmogonies of some heathen nations, as the ancient Etruscans and modern Hindoos ; and it was also adopted by Philo and other Jewish writers. 5. The order of creation, as described in Genesis, corresponds to that developed by geology. This order, according to Cuvier and Professor Jameson, is as follows : 1. The earth was covered with the sea without inhabitants. 2. Plants were created on the third day, and are found abundantly in the coal measures. 3. On the fifth day, the inhabitants of the waters, then flying things, then great reptiles, and then mammiferous animals, were created. 4. On the sixth day, man was created.

The following are the objections to this interpretation : 1. The word *day* is not used figuratively in other places of Genesis, (unless perhaps Gen. ii. 4,) though it is sometimes so used in other parts of Scripture. 2. In the fourth commandment, where the days of creation are referred to, (Exod. xx. 9, 10, 11,) no one can doubt but that the six days of labor and the Sabbath, spoken of in the ninth and tenth verses, are literal days. By what rule of interpretation can the same word in the next verse be made to mean indefinite periods? 3. From Gen. ii. 5, compared with Gen. i. 11, 12, it seems that it had not rained on the earth till the third day — a fact altogether probable if the days were of twenty-four hours, but absurd if they were long periods. 4. Such a meaning is forced and unnatural, and, therefore, not to be adopted without urgent necessity. 5. This hypothesis assumes that Moses describes the creation of all the animals and plants that have ever lived on the globe. But geology decides that the species now living, since they are not found in the rocks any lower down than man is, (with a few exceptions,) could not have been contemporaries with those in the rocks, but must have been created when man was; that is, on the sixth day. Of such a creation no mention is made in Genesis. The inference is, that Moses does not describe the creation of the existing races, but only of those that lived thousands of years earlier, and whose existence was scarcely suspected till modern times. Who will admit such an absurdity? If any one takes the ground that the existing races were created with the fossil ones, on the third and fifth days, then he must show, what no one can, why the remains of the former are not found mixed with the latter. 6. Though there is a general resemblance between the order of creation, as described in Genesis and by geology, yet when we look at the details of the creation of the organic world, as required by this hypothesis, we find manifest discrepancy, instead of the coincidence asserted by some distinguished advocates of these views. Thus the Bible represents plants only to have been created on the third day, and animals not till the fifth; and hence, at least, the lower half of the fossiliferous rocks ought to contain nothing but vegetables. Whereas, in fact, the lower half of these

6 *

rocks, all below the carboniferous, although abounding in animals, contain scarcely any plants, and those in the lowest
strata, fucoids, or sea-weeds. But the Mosaic account of
the third day's work evidently describes flowering and seed-
bearing plants, not flowerless and seedless algæ. Again :
reptiles are described in Genesis as created on the fifth day ;
but reptilia and batrachians existed as early as the time when
the lower carboniferous, and even old red sandstone strata,
were in a course of deposition, as their tracks on those rocks
in Nova Scotia and Pennsylvania evince. In short, if we
maintain that Moses describes fossil as well as living species,
we find discrepancy, instead of correspondence, between his
order of creation and that of geology. But admit that he
describes only existing species, and all difficulties vanish.

It appears, then, that the objections to this interpretation of
the word *day* are more geological than exegetical. It has
accordingly been mostly abandoned by men, who, from their
knowledge both of geology and scriptural exegesis, were best
qualified to judge. And even those who are inclined to adopt
it do also believe in the existence of a long period between
the beginning and the demiurgic days. From the earliest
times, however, in which we have writings upon the Scriptures, we find men doubting whether the demiurgic days of
Moses are to be taken in a strictly literal sense. Josephus
and Philo regarded the six days' work as metaphorical. Origen took a similar view, and St. Augustin says, " It is difficult,
if not impossible, for us to conceive what sort of days these
were." In more modern times, we find many able writers,
as Hahn, Hensler, De Luc, Professors Lee and Wait, of the
University of Cambridge, Faber, &c., adopting modifications
of the same views. Mr. Faber, however, a few years since,
abandoned this opinion ; and for the most part, geologists and

theologians prefer to regard the six days as natural days of twenty-four hours. But, generally, they would not regard the opposite opinion to be as unreasonable as it would be to reject the Bible from any supposed collision with geology. Yet, in general, they suppose it sufficient, to meet all difficulties, to allow of an indefinite interval between the " beginning " and the six days' work of creation.

In the truly scientific system of theology by the venerable Dr. Knapp, we find a proposed interpretation of the Mosaic account of the creation, that would bring it into harmony with geology. " If we would form a clear and distinct notion of this whole description of creation," says he, " we must conceive of six separate *pictures*, in which this great work is represented in each successive stage of its progress towards completion. And as the performance of the painter, though it must have natural truth for its foundation, must not be considered, or judged of, as a delineation of mathematical or scientific accuracy, so neither must this pictorial representation of the creation be regarded as literally and exactly true." He then alludes to the various hypotheses respecting the early state of the matter of the globe, and says, " Any of these hypotheses of the naturalist may be adopted or rejected, the Mosaic geogony notwithstanding." *

Thirdly. The interpretation of Genesis, for which I have contended in this lecture, does not affect injuriously any

* For a much more minute and extended account of the different modes proposed to reconcile geology and revelation, and indeed of their entire connection, I would refer to several papers in the American Biblical Repository, especially to the number for October, 1835, p. 261. The progress of science has, indeed, rendered it desirable to change a few sentences in those articles; but all their essential principles I still maintain.

doctrine of revelation. The community have, indeed, been taught to believe that the universe was all brought into existence about six thousand years ago; and it always produces a temporary evil to change the interpretation of a passage of the Bible, even though, as in this case, it be the result of new light shed upon it; because it is apt to make individuals of narrow views lose their confidence in the rules of interpretation. But when the change is once made, it increases men's confidence in the Word of God, which is only purified, but not shaken, by all the discoveries of modern science. In the present case, it does not seem to be of the least consequence, so far as the great doctrines of the Bible are concerned, whether the world has stood six thousand, or six hundred thousand years. Nor can I conceive of any truth of the Bible, which does not shine with at least equal brightness and glory, if the longest chronological dates be adopted.

Yet, fourthly. I maintain that several of these doctrines are far more strikingly and profitably exhibited, if the high antiquity of the globe be admitted. The common interpretation limits the operations of the Deity, so far as the material universe is concerned, to the last six thousand years. But the geological view carries the mind back along the flow of countless ages, and exhibits the wisdom of the Deity carrying forward, with infinite skill, a vast series of operations, each successive link springing out of that before it, and becoming more and more beautiful, until the glorious universe in which we live comes forth, not only the last, but the best of all. All this while, too, we perceive the heart of infinite Benevolence at work, either in fitting up the world for its future races of inhabitants, or in placing upon it creatures exactly adapted to its varying condition; until man, at last, the crown of all, makes it his delightful abode, with nothing to lament but his own apostasy, — with every thing perfect but himself. Can the mind enter such an almost boundless field of contemplation as this, and not feel itself refreshed, and expanded, and filled with more exalted conceptions of the divine plans and divine benevolence than could possibly be obtained within the narrow limits of six thousand years? But I will not enlarge; for I hope I may be allowed, in future lectures, to enter this rich field of thought, when we have more leisure to survey its beautiful prospects, and pluck its golden fruit.

Finally. If the geological interpretation of Genesis be true, then it should be taught to all classes of the community. It is, indeed, unwise to alter received interpretations of Scripture without very strong reasons. We should be satisfied that the new light, which has come to us, is not that of a transient meteor, but of a permanent luminary. We should, also, be satisfied, that the proposed change is consistent with the established rules of philology. If we introduce change of this sort before these points are settled, even upon passages that have no connection with fundamental moral principles, we shall distress many an honest and pious heart, and expose ourselves to the necessity of further change. But on the other hand, if we delay the change long after these points are fairly settled, we shall excite the suspicion that we dread to have the light of science fall upon the Bible. Nor let it be forgotten how disastrous has ever been the influence of the opinion that theologians teach one thing, and men of science another. Now, in the case under consideration, is there any reason to doubt the high antiquity of the globe, as demonstrated by geology? If any point, not capable of mathematical demonstration in physical science, is proved, surely this truth is established. And how easily reconciled to the inspired record, by an interpretation entirely consistent with the rules of philology, and with the scope of the passage, and the tenor of the Bible! It seems to me far more natural, and easy to understand, than that interpretation which it became necessary to introduce when the Copernican system was demonstrated to be true. The latter must have seemed to conflict strongly with the natural and most obvious meaning of certain passages of the Bible, at a time when men's minds were ignorant of astronomy, and, I may add, of the true mode of interpreting the language of Scripture respecting natural phenomena. Nevertheless, the astronomical exegesis prevailed, and every child can now see its reasonableness. So it seems to me that the child can easily apprehend the geological interpretation and its reasons. Why, then, should it not be taught to children, that they may not be liable to distrust the whole Bible, when they come to the study of geology? I rejoice, however, that the fears and prejudices of the pious and the learned are so fast yielding to evidence; and I anticipate the period, when, on this subject, the child will learn the same thing in the Sabbath school and the literary institution. Nay, I anticipate the time as not distant, when the high antiquity of the globe will be regarded as no more opposed to the Bible than the earth's revolution round the sun and on its axis. Soon shall the horizon, where geology and revelation meet, be cleared of every cloud, and present only an unbroken and magnificent circle of truth.

LECTURE III.

DEATH A UNIVERSAL LAW OF ORGANIC BEINGS ON THIS GLOBE FROM THE BEGINNING.

DEATH has always been regarded by man as the king of terrors, and the climax of all mortal evils; and by Christians its introduction into the world has generally been imputed to the apostasy of our first parents. For the threatening announced to them in Eden was, *In the day thou eatest of the forbidden fruit thou shalt surely die*, implying that if they did not eat thereof they might live. But *when the woman saw the tree was good for food, and that it was pleasant to the eyes, and a tree to be desired to make one wise, she took of the fruit thereof, and did eat, and gave also to her husband with her, and he did eat.* As the result, it is generally supposed that a great change took place in animals and plants, and from being immortal, they became mortal, in consequence of this fatal deed. But geology asserts that death existed in the world untold ages before man's creation, while physiology declares it to be a universal law of nature, and a wise and benevolent provision in such a world as ours. Now, the question is, Do not these different statements conflict with one another? and if so, is the discrepancy apparent only, or real? These are the questions which I now propose to examine, by all the light which we can obtain from the Bible and from science.

The first point to be ascertained in this investigation will be, what the Bible teaches on this subject.

In the first place, it distinctly informs us that the death which man experiences, came upon him in consequence of sin.

The declaration of Paul on this subject is as distinct as language can be. *By one man sin entered into the world, and death by sin, and so death passed upon all men, for that all have sinned.* This corresponds with the original threatening respecting the forbidden fruit. We know that our first parents ate of it; we know, also, that they died; and the apostle places these two facts in the relation of cause and effect.

In the second place, the Bible does not inform us whether the death of the inferior animals and plants is the consequence of man's transgression.

In order to prove this statement, it is necessary to show that the language of the Bible, which distinctly ascribes the introduction of death into the world, is limited to man. The first part of the sentence from Paul, just quoted, is indeed very general, and may include all organic natures. *By one man sin entered into the world, and death by sin.* What terms more general or explicit than these could be used? Yet the remainder of the sentence shows that the apostle had man mainly in his eye; *and so death passed upon all men, for that all have sinned.* The death here spoken of is limited expressly to man; and, therefore, it is not necessary to show that the same terms, in the first part of the sentence, had a more extended meaning. Death is spoken of here as the result of sin, and cannot, therefore, embrace animals and plants, which are incapable of sin. But after all, the first part of the sentence may intend to teach a general truth respecting the origin of every kind of death in the world. It will be seen in the sequel, that to such a meaning I have no objection, if it can be established.

Another very explicit passage on the introduction of death into the world is found in Corinthians : *Since by man came death, by man came also the resurrection of the dead.* Here, too, the last clause of the sentence limits the meaning to the human family. For no one will doubt that Christ is the man here spoken of, by whom came the resurrection of the dead. Now, unless the inferior animals and plants will share in a resurrection in consequence of what Christ has done, and in the redemption wrought out by him too, they cannot be included in this passage. And if neither of the texts now quoted extend in their application beyond the human race, I know of no other passage in the Bible that teaches, directly or inferentially, that death among the inferior animals or plants resulted from man's apostasy. I do not deny that there may be a connection between these events; certainly the Scriptures do not teach the contrary. But they appear to me rather to leave the question of such a connection undecided, and open for the examination of philosophers. If so, we may reason concerning the dissolution of animals, except men, without reference to the Scriptures.

Under the second part of this investigation, I shall endeavor to show that geology proves violent and painful death to have existed in the world long before man's creation.

In the oldest of the sedimentary rocks, the remains of animals occur in vast numbers; nor will any one, I trust, of ordinary intelligence, doubt but these relics once constituted living beings. Through the whole series of rocks, six miles in thickness, we find similar remains, even increasing in numbers as we ascend ; but it is not till we reach the very highest stratum, the mere superficial coat of alluvium, that we find the remains of man. The vast multitudes, then, of organized beings that lie entombed in rocks below alluvium, must

7

have yielded to death long before man received his sentence, *Dust thou art, and to dust shalt thou return.* Will any one maintain that none of these animals preceded man in the period of their existence? Then why are the remains of men not found with theirs? for his bony skeleton is as likely to be preserved and petrified as theirs. Moreover, so unlike to man and other existing tenants of the globe are many of these ancient animals, that the sure laws of comparative anatomy show us, that both races could not live and flourish in a world adapted to the one or the other. If the temperature had been warm enough for the fossil tribes, and all the circumstances of food and climate congenial to their natures, they would have been unsuited to the present races; and if adapted to the latter, the former must have perished. The difference be· tween the animals and plants dug out of the rocks in this lati· tude, and those now inhabiting the same region of country, is certainly as great as that between the animals and plants of the torrid and temperate zones; in most cases it is greater. Now, suppose that the animals and plants of the temperate zones were to change places with those between the tropics. A few species might survive, but the greater part would be destroyed. Hence, *a fortiori*, had the living beings now en tombed in the rocks been placed in the same climate with those now alive upon the globe, the like result would have followed. I say *a fortiori*; that is, for a stronger reason, the greater number must have perished; and the stronger reason is, the greater difference between fossil and living spe· cies, than between the latter in torrid and temperate latitudes. It is true that man is among the species capable of being acclimated to great extremes. And yet no physiologist will imagine that even his nature could have long survived in such a climate as formerly existed, when probably the atmosphere was loaded with carbonic acid and other mephitic gases, and with moisture and miasms, the result of a rank vegetation, and of a temperature higher than now exists in equatorial countries.

This argument, furnished by comparative anatomy, to show that man and the fossil animals could not have been contemporaries, will probably seem to have little force to those who are not familiar with the history of organic life on the globe, and the distribution of species.   It is not generally known that both animals and plants are usually confined to a particular district, and that a removal beyond its boundaries, or the access of a few more degrees of cold, or heat, than is common in the place assigned them by nature, will destroy them. To him who understands this curious history, the argument under consideration is perfectly satisfactory, to prove the existence and consequent dissolution of myriads of living beings, anterior to man.   " Judging by these indications of the habits of the animals," says the distinguished anatomist, Sir Charles Bell, " we acquire a knowledge of the condition of the earth during their period of existence ; that it was suited at one time to the scaly tribe of the lacertæ, with languid motion ; at another, to animals of higher organization, with more varied and lively habits ; and finally, we learn that at any period previous to man's creation, the surface of the earth would have been unsuitable to him.   Any other hypothesis than that of a new creation of animals, suited to the successive changes in the inorganic matter of the globe, the condition of the water, atmosphere, and temperature, brings with it only an accumulation of difficulties." — *The Hand, its Mech.,* &c. pp. 31 and 115.

But when arguing with those who do not feel the force of this argument, I would fall back upon that derived from the fact, that of the ten thousand species of animals dug out of the rocks beneath alluvium, no relic of man has been found; and ask them whether they can explain such a fact, except by the supposition that man was not their contemporary.

In his admirable Bridgewater Treatise, Dr. Buckland has conclusively shown that the same great system of organization and adaptation has always prevailed on the globe. It was the same in those immensely remote ages, when the fossil animals lived, as it now is. And there is one feature of that system which deserves notice in this argument. At present, we know that there exist large tribes of animals, called carnivorous, provided with organs expressly designed to enable them to destroy other animals, and of course to inflict on them violent and painful death. Exactly similar tribes, and in a like proportion, are found among the fossil animals. They were not always the same tribes; but when one class of carnivora disappeared, another was created to take their place, in order to keep down the excessive multiplication of other races, which appears to be the grand object accomplished by the carnivorous races. And that animals of such an organization not only lived in the ages preceding man's creation, but actually destroyed contemporary species, we have the evidence in the remains of the one animal enclosed in the body of another, by whom it was devoured for food; and both are now converted into rock, and will testify to the most sceptical, that death among animals existed in the world before man's transgression.

Under the third part of this investigation, I shall attempt to show that physiology teaches us that death is a general law of organic natures.

It is not confined to animals, but embraces also plants. As they correspond in a striking manner to animals in their

reproduction and growth, so they do in their decay and dissolution. In short, wherever in nature we find life and organization, death is inevitable. The amount of vital energy varies
in different species, and in individuals ; but in them all, it at
length becomes exhausted, and the functions cease. After a
certain period, the vessels which convey the nutritive materials, and elaborate the proximate principles, become choked
with excrementitious matter, assimilation is performed imperfectly, and gradually the vital energies are overpowered, and
yield up their charge to the disorganizing power of chemical
agencies. We can hardly see why the delicate machinery
cannot hold out longer than it does, or even indefinitely. But
experience shows us that an irresistible law of nature has fixed
the period of its operations. In the expressive language of
Scripture, which applies to plants as well as animals, *there is
no discharge in that war.*

A little reflection will convince any one, that in such a system as exists in the world, this universal decay and dissolution
are indispensable. For dead organic matter is essential to
the support and nourishment of living beings. Admit, for the
sake of the argument, (although it is obviously absurd in re
spect to the carnivorous races,) that animals might be supported by vegetable food. Yet, if plants must furnish nourishment for their successors, as well as for animals, the organic
matter must at length be exhausted. And, furthermore, how
could animals feed on plants without destroying, as they now
do, multitudes of minute insects and animalcules ? It is obvious, also, that, for a variety of reasons, the multiplication
of animals must soon be arrested, or famine would be the
result, or the world would be more than full. In short, it
would require an entirely different system in nature from the
present, in order to exclude death from the world. To the

7 *

existing system it is as essential as gravitation, and apparently just as much a law of nature.

To strengthen this argument still further, comparative anatomy testifies that large classes of animals have a structure evidently intended to enable them to feed on other tribes. The teeth of the more perfect carnivorous animals are adapted for seizing and tearing their prey, while those which feed on vegetables have cutting and grinding teeth, but not the canine. So the whole digestive apparatus in the carnivora is more simple, and of less extent, than in the herbivorous tribes, while in the former the gastric juice acts more readily upon flesh, and in the latter upon vegetables. The muscular apparatus, also, is developed in greater power in the former than in the latter, especially in the neck and fore paw. Throughout all the classes of animals, those which feed on flesh are armed with poisonous fangs, or talons, or beaks, or other formidable weapons, while the vegetable feeders are usually in a great measure defenceless. In short, in the one class we find a perfect adaptation, in all the organs, for destroying, digesting, and assimilating other animals, and in the other class, an arrangement, equally obvious, for procuring and digesting vegetables. Indeed, you need only show the anatomist the skeleton, or even a very small part of the skeleton, of an unknown animal, to enable him, in most cases, to decide, what is the food of that animal, with almost as much certainty as if he had for years observed its habits. Who can doubt, then, that when a carnivorous animal employs the weapons with which nature has furnished it for the destruction of another animal, in order to satisfy its hunger, that it acts in obedience to a law of its being, originally impressed upon its constitution by the Creator? It is true, that even the flesh-eating animals may be taught for a time to subsist upon vegetable products. But this is unnatural;

and such an animal usually pays the price of thus inverting
its original instinct, by disease and premature decay. In a
state of nature, an animal would starve rather than thus vio-
late its instinctive desires.

I will allude to only one other fact, that shows death to be
inseparable from organized beings, without a constant miraculous interference, in such a world as ours. Animal organization, in all conceivable circumstances, must be liable to
accident, from mere mechanical force, by which life would
be destroyed. It may be possible, perhaps, to conceive of a
material tenement for the soul, which should be unaffected by
all forms of mechanical violence and chemical action; if, for
instance, its constitution were analogous to that supposed
medium through which light, heat, and electricity, and perhaps gravitation, act. But, surely, our present bodies are far
enough removed from such conditions, being of all terrestrial
things the most liable to ruin from the causes above mentioned.

The conclusions from all these facts and reasonings are,
that death is an essential feature of the present system of
organized nature; that it must have entered into the plan of
creation in the divine mind originally, and consequently must
have existed in the world before the apostasy of man. Whether
the entire system of death had any connection with that event,
or whether there is any thing peculiar in the death endured
by the human family, will be questions for examination in a
subsequent part of my lecture.

In opposition to these conclusions, however, the common
theory of death maintains that, when man transgressed, there
was an entire change throughout all organic nature; so that
animals and plants, which before contained a principle of im
mortal life, were smitten with the hereditary contagion of
disease and death. Those animals which, before that event,

were gentle and herbivorous, or frugivorous, suddenly became ferocious or carnivorous. The climate, too, changed, and the sterile soil sent forth the thorn and the thistle, in the place of the rich flowers and fruits of Eden. The great English poet, in his Paradise Lost, has clothed this hypothesis in a most graphic and philosophical dress; and probably his descriptions have done more than the Bible to give it currency. Indeed, could the truth be known, I fancy that, on many points of secondary importance, the current theology of the day has been shaped quite as much by the ingenious machinery of Paradise Lost as by the Scriptures; the theologians having so mixed up the ideas of Milton with those derived from inspiration, that they find it difficult to distinguish between them.

In the case under consideration, Milton does not limit the change induced by man's apostasy to sublunary things, but, like a sagacious philosopher, perceives, also, that the heavenly bodies must have been diverted from their paths.

> " At that tasted fruit,
> The sun, as from Thyestian banquet, turned
> His course intended; else how had the world
> Inhabited, though sinless, more than now,
> Avoided pinching cold and scorching heat?"

This change of the sun's path, as the poet well knew, could be effected only by some change in the motion of the earth.

> " Some say he bid the angels turn askance
> The poles of earth, twice ten degrees and more,
> From the sun's axle; they with labor pushed
> Oblique the centric globe."

Next we have the effect upon the lower orders of animals described.

> " Discord first,
> Daughter of sin, among the irrational
> Death introduced: through fierce antipathy,
> Beast now with beast 'gan war, and fowl with fowl,
>   And fish with fish ; to graze the herb all leaving,
> Devoured each other."

The question arises here, whether such views are sustained by the Bible and by science. Few, I presume, would seriously maintain that the act of our first parents, which produced what Dr. Chalmers calls " an unhingement " of the human race, resulted likewise in a change in the motion of the earth and the heavenly bodies ; since the Bible so clearly describes the previous ordination of days, years, and seasons, on the fourth day of creation. And is there any thing in the language of the Bible that will justify the opinion that such changes as this theory supposes took place in the productions of the earth, and in the nature of its animals? No anatomist can surely be made to believe that, without a constant miracle, our carnivorous animals can have become herbivorous, without such a change in their organization as must have amounted to a new creation. And such a metamorphosis can hardly have passed unnoticed by the sacred writer. True, only the gramineous and herbaceous substances are in the Bible given to the inferior animals for food, while the fruits are assigned to man. But this passage seems only to be a designation of one part of vegetable productions to men, and another to other animals, and can hardly be supposed to preclude the idea that there might be other tribes requiring animal food.

The sentence pronounced upon the serpent for his agency in man's apostasy seems, at first view, favorable to the opinion that animal natures experienced at the same time important changes; for he is supposed to have been deprived of limbs, and condemned henceforth to crawl upon the earth, and to make the dust his food. But is it the most probable interpretation of this passage, which makes the tempter a literal serpent, or only a symbolical one? The naturalist does not surely find that serpents live upon dust, for they all are carnivorous, and they are as perfectly adapted to crawl upon the ground as other animals to different modes of progression; and though *cursed above all cattle*, they are apparently as happy as other animals. Hence the probability is, that an evil spirit is described in Genesis under the name and figure of a serpent. This conclusion is supported by other parts of Scripture, where the tempter is in several places declared to be *the devil, the old serpent*, and *the great dragon*.

A part of the sentence passed upon man seems, also, at first view, to imply an important change in the vegetable productions of the earth; for the ground is cursed for man's sake: it would henceforth produce to him thorns and thistles, and in the sweat of his brow must he eat of the fruits of it, all the days of his life. Now, will not the condition and character of Adam show how this curse might be fulfilled, without any change in the productions of the soil? The garden of Eden, where man had lived in his innocence, was doubtless some sunny and balmy spot, where the air was delicious, and the earth poured forth her abundant fruits spontaneously; and although he was called to keep and dress that garden, yet, with a contented and holy heart, and with no factitious wants, the work was neither labor nor sorrow. But now he is driven from that garden into regions far less fertile, where the sterile soil can be made to yield its fruits only by the sweat of the brow, and where the thorn and the thistle dispute their right of soil with salutary plants; and in his heart, too, unholy and unsubdued passions have place, which will infuse sorrow into all his labors.

As I have remarked in another place, I cannot see why the functions of animal and vegetable organization might not have gone on forever without decay and death, if such had been the Creator's will. In other words, I do not see why the operation of the organs should at length be impeded and cease, as we know they do universally. Hence I can conceive that it might have been otherwise originally; and in the case of man it is possible, as we shall see farther on, that a change of this sort may have taken place at the time of his apostasy. But, after all, it strikes me that the Bible furnishes very clear evidence that the same system of decay and death prevailed before the apostasy which now prevails. The command given, both to animals and to man, to be fruitful and multiply, implies the removal of successive races by death; otherwise the world would ere long be overstocked. A system of death is certainly a necessary counterpart to a system of reproduction; and hence, where we know the one to exist, the presumption is very strong that the other exists also. There is no escape from this inference, except to call in the aid of miraculous power to preserve the proper balance among different races of animals, by preventing their multiplication. Such an interference I am always ready to admit, where the Scriptures assert it. But to imagine a miracle without proof, merely to escape a fair conclusion, is, to say the least, very wretched logic. God never introduces a miracle where he can employ the ordinary agency of nature for accomplishing his purposes. Nor should we resort to one without the express testimony of the Bible, which, on this subject, is our only source of evidence.

We have in Scripture the same kind of proof that plants were subject to decay and death, before the fall, as we have in respect to animals. For in the account of the creation of plants on the third day, we find them described as bearing seeds; and does not this clearly imply the same system of reproduction which now exists throughout the vegetable kingdom? In short, an unprejudiced mind, in reading the history of the world in Genesis, before and after the fall, can hardly fail of the conviction, that animals and plants were originally created on the same plan, as to reproduction, decay, and death, which now prevails. Great, indeed, must have been the change at the fall, if, previous to that time, their structure excluded all the organs and means of reproduction; as must have been the case if decay and death were also excluded. And it is strange that the sacred writer should take no notice of such a change. He states the effect of sin upon the three parties directly concerned in it, viz., the tempter, Adam, and Eve; and if a transformation of all vegetable and animal natures, great enough almost to constitute a new creation, did take place, it could hardly have been passed in silence. Even in the case of man, we have no remarkable physical change. The effect seems to have been chiefly confined to his intellectual constitution, where we should expect the effect of sin to be primarily felt. There, indeed, in man's noblest part, has the havoc been the most terrific, and powerfully has its operation there reacted upon the body, so as to make death, in the case of man, the king of terrors.

We find, then, insuperable objections to the prevalent notion that an entire revolution took place at the fall in the material world, and especially in organic nature. Those passages of Scripture which, literally interpreted, seem to imply some changes of this sort, are easily understood as vivid figurative representations of the effects of sin upon men, while their literal interpretation would involve us in inextricable difficulties. We rest, therefore, in the conclusion, that, whatever connection there may be between death and the existing system of organic and inorganic nature, no important change took place at the time of man's first transgression; in other words, the present system is that which was originally determined upon in the divine mind, and not the original plan altered after man's transgression.

The fourth step in the investigation of this subject leads me to attempt to show that, in the present system of the world, death, to the inferior animals, is a benevolent provision, and to man, also, when not aggravated or converted into a curse by his own sin.

In examining this point, as well as many others in natural theology, where the existence of evil is concerned, we must assume that the present system of the world is the best which infinite wisdom and benevolence could devise. And this we may consistently do. For the prominent design throughout nature appears to be beneficial to animal natures, and suffering is only incidental, and happiness, moreover, is superadded to the functions of animals, where it is unnecessary to the perfect performance of the function. We may be certain, therefore, that the Author of such a system can neither be malevolent nor indifferent to the happiness of animals, but must be benevolent; and, therefore, the system must be the best possible, since such a Being could constitute no other.

Now, death being an essential feature of such a system, we should expect to find it, as a whole, a benevolent provision. But, in the case of man, the Bible represents it as a penal

8

infliction, and such is its general aspect in the human family
So far as the mere extinction of life is concerned, it is the
same in man as in other animals; but sin arms it with a
deadly sting, by pointing the offender to a world of retribution, as he sees the menacing dart of the great destroyer aimed at his heart. And, indeed, through all his
days, man's power of anticipation keeps death ever before
him, as the end of all his present enjoyments, and the commencement, it may be, of unmitigated suffering. But the
inferior animals, being incapable of sin, find none of these
aggravations to give keenness to their final sufferings. No
anticipation of death keeps it ever in view, as a terrific
enemy. No guilty conscience points them to a righteous
throne of judgment, where they must be arraigned. But
when the stroke comes, it falls unexpectedly, and the mere
physical suffering is all that gives severity to their dissolution.

In the case of man, too, there is the sundering of ties too
strong for any thing but death to break; — ties which bind him
to kindred, friends, and country; and often this separation
constitutes the most painful part of the closing scene. But in
the case of animals, we have no reason to suppose these
attachments, so far as they exist, to be very strong; nay, in
most cases they are certainly very weak. And even did they
exist, the brute would not be conscious that death would remove him from the society of his beloved companions.

The inferior animals, also, usually die either a violent and
sudden death, inflicted by some carnivorous enemy, or in extreme old age, by mere decay of the natural powers, without
disease. The violent death can usually have in it little of
suffering; and the slow decay still less. But although some
men die violent deaths, how few survive to extreme old age,

and sink at last almost unconsciously into the grave, because the vital energies are exhausted ! Were this the case, the physical terrors of death would be almost taken away, and we should pass as quietly into eternity as a lamp goes out when the oil is exhausted. But in general we see a constitution yet unbroken, struggling with fierce disease, and yielding to its fate only with terrific agonies; because sin has early implanted the seeds of disease in the constitution.

Imagine, now, that death should come upon a man in the course of nature ; that is, without disease, and with little suffering, and with no painful forebodings of conscience. Suppose, moreover, that the dying individual should feel that the change passing upon him would assuredly introduce him to a new and spiritual body, undecaying, and adapted to the operations of the mind; that it would, in fact, be *the building of God, the house not made with hands, eternal in the heavens ;* and that the soul, after death, would enter into free and full communion with all that is great and ennobling in the universe; and that joys, inconceivable and eternal, would henceforth be its portion : O, how different would such a death be from what we usually witness ! Yet, were men all to accept of the offered ransom from sin and death, and, under the guidance of pure religious principle, were to pay a strict regard to hygienic laws, such would be, for the most part, the character of the death they would experience. The excepted cases would be those of violent and sudden death from accident, or of disease from unavoidable exposure, and they would be comparatively few. So that, in fact, an observance of the laws, physical and moral, which God has ordained, would change almost the entire aspect of death, even in this fallen world.

These remarks seem necessary in order to obtain a correct

idea of the character of death, when not aggravated by the sins of men. For those aggravations seem superadded, in the case of men, as penal inflictions for their sins; and we ought to leave them out of the account, when we are considering death as a benevolent provision. I do not contend that death, even in its mildest forms, is no evil; nor that the apostasy of man was not the cause of its introduction into the world. These points I shall consider in another place. But I contend that, in the present system of the world, death, when not aggravated by the sins of men, is to be regarded as a benevolent provision, bringing with it more happiness than misery; although, had sin never existed, a system productive of still greater enjoyment might have been adopted in this world. But as the arrangements of the world now are, death affords the following evidences of infinite benevolence and wisdom.

In the *first place*, it is a transfer from a lower to a higher state of existence.

Let me here be understood distinctly as speaking only of the death of those accountable beings, who, by the transforming power of grace, have become prepared for a higher and perfectly holy state of being. For the death of all others can be looked on only in the light of a terrible penal infliction. But the righteous, when they die, — and all may, if they will, become righteous, — have before them the certain prospect of immortal happiness, such as *eye hath not seen, nor ear heard, neither hath it entered the heart of man to conceive.* They enter upon *fulness of joy, and pleasures forevermore;* and therefore death to them is infinite gain.

Whether the inferior animals will exist again after death is a more doubtful point. There is certainly nothing in Scripture decisive against their future existence; for the

passage in Psalms which says, that *man that is in honor and abideth not is like the brutes that perish*, if understood to mean the annihilation of animals, would prove also the annihilation of wicked men. And while most men of learning and piety have suspended their opinion on the existence of the inferior animals after death, for want of evidence, some have been decided advocates of the future happy existence of all beings, who exhibit a spark of intelligence. Not a few distinguished German theologians and philosophers regard the whole visible creation, both animate and inanimate, as at present in a confined and depressed state, and struggling for freedom. On this principle Tholuck explains that most difficult passage in Romans, which declares *that the whole creation groaneth and travaileth together in pain until now*. He supposes this "bound or fettered state of nature," both animate and inanimate, to have a casual connection with sin, and the death accompanying it among men ; and, therefore, when men are freed from sin and death, *the creation itself, also, shall be delivered from the bondage of corruption into the glorious liberty of the children of God*. The kingdom of God, according to Tholuck, Martin Luther, and many other distinguished theologians, will not be transferred to heaven at the end of the world, but be established on earth, where all these transformations of the animate and inanimate creation will take place.

This exposition surely carries with it a great deal of naturalness and probability ; and if it be true, death to the inferior animals must surely be an indication of great benevolence on the part of the Deity, since it introduces them to a higher state of existence. But if it be rejected, still the general principle is eminently applicable to the case of man.

In the *second place,* the system of a succession of races

8*

of animals on earth, which death alone would render possible, secures a much greater collective amount of happiness than a single race of animals, endowed with earthly immortality. I sustain this position by three arguments. The first is, that young animals enjoy more, in the same period of time, than those more advanced in age. This may result, in part, in the present organization of animals, from the superior health and vigor enjoyed by the young. But it is due, also, in part, and largely, to the novelty of the scenes presented in early life. And so far as it results from the latter cause, it proves that a succession of races would enjoy more than a single race continued indefinitely, because the successive races would always be comparatively young. A single continuous race might, indeed, be supposed always possessed of the unabated vigor and health of youth; but, of necessity, objects must soon lose the charm of novelty, and, therefore, produce less of enjoyment. The second argument is, that a succession of races admits of the contemporaneous existence of a greater number of species than could coëxist were none removed by death. If only one undying race occupied the globe, it must subsist exclusively on vegetable food. Whereas much the largest part of the species that now live are carnivorous or omnivorous. All the enjoyment of these flesh-eating animals is, therefore, so much clear gain to the stock of happiness, with the exception of the suffering which death inflicts. Now, but few of the inferior animals perish by disease. Some die by old age, and these suffer almost nothing. But the greater part are suddenly destroyed by the violent assault of the carnivorous races. And as the pangs of death are momentary, and there are no anticipations of its approach, nor sunderings of the ties of affection, nor dread of an hereafter, the suffering endured must be an exceedingly small drawback upon the enjoyment of the whole life. It is far less than it would be, if animals were left to perish by famine, or by slow degrees, from deficient nourishment; so that the existence of the carnivorous races, seeming at first view intended to convert the world into a vast Golgotha, does in fact add greatly to the amount of enjoyment, because it so prodigiously multiplies the number of species of animals, and lessens the sufferings of death. In the third place, death exerts a salutary moral influence upon man, and, as a consequence, swells the amount of his happiness. And although this consideration affects only one species, yet man's position on the scale of being makes his happiness an object of no small importance.

The final conclusions at which we arrive, then, are, first, that death is a fixed and universal law of nature, essential to the existence of the present system of the world; and secondly, that, like all other laws of nature, it exhibits marks of benevolence, and wise adaptation on the part of the Author of nature. The question will indeed arise in every reflecting mind, why a Being of infinite power and wisdom could not have secured to his creatures the benefits resulting from a system of death, without the attendant suffering. But this question resolves itself into the inquiry, why evil exists at all; and although, in my own view, it exists most probably as a means of greater happiness to the universe, yet on this point the wisest minds have differed and been baffled, and equally perplexing is it to every form of religion. Hence it is no objection to any views we may adopt, that they leave this question where they found it.

The fifth and last step in our investigation of this subject is to show how science, experience, and revelation may be reconciled on the subject of death.

We have seen that geology is not alone in proving death

to be a law of nature, essential to the present system of the
world, and, indeed, indicative of divine wisdom and benevolence.   For anatomy and physiology, as well as experience,
teach us the same truths.   And natural theology shows that,
if death is a law of organic nature, it must have entered into
the plan of the universe in the divine mind, and was not the
result of any change of organic nature subsequent to the fall
of man.   Can these views be reconciled with the declarations
of Scripture, which certainly represent death among the
human family, if not among the lower animals, to be the
consequence of sin?

There are three suppositions by which all apparent discrepancy between science and revelation, on this subject, may be
removed.   I shall present them, with the arguments in their
favor, leaving to others to decide which is most reasonable.
For they are independent of one another, though not inconsistent; and, therefore, even though different persons should
prefer different theories, they need not be regarded as in opposition to one another.

The first theory proceeds on the supposition that death is
a universal law of organic nature, from which man was exempted so long as he obeyed the law of God.   But I will
present it in the language of its distinguished author.   " In
the state of pristine purity," says Dr. J. Pye Smith, " the
bodily constitution of man was exempted from the law of
progress towards dissolution, which belonged to the inferior
animals.   It must have been maintained in that distinguished
peculiarity by means to us unknown; and it would seem
probable that, had not man fallen by his transgression, he,
and each of his posterity, would, after faithfully sustaining
an individual probation, have passed through a change without dying, and have been exalted to a more perfect state of
existence." — *Scrip. and Geol.* 4th ed. p. 208.

According to this theory of Dr. Smith, man saw all other organic beings around him subject to decay and death, while he, as a special favor, remained unaffected by the general law. The penalty of disobedience was, that he would forfeit this enviable distinction, and be subjected to death more revolting than the brutes. The reward of obedience was a continued immunity from evil, and a final translation, without suffering, to a more exalted condition. And certainly the nature of the case furnishes a strong presumptive argument to show that man did thus stand exempted from the decay and death which reigned all around him. If not, what weight or meaning would there be in the penalty? If he had not seen death in other animals, how could he have any idea of the nature of the threatening? And we may be sure that God never promulgates a penalty without affording his subjects the means of comprehending it.

I have already intimated that I could hardly see why there exists in all organic natures a tendency to decay and death, except in the will of the Creator. May not that tendency result, like the varieties among men, from some slightly modifying cause implanted by the Deity in the nature of the animal or plant? And if so, might not an opposite tendency be imparted to one or more species, so that the decay and death of the one, and the continued existence of the other, might be equally well explained on physiological principles? If this suggestion be admitted, it would not be necessary to resort to any supernatural or miraculous agency to show how sinless man in paradise might have stood unaffected by decay, the common lot of all other races. It must be confessed, however, that it is not as easy to see how, by any natural law, he could have been proof against mechanical violence and chemical agencies; there we must admit miraculous protection, or a self-restoring power more wonderful than that possessed by the polypi.

These views receive strong confirmation from the history of the tree of life, that grew in the garden of Eden. The very name implies that it was intended to give or preserve life. That it had in it a power to preserve life is evident from the sentence pronounced on man. *And the Lord God saith, Behold, the man hath become as one of us, to know good and evil; and now, lest he should put forth his hand, and take also of the tree of life, and live forever, therefore the Lord God sent him forth from the garden of Eden.* Now, it appears to me to be in perfect harmony with the principles of physiology to suppose that there might be a virtue in the tree of life — either in its fruit or some other part — to arrest that tendency to decay and dissolution which we now find in all animal bodies. It does seem that it would require only some slight modification of the present functions of the human frame to keep the wheels of life in motion indefinitely. When in Eden, man had access to this sure defence against disease. But after he had sinned, he must forfeit this privilege, and, like the plants and inferior animals, submit to the universal law of dissolution. Surely, of all the expositions that have been given of the meaning of this passage, this is the most rational, and it does throw an air of great plausibility over Dr. Smith's views.

It will occur to every reflecting mind that we have in Scripture a few interesting examples of that change, without dying, from the present to a higher state of being, which the theory of Dr. Smith supposes would have been the happy lot of all mankind had they not sinned. *By faith Enoch was translated, that he should not see death. He walked with God, and he was not · for God took him.* Glad'y would philosophys here interpose a thousand questions as to the manner in which this wonderful change took place ; but the Scriptures are silent. It was enough for the heart of piety that God was the author of the change. And so, in the case of Elijah, we have the sublimely simple description only — *And it came to pass, as they still went on and talked, that, behold, there appeared a chariot of fire, and horses of fire, and parted them both asunder; and Elijah went up by a whirlwind into heaven.* Except the transfiguration of Christ, which appears to have been of an analogous character, these are all the actual examples of translation on record. But the apostle declares that, in the closing scene of this world's history, this same change shall pass upon multitudes. *Behold, I show you a mystery. We shall not all sleep; but we shall all be changed, in a moment, in the twinkling of an eye, at the last trump; for the trumpet shall sound, and the dead shall be raised incorruptible, and we shall be changed.* Abundant evidence is, therefore, before us, that the great change which death now causes us to pass through with fear and dread, might as easily have been, for the whole human family, a transition delightful in anticipation and joyful in experience.

The second theory which will reconcile science and revelation on the subject of death, is one long since illustrated by Jeremy Taylor. And since he could have had no reference to geology in proposing it, because geology did not exist in his day, we may be sure, either that he learnt it from the Bible, or that other branches of knowledge teach the existence of death as a general law of nature, as well as geology.

"That death, therefore," says Taylor, " which God threatened to Adam, and which passed upon his posterity, is not the going out of this world, but the manner of going. If he had staid in innocence, he should have gone placidly and fairly, without vexatious and afflictive circumstances; he should not have died by sickness, defect, misfortune, or unwillingness. But when he fell, then he began to die; the same day, (God said,) and that must needs be true; and, therefore, it must mean upon that very day he fell into an evil and dangerous condition, a state of change and affliction; then death began; that is, man began to die by a natural diminution, and aptness to disease and misery. Change or separation of soul and body is but accidental to death; death may be with or without either; but the formality, the curse, and the sting, — that is, misery, sorrow, fear, diminution, defect, anguish, dishonor, and whatsoever is miserable and afflictive in nature, — that is death. Death is not an action, but a whole state and condition; and this was first brought in upon us by the offence of one man."

In more recent times, the essential features of these views of Taylor have been adopted by the ablest commentators and theologians, and sustained by an appeal to Scripture.* The position which they take is, that the death threatened as the penalty of disobedience has a more extended meaning than physical death. It is a generic term, including all penal evils; so that when death is spoken of as the penalty of sin, we may substitute the word *curse*, *wrath*, *destruction*, and the like. Thus, in Gen. ii. 17, we might read, *In the day thou eatest thereof, thou shalt surely be cursed*; and in Rom. v. 12, *By one man sin entered into the world, and the curse by sin*, &c. In his commentary on this passage, Professor Stuart says, "I see no *philological* escape from the conclusion that death, in the sense of *penalty for sin in its full measure,*

* See Stuart and Hodge on Rom. v. 12; also Chalmers's Lectures on Romans, Lecture 26; and Harris's Man Primeval, p. 178.

must be regarded as the meaning of the writer here." The same may be said of many other passages of Scripture, where the term *death* is used.

According to this exposition, the death threatened as the penalty of transgression embraces all the evils we suffer in this life and in eternity; among which the dissolution of the body is not one of the worst. Indeed, some writers will not admit that this was included at all in the penalty. Such, of course, find no difficulty in the geological statement that literal death preceded man's existence. But from the declaration in 1 Cor. xv. 22, *As in Adam all die, even so in Christ shall all be made alive*, it seems difficult to avoid the conclusion, that the death of the body was brought in upon the race by Adam's transgression. According to Taylor's view, however, we might reasonably suppose that what constituted the death threatened to Adam was not the going out of the world, but the manner of going, and that, had he continued holy, a change of worlds might have taken place, but it would not have been death.

Now, there are some facts, both in experience and revelation, that give to these views an air of probability. One is, the mild character of death in many cases, when attended by only a few of the circumstances above enumerated, as constituting its essence. I believe that experience sustains the conclusion already drawn as to the inferior animals, when not aggravated by human cruelty. Pain is about the only circumstance that gives it the character of severity; and this is usually short, and not anticipated. Nor can it be doubted, as a general fact, that, as we descend along the scale of animals, we find the sensibility to suffering diminish. But in the human family we find examples still more to the point. In all those cases in which there is little or no disease, and a man

9

in venerable old age feels the powers of life gradually give
way, and the functions are feebly performed, until the heart
at length ceases to beat, and the lungs to heave, death is
merely the quiet and unconscious termination of the scene,
so far as the physical nature is concerned. The brain par-
takes of the gradual decay, and thus the man is scarcely conscious of the failure of his powers, because his sensibilities
are so blunted; and therefore, apart from sin, his mind feels
little of the anguish of dissolution, and he quietly resigns himself into the arms of death, —

> " As sweetly as a child,
> Whom neither thought disturbs, nor care encumbers,
> Tired with long play, at close of summer's day,
> Lies down and slumbers."

If now, in addition to this physical preparation for his departure, the man possesses a deep consciousness of forgiven
sin, and a firm hope of future and eternal joy, this change,
which we call death, becomes only a joyful translation from
earth to heaven; and though the man passes from our view, —

> " He sets,
> As sets the morning star, which goes not down
> Behind the darkened west, nor hides obscured
> Among the tempests of the sky, but melts away
> Into the light of heaven."

Nay, when such faith and hope form an anchor to the soul,
.t is not necessary that the physical preparation, which I have
described, should exist. The poor body may be torn by fierce
disease, nay, by the infernal cruelties of martyrdom, and yet
faith can rise — often has risen — over the pains of nature,
in joyful triumph; and in the midst of the tempest, with her

anchor fastened to the eternal Rock, she can exclaim, *O death, where is thy sting ! O grave, where is thy victory ! Thanks be to God, which giveth me the victory through my Lord Jesus Christ.* Surely such a dissolution as this cannot mean the death mentioned in the primeval curse.

Look now at the contrast. Behold a man writhing in the fangs of unrelenting disease, and feeling at the same time the scorpion sting of a guilty conscience. His present suffering is terrible, but that in prospect is more so ; yet he cannot bribe the king of terrors to delay the fatal stroke.

> "The foe,
> Like a stanch murderer, steady to his purpose,
> Urges the soul through every nook and lane of life."

It were enough for an unruffled mind to bear the bodily anguish of that dying hour. But the unpardoned sins of a whole life, and the awful retributions of a whole eternity, come crowding into that point of time ; and no human fortitude can stand under the crushing load. This, this is emphatically death ; the genuine fruit of sin, and therefore in correspondence with the original threatening.

If we turn now to the Scriptures, we shall find some passages in striking agreement with the opinion that the death threatened to man was not the mere dissolution of the body and soul ; not a mere going out of the world, but the manner of going.

This is, indeed, made exceedingly probable by the facts already stated respecting the translation of Enoch and Elijah, and those alive at the coming of Christ. For the sacred writers do not call this death, although it be a removal out of the world, and a transformation of the natural into the spiritual body. Hence, upon the material part of men, the same effects were produced as result from ordinary death, and the subsequent resurrection.

If we recur to the original threatening of death as the consequence of sin, we shall find a peculiarity in the form of expression, which our English translators have rendered by the phrase *thou shalt surely die;* but literally it should be, *dying thou shalt die.*

This mode of expression is indeed very common in the Hebrew language ; but it certainly was meant to indicate an intensity in the meaning, as in the phrase *blessing I will bless thee, and multiplying I will multiply thee;* that is, I will greatly multiply thee. Must it not imply, in the case under consideration, at least that the death which would be the consequence of transgression, would possess an aggravated character ? May it not imply as much as Taylor's theory supposes ? Might it not be intended to teach Adam that, when he died, his death should not be simply the dissolution of the animal fabric, and the loss of animal life, as he witnessed it in the inferior creatures around him ; but a change far more agonizing, in which the mental suffering should so much outweigh the corporeal as to constitute, in fact, its essence ? I do not assert that this passage has such an extended meaning, but I suggest it. And I confess that I do not see why its peculiarity of form is understood in our common translation to imply certainty rather than intensity.

There is another part of the threatening that deserves consideration. It says, that man should not only die, but die the very day of the offence. Now, if by death we understood merely a removal out of the world, or a separation of soul and body, the threatening was not executed after the forbidden fruit was tasted. But if it meant also, and chiefly, a state of sorrow, pain, and suffering, a liability to disease and fatal

accident, the goadings of a guilty conscience, and the consequent fear of punishment beyond the grave, then death began
on the very day when man sinned, and the dissolution of the
soul and body was but the closing scene of the tragedy.

The beautiful passage in the First Epistle to the Corinthians,
already quoted, where the Christian, in view of death, exult-
ingly exclaims, *O death, where is thy sting! O grave, where
is thy victory!* will doubtless occur to all who hear me, in this
connection. Here the sting of death is expressly declared to
be sin, and that the pardoned Christian obtains the victory over
it. To him all that renders this king of terrors formidable is
gone. Its physical sufferings may indeed be left, but these
are hardly worth naming, when that which constitutes the
sting of this great enemy —unpardoned guilt — is taken away.
Little more than his harmless shadow is left. Worlds, indeed,
are to be exchanged, and so they must have been if Adam
had never been driven from paradise. The eyes, too, must
close on beloved friends; but how soon to open them upon
the bright glories of heaven! In short, the strong impression
of this passage upon the mind is, that the essential thing in
death is unpardoned sin; and therefore the death threatened
to Adam may have been only the terrible aggravations of a
departure out of this world, which have followed in the train
of transgression.

Another striking passage, bearing upon the same point, is
the declaration of Paul, that *Jesus Christ hath abolished death,
and brought life and immortality to light through the gospel.*

The apostle does not surely mean that Christians are freed
from what is commonly called death, since universal experience shows that animal life in them is as sure to be extin-
guished, and the soul to be separated from the body, as in
others. But so different is death now, since Christ has brought

9 *

to light a future and an immortal life, and by the sacrifice of himself shown how the heart may be reconciled to God, and sin forgiven, and faith inspired, that, in fact, while the shadow of death still occupies the passage to eternity, its substance is gone.

That death, which sin introduced, Christ has abolished, because, by his sacrifice and his grace, he has conquered sin.

Upon the whole, though we may not be convinced that either of the theories that have been explained is directly taught in the Scriptures, or can be shown to be infallibly true, yet they are sustained by probable evidence enough to remove the apprehension that there is any real discrepancy between geology and revelation on the subject of death. Between these theories there is but a slight difference. They are in fact but modifications of the same general principles; and I say it would be more philosophical to admit the truth of either of them, than a disagreement between science and Scripture, since the truth of both geology and revelation is sustained by such a mass of independent evidence.

An objection, however, may be stated against both of these theories, on the ground that they seem to imply that death would have existed in the world, irrespective of the sin of man, and therefore they lessen our sense of the evil of sin.

It may be doubted, I think, whether these theories do necessarily imply that there was no connection between the sin of man and the introduction of death into the world. But, admitting that they do, is it certain that inadequate views of sin are the result? For poetic effect, we admire the sublime sentimentalism of Milton : —

> "Earth felt the wound; and Nature, from her seat,
> Sighing through all her works, gave signs of woe
> That all was lost."

But, after all, the deepest impression we get of the evil of sin is derived from contemplating its effects upon man, and especially the immortal mind. Witness its lofty powers bowed down in ignominious servitude to base corporeal appetites and furious and debasing passions. See how the understanding is darkened, the will perverted, and the heart alienated from all that is holy. See reason and conscience dethroned, and selfishness reigning in gloomy and undisputed tyranny over the immortal mind, while appetite and passion have become its obsequious panders. See how the affections turn away with loathing from God, and what a wall of separation has sprung up between man and his Maker; how deeply and universally he has revolted from his rightful sovereign, and has chosen other gods to rule over him. Consider, too, what havoc has been made in the body, that curious and wonderful workmanship of the Almighty; how the unbridled appetites have sown the seeds of disease therein, and how pain, languor, and decay assail the constitution as soon as we begin to live, and cease not their attacks till they triumph over the citadel of life. Consult the history of the world, and what a lazar-house and a Golgotha has it been! What land has not been drenched in human blood, poured out in ferocious war! What oceans of tears has the thirsty soil drank up! What breeze has ever blown over the land which has not been loaded with sighs, and groans, and the story of wrong and oppression, of treachery and murder, of suicide and assassination, of blasted hopes and despairing hearts! These, therefore, are the genuine fruits of sin. This, this is death. And, need I add that these are but the precursors of the second death?

The third theory respecting death takes a more comprehensive view of the subject, and traces its origin to the divine plan of the creation.

In creating this world, God did not act without a plan previously determined upon in all its details. Of course, man's character and condition formed prominent items in that plan. His apostasy, too, however some would hesitate to regard it as predetermined, all will allow to have been foreknown. Now, I maintain that God, in the beginning, adapted every other being and event in the world to man's character and condition, so that there should be entire harmony in its system.   And since, either in the divine appointment, or in the nature of things, there is an inseparable connection between sin and death, the latter must constitute a feature of the system of the world, because a free agent would introduce the former.   Death would ultimately exist in the world, and, therefore, all creatures placed in such a world must be made mortal, at whatever period created.   For mortal and immortal natures could not exist in the same natural constitution, nor could a condition adapted to undying creatures be changed into a state of decay and death without an entirely new creation.   Death, therefore, entered into the original plan of the world in the divine mind, and was endured by the animals and plants that lived anterior to man.   Yet, as the constitution of the world is, doubtless, very different from what it would have been if sin had not existed in it, and as man alone was capable of sin, it is proper to regard man's transgression as the occasion of all the suffering and death that existed on the globe since its creation.

It will probably be objected to this theory, that it is unjust to make animals suffer for man's apostasy, especially before it took place.

I do not see why such suffering is any more unjust before than after man's transgression ; and we know that they do now suffer in consequence of his sin.   But this suffering is not to be regarded in the light of punishment; and if it can only be proved that benevolence predominates in the condition of animals, notwithstanding their sufferings, divine justice and benevolence are vindicated; and can there be any doubt that such is the fact? Death is not necessarily an evil to any animals. It may be a great blessing, by removing them to a higher state of existence. In the case of the inferior animals, it is but a small drawback upon the pleasure of life, even though they do not exist hereafter. We have endeavored to show that even the existence of carnivorous races is a benevolent provision. That animals are placed in an inferior condition, in consequence of man's apostasy, is no more cause of complaint than that man is made a little lower than the angels.

Another objection to these views is, that it makes the effect precede the cause ; for it represents the pre-Adamic animals as dying in consequence of man's transgression.

I do not maintain that the death of animals, before or after Adam, was the direct and natural consequence of his transgression. Nay, I am endeavoring to show directly the contrary. But, then, the certainty of man's apostasy might have been the grand reason in the divine mind for giving to the world its present constitution, and subjecting animals to death. Not that God altered his plan upon a prospective knowledge that man would sin ; but he made this plan originally, that is from eternity, with that event in view, and he made it different from what it would have been, if such an event had not been certain. If this be true, then was there a connection between man's sin and the death that reigned before his exist ence ; though, in strict accuracy of speech, one can hardly be called the cause of the other. And yet it was, as I maintain, occasioned by man's sin, and shows the wide-spread influence of that occurrence, even more strikingly than the ordinary theory of death.

A third objection to this theory is, that it represents God as putting man in a place of punishment before he had sinned; or, at least in a state where death was the universal law, and where he must die, though he should keep the law of God.

There are three suppositions, either of which will meet this difficulty.

We may suppose, with Jeremy Taylor, that the death threatened to Adam consisted, not in going out of the world, but in the manner of going. If he had not sinned, the exchange of worlds would have been without fear or suffering, and an object of desire rather than aversion. Christ has not secured to the believer the privilege of an earthly immortality, but has taken away from a removal out of the world all that constitutes death.

Or we may suppose, with Dr. J. Pye Smith, that, while man should continue to keep the divine law, he would be secured from that tendency to decay and dissolution, which was the common lot of all other creatures, until the time hould come for his removal, without suffering or dread, to a ligher state of existence. And that a means of immunity from death existed in the garden of Eden we learn from the Scriptures. For there stood the tree of life, whose fruit had the power to make man live forever, and, therefore, he must be banished from the spot where it grew.

Or, finally, we may suppose that God fitted up for man some balmy spot, where neither decay nor death could enter, and where every thing was adapted for a being of perfect holiness and happiness. His privilege was to dwell there, so long as he could preserve his innocence, but no longer. And surely this supposition seems to accord with the description of the garden of Eden, man's first dwelling-place. There every thing seems to have been adapted to his happiness; but sin drove him out among the thorns and thistles, and a cherubim and a flaming sword forbade his return to the tree of life.

Either of these suppositions will meet the difficulty suggested by the objection; or they may all be combined consistently. Let us now look at some of the advantages of the third theory above advanced.

In the first place, it satisfactorily harmonizes revelation with geology, physiology, and experience, on the subject of death. It agrees with physiology and experience in representing death to be a law of organic being on the globe. Yet it accords with revelation, in showing how this law may be a result of man's apostasy; and with geology, also, in showing how death might have reigned over animals and plants before man's existence. To remove so many apparent discrepancies is surely a presumption in favor of any theory.

In the second place, the fundamental principle of this theory is also a fundamental principle of natural and revealed theology, viz., that all events in this world entered originally into the plan or purpose of the Deity. To suppose that God made the world without a plan previously determined upon, is to make him less wise than a human architect, who would be charged with great folly to attempt building even a house without a plan. And to suppose that plan not to extend to every event, is to rob God of his infinite attributes.

In the third place, this theory falls in with the common interpretation of Scripture, which refers the whole system of suffering, decay, and death in this world to man's apostasy. And although the general reception of any exegesis of Scripture does not prove it to be correct, it is certainly gratifying when a thorough examination proves the obvious sense of a passage to be the true one. For to disturb the popular interpretation is, with many, equivalent to a denial of Scripture.

In the fourth place, this theory shows us the infinite skill and benevolence of Jehovah in educing good from evil.

The free agency of man was an object in the highest degree desirable. Yet such a character made him liable to fall; and God knew that he would fall. To human sagacity that act would seem to seal up his fate forever. But infinite wisdom saw that the case was not hopeless. It placed him in a state of temporal suffering and temporal death, that he might still have a chance of escaping eternal suffering and eternal death. The discipline of such a world was eminently adapted to restore his lost purity, and death was probably the only means by which a fallen being could pass to a higher state of existence. That discipline, indeed, if rightly improved, would probably fit him for a higher degree of holiness and happiness than if he had never sinned ; so as to make true the paradoxical sentiment of the poet, —

"Death gives us more than was in Eden lost."

Misimproved, this discipline would result in an infinite loss, far greater than if man never passed through it. But this is all the fault of man ; while all the benefit of a state of probation is the result of God's infinite wisdom and benevolence.

In the fifth place, this theory relieves us from the absurdity of supposing that God was compelled to alter the plan of creation after man's apostasy.

The common theory does convey an idea not much different from this. It makes the impression that God was disappointed when man sinned, and being thereby thwarted in his original purpose, he did the best he could by changing his plan, just as men do when some unexpected occurrence interferes with their short-sighted contrivances. Now, such an anthropomorphic view of God is inexcusable in the nineteenth century. It was necessary to use such representations in the early ages of the world, when pure spiritual ideas were unknown; and hence the Bible describes God as repenting and grieved that he had made man. But with the light of the New Testament and of modern science, we ought to be able to enucleate the true spiritual idea from such descriptions. The theory under consideration does not reduce God to any after-thought expedients, but makes provision for every occurrence in his original plan; and, of course, shows that every event takes place as he would have it, when viewed in its relations to the great system of the universe.

In the sixth place, this theory sheds some light upon the important question, why God permitted the introduction of death into the world.

It is difficult for some persons to conceive why God, when he foresaw Adam's apostasy, did not change his plan of creation, and exclude so terrible an evil as death. But according to this theory, he permitted it, because it was a necessary part of a great system of restoration, by which the human race might, if not recreant to their true interests, be restored to more than their primeval blessedness. It was not introduced as a mere punishment, but as a necessary means of raising a fallen being into a higher state of life and blessedness; or, if he perversely spurned the offered boon, of sinking him down to the deeper wretchedness which is the just consequence of unrepented sin, without even the sympathy of any part of the created universe.

Finally. This subject throws some light upon that strange mixture of good and evil, which exists in the present world. We have seen, indeed, that benevolence decidedly predominates in all the arrangements of nature; and we are called upon continually to admire the adaptation of external nature to the human constitution. A large portion of our sufferings

10

here may also be imputed to our own sins, or the sins of others ; and these we cannot charge upon God.   But, after all, it
seems difficult to conceive how even a sinless man could escape
a large amount of suffering here ; enough, indeed, to make
him often sigh for deliverance and for a better state.   How
many sources of sufferings there are in unhealthy climates,
mechanical violence, and chemical agents ; in a sterile soil,
in the excessive heats of the tropical regions, and extreme
cold of high latitudes ; in the encroachments and ferocity of
the inferior animals ; in poisons, mineral, vegetable, and animal ; in food unfitted to the digestive and assimilating organs ;
in the damps and miasms of night ; and in the frequent necessity for over-exertion of body and mind ! And then, how many
hinderances to the exercise of the mental powers, in all the
causes that have been mentioned ! and how does the soul feel
that she is imprisoned in flesh and blood, and her energies
cramped, and her vision clouded, by a gross corporeal medium !   And thus it is, to a great extent, with all nature,
especially animal nature ; and I cannot but believe, as already
intimated, that Paul had these very things in mind when he
said, *The whole creation groaneth and travaileth together in
pain until now, and waiteth for the manifestation of the sons
of God ;* that is, for emancipation from its present depressed
and fettered condition.   In short, while there is so much in
this world to call forth our admiration and gratitude to God,
there is enough to make us feel, also, that it is a fallen condition.   It is not such a world as infinite benevolence would
provide for perfectly holy beings, whom he desired to make
perfectly happy, but rather such a world as is adapted for a
condition of trial and preparation for a higher state, when
both mind and body would be delivered from the fetters that
now cramp their exercise.

    Now, the theory which I advocate asserts that this peculiar

condition of the world resulted from the divine determination, upon a prospective view of man's transgression. It may, therefore, be properly regarded as occasioned by man's transgression, but not in the common meaning attached to that phrase, which is, that, before man's apostasy, the constitution of the world was different from what it now is, and death did not exist. This theory supposes God to have devised the present peculiar mixed condition of the world, as to good and evil, in eternity, in order to give man an opportunity to rescue himself from the penalty and misery of sin; and in order to introduce those who should do this into a higher state of existence. The plan, therefore, is founded in infinite wisdom and benevolence, while it brings out man's guilt, and the evil of sin, in appalling distinctness and magnitude.

But, after all, how little idea would a man have of the entire plot of a play, who had heard only a part of the first act! How little could he judge of the bearing of the first scene upon the final development! Yet we are now only in the first act of the great drama of human existence. Death shows us that we shall ere long be introduced into a second act, and affords a presumption that other acts — it may be in an endless series — will succeed, before the whole plot shall have passed before us; and not till then can we be certain what are all the objects to be accomplished by the introduction of sin and death into our world. And if thus early we can catch glimpses of great benefit to result from these evils, what full conviction, that infinite benevolence has planned and consummated the whole, will be forced upon the mind, when the vast panorama of God's dispensations shall lie spread out in the memory! For that time shall Faith wait, in confident hope that all her doubts and darkness shall be converted into noonday brightness.

LECTURE IV.

THE NOACHIAN DELUGE COMPARED WITH THE GEOLOGICAL DELUGES.

THE history of opinions respecting the deluge of Noah is one of the most curious and instructive in the annals of man. In this field, Christians have often broken lances with infidels, and also with one another. The unbeliever has confidently maintained that the Bible history of the deluge is at war with the facts and reasonings of science. Equally confident has been the believer that nature bears strong testimony to its occurrence. Some Christians, however, have asserted, with the infidel, that no trace remains on the face of nature of such an event. And as this is a subject which men are apt to suppose themselves masters of, when they have only skimmed the surface, the contest between these, different parties has been severe and protracted. Almost every geological change which the earth has undergone, from its centre to its circumference, has, at one time or another, been ascribed to this deluge. And so plain has this seemed to those who had only a partial view of the facts, that those who doubted it were often denounced as enemies of revelation. But most of these opinions and this dogmatism are now abandoned, because both Nature and Scripture are better understood. And among well-informed geologists, at least, the opinion is almost universal, that there are no facts in their science which can be clearly referred to the Noachian deluge; that is, no traces in nature of that event; and on the other hand, that there is nothing in the Mosaic account of the deluge which would necessarily lead us to expect permanent marks of such a catastrophe within or upon the earth.

If such be the case, you will doubtless inquire, what connection there is between geology and the revealed history of the deluge, and why the subject should be introduced into this series of lectures. I reply, that so recently have correct views been entertained on this subject, and so little understood are they, that they need to be defined and explained. And if the distribution of animals and plants on the globe come within the province of geology, then this science has a very important point of connection with the history of the deluge, as will appear in the sequel. And finally, the history of opinions on this subject is full of instruction to those who undertake to reason on the connection between science and religion. Obviously, then, my first object should be to give a brief history of the views that have been entertained respecting the deluge of Noah, so far as they have been supposed to have any connection with geology.

It is well known, that in the written and unwritten traditions of almost every nation and tribe under heaven, the story of a general deluge has been prominent; and probably, in all these cases, some attempt has been made to explain the manner in which the waters were brought over the land. But most of these reasonings, especially in ancient times, are too absurd to deserve even to be recited. Indeed, it is not till the beginning of the sixteenth century, that we find any discussions on the subject worthy of notice. At that time, some excavations at Verona, in Italy, brought to light many fossil shells, and awakened a question as to their origin. Some maintained that they were only *simulacra,* or resemblances

10 *

to animals, but never had a real existence. They were supposed to have been produced by a certain " *materia pinguis*,"
or " fatty matter," existing in the earth. Others maintained
that they were deposited by the deluge of Noah. Such, indeed, was the general opinion ; but Fracastoro and a few
others maintained that they were once real animals, and could
not have been brought into their present condition by the last
deluge. For more than three hundred years have these questions been more or less discussed ; and though decided many
years ago by all geologists, not a few intelligent men still
maintain, that petrified shells are mere abortive resemblances
of real beings, or that they were deposited by the deluge.

The advocates of the diluvial origin of petrifactions soon
found themselves hard pressed with the question, how these
relics could be scattered through strata many thousand feet
thick, by one transient flood. They, therefore, came to the conclusion, in the words of Woodward, a distinguished cosmogonist of the eighteenth century, that the " whole terrestrial globe
was taken to pieces and dissolved at the flood, and the strata
settled down from this promiscuous mass, as any earthy sediment from a fluid." During that century, many works appeared upon cosmogony, defending similar views, by such
men as Burnet, Scheuchzer, and Catcott. Some of these
works exhibited no little ability, mixed, however, with hypotheses so extravagant that they have ever since been the butt
of ridicule. The very title of Burnet's work cannot but pro-
voke a smile. It is called " The Sacred Theory of the Earth,
containing an Account of the Original of the Earth, and of all
the general Changes it hath already undergone, or is to undergo,
till the Consummation of all Things." He maintained that the
primitive earth was only " an orbicular crust, smooth, regular,
and uniform, without mountains and without a sea." This crust

rested on the surface of a watery abyss, and, being heated by the sun, became chinky; and in consequence of the rarefaction of the included vapors, it burst asunder, and fell down into the waters, and so was comminuted and dissolved, while the inhabitants perished. Catcott's work was confined exclusively to the deluge, and exhibited a good deal of ability. He endeavored to show, that this dissolution of the·earth by the deluge was taught in the Scriptures, and his reasoning on that point is a fine example of the state of biblical interpretation in his day. "As there are other texts," says he, "which mention the dissolution of the earth, it may be proper to cite them. Ps. xlvi. 2. *God is our refuge; therefore will we not fear though the earth be removed*, [be changed, be quite altered, as it was at the deluge.] *God uttered his voice, the earth melted*, [flowed, dissolved to atoms.] Again, Job xxviii. 9. *He sent his hand* [the expansion, his instrument, or the agent by which he worked] *against the rock, he overturned the mountains by the roots, he caused the rivers to burst forth from between the rocks*, [or broke open the fountains of the abyss.] *His eye* [symbolically placed for light] *saw* [passed through, or between] *every minute thing*, [every atom, and so dissolved the whole.] *He* [at last] *bound up the waters from weeping*, [i. e. from pressing through the shell of the earth, as tears make their way through the orb of the eye; or, as it is related, (Gen. viii. 2,) *He stopped the fountains of the abyss and the windows of heaven*,] *and brought out the light from its hiding-place*, [i. e., from the inward parts of the earth, from between every atom where it lay hid, and kept each atom separate from the other, and so the whole in a state of dissolution; his bringing out those parts of the light which caused the dissolution would of course permit the agents to act in their usual way, and so reform the earth."] — *Treatise on the Deluge*, p. 43, (London, 1761.)

We can hardly believe at the present day, that a logical and scientific mind, like that of Catcott, could satisfy itself, by such a dreamy exegesis, that the Scriptures teach the earth's dissolution at the deluge ; especially when they so distinctly describe the waters of the deluge, as first rising over the land, and then sinking back to their original position.   Still more strange is it how Burnet could have thought it consistent with Scripture to suppose the earth, before the flood, " to have been covered with an orbicular crust, smooth, regular, and uniform, without mountains and without a sea," when the Bible so distinctly states, as the work of the third day, that *the waters under the heavens were gathered together unto one place, and the dry land appeared ;* and that *God called the dry land earth, and the gathering together of the waters he called seas ;* and further, that, by the deluge, *all the high hills were covered.*   Yet these men doubtless supposed that, by the views which they advocated, they were defending the Holy Scriptures.   Nay, their views were long regarded as exclusively the orthodox views, and opposition to them was considered, for one or two centuries, as virtual opposition to the Bible.   Truly, this, in biblical interpretation, was straining at a gnat and swallowing a camel.

It is quite convenient to explain such anomalies in human belief, by referring them to the spirit of the age, or to the want of the light of modern science.   But in the present case, we cannot thus easily dispose of the difficulty.   For in our own day, we have seen these same absurdities of opinion maintained by a really scientific man, selected to write one of the Bridgewater Treatises, as one of the most learned men in Great Britain.   I refer to Rev. William Kirby, evidently a thorough entomologist and a sincere Christian.   But he adopts the opinion, not only that there exists a subterranean abyss of waters, but a subterranean metropolis of animals, where the huge leviathians, the gigantic saurians, dug out of the rocks by the geologist, still survive ; and this he endeavors to prove from the Bible. For this purpose he quotes the passage in Psalms, *though thou hast sore broken us in the place of dragons, and covered us with the shadow of death.* His exposition of this text is much in the style of that already given from Catcott. Following that writer and Hutchinson, he endeavors to show, by a still more fanciful interpretation, that the phrase " windows of heaven," in Genesis, means cracks and volcanic rents in the earth, through which air and water rushed inwardly and outwardly with such violence as to tear the crust to pieces. This was the effect of the increasing waters of the deluge ; the bringing together of these comminuted particles, so as to form the present strata, was the work of the subsiding waters.

These views will seem very strange to those not familiar with the history of geology. But we shall find their origin, if a few facts be stated respecting what has been called the physico-theological school of writers, that originated with one Hutchinson, in the beginning of the eighteenth century. He was a disciple of the distinguished cosmogonist Woodward. But he attacked the views of his master, as well as those of Sir Isaac Newton on gravitation, in a work which he published in twelve octavo volumes, entitled " *Moses's Principia.*" He there maintains that the Scriptures, when rightly understood, contain a complete system of natural philosophy.

This dogma, advocated by Hutchinson with the most intolerant spirit, constitutes the leading peculiarity of the physico-theological school, and has been very widely adopted, and has exerted a most pernicious influence both upon religion and upon science. It is painful, therefore, to find so learned and excellent a man as Mr. Kirby so deeply imbued with it, so long after its absurdity has been shown again and again. It is devoutly to be wished that the cabalistic dreams of Hutchinsonianism are not to be extensively revived in our day. And, indeed, such is the advanced state of hermeneutical knowledge, that we have little reason to fear it. Nevertheless, its leaven is yet by no means thoroughly purged out from the literary community.

It was one of the settled principles of the physico-theological school, that, since the creation, the earth has undergone no important change beneath the surface, except at the deluge, because it was supposed that the Bible mentions no other event that could produce any important change. Hence all marks of changes in the rocks since their original creation must be referred to the deluge. And especially when it was found that most of the petrifactions in the rocks were of marine origin, not only were they supposed to be the result of the deluge, but a most conclusive proof of that event. And this opinion is even yet very widely received by the Christian world. The argument in its favor, when stated in a popular manner to those not familiar with geology, is indeed quite imposing. For if the land, almost every where, even to the tops of some of its highest mountains, abounds in sea shells, this is just what we should expect, if the sea flowed over those mountains at the deluge. But the moment we come to examine the details respecting marine petrifactions, we see that nothing can be more absurd than to suppose them the result of a transient deluge. Yet this view is maintained in nearly all the popular commentaries of the present day upon Genesis, and in many respectable periodicals. It is taught, therefore, in the Sabbath school and in the family; and the child, as he grows up, is shocked to find the geologist assailing it; and when he finds it false, he is in danger of becoming jealous of the other evidences of Christianity which he has been taught.

Another branch of the modern physico-theological school, embracing men who have read too much on the subject of geology to be able to believe in the dissolution of the globe by the deluge, have adopted a more plausible hypothesis. They suppose that between the creation and the deluge, or in sixteen hundred and fifty-six years, according to the received chronology, all the present fossiliferous rocks of our continents, more than six miles in thickness, were deposited at the bottom of the ocean. By that event, they were raised from beneath the waters, and the continents previously existing sunk down and disappeared; so that the land now inhabited was formerly the ocean's bed. To prove that such a change took place at the deluge, Granville Penn and Fairholme quote the declaration of God, in Genesis, respecting the flood — *I will destroy them,* (i. e., men,) *and the earth, or with the earth;* also the statement of Peter — *The world that then was, being overflowed with water, perished.* The terms *earth* and *world* may mean either the solid globe, or the animals and plants upon it. If in these passages they have the latter meaning, then they simply teach that the deluge destroyed the natural life of organic beings. If they have the former meaning, then the inquiry arises, What are we to understand by the destruction here described? It may mean annihilation, or it may imply ruin in some respects. That annihilation did not result from the deluge is evident from the case of men, who suffered only temporal death, and even this was not universal; and we know, also, that the matter of the earth did not perish. We must resort, therefore, to the sacred history to learn how far the destruction extended

That history seems very plain. There was a rain of forty days, and the fountains of the great deep were broken up; that is, as Professor Stuart happily expresses it, "The ocean overflowed while the rain descended in vast quantities." The waters gradually rose over the dry land, and after a hundred and fifty days, began to subside, and at the end of a year and a few days they were gone. Such an overflowing could not take place without producing the almost entire destruction of organic life, and making extensive havoc with the soil, especially as a wind assisted in driving these waters from the land. But there is nothing in the narrative that would lead us to suppose either a comminution or dissolution of the earth, or the elevation of the ocean's bed. The same land which was overflowed is described as again emerging. Indeed, a part of the rivers proceeding out of the garden of Eden are the same as those now existing on the globe. We must then admit that our present continents, — certainly the Asiatic, — are the same as the antediluvian, or deny that the account of Eden, in Genesis, is a part of the Bible. The latter alternative is preferred by Penn and Fairholme. Surely such men ought to be cautious how they censure geologists for modifying the meaning of some verses in Genesis, when they thus, without any evidence of its spuriousness, unceremoniously erase so important a passage.

I might add to all this that the facts of geology forbid the idea that our present continents formed the bed of the ocean at so recent a date as that of Noah's deluge, and that the supposition that all organic remains were deposited during the two thousand years between the six days' work and the deluge is totally irreconcilable with all correct philosophy. Why, during the time when the fossiliferous rocks were in a course of formation, four or five entirely distinct races of animals and plants successively occupied the land and the waters, and passed away in regular order ; and these races were so unlike, that they could not have been contemporaneous. Who will maintain that all this took place in the short period of two thousand years ? I am sure that no geologist will.

But modern geologists have, until recently, supposed that the traces of Noah's deluge might still be seen upon the earth's surface. I say its surface ; for none of them imagined those effects could have reached to a great depth. Over a large part of the northern hemisphere they found extensive accumulations of gravel and bowlders, which had been removed often a great distance from their parent rocks, while the ledges beneath were smoothed and striated, obviously by the grating over them of these piles of detritus. How very natural to refer these effects to the agency of currents of water ; just such currents as might have resulted from a universal deluge. But the inference was a hasty one For when geologists came to study the phenomena of drift or diluvium, as these accumulations of travelled matter are called, they found that currents of water alone would not explain them all. Some other agency must have been concerned ; and the general opinion now is, that drift has been the result of the joint action of water and ice ; and nearly all geologists suppose that this action took place before man's existence on the globe. Some suppose it to have been the result of oceanic currents, while yet our continents were beneath the waters ; others think that the northern ocean may have been thrown southerly over the dry land by the elevation of its bed ; and others maintain that vast masses of ice may formerly have encircled high latitudes, whose glaciers, melting away, may have driven towards the equator the great quantities of drift and

11

bowlders which have been carried in that direction. In short, it is now found that this is one of the most difficult problems in geology ; and while most geologists agree that both ice and water have been concerned in producing the phenomena, the time and manner of their action are not yet very satisfactorily determined. They may have acted at different periods and in divers manners ; but all the phenomena could not have been the result of one transient deluge.

From the facts that have now been detailed, it appears that on no subject of science connected with religion have men been more positive and dogmatical than in respect to Noah's deluge, and that on no subject has there been greater change of opinion. From a belief in the complete destruction and dissolution of the globe by that event, those best qualified to judge now doubt whether it be possible to identify one mark of that event in nature.

I shall now proceed to state, in a more definite form, the views of this subject entertained by the most enlightened judges of its merits at the present day.

In the first place, most of the cases of accumulations of drift, the dispersion of bowlders, and the polish and striæ upon rocks in place, occurred previous to man's existence upon the globe, and cannot have been the result of Noah's deluge.

From the arguments for sustaining this position I shall select only a part.

The first is, that the organic remains found in the alluvium considerably above the drift, which always lies below the alluvium, are many of them of extinct species. Whether the genuine drift — a heterogeneous mass of fragments, driven pellmell together — contains any organic relics, is to me very doubtful. But if the stratified deposits subsequent to the drift present us with beings no longer alive on the globe, much more would the drift. Now, the presumption is, that extinct animals and plants belong to a creation anterior to man, especially if they exhibit a tropical character, — as those do which are usually assigned to the drift, — since we have no evidence of a tropical climate in northern latitudes till we get back to a period far anterior to man.

Secondly. No remains of man or his works have been found in drift, nor indeed till we rise almost to the top of the alluvial deposit. Even ancient Armenia has now been examined geologically, with sufficient care to make it almost certain that human remains do not exist there in drift, if drift is found there at all; of which there may be a question.

Thirdly. The agency producing drift must have operated during a vastly longer period than the three hundred and eighty days of Noah's deluge. It would be easy to show to a geologist that the extensive erosions which are referrible to that agency, and the huge masses of detritus which have been the result, must have demanded centuries, and even decades of years. Nor will any supposed increase of power in the agency explain the results, without admitting a long period for their action.

Fourthly. Water appears to have been the principal agent in the Noachian deluge; but in the production of drift, ice was at least equally concerned.

Finally. The phenomena of deltas, terraces, and ancient sea-beaches, make the period of the drift immensely more remote than the deluge of Noah, since these phenomena are all posterior to the drift period. I need not go into the details of this argument here, since I have drawn them out in my second lecture. But of all the arguments ever adduced to prove the great length of time occupied in geological changes, this — which, so far as the terraces are concerned, has never before, I believe, been adduced — seems to me the most convincing to those who carefully examine the subject.

We may be sure, then, that the commencement of the drift period, and the deluge of Noah, cannot have been synchronous. But the drift agency, connected, as nearly all geologists seem now to be ready to admit, with the vertical movements of continents, may have operated, and undoubtedly has, at various periods, and very possibly, in some parts of the world, long posterior to the period usually called the drift period. I agree, therefore, in opinion with one of the most eminent and judicious of the European geologists, Professor Sedgwick of Cambridge, when he says, " If we have the clearest proofs of great oscillations of sea level, and have a right to make use of them, while we seek to explain some of the latest phenomena of geology, may we not reasonably suppose, that, within the period of human history, similar oscillations have taken place in those parts of Asia which were the cradle of our race, and may have produced that destruction among the early families of men, which is described in our sacred books, and of which so many traditions have been brought down to us through all the streams of authentic history ? " — *Geology of the Lake District*, p. 14.

Secondly. Admitting the deluge to have been universal over the globe, it could not have deposited the fossil remains in the rocks.

This position is too plain to the practical geologist to need a formal argument to sustain it. But there are many intelligent men, who do not see clearly why the remains of marine animals and plants may not be referred to the deluge. And if they could be, then all the demands of the geologist for long periods anterior to man are without foundation. But they cannot be, for the following reasons : —

First. On this supposition the organic remains ought to be confusedly mingled together, since they must have been brought over the land promiscuously by the waters of the deluge ; but they are in fact arranged in as much order as the specimens of a well-regulated cabinet. The different rocks that lie above one another do, indeed, contain some species that are common ; but the most are peculiar. It is impossible to explain such a fact if they were deposited by the deluge.

Secondly. On this theory, at least, a part of the organic remains ought to correspond with living animals and plants, since the deluge took place so long after the six days of creation. But with the exception of a few species near the top of the series, the fossil species are wholly unlike those now alive.

Thirdly. How, by this theory, can we explain the fact, that there are found in the rocks at least five distinct races of animals and plants, so unlike that they could not have been contemporaries ? or for the fact, that most of them are of a highly tropical character ? or for the fact, that as we rise higher in the rocks, there is a nearer and nearer approach to existing species ?

Fourthly. This theory requires us to admit, that in three hundred and eighty days the waters of the deluge deposited rocks at least six miles in thickness, over half or two thirds of our existing continents ; and these rocks made up of hundreds of thick beds, exceedingly unlike one another in composition and organic contents. Will any reasonable man believe this possible without a miracle ?

But I need not multiply arguments on this point. It is a theory which no reasonable man can long maintain after studying the subject. And if it be indeed true, that neither in the

11 *

drift, nor in the fossiliferous rocks, can we discover any traces of the deluge, then we shall find them nowhere on the globe. But

Thirdly. There are no facts in geology that afford any presumption against the occurrence of the Noachian deluge, but rather the contrary.

The geologist says only, that if any traces of it exist, he cannot distinguish them from the effects of other analogous agencies that have operated on the globe at various periods. Some parts of the globe do not exhibit marks of any powerful aqueous action, such as high northern and southern latitudes do exhibit. But the sacred record, in its account of the access and subsidence of diluvial waters, does not require us to suppose any great degree of violence in their action on the surface ; and although currents somewhat powerful must have been the result, yet they may not have existed every where, nor have always left traces of their passage where they did exist. On the other hand, the geologist will admit, as we have already seen, that in the elevation and subsidence of mountains and continents, and in volcanic agency generally, of which geology contains so many examples, we have an adequate cause for extensive, if not universal, deluges ; nor can he say how recently this cause may have operated beneath certain oceans, sufficiently to produce the deluge of the Scriptures. So that, in fact, we have in geology a presumption in favor of, rather than against, such a deluge. Nay, some, who have examined Armenia, have thought they found there a deposit which could be referred to the deluge of Noah ; but I have no access to any facts on this point.

Fourthly. There are reasons, both in natural history and in the Scriptures, for supposing that the deluge may not have been universal over the globe, but only over the region inhabited by man.

This is a position of no small importance, and will, there-fore, require our careful examination. And in the beginning, I wish to premise, that I assume the deluge to have been brought about by natural operations, or in conformity with the laws of nature. I feel no reluctance in admitting it to have been strictly miraculous, provided the narrative will al-low of such a conclusion. But if it was miraculous, then we must give up the idea of philosophizing about it, and believe the facts simply on the divine testimony. For how can we philosophize upon an event that is brought about by the direct efficiency of God, and without reference to existing natural laws, and, it may be, in contravention of them, unless, indeed, the history contains such contradictions as even infinite power and wisdom could not make harmonious ? Some writers en-deavor to show the conformity of the sacred history of the deluge to established natural laws, until they meet with some objection too strong to be answered, when they turn round and declare the whole occurrence to have been miraculous. This I conceive to be absurd, and I shall accordingly proceed on the supposition that the whole event was a penal infliction, brought about by natural laws ; or, at least, if there was any thing miraculous, it consisted in giving greater power to nat-ural operations, without interfering with the regular sequence of cause and effect. And does not the narrative leave the im-pression on the mind of the reader, that it was brought about by natural means ? The sacred writer distinctly assigns two natural causes of the increase of the waters, viz., a rain of forty days and the breaking up of the fountains of the great deep, which doubtless means an overflow of the ocean ; and, to hasten the subsidence of the waters, it is said that God made a wind to blow over the surface. It is no proof of mi-raculous agency, that the whole work is referred to the immediate power of God, for it is well known that this is the usual mode in which the sacred writers speak of natural events.

The first difficulty in the way of supposing the flood to have been literally universal, is the great quantity of water that would have been requisite.

The amount necessary to cover the earth to the tops of the highest mountains, or about five miles above the present oceans, would be eight times greater than that existing on the globe at this time. From whence could this immense volume of water have been derived ? A great deal of ingenuity has been devoted to give an answer to this inquiry. By some it has been supposed, that most of the earth's interior is occupied by water, and the theorist had only to devise means for forcing it to the surface. One does this by the forcible compression of the crust ; another, by the expansive power of internal heat ; another, by the generation of various gases through galvanic action. Others have maintained that the antediluvian continents were sunk beneath the ocean at that time, though such find it hard to tell us why there was a rain of forty days upon land that was ready to subside beneath the ocean. Others have resort to a comet's impinging against the earth, and throwing the waters of the ocean over the land. But they were not aware that comets are mere vapor. Others suppose (and surely theirs is the most plausible theory) that the elevation of the bed of some ocean, by volcanic agency, threw its waters over the adjoining continents, and the mighty wave thus produced would not stop till it had swept over all other continents and islands. But in this case, it is evident that the continent first overflowed must have been left dry before the wave had reached other continents, so that, in fact, all parts of the earth would not have been enveloped simultaneously ; and besides, how unlike such a violent rushing of the waters over the land is the scriptural account! In short, so unsatisfactory have been most of the theories to account for the water requisite to produce a universal deluge, that most writers have resorted, in the end, to miraculous agency to obtain it. And that, in fact, is the most satisfactory mode of getting over this difficulty, if the Scriptures unequivocally teach the universality of the deluge.

A second objection to such a universality is, the difficulty of providing for the animals in the ark.

Calculations have indeed been made, which seemed to show that the ark was capacious enough to hold the pairs and septuples of all the species. But, unfortunately, the number of species assumed to exist by the calculators was vastly below the truth. It amounted only to three or four hundred; whereas the actual number already described by zoölogists is not less than one hundred and fifty thousand; and the probable number existing on the globe is not less than half a million. And for the greater part of these must provision have been made, since most of them inhabit either the air or the dry land. A thousand species of mammalia, six thousand species of birds, two thousand species of reptiles, and one hundred and twenty thousand species of insects are already described, and must have been provided with space and food. Will any one believe this possible, in a vessel not more than four hundred and fifty feet long, seventy-five feet broad, and forty-five feet high?

The third and most important objection to this universality of the deluge is derived from the facts brought to light by modern science, respecting the distribution of animals and plants on the globe.

It was the opinion of Linnæus that all animals and plants had their commencement in a particular region of the earth, from whence they migrated into all other parts of its surface. And had no new facts come to light since his day, to change the aspect of the subject, one would hesitate long before adopting views opposed to so distinguished a naturalist. But new facts, in vast numbers, have been multiplying ever since his day, and zoölogists and botanists now almost universally adopt the opinion, early promulgated by Dr. Prichard, in his admirable work on the Physical History of Man, that there must have been several centres of creation, from which the animals and plants radiated only so far as the climate and food were adapted to their natures, except a few species endowed with the power of accommodating themselves to all climates. Certain it is that they are now thus distributed; and it is inevitable death for most species to venture beyond certain limits. If tropical animals and plants, for instance, were to migrate to the temperate zones, and especially to the frigid regions, they could not long survive; and almost equally fatal would it be for the animals and plants of high latitudes to take up their abode near the equator. But even within the tropics we find distinct species of animals and plants on opposite continents. Indeed, naturalists reckon a large number of botanical and zoölogical districts, or provinces, as they are called, within which they find certain peculiar groups of animals and plants, with natures exactly adapted to that particular district, but incapable of enduring the different climate of adjoining districts. They differ considerably as to the number of these districts, because the plants and animals of our globe are by no means yet fully described, and because the districts assigned to the different classes do not fully coincide; but as to the existence of such a distribution, they are of one opinion. The most reliable divisions of this kind make twenty-five botanical provinces, and five kingdoms and fourteen provinces among animals.*

The fact that man, and some of the domesticated animals, and a few plants, are found in almost every climate, has, until recently, blinded the eyes of naturalists to the manner in which the great mass of animals and plants are confined within certain prescribed limits. But so soon as the general fact is stated, we immediately recur to abundant proof of its truth. We should be disposed to question the veracity of that traveller who should visit a new and remote country, and describe its vegetable and animal productions as essentially the same as in our own ; and all because the analogy of other portions of the globe leads us to expect that a new geographical province shall present us with a peculiar *fauna* and *flora ;* that is, with peculiar groups of animals and plants.

It is obvious that the facts which have been stated have an important bearing upon the mode in which the animals were brought together to enter the ark, and were afterwards distributed through the earth, if the deluge were universal. Certain it is that, without miraculous preservation, they could never have been brought together, nor again dispersed. We have reason to suppose that the ark was constructed in some part of the temperate zone. Now, suppose the animals of the torrid zone at the present day to attempt, by natural means, to reach the temperate zone ; who does not know that nearly all of them must perish ? Nor is it any easier to conceive how, after the flood, they could have migrated into all continents, and islands, and climates, and how each species should have found the place exactly fitted to its constitution, as we now find them. Indeed, the idea of their collection and

* Johnston's Physical Atlas, pp. 66, 76, (Philadelphia edition, 1850.)

dispersion in a natural way is altogether too absurd to be believed. And we must, therefore, resort to a miracle, or suppose a new creation to have taken place after the deluge, or admit the flood to have been limited. If the latter supposition be not inconsistent with the Bible, it completely relieves the difficulty. If we suppose the limited region of Central Asia, where man existed, to have been deluged, and pairs and septuples of the most common animals in that region only to have been kept alive in the ark, the entire account will harmonize with natural history. The question, then, whether such a view is consistent with the Bible, becomes of great interest; and to this point I beg leave next to direct your attention.

If we understand the scriptural account to denote a literal universality, it is certainly very natural to inquire why such universality was necessary, since the deluge is represented as a penal infliction upon man. For it seems difficult to believe as some writers have attempted to prove, that the human family had become very numerous, or had extended far beyond the spot where they were first planted, in less than two thousand years; especially when we recollect how few were the children of patriarchs whose age amounted to many centuries, and how very probable it is that the extreme wickedness of most of the antediluvians tended to their extinction rather than their multiplication. Why, then, for the sake of destroying man, occupying probably only a limited portion of one continent, was it necessary to depopulate all other continents and islands, inhabited only by irresponsible animals, who had no connection with man? If the Scriptures unequivocally declare that such was the fact, we are bound to believe it on divine testimony. But if their language admits of a different interpretation, it seems reasonable to adopt it.

And here I am willing to acknowledge that the language of the Bible on this subject seems, at first view, to teach the universality of the flood, unequivocally. *The waters*, say they, *prevailed exceedingly upon the earth, and all the high hills that were under the whole heaven were covered.* Again : *Behold, I, even I, do bring a flood of waters upon the earth to destroy all flesh, wherein is the breath of life, from under heaven ; and every thing that is in the earth shall die.* If such language be interpreted by the same rules which we should apply to a modern composition, it could in no way be understood to teach a limited deluge or a partial destruction. But in respect to this ancient record, two considerations are to be carefully weighed.

In the first place, the terms employed are not to be judged of by the state of knowledge in the nineteenth century, but by its state among the people to whom this revelation was first addressed. When the earth was spoken of to that people, (the ancient Jews,) they could not have understood it to embrace a much wider region than that inhabited by man, because they could not have had any idea of what lay beyond those limits. And so of the phrase *heaven ;* it must have been coëxtensive with the inhabited earth only. And when it was said that all animals would die by the deluge, they could not have supposed the declaration to embrace creatures far beyond the dwellings of men, because they knew nothing of such regions. Why, then, may we not attach the same limited meaning to these declarations ? Why should we suppose that the Holy Spirit used terms, adapted, indeed, to the astronomy and geography of the nineteenth century, but conveying only a false idea to those to whom they were addressed ?

In the second place, in all ages and nations, and especially

12

among ancient ones, " universal terms are often used to signify only a very large amount in number or quantity." —
Dr. Smith, *Scrip. and Geol.* p. 212, 4th ed. — The Hebrew
בֹּל, (*kol*,) the Greek πας, and the English *all*, are alike employed in this manner, to signify *many*. There are some very
striking cases of this sort in the Bible. Thus in Genesis it is
said that *all countries came into Egypt to Joseph to buy corn,
because the famine was sore in all lands.* This certainly could
apply only to the well-known countries around Egypt; for
transportation would have been impossible to the remotest
parts of the habitable globe. In the account of the plagues
that came upon Egypt, it is said that *the hail smote every
herb of the field, and brake every tree of the field ;* but, in a
few days afterwards, it is said of the locusts that *they did eat
every herb of the land and all the fruit of the trees which
the hail had left. This day*, said God to the Israelites, while
yet in their journeyings, *will I begin to put the fear of thee
and the dread of thee upon the face of the nations under all
the heavens.* But it is obvious that only the nations contigu-
ous to the Israelites, chiefly the Canaanites, are here meant.
In the New Testament, it is said that, at the time of the pen-
tecost, there were dwelling at Jerusalem *Jews, devout men,
out of every nation under heaven.* Yet, in the enumeration,
which follows this passage, of the different places from which
those Jews had come, we find only a region extending from
Italy to Persia, and from Egypt to the Black Sea. It could
have been a district of only about that size which Paul meant,
when he said to the Colossians that *the gospel was preached
to every creature which is under heaven.* In the First Book of
Kings, it is said that *all the earth sought the presence of Solomon, to hear his wisdom ;* — a passage which requires as much
limitation as the others above quoted. A similar mode of

expression is employed by Christ, when he says of the queen of Sheba that *she came from the uttermost parts of the earth to hear the wisdom of Solomon ;* for her residence, being probably on the Arabian Gulf, could not have been more than twelve or fourteen hundred miles from Jerusalem. A like figurative mode of speech is employed in the description of Peter's vision, in which he saw a great sheet let down to the earth, *wherein were all manner of four-footed beasts of the earth, and wild beasts, and creeping things, and fowls of the air.* Who will suppose, since it is wholly unnecessary for the object, which was to convince Peter that the Mosaic distinction into clean and unclean beasts was abolished, that he here had a vision of all the species of terrestrial vertebral animals on the globe ?

It would be easy to multiply similar passages. In many of them we should find that the phrase *all the earth* signifies the land of Palestine ; in a few, the Chaldean empire ; and in one, that of Alexander of Macedon.

Now, so similar is the phraseology of the passages just quoted to that descriptive of the deluge, so universal are the terms, while we are sure that their meaning must be limited, that we are abundantly justified in considering the deluge as limited, if other parts of the Bible, or the facts of natural history, require such a limitation. Indeed, so obviously analogous are the passages quoted to the Mosaic account of the deluge, that distinguished writers have regarded the deluge as limited, long before geology existed, or natural history had learned the manner in which organic life is distributed on the globe ; nay, at a period when naturalists, with Linnæus at their head, supposed animals and plants to have proceeded from one centre : — an opinion that seemed to sustain the notion of the universality of the flood. The inference, then, that it was limited, must have been made chiefly on exeget ̓ cal grounds.

" I cannot see," says Bishop Stillingfleet, more than a cen tury ago, " any urgent necessity from the Scripture to assert that the flood did spread over all the surface of the earth. That all mankind, those in the ark excepted, were destroyed by it, is most certain, according to the Scriptures. The flood was universal as to mankind; but from thence follows no necessity at all of asserting the universality of it as to the globe of the earth, unless it be sufficiently proved that the whole earth was peopled before the flood, which I despair of ever seeing proved." — *Origines Sacræ*, B. III. chap. 4, p. 337, ed. 1709.

Matthew Poole, well known for his valuable and extensive commentaries on the Bible, thus expresses himself : " It is not to be supposed that the entire globe of the earth was cov-ered with water. Where was the need of overwhelming those regions in which there were no human beings? It would be highly unreasonable to suppose that mankind had so increased before the deluge as to have penetrated to all the corners of the earth. It is, indeed, not probable that they had extended themselves beyond the limits of Syria and Mesopotamia. Absurd it would be to affirm that the effects of the punishment inflicted upon men alone applied to places in which there were no men. If, then, we should entertain the belief that not so much as the hundredth part of the globe was overspread with water, still the deluge would be univer-sal, because the extirpation took effect upon all the part of the globe which was inhabited. If we take this ground, the difficulties which some have raised about the deluge fall away as inapplicable, and mere cavils; and irreligious persons have no reason left them for doubting the truth of the Holy Scrip-tures." — *Synopsis on Gen.* vii. 19.

Poole wrote nearly two centuries ago. In more recent times, we find authorities equally eminent for learning and candor adopting the same views. "Interpreters," says Dathe, " do not agree whether the deluge inundated the whole earth, or only those regions then inhabited.   I adopt the latter opinion. The phrase *all* does not prove the inundation to have been universal. It appears that in many places בֹּל (*kol*) is to be understood as limited to the thing or place spoken of. Hence all the animals said to have been introduced into the ark were only those of the region inundated. So, also, only those mountains are to be understood, which were surmounted by the waters." — *Pentateuchus a Dathio*, p. **63.**

But no modern writer has treated this subject with so much candor and ability — and the same may be said of his whole work on the " Relation of the Holy Scriptures to some Parts of Geological Science " — as Dr. John Pye Smith. We can say of him, what we can say of very few men, that he is accurately acquainted with all the branches of the subject. Eminent as a theologian and a philologist, and fully possessed of all the facts in geology and natural history, he gives us his opinion, not as a young man, fond of novelties, but in the full maturity of judgment and of years. " From these instances," says he, " of the scriptural idiom in the application of phraseology similar to that in the narrative concerning the flood, I humbly think that those terms do not oblige us to understand a literal universality ; so that we are exonerated from some otherwise insuperable difficulties in natural history and geology. If so much of the earth was overflowed as was occupied by the human race, both the physical and the moral ends of that awful visitation were answered." — *Scrip. and Geol.* p. **214,** 4th ed.

" Let us now take the seat of the antediluvian population,"
12 *

continues Dr. Smith, "to have been in Western Asia, in which a large district, even at the present day, lies considerably below the level of the sea. It must not be forgotten that six weeks of continued rain would not give an amount of water forty times that which fell on the first, or a subsequent day, for evaporation would be continually carrying up the water to be condensed, and to fall again ; so that the same mass of water would return many times. If, then, in addition to the tremendous rain, we suppose an elevation of the bed of the Persian and Indian Seas, or a subsidence of the inhabited land towards the south, we shall have sufficient cause in the hands of almighty justice for submerging the district, covering its hills, and destroying all living beings within its limits, except those whom divine mercy preserved in the ark. The drawing off of the waters would be effected by a return of the bed of the sea to a lower level, or by the elevation of some tracts of land, which would leave channels and slopes for the larger part of the water to flow back into the Indian Ocean, while the lower part remained a great lake, or an inland sea, the Caspian." — p. 217.

It is a circumstance favoring the above suggestions of Dr. Smith, that there is a tract of country ten degrees of latitude in breadth, embracing most of Asia Minor, ancient Armenia and Georgia, and part of Persia, extending at least as far east as the Caspian Sea, and probably much farther, in which volcanic agency has been in operation at a comparatively recent period. I am not aware that we have evidence of any eruption of lava in those regions, within historic times, except, perhaps, some mud volcanoes in the Caucasian range. The Katekekaumene, or Burnt District, of Asia Minor, and Mount Ararat, probably experienced eruptions at a date somewhat earlier, though at a comparatively recent date. Yet important changes of level may have been the result of volcanic agency in Central Asia, as recently as the Noachian deluge, without leaving any traces which would be obvious, without more careful observation than has yet been made in those regions. Especially might a subsidence of the surface have taken place, and not have left any striking evidence of its occurrence. Still more difficult would it now be to discover the marks of vertical movements in the bed of the Indian Ocean at the time of the deluge.

I will venture to add another suggestion. If the bed of the Indian Ocean was uplifted by volcanic matter, struggling to get vent, vapor enough might have been liberated to account, on natural principles, for the forty days' rain of the deluge. For it is well known that in volcanic eruptions drenching rains are often the result of the sudden condensation of the aqueous vapor.

We are here met, however, by a serious objection to the hypothesis, which gives only a limited extent to the deluge. If the present Mount Ararat, in Armenia, is the mountain on which the ark first rested, a deluge which covered its top must, by its flux and reflux, have overspread nearly all other portions of the globe, for that mountain rises seventeen thousand seven hundred feet above the ocean. But we are informed by Jerome, that the name Ararat was given generally to the mountains of Armenia; (indeed, that is the meaning of the name ;) and long before geology existed, Shuckford suggested that some spot farther east corresponds better with the scriptural account of the place where the ark rested. For it is said of the families of the sons of Noah, that, as they journeyed from the east, they found a plain in the land of Shinar. Now, Shinar, or Babylonia, lies nearly south of the Armenian Ararat, and the probability, therefore, is, that the true Ararat, from whose vicinity the descendants of Noah probably emigrated, lay much farther to the south. Again, if the ark rested upon the present Ararat, it is impossible, except by a miracle, that those who came out of it could have reached the plain below; for so exceedingly difficult of access is it, that it is doubtful whether, since the deluge, any one ever succeeded in reaching its summit, till the year 1829. Indeed, it is an article in the creed of the Armenian church that its ascent is impossible. That the almost universal tradition of Eastern nations should have fixed upon that mountain as the resting-place of the ark is not strange, considering that there is no mountain in all Asia so striking to behold.

But upon the whole, the probability is strong that some other elevation, less lofty and steep, was the radiating point of the postdiluvian races of man and other animals. The fact of Noah's sending forth a dove from the ark, which came back in the evening with an olive leaf in her mouth, strengthens the preceding view. For neither upon the present Ararat, nor around it, does the olive grow, because it is too cold. Indeed, all its upper part is covered with perpetual ice. But if the Ararat of Scripture lay nearer the tropics, the olive might find upon it a congenial spot. A distinguished botanist adduced the fact about the olive as evidence against the Bible. But how easily refuted, if the theory now under examination be true !

In favor of this supposition, I might have urged another consideration, which, in my mind, has no little weight. It is impossible that the waters of the deluge should have covered the earth for a year, without destroying nearly all the existing vegetation. Yet nothing is said of the preservation of seeds in the ark ; and if they had been preserved, certainly nothing but miraculous power, and that of the most remarkable kind, could have scattered them through the remotest continents and islands, so as to form distinct botanical districts, such as have been described. The olive, from which a leaf was plucked by the dove sent out of the ark, was probably situated upon elevated ground, and where it remained but a short time beneath the waters, and therefore did not lose its vitality.

It is probable that the theory which makes the deluge limited in extent will meet with more favor than any other, with candid and intelligent men, to meet the suggested difficulties of the case. But some, who are unwilling to abandon the idea of the universality of the deluge, avoid these difficulties by supposing a new creation to have taken place at that epoch. That such a new creation occurred at the commencement of several geological periods can hardly admit a doubt. And a presumption is hence derived in favor of a similar act at the beginning of the postdiluvian period, preceded as it was, like the other geological periods, by an almost entire destruction of organic life.

The principal objection to this view is, that no notice is taken of such a new creation in the Bible. And it would seem that an event of so much importance would hardly be passed in silence ; and yet the bringing into existence new races of the inferior animals and plants could have but little bearing upon the object of revelation, which respects almost exclusively the spiritual condition of man. One, however, can hardly see why pairs and septuples of the animals, even in a limited district, need to have been preserved in the ark, if a new creation were to follow the coming catastrophe ; nor why the creation of the antediluvian animals, so soon to perish, should have been so particularly described, while no notice was taken of the postdiluvian races, which were to occupy the earth so much longer time.

A third theory has been suggested by some, embracing both those which have been described. They admit the deluge to have been of limited extent, but suppose this limitation not to be sufficient to explain all the facts of revelation and of science, without a new creation also, at the commencement of the postdiluvian period. They suppose, indeed, that geology and natural history teach the occasional extinction of species, and the creation of others, even in our own times. And in regard to this latter view, it may at least be said that it is not contradicted by the Bible. Nay, one would almost suppose that the Psalmist were describing such a state of things when he says, *Thou hidest thy face; they* [animals] *are troubled. Thou takest away their breath; they die and return to their dust. Thou sendest forth thy spirit; they are created; and thou renewest the face of the earth.* The resemblance between this language and that employed to describe the original creation is striking. Indeed, the same word (*bawraw*) is used.

Without attempting to decide which of these theories has the highest claim upon our belief, it is sufficient to remark, that either of them reconciles the facts of geology and natural history with the inspired record; nor does the adoption of either of them require us to put a forced and unnatural construction upon the language of the Bible. Even then, if we should admit that a construction agreeing with these theories is not the most natural meaning, yet if the facts of natural history unequivocally require such an interpretation to harmonize the Bible with nature, it is assuredly one of those cases where science must be allowed to modify our exegesis of Scripture. In the view of sound philosophy, such modification at once disarms scepticism of its cavils.

With two remarks of a practical character, I close the discussion of this subject.

First. The history of opinions respecting the Noachian deluge furnishes a salutary lesson to those employed in the examination of analogous subjects. We have seen these opinions assume almost every possible shape ; yet, until recently they have all been maintained with the most positive and dogmatic assurance ; and each particular theory has been regarded as involving the essence of the Bible, as being the *articulus stantis vel cadentis ecclesiæ*, and whoever denied it virtually denied the Bible. But all reasonable and truly scientific men are fast coming to the conclusion, that the deluge has had very little to do with the present configuration of the globe, and that it is doubtful whether any trace of its occurrence will ever be found in nature ; so that, on the one hand, all the alarms and denunciations of misguided Christians on this subject might have been spared ; and, on the other hand, if the hasty exultation of the infidel, in his supposed discovery of discrepancy between nature and Moses, had been suppressed until the subject was understood, he would not have experienced the mortification of entire defeat.

It is, indeed, very humiliating to human nature to find so many of the wise, the talented, and the religious so confident and zealous, yet so erroneous. But it is a salutary lesson. It shows us the vast importance of being thoroughly acquainted with a subject before we dogmatize upon it. It should not, indeed, discourage us, and produce a universal scepticism on all subjects not admitting a mathematical demonstration ; but it should make us cautious in examining the grounds of our conclusions, and modest in maintaining them.

Secondly. It is interesting to observe how, amid all the diversities and fluctuations of opinion on this subject, the Bible has remained unaffected.

The infidel felt confident that the arrows which he drew from this quiver would certainly pierce Christianity to the heart. But they rebounded from her adamantine breastplate, blunted and broken; and no one will have the courage to pick them up and hurl them again. The physico-theological school at one time felt certain, that no other theory but an entire dissolution of the crust of the globe at the deluge, could possibly be made consistent with the Bible. More recently, it has been supposed equally necessary, to reconcile geology and revelation, that we should admit the antediluvian continents to have sunk beneath the ocean at that time. Still later, it has been thought quite certain that the surface of the earth bore the most striking marks of a universal deluge, probably identical with that of Scripture. At length, the extreme opinion is now generally reached, that no trace of the deluge of Noah remains. And equally wide and well established is the belief that, amid all these fluctuations of theory, the Bible has stood as an immovable rock amid the conflicting waves. The final result is, that we have only slightly to modify the interpretation of the Mosaic account, in conformity with the laws of language, to make it entirely consistent with the notion that all traces of the deluge have disappeared. Thus, in the midst of human opinions, veering to every point of the compass, the Bible has ever remained fixed to one point. Not so with false systems of religion. The Hindoo religion contains a false astronomy, as well as anatomy and physiology; and the Mohammedan Koran distinctly advances the Ptolemaic hypothesis of the universe; so that you have only to prove these religions false in science in order to destroy their claim to infallibility. But the Bible, stating only facts, does not interfere with, neither is affected by, the hypotheses of philosophy. Often, indeed, in past ages, have men set up their hypotheses as oracles in the temple of nature, to be consulted rather than the Bible. But, like Dagon before the ark, they have fallen to the earth, and been broken in pieces before the Word of God; while this has ever stood and ever shall stand, in sublime simplicity and undecaying strength, amid the wrecks of every false system of philosophy and religion.

13

LECTURE V.

THE WORLD'S SUPPOSED ETERNITY.

In our attempts thus far to elucidate the religion of geology, our attention has been directed to those points where this science has been supposed to conflict with revelation ; and I trust it has been made manifest that the collision was rather with the interpretation than with the meaning of Scripture ; and that, in fact, geology, instead of coming into collision with the Bible, affords us important aid in understanding it aright. We now advance to a part of the subject which has a more direct bearing upon natural religion. And here, if I mistake not, we shall find the illustration of religious truth from this science, as we might expect, more direct and palpable.

The subject to which I wish first to call your attention is the world's eternity, or the eternal existence of matter. This was the universal belief of the philosophers of antiquity, and, indeed, of most reasoning minds where the Bible has not been known. The grand argument by which this opinion was sustained is the well-known *ex nihilo nihil fit*, (nothing produces nothing.) Hence men inferred that not even the Deity could create matter out of nothing ; and, therefore, it must be eternal. Most of the ancient philosophers, however, did not hence infer the non-existence of the Deity. But they endeavored to reconcile the existence of eternal matter with an eternal Spirit. They supposed both to be self-existent and

coëxistent. From this rational thinking principle they supposed all good to be derived ; while from the material irrational principle all evil sprung. Plato taught that God, of his
own will, united himself with matter, although he did not
create it, and out of it produced the present world ; so that
it was proper to speak of the world as created, although the
matter was from eternity. Aristotle and Zeno taught that
God's union with matter was necessary ; and hence they considered the world eternal. In the opinion of Epicurus, God
was entirely separated from matter, which consisted of innu-
merable atoms, floating about from eternity, like dust in the
air, until at last they assumed the present form of the world.

In modern times, the belief in the eternity of matter has
usually been connected with, or made the basis of, a refined
and popular system of atheism. I refer to the pantheism of
Spinoza. He maintains that there exists in the universe but
one substance, variously modified, whose two principal attributes are infinite extension and infinite intelligence. This
substance, the τò πᾶν of Spinoza, he regarded as God ; and
hence his system is called *Pantheism.* Under various modifications, it has been adopted by many sceptical minds, and is,
undoubtedly, the most common and plausible system of
atheism extant. Other modern writers, among whom may be
mentioned that anomalous philosopher Bayle, have advocated
the views of the ancients respecting the eternity of matter.

It may seem strange, but it is true, that some Christian philosophers and divines have been, in ancient and modern times,
the advocates of the eternity of matter. The ancient Christians
adopted it from Plato. Thus we find Justin Martyr maintaining that God formed the world from an eternal, unorganized
material. And the schoolmen, who followed Aristotle, taught
that " God had created the world from eternity." On this

ground, even some Protestant theologians have asserted that
it was absurd to speak of an eternal God who is not an eternal Creator.

A principle which has thus been adopted by so many
acute minds unenlightened by revelation, and by some
who possessed that divine testimony, must be sustained by
some plausible arguments. The principal one relied on is,
that the changes which are going on in the material world
are proved to be only transmutations, which follow one
another in series that return into themselves, and which may,
therefore, have been going on from eternity; and if this be
admitted, it is as easy to suppose matter to be self-sustained,
and to have fallen into its present order of itself, as to suppose the interference of an infinite Spirit. "How do we
know," says Dr. Chalmers, in stating the atheistic argument,
"that the world is a consequent at all? Is there any greater
absurdity in supposing it to have existed, as it now is, at any
specified point of time, throughout the millions of ages that are
past, than that it should so exist at this moment? Does what
we suppose might have been then, imply any greater absurdity, than what we actually see to be at present? Now, might
not the same question be carried back to any point or period
of duration, however remote? or, in other words, might we
not dispense with a beginning for the world altogether?"
"For aught we can know *a priori*," says Hume, "matter
may contain the source or spring of order originally within
itself as well as mind does; and there is no more difficulty in conceiving that the several elements, from an internal, unknown cause, may fall into the most exquisite arrangement, than to conceive that their ideas, in the great universal
mind, from a like internal cause, fall into that arrangement.
If this material world rests upon a similar ideal world, this

ideal world must rest upon some other, and so on without end. It were better, therefore, never to look beyond the present material world. By supposing it to contain the principle of its order within itself, we really assert it to be God ; and the sooner we arrive at that divine Being, so much the better."

Now, in what manner have these ingenious arguments been met ? Until quite recently, no one has supposed that any light on this subject could be derived from geology. Indeed, even now, by many, that science is regarded as favoring the idea of the world's eternity. Neither has it been thought that, on a question of natural theology, like this, it was proper to appeal to the Bible. Philosophers and divines, however, have attempted to reply to these arguments, irrespective of geology and revelation ; and they have generally convinced themselves that they have been successful. But to my mind, I must confess, this has always appeared the weakest spot in natural religion. Some of the arguments to prove the world not eternal do, indeed, appear, at first statement, very profound ; but they rather silence than convince ; and the longer we reflect upon them, the more apt are we to doubt their force.

And here I am constrained to bear testimony to the masterly manner in which this subject has been treated by Dr. Chalmers. Perceiving that the defences of natural religion on this subject were weak, in spite of much show of strength, he has laid out his giant force of intellect in clearing away the rubbish and building a rampart of rock. His remarkable skill in seizing upon and bringing out prominently the great principles of a difficult subject, and turning them round and round till they fill every eye, is here most happily exerted.

Let us now proceed, in the first place, to examine the arguments that have been adduced to prove the non-eternity of

13 *

the world, independent of geology and revelation ; and in the second place, to derive from these two sources of evidence the true ground on which that proposition rests.

The first supposed proof that the world has not eternally existed is derived from what is called the *a priori* argument for the existence of the Deity, originally proposed by the monk Anselmus, and afterwards more fully illustrated in England by Dr. Samuel Clarke. Take the following brief summary of this argument, as applied to the eternity of matter, in the words of Dr. Crombie.

" Whatever has existed from eternity, independent and without any external cause, must be self-existent. Whatever is self-existent must exist necessarily, by an absolute necessity in the nature of the thing. This is also self-evident. It follows, therefore, that unless the material world exist necessarily, by an absolute necessity in its own nature, so that it must be a contradiction to suppose it not to exist, it cannot be independent and eternal. In order to disprove this absolute necessity, he [Dr. Clarke] reasoned thus : If matter be supposed to exist necessarily, then in that necessary existence is included the power of gravitation, or it is not. If not, then in a world merely material, and in which no intelligent being presides, there never could have been any motion. But if the power of gravitation be included in the pretended necessary existence of matter, then it follows necessarily, that there must be a vacuum ; it follows, likewise, that matter is not a necessary being. For if a vacuum actually be, then it is plainly more than possible for matter not to be."

Is it not passing strange that such a dreamy argumentation as this — and it is a fair sample of Dr. Clarke's extended work on the existence of the Deity — should have been re-garded as sound logic by many of the acutest minds, and that a majority even of the ablest metaphysicians, up almost to the present day, should have felt satisfied with it? A few minds, indeed, long ago perceived its fallacy, among whom was Alexander Pope, who thus sarcastically describes it : —

> " Be that my task, replies a gloomy Clarke,
> Sworn foe to mystery, yet divinely dark.
> Let others creep by timid steps and slow,
> On plain experience lay foundation low,
> By common sense to common notions bred,
> And last to nature's cause through nature led,
> All-seeing in thy mists, we need no guide,
> Mother of arrogance, and source of pride !
> We nobly take the high *priori* road,
> And reason downward till we doubt of God."
>
> *Dunciad,* Book IV.

It is impossible, on this occasion, to go into a formal refutation of this famous argument. But this is unnecessary ; since, as Dr. Chalmers says, it " has fallen into utter disesteem and desuetude." Indeed, the language of Dr. Thomas Brown on this subject is not too severe, when he says, that he " conceives the abstract arguments that have been adduced to show that it is impossible for matter to have existed from eternity, by reasoning on what has been termed necessary existence, and the incompatibility of this necessary existence with the qualities of matter, to be relics of the mere verbal logic of the schools, as little capable of producing conviction as any of the wildest and most absurd of the technical scholastic reasonings on the properties, or supposed properties, of entity and nonentity."

In the second place, it has been argued with much apparent plausibility, by Dr. Paley, that wherever we find a complicated organic structure, adapted to produce beneficial results, its origin must be sought beyond itself; and since the world abounds with such organisms, it cannot be eternal; that is, the mere existence of animals and plants proves their non-eternity.

Now, without asserting that there is no force in this argument, I have two remarks to make upon it. The first is, to quote the reply to it, which such a writer as David Hume has given, in language which I have just repeated. " For aught we can know *a priori*," says he, " matter may contain the source or spring of order originally within itself, as well as mind does; and there is no more difficulty in conceiving that the several elements, from an internal unknown cause, may fall into the most exquisite arrangement, than to conceive that their ideas in the great universal mind, from a like internal unknown cause, fall into that arrangement. To say that the different ideas, which compose the reason of the Supreme, fall into order of themselves, and by their own nature, is really to talk without any precise meaning. If it has a meaning, I would fain know why it is not as good sense to say, that the parts of the material world fall into order of themselves and by their own nature. Can the one opinion be intelligible while the other is not so ? "

Fairly to meet this reasoning of the prince of sceptics is not an achievement of dulness or ignorance. In order to do it triumphantly, we want, what Dr. Paley could not find, a distinct example of the creation of numerous organic beings by some cause independent of themselves. I say, he could not find such an example; for on a question of natural theology, he did not think it proper to appeal to the Bible; nor had geology, when he wrote, revealed her astonishing record on this subject. But as it is now developed, it puts an end to all controversy as to the origin of the organic world.

My second remark, however, on this argument is, that even

admitting its correctness, it only proves the commencement of organic natures, but does not show that the matter of which they are composed may not have been eternal.

In the third place, an argument against the eternal existence of matter has been derived by Sir John Herschel, one of the most distinguished natural philosophers of the day, from the atomic constitution of bodies, as made known to us by chemistry. This science makes it certainly probable, that even the infinitesimal particles of matter have a definite and peculiar shape, and size, and weight, in each of the elements. " Now," says this writer, " when we see a great number of things precisely alike, we do not believe this similarity to have originated, except from a common principle independent of them." " The discoveries alluded to effectually destroy the idea of an external self-existent matter, by giving to each of its atoms the essential characters at once of a manufactured article and a subordinate agent."

To this argument the atheist's reply would be essentially the same as that last considered; and in one respect it would even be more forcible, because the atomic constitution of bodies, being less complex, is less obviously the result of foreign agency, and may more easily be regarded as the necessary property of eternal matter. On the other hand, however, it is more obviously an attribute of the original constitution of matter than organic structure; and if it does require an independent agency for its production, it seems difficult to conceive of the existence of matter in a previous state. So that, in this point of view, this argument is more forcible than the last; and it is no small evidence that it has real strength, that it comes to us from one of the most acute and impartial minds in Europe.

In the fourth place, it is maintained that the idea of an

eternal succession, or chain of being, which the atheistic advocates of the world's eternity defend, is highly absurd, and even mathematically false.

The atheist mainly relies upon this notion of an eternal series of things; for if he can defend that opinion, he will overturn the main argument of the Theist for the divine existence, viz., that from design in the works of creation. On this ground, therefore, he should be fairly met. Has he been so met by the reasoning that has usually been employed to refute his opinion? As a fair sample of it, I will here quote the leading points of the argument, as given by one of the most popular and able theologians of our country. " It is asserted by atheists," says Dr. Dwight, " that there has been an eternal series of things. The absurdity of this assertion may be shown in many ways.

" First. Each individual in a series is a unit. But every collection of units, however great, is with intuitive certainty numerable, and, therefore, cannot be infinite."

" Secondly. Every individual in the series (take for example a series of men) had a beginning. But a collection of beings must, however long the series, have had a beginning. This, likewise, is intuitively evident."

" Thirdly. It is justly observed by the learned and acute Dr. Bentley, that in the supposed infinite series, as the number of individual men is alleged to be infinite, the number of their eyes must have been twice, the number of their fingers ten times, and the number of the hairs on their heads many thousand times, as great as the number of men."

" Fourthly. It is also observed by the same excellent writer, that all these generations of men were once present." — *Dwight's Theology*, vol. ii. p. 24.

How is it possible that such reasoning should have satisfied logical and philosophical minds? Would it not be equally good to disprove the demonstrated principles of mathematics which relate to infinite quantities? For in mathematics an infinite series of units is a familiar phrase; and it is also common to speak of one infinite quantity as twice, or ten times, or many thousand times, greater than another, and that, too, in just such cases as the one referred to above.

True, mathematical infinites are in some respects different from metaphysical infinites; but it is the former that belong to this argument, since the supposed infinite succession of organic beings forms a mathematical series.

An acute writer in our own country, however, has recently attempted to show that " there can be no number actually infinite, and therefore no infinite number of generations." *
That the mathematician cannot actually present before us the whole of an infinite series, is indeed most certain ; for such power belongs only to an Infinite Being. But does the fact that man's faculties are limited, prove that an arithmetical process cannot be carried on from eternity to eternity? Because man cannot put upon paper the series of numbers representing the miles in infinite space, or the hours in infinite duration, is there, therefore, no such thing as infinite space, or infinite duration? Certainly not, if this reasoning be correct.

In spite, however, of such mathematical metaphysics, is it not an intelligible statement of the atheist, when he says of any generation of men and animals in past time, that there was another that preceded it; and unless you have matter-of-fact proof to the contrary, how will you disprove his assertion? You may show him that practically he can never

* Rev. Joseph Tracy, Bibliotheca Sacra, Oct. 1850, p. 614.

exhibit a series, even of numbers, extending eternally backward ; but he may, in return, challenge you to put your finger upon the first link of the chain of organic nature. If you attempt it, he will reply that other links preceded the one you have named, and that, as far as you choose to run backward, he can go farther; in other words, by the very supposition which he makes, he excludes a beginning to organic nature, and, therefore, all reasoning which assumes such a beginning is of no force against his conclusions. If a series which may thus be extended indefinitely backward be not infinite in a metaphysical sense, it is to common sense.

Let me not be thought to be an advocate in any sense for the unsupported notion of an infinite series of organic beings. But the question is, whether those who, in spite of common sense, have maintained this opinion, have been fairly refuted by such metaphysical evasions as I have quoted. The truth is, that, in order to end this dispute, the Theist needs to bring forward at least one example in which the commencement of some race of animals can be fairly pointed out; and I know not where such an example can be found, save in the Bible and geology.

In the fifth place, the changing state of the world has been regarded as incompatible with the world's eternity. This argument is thus stated by Bishop Sumner: "If the universe itself is the first eternal being, its existence is necessary, as metaphysicians speak ; and it must be possessed of all those qualities which are inseparable from necessary existence. Of this nature are immutability and perfection. For change is the attribute of imperfection, and imperfection is incompatible with that Being, which is, as the hypothesis affirms, independent, and, therefore, can have no source of imperfection. To suppose, therefore, of the first independent Being, that it could have existed otherwise than it is, is no less contrary to the idea of necessity, with which we set out, than to suppose it not to exist at all."

This reasoning is not destitute of plausibility. For there is scarcely any lesson more forcibly impressed on short-lived man than the mutability of the world. And it is indeed true that change is its most striking attribute. But when we look at the subject philosophically, we find that all this mutability is consistent with the most perfect ultimate stability; nay, that the change is essential to secure the stability. Apart from what revelation and geology teach, these changes in nature form cycles, which, like those in astronomy, are perfectly consistent with the eternal permanence of the general system to which they belong. In the motions of the heavenly bodies, a considerable amount of irregularity and oscillation about a mean state does not tend to the ruin, but rather to the preservation, of the system, provided the anomalies do not extend beyond certain limits. It is just so with other changes that are going on around us. All of them are, in fact, as much regulated by mathematical laws as the perturbations of the heavenly bodies; although those laws are more complicated and difficult to bring out in distinct formulæ in the former case than in the latter. Yet even in astronomy, it is not many years since the mutual disturbances among the heavenly bodies were supposed to be the certain precursors of ruin to the system. It was not till the famous problem of the three bodies was solved, by the use of the most refined mathematical analysis, that astronomers learnt the true operation of those causes of disturbance among the heavenly bodies which exist in their mutual attractions. It was then found that, so balanced are they in their action, and so narrow their limits, that they can never affect the stability of the system;

14

or, rather, they secure that stability. It is, indeed, true, that
when changes in nature go on increasing or decreasing in
magnitude indefinitely, they clearly indicate a beginning and
an end to the system to which they belong. And it was
on this principle that the earlier astronomers predicted that
the celestial perturbations would ultimately bring the universe
to a state of chaos. They found, for instance, that the moon's
orbit was decreasing in size, and they inferred that, ultimately, that luminary must come to the earth. But they now
know it to be mathematically certain that, after a long period,
the diminution of the orbit will cease ; it will begin to expand,
and go on expanding, until the opposite point of oscillation
is reached, when it will again diminish ; and in this manner,
if God's will permit, perform its eternal round. Just so it is
with all the irregularities of the solar system.

> "Yonder starry sphere
> Of planets, and of fixed, in all her wheels,
> Resembles nearest mazes intricate,
> Eccentric, intervolved, yet regular ;
> Then most, when most irregular they seem."

And so it is with all the natural changes which we witness
around us, and with all which science shows us to have taken
place on the globe, excepting some which geology discloses,
and perhaps one which astronomy renders probable. Let us
look at some of those changes which the argument under
consideration regards as inconsistent with the world's eternity.

Nearly all the changes in nature with which we are acquainted belong to three classes, — the mechanical, the chemical, and the organic. Astronomical changes are purely
mechanical ; and hence the ease with which they may be calculated by mathematics. The universal system of death,

which reigns over all animals and plants, is the result of organic laws; and it is this which probably gives to man the strongest impression of the transient nature of sublunary things. But just consider the antagonist agencies to this universal destroyer. I refer to the equally universal system of reproduction, and to the law by which permanence of species is secured. The consequence is, that, while every individual animal and plant dies, the species survives. In the whole history of the animals and plants now existing on the globe, only eight or ten certain examples are on record in which a species has become extinct, and those are some large birds, such as the dinornis and dodo, once inhabitants of the Isle of Bourbon and New Zealand. Every one of the human family, every elephant, every ox, every lion, &c., die, but man, as a species, still lives; and so does the elephant, the ox, and the lion; and most obviously this is a law of nature. How easy, then, for the atheist to evade the force of your argument against the world's eternity, drawn from the ravages of death! He has only to suppose the havoc of individuals by death always to have been repaired by the equivalent operation of reproduction, and that these two agencies have been balanced against each other from eternity; and how will you prove this impossible, except by the absurd metaphysical arguments already considered?

Atmospheric and aqueous changes often, and, indeed, generally, appear more chaotic and destitute of a controlling force than any others in nature. When the winds are let loose from their prison-house; when the heavens become dark, and the clouds, rent by the lightnings, pour down their contents, and the swollen torrents carry desolation down the mountain's side and over the wide plain; when the ocean rolls in upon the land its giant waves; when the tornado sweeps all before it, in rich tropical regions; or when the sirocco sends its hot blast, loaded with sand, over the devoted surface, — in all these cases, how difficult for us to conceive that all this uproar among the elements is limited and controlled by laws as fixed and unalterable as those which regulate the heavenly bodies! Nevertheless, it must be so; and although the winds and the waters seem to be rioting at their pleasure, there are, in fact, at work antagonist agencies, which will confine their wild war to a narrow field, and soon bring them again into peaceful submission. For such has always been the case, and the limits of their irregularities are no wider now than six thousand years ago. In other words, the repressing agency has always been superior to the destroying force, when the latter has risen to a certain limit; and I doubt not but the profounder mathematics of angelic minds might as easily calculate the anomalies and perturbations of winds and waves as the formulas of La Place can determine those of the solar system. And if such constancy has existed for six thousand years in meteorological changes, — of all others in nature apparently the most irregular, — why, the atheist will ask, may not that constancy have been eternal? And with equal reason may he ask the same in respect to all changes resulting from mechanical, chemical, and organic laws, which we witness in nature, except those which come within the province of geology, and even concerning some of those; and what changes in the material world do not result, directly or remotely, from one or two, or all of these laws? Yet, in regard to all these changes, there is no inconsistency in supposing them to have gone on in an eternal series; and hence they furnish no proof of the non-eternity of the world.

In the seventh and last place, the recent origin of society, as shown by historical monuments, is regarded as evidence of the recent origin of the world. This argument was well understood as long ago as the days of Lucretius, who states it very clearly in the oft-quoted lines, —

> "Si nulla fuit genitalis origo,
>   Terrarum et cœli, semperque eterna fuit,
>   Cur, supra bellum Thebanum et funera Trojæ,
>   Non alias alii quoque res cecinere poetæ?"

This argument, though it has been met by a plausible reply, is certainly of great importance in its bearing upon the recent origin of the human race, which, as we shall shortly see, is a point of much interest. But it is obvious that it proves nothing respecting the origin of matter, since this might have had an eternal existence before man was placed upon it. We need not, therefore, be delayed by its discussion.

Such is a fair summary, as I believe, of the arguments usually adduced, aside from the Bible and geology, to prove the non-eternity of the world. I am not prepared to say that they amount to nothing; but I do believe that they perplex, rather than convince, and that some of them are mere metaphysical quibbles.

They do not produce that instantaneous conviction which most of the arguments of natural theology force upon the mind; and it is easy to see how a man of a sceptical turn should rise from their examination entirely unaffected, or affected unfavorably. Let us now, therefore, turn to geology, and inquire whether its archives will afford us any clearer light upon the subject.

And here we must confess, at the outset, that geology furnishes us no more evidence than the other sciences of the creation of the matter of the universe out of nothing. But it does furnish us with examples of such modifications of matter

14 *

as could be effected only by a Deity. Suppose, then, we should be obliged to acknowledge to the atheist, that we yield to him the point of matter's eternal existence, if he pleases, because we can find nowhere in nature decisive evidence of its creation, and then take our stand upon the arrangements and metamorphoses of matter. Or, rather, suppose we say to him, that we shall not contend with him as to the origin of matter, but challenge him to explain, if he can, without a Deity, its modifications, as taught by geology. If that science does disclose to us such changes on the globe as no power and wisdom but those of an infinite God could produce, then of what consequence is it, so far as religion is concerned, whether we can, or cannot, demonstrate the first creation of matter? I can conceive of no religious truth that would be unfavorably affected, though we should admit that this point cannot be settled. Let us, then, at least for the sake of argument, admit that it cannot be, and proceed to inquire whether, aside from this point, geology does not teach us all that is necessary to establish the most perfect system of Theism. I shall select four examples from that science, each of which is independent of the others in its bearing upon the subject, since in this way the argument will become cumulative ; and if some are not satisfied with one example, the others may produce conviction.

In the first place, geology teaches that the time has been when the earth existed as a molten mass of matter, and, therefore, all the animals and plants now existing upon its surface, and all those buried in its rocky strata, must have had a beginning, or have been created. I should be sustained by many probabilities, were I to go farther, and maintain that the time was when the globe existed in a gaseous state — an opinion very widely adopted by able philosophers of the present day.

But as this view is more hypothetical than my first position, which makes the earth a liquid mass, and as nothing would be gained to the argument by supposing it in a gaseous state, I shall not press that point. That it was once in a state of fusion is probable from the very great heat still remaining in its interior. But more direct proof of this results from the facts, now admitted by almost all geologists, that the unstratified rocks have all been melted, and that the stratified class have all, or nearly all, been the result of disintegration and abrasion of the unstratified masses. A striking confirmation of this opinion is the spheroidal figure of the earth, — a figure precisely such as the globe would have assumed in consequence of rotation, had it been in a fluid state. In fine, so many and so decisive are the facts which point to the original igneous fluidity of the globe, that no competent judge thinks of doubting that all the matter of which it is composed, certainly its crust, has some time or other been in that state. It is, however, the opinion of some geologists of distinction, that the whole of it was not in fusion at the same time, and that its different portions have passed successively through the furnace. But this view of the subject scarcely affects my argument, since at whatever period the fusion of any part took place, the destruction of organic life, if it existed, must have been the consequence. The essential thing is, to show that such was once the state of the earth that animals and plants could not have existed on it. For if such was the case, their creation must have been a subsequent operation ; and if this did not require an infinite Being to accomplish it, no result in nature would demand his agency.

To prove the original igneous fluidity of the globe, we might have adopted another course of argument. All will admit that the present temperature of the interior of the earth is far

more elevated than that of the surrounding planetary spaces
The inevitable result is, from the known laws of heat, that its
radiation into the celestial spaces is constantly going on, and
consequently the earth's temperature is being constantly lowered.   Who can tell us now when this process of refrigeration commenced ?   If no one, then there must have been a
time when the heat was great enough to fuse the whole globe.
And the facts already stated confirm such an inference.   For
all the efforts hitherto made to show that the earth may be
passing through regions of various temperatures, in its march
around the centre of centres, amount to nothing more than
dreamy conjecture.

In order to feel the force of the argument, sustained by so
many facts in geology, just picture to yourselves this vast
globe as a mass of liquid fire.   From such a world every thing
organic must have been excluded, and every thing combustible consumed, and only such combinations of matter have
existed as incandescent heat could not decompose.   Compare
such a world with that now teeming with life, and beauty, and
glory, which we inhabit ; and say, must not the transition to
its present condition have demanded the exercise of infinite
power, infinite wisdom, and infinite benevolence ?   You can,
indeed, conceive how a solid crust might have formed over
the vast fiery ocean, by the simple radiation of heat ; and then,
too, by natural laws, might the vapors have been condensed
into oceans and clouds, while volcanic force within might
have lifted up our continents and mountains above the flood.
But what a picture of desolation and ruin would such a world
present, while unadorned with vegetation, and with no voice
of life to break the stillness of universal death ! Here is, then,
the precise point where we need the interference of a Deity.
Admit, if you please, that atheism, with its eternal matter and

the laws of nature at command, might form a world without inhabitants. Who does not see, that to bestow organization, and life, and instinct, to say nothing of intellect, upon brute matter, is the loftiest prerogative of Jehovah? especially to fill so vast a world as ours with its teeming millions, exhibiting ten thousand diversities of size, form, and structure.

Let the atheist then exult in the belief of an eternal world. Geology shows him that it must have been without inhabitants; and that, therefore, the most wonderful part of the creation still remains to be accounted for; while physiology teaches that the interference of an infinite Deity can alone solve the enigma.

My second example from geology to disprove the notion of an eternal series of animals and plants on the globe, is derived from the history of organic remains. That history shows us clearly, that the earth, since its creation, has been the seat of several distinct economies of life, each occupying long periods, and successively passing away. During each of these periods, distinct groups of animals and plants have occupied the earth, the air, and the waters. Each successive group has been entirely distinct from that which preceded it, though each group was exactly adapted to the existing state of the climate and the food provided; so that, had the different groups changed places with one another, they must have perished, because their constitutions were adapted only to the state of things during the period in which they actually lived. A distinguished naturalist has recently declared that " he has discovered, in surveying the entire series of fossil animal remains, five great groups, so completely independent that no species whatever is found in more than one of them." — *Deshayes.*

Including the existing races, this would give us six entirely distinct groups of organic beings that have lived in succession upon this globe since it became a habitable world. But even

if it should be found that a few species are common to adjoining groups, the great truth would still remain, that the
different groups were too much unlike to be contemporaries,
and that consequently a new creation must have taken place
whenever each new group commenced its course.

It is probable the earth has changed its inhabitants more
than the six times that have been mentioned ; some think as
many as twelve times.   But a larger number cannot yet be
proved so clearly ; and could they be, they would add nothing
to this argument ; for it rests mainly on the fact that this
change of organic life has even once been complete.   We
may, however, very safely assume that the present animals
and plants are the sixth group that have occupied the globe.*

These facts being admitted, and who does not see the necessity of divine interference, whenever one race of animals and
plants passed from the earth in order to repeople it ?   It is not
difficult to conceive how volcanic fires, or aqueous inundations, may have carried universal destruction over the globe,
and bereft it of inhabitants.   But where, save in the fiat of
an infinite Deity, is the power that can make this universe of
death teem again with life and beauty ?   In the powerful language of Dr. Chalmers, we may inquire, " Is there aught in
the rude and boisterous play of a great physical catastrophe
that can germinate those exquisite structures, which, during
our yet undisturbed economy, have been transmitted in pacific
succession to the present day ?   What is there in the rush,
and turbulence, and mighty clamor of such great elements, of
ocean heaved from its old resting-place, and lifting its billows
above the Alps and the Andes of a former continent, — what
is there in this to charm into being the embryo of an infant
family, wherewith to stock and to repeople a now desolate

* See the Frontispiece.

world ?   We see in the sweeping energy and uproar of this
elemental war enough to account for the disappearance of
all the old generations, but nothing that might cradle any
new generations into existence, so as to have effloresced on
ocean's deserted bed the life and loveliness which are now
before our eyes.   At no juncture, we apprehend, in the history of the world, is the interposition of the Deity more manifest than at this ; nor can we better account for so goodly a
creation emerging again into new forms of animation and
beauty from the wreck of the old one, than that the spirit of
God moved on the face of chaos, and that nature, turned by
the last catastrophe into a wilderness, was again repeopled
at the utterance of his word."

Sir Isaac Newton has said, that " the growth of new systems out of old ones, without the mediation of a divine power,
seems to me apparently absurd."   He seems in this passage
to have referred only to the arrangements of matter, " with
respect to size, figure, proportions, and properties," and not
to the principle of life, of instinct, or of intellect.   But when
the latter are taken into the account, it must be superlatively
absurd to suppose new systems can grow out of old ones by
merely natural operations.   He, indeed, who can bring himself to believe, with a certain writer, that " the instincts of animals are nothing more than inert and passive attractions, derived from the power of sensation, and the instinctive operations of animals nothing more than crystallizations produced
through the agency of that power," — such a man could probably easily persuade himself that, by the help of galvanism,
animals and plants might be the result of natural operations.
Such doctrines, however, we shall examine in another lecture.

My third example from geology, showing the non-eternity
of the present condition of the globe, is the fact of the disap-

pearance of several large species of animals since the commencement of the most recent or alluvial geological period.
Certain large pachydermatous and other animals, such as the
fossil elephant, the mastodon, the megatherium, the mylodon,
the megalonyx, the glyptodon, the fossil horse, ox, deer, &c.,
also nine or ten species of huge birds — the dinornis, the
palapteryx, aptornis, notornis, and nestor of New Zealand,
the dodo of Mauritius and Bourbon, and the pezohaps or
solitaire of Rodriguez, — have ceased to exist since the tertiary
period ; some of them — the birds, for instance — since
man's creation. Now, if any important species of animals
from time to time disappear from any system of organic life,
it shows a tendency to ruin in that system ; for such is the
intimate dependence of different beings upon one another,
that you cannot blot out one, certainly not a large number,
without disturbing the healthy balance between the whole,
and probably bringing the whole to ultimate ruin. At any
rate, if several species die out by natural processes, no reason
can be given why others should not, in like manner, disappear. And to prove that any organic system shows a
tendency to ruin is to show that it had a beginning.

My third example from geology, demonstrating the special
interference of the Deity in the affairs of this world, is the
fact of the comparatively recent commencement of the human
race. That man was among the very last of the animals
created is made certain by the fact that his remains are found
only in the highest part of alluvium. This is rarely more
than one hundred feet in thickness, while the other fossiliferous strata, lying beneath the alluvium, are six miles thick.

Hence man was not in existence during all the period in
which these six miles of strata were in a course of deposition,
and he has existed only during the comparatively short period

in which the one hundred feet of alluvium have been formed; nay, during only a small part of the alluvial period. His bones, having the same chemical composition as the bones of other animals, are no more liable to decay; and, therefore, had he lived and died in any of the periods preceding the alluvial, his bones must have been mixed with those of other animals belonging to those periods. But they are not thus found in a single well-authenticated instance, and, therefore, his existence has been limited to the alluvial period. Hence he must have been created and placed upon the globe — such is the testimony of geology — during the latter part of the alluvial period.

I might include in this example nearly all the other species of existing animals and plants, since it is only a very few of these that are found fossil, and such species are limited to the tertiary strata. But since this might make some confusion in the argument, and since man is confessedly at the head of the existing creation, I prefer to let his case stand out alone, and to regard it *instar omnium*.

Here, then, we have a case in which geology can lay her finger upon the precise epoch, in the revolutions of our globe, in which the most complicated, perfect, and exalted being that ever dwelt upon its surface first began to be. It was not the commencement of a mere zoöphyte, or cryptogamean plant, in which we see but little superiority to unorganized matter, except in their possession of a low degree of vitality. But we have a being complicated enough to contain a million of parts, endowed with the two great attributes of life, sensibility and contractility, in the highest degree, and, above all, possessing intellect and moral powers far more wonderful than organization and animal life.

As to the period when the creation of such a being, by the

15

most astonishing of all miracles, took place, I believe there is no diversity of opinion. At least, all agree that it was very recent; nay, although geology can rarely give chronological dates, but only a succession of events, she is able to say, from the monuments she deciphers, that man cannot have occupied the globe more than six thousand years.

Now, if it was difficult to conceive how successive races of the inferior animals and plants could have originated in the laws of nature, without the special interference of the Deity, that difficulty increases in a rapid ratio as we ascend on the scale of organization and intellect, and attempt in the same manner to account for the origin of man without the miraculous agency of Deity. The thorough-going material-ist, however, does not shrink from the effort. "Thought," says Bory de St. Vincent, " being the necessary result of a certain kind of organization, wherever this order is estab-lished, thought is necessarily derived from it; and it is no more possible for the molecules of matter, arranged in a certain manner, not to produce thought, than for brass, when smitten, not to return a sound, or for creatures formed by this matter, after such and such laws, not to walk, not to breathe, not to reproduce; in a word, not to exercise any of the facul-ties which result from their peculiar mechanism of organiza-tion." — *Dict. Clas. D. Hist. Nat.* art. *Matière.*

This may seem, upon a superficial view, to be settling this matter at once. But it merely shifts the difficulty from one part of the subject to another. Admitting the premises of the materialist to be correct, it does indeed show us the prox-imate cause of thought. But the mind immediately inquires how a certain organization became possessed of such won-derful power. Is it inherent in matter, or is it a power com municated to organization by a supreme Being? If the

MAN'S CREATION MIRACULOUS.

latter, it is just what the Theist contends for; if the former, then there is just as much necessity for the original interposition of the Deity, in order to give matter such an astonishing power, as there is, on the theory of the immaterialist, to impart a spiritual and immortal principle to matter. The materialist will, indeed, say that matter has possessed this power from eternity. But this supposition, evidently absurd, does in fact invest matter with the attributes of Deity; since those attributes, and those alone, are sufficient to account for the phenomena. And besides, how is the fact to be explained that this power was not exerted till six thousand years ago?

But with the exception of the materialist, I am sure that most reasoning minds will feel as if the creation of the human family was one of the most stupendous, perhaps the most stupendous, exercise of infinite power and wisdom which the universe exhibits. If any change whatever demands a Deity for its accomplishment, it must be this; and, therefore, geology presents, in the case of man, the most striking example which nature could furnish of a beginning of organic and intellectual life on the globe. It shows us that there was a time, and that not remote, when the first link of the curious chain of the human family, now constantly lengthening by inflexible laws, was created.

I might now refer to certain recent discoveries in astronomy, which have the same bearing upon the general argument as the examples that have been quoted from geology, although less decisive. After the famous demonstration of the eternity of the universe by La Grange, provided the present laws of gravity alone control it, we could hardly expect that, so soon, even astronomy would furnish proof of a disturbing cause, which must ultimately and inevitably bring ruin among the heavenly bodies, if some counteracting agency be not exerted.

Yet such a source of derangement exists in the supposed medium extending through all space, which has already shown its retarding influence upon Enke's, Biela's, and Halley's comets. And who can say that some of the vast periods which geology discloses may not have been commensurate with those intervening between catastrophes among the heavenly bodies as the result of the universal resisting ether? At present, however, we can say only that we know such long periods have existed in geology, and probably in astronomy. And their mere existence is fatal to the idea of the eternity of the world in its present state.

If, then, geology can clearly demonstrate the present state of the globe to have had a beginning; if she can show us the period, by fair induction, when one liquid, fiery ocean enveloped the whole earth; if she can show us five or six economies of organic life successively flourishing and passing away; if she can trace man back to his origin at a comparatively recent date; if, in fact, she can show us that the most important operations on the globe, and the most complicated and exalted organic races, had a beginning; and if astronomy affords glimpses of similar changes, — then why may we not safely leave the subject of the world's eternity an undecided question, consistently with the most perfect Theism? If we can prove that the power, the wisdom, and the benevolence of the Deity have again and again interfered with the regular sequence of nature's operations, and introduced new conditions and new and more perfect beings, by using the matter already in existence, what though we cannot, by the light of science, run back to the first production of matter itself? What though the atheist should here be allowed to maintain his favorite theory that matter never had a beginning? What doctrine of natural religion is thereby unfavorably affected, if we can only show the interposition of the Deity in all of matter's important modifications? Such an admission would not prove matter to be eternal, but only that science has not yet placed within the reach of man the means of proving its non-eternity. And really, such an admission would be far more favorable to the cause of truth than to rely, as theologians have done, on metaphysical subtilties to prove that matter had a beginning. For the sceptical mind will not merely remain unconvinced by such arguments, but be very apt to draw the sweeping inference that all the doctrines of natural and revealed religion rest on similar dreamy abstractions.

But is natural theology in fact destitute of all satisfactory proof that the matter of the universe had a beginning? Such proof, it seems to me, she will seek in vain in the wide fields of physical and mathematical science; and the solution of the question which metaphysics offers, as we have seen, does not satisfy. But there are sources of evidence on this point which seem to me of the most satisfactory kind.

In the first place, we may derive from science some presumptive proof of a commencement of the matter of the universe. The fact that the organic races on the globe had a beginning affords such proof. For matter could not have originated itself; nor is there any proof of its eternal existence; and to assume that it did eternally exist, without proof, is far more unphilosophical than to admit its origination in the divine will. For since God has complete control over matter, it is probable that he created it with such properties as he wished it to possess. And furthermore, to the power and wisdom that could set in motion the heavenly bodies, and create and adapt existing organisms out of preëxistent matter, we can assign no limits, and hence conclude them to be infinite.

15 *

Therefore they are sufficient to the production of matter, which could not have demanded more than infinite wisdom and power.

Now, in confirmation of these presumptions, we may appeal to the Bible. It is true that writers have been accustomed to consider it contrary to sound logic to draw from revelation any support or illustrations of natural religion. But why should an historical fact possess less value, if transmitted to us through the channel of sacred, rather than profane, writers? Now, it would be regarded as perfectly good reasoning to seize upon any facts stated by heathen philosophers and historians, illustrative of natural religion. But the Scriptures carry with them, to say the least, quite as strong evidence of their authenticity and claims to be credited, as any ancient uninspired writer. We place them on the same ground as any other history, and demand for them only that they should be believed so far as we have testimony to their authenticity. If a man, after careful examination of their evidences, comes to the conclusion that they are mere fables, then to him their testimony is of no value to prove or illustrate any truth of natural religion. But if he is convinced that they are worthy of credence, then their statements may decide a point about which the light of nature leaves him in uncertainty. In this way the Bible is used by the natural theologian, just as he would employ any curious object in nature — say, the human hand, or the eye. These organs exist, and their mechanism is to be accounted for either with or without a God. And so the Bible exists, and its contents are to be accounted for ; and if they clearly evince the agency of a Deity, then we may use them, just as we would use the eye or the hand, to prove or illustrate important truths in natural theology.

But the testimony of the Bible, as to the origin of the

world, is most explicit and decided. It declares that *in the beginning God created the heavens and the earth ; and that the worlds were formed by the word of God, so that the things which are seen were not made of things which do appear.* The obvious meaning of this latter passage is, that the material universe was created out of nothing. (τα μη φαινομενα.) How much more satisfactory this simple and consistent statement, than a volume of abstract argument to prove the non-eternity of the world !

Now, if the testimony of the Scriptures on all other points has been found correct, why should we not receive with unhesitating credence, and even with joy, the sublime announcement with which that volume opens ? True, we are not compelled to admit this statement, in order to save Theism from refutation, because geology shows us the commencement of several economies on the globe, which point us to a divine Author. But the doctrine of matter's creation out of nothing gives a desirable completeness to the system.

In looking back upon the subject, which has thus been discussed, too briefly for its merits, but too prolixly for your patience, several important inferences force themselves upon our attention.

And first, it furnishes a satisfactory reply to a well-known objection, otherwise unanswerable, against the argument from design in nature to prove the existence of a Deity. We present ten thousand examples of exquisite design and adaptation in nature to the atheist. He admits them all ; but says, it was always so, and therefore requires no other Deity but the power eternally inherent in nature. At your metaphysical replies to his objections he laughs ; but when you take him back on geological wings, and bid him gaze on man, just springing, with his lofty powers, from the plastic hands of his Creator,

and then, still earlier, you point him to system after system of
organic life starting up in glorious variety and beauty on the
changing earth, and even still nearer the birth of time, you
show him the globe, a glowing ocean of fire, swept of all
organic life, he is forced to exclaim, " A God ! a personal
God ! an infinitely wise and powerful God ! " What though
he still clings to the notion of matter's eternity ? you have
forced him to see the hand of Deity in its wonderful arrangements and metamorphoses ; the hand of such a Deity as might
have brought it into existence in a moment, by the word of
his power.*

Secondly. The subject presents us with a new argument for
the existence of a God, or rather a satisfactory modification
of the argument from design. In that argument, as derived
from other sciences, the Theist finds, indeed, multiplied and
beautiful proofs of adaptation and apparent design ; but then he
cannot, as already observed, from those sciences derive proof
of the commencement either of matter or its arrangements ;
and then, too, the sceptic, with plausible ingenuity, can take
his stand upon law as the efficient agent in nature's movements and harmonies. But when geology shows us, not the
commencement of matter, but of organism, and presents us
with full systems of animals and plants springing out of inorganic elements, where is the law that exhibits even a tendency
to such results ? Nothing can explain them but the law of
miracles ; that is, creation by divine interposition. Thus is
the idea of a Deity forced nakedly upon us, as the only possible solution of the enigmas of creation. The metaphysical

---

* The subject of this inference is treated with great ability and
candor in the *Biblotheca Sacra* for November, 1849, by my friend and
colleague, Rev. Joseph Haven, Jr., professor of intellectual and moral
philosophy in Amherst College.

Theist must waste half his strength in battling the questions
about the beginning of matter, and the laws of matter; nor
can he ever entirely dislodge the enemy from these strongholds
of atheism.   But the geological Theist takes us at once into a
field where work has been done, which neither eternal law,
nor eternal matter, but an infinite personal Deity only, could
accomplish.

   In conclusion, I would merely refer to the interesting fact,
that geology should prove almost the only science that presents us with exigencies demanding the interposition of creating power.   And yet, up to the present time, geology has
been looked upon by many Christian writers with jealous eye,
because it was supposed to teach the world's eternity, and
so to account for natural changes by catastrophes and the
gradual operation of existing agencies, as to render a Deity
unnecessary, either for the creation or regulation of the world.
One of these writers has even most uncharitably and unreasonably said, that " the mineral geology, considered as a science, can do as well without God (though in a question concerning the origin of the earth) as Lucretius did." — Granville
Penn, *Comparative Estimate*, &c. — How much ground there
is for such an allegation, let the developments made in this
lecture answer.   Surely, in this case, geology has followed
the directions of the Oriental poet : —

> " Learn from yon Orient shell to love thy foe,
>   And strew with pearls the hand that brings thee woe ;
>   Free, like yon rock, from base, vindictive pride,
>   Emblaze with gems the wrist that rends thy side.
>   Mark where yon tree rewards the stony shower
>   With fruit nectareous or the balmy flower.
>   All nature calls aloud, — ' Shall man do less
>   Than heal the smiter, and the railer bless ? ' "

Misunderstood or misinterpreted though this science has been, she now offers her aid to fortify some of the weakest outposts of religion.   And thus shall it ever be with all true science.   Twin sister of natural and revealed religion, and of heavenly birth, she will never belie her celestial origin, nor cease to sympathize with all that emanates from the same pure home.   Human ignorance and prejudice may for a time seem to have divorced what God has joined together.   But human ignorance and prejudice shall at length pass away, and then science and religion shall be seen blending their parti-colored rays into one beautiful bow of light, linking heaven to earth and earth to heaven.

LECTURE VI.

GEOLOGICAL PROOFS OF THE DIVINE BENEVOLENCE.

THE subject of the present lecture is the divine benevolence, as taught by geology. But what connection, it will be
asked, can there be between the history of rocks and the benevolence of God ?   Do not the leading points of that history
consist of terrible catastrophes, aqueous or igneous, by which
the crust of the earth has been dislocated and upheaved,
mountains lifted up and overturned, the dry land inundated,
now by scorching lava, and now by the ocean, sweeping from
its face all organic life, and entombing its inhabitants in a
stony grave ?   Who can find the traces of benevolence in the
midst of such desolation and death ?   Is it not the very place
where the objector would find arguments to prove the malevolence, certainly the vindictive justice, of the Deity ?

This, I am aware, is a not unnatural *prima facie* view of
this subject. But it is a false one. Geology does furnish
some very striking evidence of divine benevolence ; and if
I can show this, and from so unpromising a field gather decisive arguments on this subject, they will be so much clear
gain to the cause of Theism. This is what, therefore, I shall
now attempt to do.

*In the first place, I derive an argument for the divine be-
nevolence from the manner in which soils are formed by the
disintegration and decomposition of rocks.*

Chemical analysis shows us that the mineral **constituents** of rocks are essentially the same as those of soils; and that the latter differ from the former, in a pulverized state, only in containing animal and vegetable matter. Hence we cannot doubt but the soils originated from the rocks. And, in fact, the process of their production is continually going on under our eyes. Wherever the rocks are exposed to atmospheric agencies, they are seen to crumble down; and, in fact, most of them, having been long exposed, are now covered with a deposit of their own ruins, forming a soil over them. This process is in part decomposition and in part disintegration; and as we look upon rocks thus wasting away, we are apt to be impressed with the idea that it is an instance of decay in nature's works, which, instead of indicating benevolence, can hardly be reconciled with divine wisdom. But when we learn that this is the principal mode in which soils are produced, that without it vegetation could not be sustained, and that a world like ours without plants must also be without animals, this apparent ruin puts on the aspect of benevolence and wise design.

My second argument in proof of the divine benevolence is derived from the disturbed, broken, and overturned condition of the earth's crust.

To the casual observer, the rocks have the appearance of being lifted up, shattered, and overturned. But it is only the geologist who knows the vast extent of this disturbance. He never finds crystalline, non-fossiliferous rocks, which have not been more or less removed from their original position; and usually he finds them to have been thrown up by some powerful agency into almost every possible position. The older fossiliferous strata exhibit almost equal evidence of the operation of a powerful disturbing force, though sometimes found in their original horizontal position. The newer rocks have experienced less of this agency, though but few of them have not been elevated or dislocated. Mountainous countries exhibit this action most strikingly. There it is shown sometimes on a magnificent scale. Entire mountains in the Alps, for instance, appear not only to have been lifted up from the ocean's depths, but to have been actually thrown over, so as to bring the lowest and oldest rocks at the top of the series. The extensive range of mountains in this country, commencing in Canada, and embracing the Green Mountains of Vermont, the Highlands of New York, and most of the Alleghany chain as far as Alabama, a distance of some twelve hundred miles, has also been lifted up, and some of the strata, by a lateral force, folded together, and then thrown over, so as now to occupy an inverted position. Let us now see wherein this agency exhibits benevolence.

If these strata had remained horizontal, as they were originally deposited, it is obvious that all the valuable ores, minerals, and rocks, which man could not have discovered by direct excavation, must have remained forever unknown to him. Now, man has very seldom penetrated the rocks below the depth of half a mile, and rarely so deep as that; whereas, by the elevations, dislocations, and overturnings that have been described, he obtains access to all deposits of useful substances that lie within fifteen or twenty miles of the surface; and many are thus probably brought to light from a greater depth. He is indebted, then, to this disturbing agency for nearly all the useful metals, coal, rock salt, marble, gypsum, and other useful minerals; and when we consider how necessary these substances are to civilized society, who will doubt that it was a striking act of benevolence which thus introduced disturbance, dislocation, and apparent ruin into the earth's crust?

16

Another decided advantage resulting from this disturbing agency is the formation of valleys.

If we suppose the strata spread uniformly over the earth's entire surface, then the ocean must envelop the whole globe. But, admitting such interruptions in the strata to exist as would leave cavities, where the waters might be gathered together into one place, and the dry land appear, still that dry land must form only an unbroken level. Streams of water could not exist on such a continent, because they depend upon inequalities of surface; and whatever water existed must have formed only stagnant ponds, and the morasses which would be the consequence would load the air with miasms fatal to life; so that we may safely pronounce the world uninhabitable by natures adapted to the present earth. But such, essentially, must have been the state of things, had not internal forces elevated and fractured the earth's crust. For that was the origin of most of our valleys — of all the larger valleys, indeed, which checker the surface of primary countries. Most of them have been modified by subsequent agencies; but their leading features, their outlines, have been the result of those internal disturbances which spread desolation over the surface. We are apt to look upon such an agency as an exhibition of retributive justice, rather than of benevolence. And yet that admirable system for the circulation of water, whereby the rain that falls upon the surface is conveyed to the ocean, whence it is returned by evaporation, depends upon it. It imparts, to all organic nature, life, health, and activity; and had it not thus ridged up the surface, stagnation and death must have reigned over all the earth. In the unhealthiness of low, flat countries, at present, we see the terrible condition of things in a world without valleys. Can we doubt, then, that it was the hand of benevolence that drove the ploughshare of ruin through the earth's crust, and ridged up its surface into a thousand fantastic forms?

It will more deeply impress us with this benevolence to remember that most of the sublime and the beautiful in the scenery of a country depends upon this disturbing agency. Beautiful as vegetable nature is, how tame is a landscape where only a dead level is covered with it, and no swelling hills, or jutting rocks, or murmuring waters, relieve the monotonous scene! And how does the interest increase with the wildness and ruggedness of the surface, and reach its maximum only where the disturbance and dislocation have been most violent!

Some may, perhaps, doubt whether it can have been one of the objects of divine benevolence and wisdom, in arranging the surface of this world, so to construct and adorn it as to gratify a taste for fine scenery. But I cannot doubt it. I see not else why nature every where is fitted up in a lavish manner with all the elements of the sublime and beautiful, nor why there are powers in the human soul so intensely gratified in contact with those elements, unless they were expressly adapted for one another by the Creator. Surely natural scenery does afford to the unsophisticated soul one of the richest and purest sources of enjoyment to be found on earth. If this be doubted by any one, it must be because he has never been placed in circumstances to call into exercise his natural love of the beautiful and the sublime in creation. Let me persuade such a one, at least in imagination, to break away from the slavish routine of business or pleasure, and in the height of balmy summer to accompany me to a few spots, where his soul will swell with new and strong emotions, if his natural sensibilities to the grand and beautiful have not become thoroughly dead within him.

We might profitably pause for a moment at this enchanting season of the year, (June,) and look abroad from that gentle elevation on which we dwell, now all mantled over with a flowery carpet, wafting its balmy odors into our studies. Can any thing be more delightful than the waving forests, with their dense and deep green foliage, interspersed with grassy and sunny fields and murmuring streamlets, which spread all around us? How rich the graceful slopes of yonder distant mountains, which bound the Connecticut on either side! How imposing Mount Sugar Loaf on the north, with its red-belted and green-tufted crown, and Mettawampe too, with its rocky terraces on the one side, and its broad slopes of un-broken forest on the other! Especially, how beautifully and even majestically does the indented summit of Mount Hol-yoke repose against the summer sky! What sunrises and sunsets do we here witness, and what a multitude of permu-tations and combinations pass before us during the day, as we watch from hour to hour one of the loveliest landscapes of New England!

Let us now turn our steps to that huge pile of mountains called the White Hills of New Hampshire. We will ap-proach them through the valley of the Saco River, and at the distance of thirty miles they will be seen looming up in the horizon, with the clouds reposing beneath their naked heads. As the observer approaches them, the sides of the valley will gradually close in upon him, and rise higher and higher, until he will find their naked granitic summits almost jutting over his path, to the height of several thousand feet, seeming to form the very battlements of heaven. Now and then will he see the cataract leaping hundreds of feet down their sides, and the naked path of some recent landslip, which carried death and desolation in its track. From this deep and wild chasm he will at length emerge, and climb the vast ridge, until he has seen the forest trees dwindle, and at length disappear; and standing upon the naked summit, immensity seems stretched out before him. But he has not yet reached the highest point; and far in the distance, and far above him, Mount Washington seems to repose in awful majesty against the heavens. Turning his course thither, he follows the narrow and naked ridge over one peak after another, first rising upon Mount Pleasant, then Mount Franklin, and then Mount Monroe, each lifting him higher, and making the sea of mountains around him more wide and billowy, and the yawning gulfs on either side more profound and awful, so that every moment his interest deepens, and reaches not its climax till he stands upon Mount Washington, when the vast panorama is completed, and the world seems spread out at his feet. Yet it does not seem to be a peopled world, for no mighty city lies beneath him. Indeed, were it there, he would pass it almost unnoticed. For why should he regard so small an object as a city, when the world is before him ? — a world of mountains, bearing the impress of God's own hand, standing in solitary grandeur, just as he piled them up in primeval ages, and stretching away on every side as far as the eye can reach. On that pinnacle of the northern regions no sound of man or beast breaks in upon the awful stillness which reigns there, and which seems to bring the soul into near communion with the Deity. It is, indeed, the impressive Sabbath of nature ; and the soul feels a delightful awe, which can never be forgotten. Gladly would it linger there for hours, and converse with the mighty and the holy thoughts which come crowding into it ; and it is only when the man looks at the rapidly declining sun that he is roused from his revery and commences his descending march.

16 *

Let such a man next accompany me to Niagara.   We will pass by all minor cataracts, and place ourselves at once on the margin of one that knows no rival.   Let not the man take a hasty glance, and in disappointment conclude that he shall find no interest and no sublimity there.   Let him go to the edge of the precipice, and watch the deep waters as they roll over, and, changing their sea-green brightness for a fleecy white, pour down upon the rocks beneath, and dash back again in spray high in the air.   Let him go to the foot of the sheet, and look upward till the cataract swells into its proper size. Let him, on the Canada shore, take in the whole breadth of the cataract at once ; and as he stands musing, let him listen to the deep thunderings of the falling sheet.   Let him go to Table Rock, and creep forward to its jutting edge, and gaze steadily into the foaming and eddying waters so far beneath him, until his nerves thrill and vibrate, and he involuntarily shrinks back, exclaiming, —

> "How dreadful
> And dizzy 'tis to cast one's eyes so low !
>   I'll look no more,
> Lest my brain turn."

Next, let him stand upon that rock till the sun approaches so near the western horizon that a glorious bow, forming an almost entire circle on the cataract and the spray, shall clothe the scene with unearthly beauty, and, in connection with the emerald green of the waters, give it a brilliancy fully equal to its sublimity.   And finally, if he would add the emotions of moral to natural sublimity, let him follow to Ontario, the deep gulf through which all these waters flow, and, gathering up the evidence, which he will find too strong to resist, that they themselves have worn that gulf backward seven miles, let him try the rules of geological arithmetic to see if he can reach the period of its commencement. Surely, when he reviews the emotions of that day, he will never again doubt that the magnificent scenery of our world is the result of benevolent design on the part of the Creator.

If, now, we cross the Atlantic, we shall easily find scenes of natural beauty and sublimity, that have long elicited the wonder and delight of thousands of genuine taste. Shall we turn our steps first to the valleys and mountains of Wales? To an American eye, indeed, they lack one important feature, in being so destitute of trees. But then their wild aspect, their ragged and rocky outlines, present a picture of the sublimity of desolation rarely equalled. And as you ascend the mountains, — Snowdon, for instance, the highest of them all, — you find their summits, not rounded, as our American mountains, by former drift agency, nor forming continuous ridges, but shooting up in ragged peaks and edges, as if they formed the teeth of mother earth; although, in fact, it was the tooth of time that has gnawed them into their present forms. As you approach the summit, you feel animated in anticipation of the splendid prospect about to open upon you. But the clouds begin to gather, and soon envelop the mountain top; and though you reach the pinnacle, the dense mist limits your vision to a circle of a few rods in diameter. But ere long the vapor begins to break away, and the lofty cliffs and deep caverns around you are revealed. Now and then, the lake, so often found in the recesses of these mountains, is half seen through the opening cloud, and, magnified by the obscurity, it seems more distant and grand than if distinctly visible. Gradually the clouds open in various directions, disclosing gulf after gulf, lake after lake, mountain after mountain, and, finally, the Irish Channel, dotted with sails; and the whole scene lies spread out before you in glories that cannot be described. You are standing upon the pinnacle of England, and you feel as if almost the whole of it lay within the circle of vision. After enjoying so splendid a scene, you are thankful that the cloud hid it at first from your sight, and so much enhanced your pleasure by opening vista after vista, till the whole became one magnificent circle of picturesque beauty and sublimity.*

To relieve the mind after gazing long on such scenes of rugged grandeur, let us turn our course southerly, and follow down the romantic banks of the Wye, where every turn presents some new beauties, occasionally disclosing the ruins of some old castle, or magnificent abbey, (Tinton,) and at length Bristol, with its aristocratic adjunct, Clifton, turns your thoughts from the works of nature to those of man. And yet, even Clifton's elegant Crescent is but a meagre show by the side of the magnificent gorge which the Avon has cut in the rocks just before it enters Bristol Channel.

Passing over to the Isle of Wight, and traversing its shores, we shall witness many unique examples of natural beauty, swelling sometimes into sublimity, — such are the chalk cliffs near its western extremity, from two hundred to six hundred feet high, — sometimes hollowed out into magnificent domes, and the pillars of chalk, called *Needles*, in the midst of the sea, alive with sea gulls and cormorants, and forming the

* In this description I have attempted to give exactly the experience of myself and John Tappan, Esq., with our wives, who ascended Snowdon in June, 1850. A few days after, we ascended Cader Idris, another mountain of Wales, near Dolgelly, where the views were perhaps equally wild and sublime, with the addition of a vast number of trap columns, and a pseudo-crater, with its jagged and frowning sides.

remnants of the chalk bridge that once united the island to England. There, too, Alum Bay, with its many-colored strata of clay, unites the interesting in geology with the picturesque in scenery.

Along the southern coast, also, are the stupendous cliffs and the romantic under-cliffs, as well as the ragged *chines*, where an almost tropical climate attracts the invalid, while the cool sea breezes draw thither the wealthy and the fashionable.

But if sublime scenery pleases us more, we must traverse the Highlands of Scotland, —

" Land of brown heath and shaggy furze,"

land of lofty and naked mountains, embosoming lakes of great beauty, and full of historic and poetic interest.

Passing over Loch Lomond, the queen of Scottish lakes, you go through the long shadow of Ben Lomond, propped by many lesser mountains. Rising into the Highlands, the sterility and wildness increase, and reach their maximum in Glencoe, whose wildness and sublimity are indeed indescribable ; but if seen, they can never be forgotten. Still farther north, Ben Nevis lifts its uncovered head above all other mountains in the British Isles ; so high, indeed, that often, during the whole summer, it retains a portion of its snowy, wintry mantle.

Yet farther north, we come to the unique terraces, called the *Parallel Roads of Glen Roy,* formerly supposed to be the work of giants ; but now, that they are known to be the product of nature, proving not only objects of great scenographical interest, but a problem of special importance and difficulty in geology.

If we should pass from Scotland to the north-east part of Ireland, taking Staffa in our way, we should find in the basaltic columns of Fingal's Cave, and the Giant's Causeway, what seems, at first view, to be stupendous human structures, or rather the architecture of giants. But you soon find it to be only an example —

> " Where nature works as if defying art,
> And, in defiance of her rival powers,
> By these fortuitous and random strokes,
> Performing such inimitable feats,
> As she, with all her rules, can never reach."

Let any one sail along the coast for a few miles at the Giant's Causeway, enter some of the deep and echoing caverns, overhung by the basaltic mass, and see the columns rising tier above tier, sometimes four hundred feet in height, and assuming every wild and fantastic shape ; or let him walk over the acres of columns, whose tops are as perfectly polygonal and as accurately fitted to one another as the most skilful architect could make them, and he will confess how superior Nature is, when she would present a model for human imitation ; and how with accurate system she can combine the wildest disorder, and thus delight by symmetry, while she awes by sublimity.

Let us next pass over to continental Europe. We have reached the Rhine at Bonn, and the steamboat takes us at once into the midst of the romantic Drachenfels, or seven mountains, the result of volcanic agency, and still presenting more or less of the conical outline peculiar almost to modern volcanoes. These are the commencement of the romantic scenery of the Rhine. From thence to Bingen, some sixty or seventy miles, that river has cut its way through hills and mountains, sometimes rising one thousand feet. Along their base, the inhabitants have planted many a well-known town, while old castles, half crumbled down, recall continually the history of feudal ages ; and here, too, springs up a multitude of remembrances of startling events in more recent times. The mind, indeed, finds itself drawn at one moment to some historical monument, and the next to scenery of surpassing beauty or sublimity ; now the bold, overhanging rock, now the deep recess, now the towering mountain, now the quiet dell with its romantic villages; while every where on the north bank, the vine-clad terraces show us what wonders human industry can accomplish.

Nor does the Rhine lose its interest when we have emerged from its *Ghor* into its more open valley, from Bingen to Basle, in Switzerland. On its right bank, the Vosges Mountains, and on its left, the Black Forest, with not infrequent volcanic summits, afford a fine resting-place for the eye, as the rail car bears us rapidly over the rich intervening level. Or if we turn aside, — as to Heidelberg, on the Neckar, — what can be a more splendid sight than to stand by the old castle above the town, and look down the valley as the sun is sinking in the west !

But after all, it is in Switzerland, and there only, that we meet with the climax of scenographical wonders. Nowhere else can we find such lakes in the midst of such mountains ; such pleasant valleys bordered by such stupendous hills ; such gorges, and precipices, and passes, and especially such glaciers ; such avalanches, such snow-capped mountains, while vegetation at their base, and far up their sides, is fresh and luxuriant.

Embark, for instance, at Zurich, and, crossing its beautiful lake, direct your course towards Mount Righi. As the heavy diligence lifts you above the lake, you begin to catch glimpses of the grandeur of the Swiss mountains to the south, piercing

the clouds far off. Passing the romantic Zug, you come to
the valley between the Rossberg and the Righi, and the
denuded face of the former tells you whence came the mass
of ruins over which you clamber, and which buried the villages
of Goldau, Bussingen, and Rothen several hundred feet deep
with blocks of stone and soil. Long and steep is your ascent
of Righi, nearly six thousand feet above the sea. But the
views you obtain by the way become wider and grander at
every step. Reaching the summit near sunset, you may be
gratified by a panoramic view of a large part of Switzerland,
embracing its wildest and grandest scenery. Yet, if the
clouds prevent, you wait for the morning, in the hope of being
more fortunate. With the earliest dawn you awake, and
proceed to the summit of the mountain, where hundreds,
perhaps, from all civilized lands, are congregated, to witness
the rising of the sun. But a dense cloud envelops the
mountain, and hope almost dies within you. Wait, however,
a few moments, and the rising sun will depress the clouds
below the mountain's summit, and a scene of glory shall
open upon you, which can never be erased from your memory. Look now, for the sun's first rays have shed a flood of
glory over the clouds which now fill the valleys beneath your
feet. A fleecy white predominates; but the colors of the
prism tinge the edges of the clouds, and no part of the solid
earth rises above them, save the pinnacle on which you
stand, and to the south the higher peaks of the Bernese Alps,
— the Jungfrau, the Eiger, the Shreckhorn, and the Wetter-
horn, — covered with snow and glaciers, and seeming too
pure to belong to earth. Indeed, the whole scene seemed to
me to be unearthly; the fittest emblem that my eyes ever rested
upon of celestial scenes; and one cannot repress the desire,
when looking upon it, to be borne away on wings over the

glorious scene, and to repose for a time upon the gorgeous
bed, forgetful of the lower world. Yet when, at length, the
clouds begin to break away, and disclose the deep valleys
and blue lakes, — places made immortal by the deeds of such
patriots and reformers as Tell and Zuinglius, — we feel again
the attractions of earth; and as we descend to Lake Lucerne,
we have before us such scenery as scarcely any other part
of the world can furnish. And these scenes continue, in
ever-changing aspects, wherever we wander along this enchanting lake; and though the exhausted brain fails at length,
the objects of interest do not.

From this lake we might turn our course easterly, and
soon find ourselves amid the glacial regions of the Oberland
Alps — scenes full of deep and thrilling interest. But let us
rather turn southerly, and, following down the great valley of
Switzerland, find our way among the Alps of Savoy, where the
same phenomena attain their maximum of interest and sublimity, and the great monarch of the Alps is seen, wearing
his hoary crown. As we pass along towards Lake Lehman,
if the air be clear, the Bernese Alps loom up in unrivalled
majesty; and as we sail over Lake Lehman, Mont Blanc, with
some of its nearly equal associates, shows its distant yet impressive form. Passing without notice the almost unrivalled
beauties of Lehman, and following up the Arve through its stupendous gorges, we catch views of Mont Blanc, as we approach
it, that possess overpowering sublimity. At length, Chamouny
is reached — a lovely vale in the midst of Alpine wonders.
From thence we first ascend the Flegère, thirty-five hundred
feet above the valley, and sixty-five hundred above the
ocean; and there we get a fine view of Mont Blanc and the
Aiguilles, or Needles. Here distances are vastly diminished
to the eye, and you seem in near proximity even with Mont

17

Blanc; and, in fact, should any adventurous visitors have reached the top of that mountain, a good spy-glass will show them from this spot.*

On the opposite side of the valley from the Flegere, and at about the same height, is Montanvert, the most convenient spot for traversing the glacier called the Mer de Glace. If, however, one would see the lower extremity of that glacier, and the Arveron issuing from it, he must pass along the right hand side of the stream, and then he can follow up the glacier to Montanvert; and strange would it be if, in doing this, he should not hear and see the frequent avalanche.

We have now reached the field where everlasting war is carried on between heat and cold, summer and winter. Below us, verdure clothes the valleys, and climbs up the slopes of the hills; and there the shepherd watches his flocks. Above us there are fields of ice stretching many a league, save where some needle-shaped summit of naked rock, too steep for snow to rest upon, shoots up in lonely grandeur thousands of feet, and defies the raging elements. From these oceans of ice shoot forth down the valleys enormous glaciers, appearing like vast rivers of ice, winding among the hills, and pushing, at the rate of a few inches each day, far into regions

---

* When I visited this spot, in September, 1850, I was so fortunate as to get sight of a party that had just commenced the descent from the summit of Mont Blanc. To the naked eye they were invisible, but the whole train could be distinctly seen through a telescope. This was the third party that had ascended that mountain in the summer of 1850. I doubt not that the dangers have been exagger ated, and that the excursion will become common.

There are other points of great interest around Chamouny, whic I have not noticed, some of which I visited, but not all. I hav mentioned only the most common.

of vegetation; one year encroaching upon the shepherd's pasture ground, and anon, by the access of heat, driven back towards the summit; hurling down, from time to time, as they push forward, the thundering avalanche.

Without difficulty at Montanvert we can enter upon the glacier, and in spite of the deep *crevasse*, and the elemental war, which always rages in those lofty regions, we may make our way to their source. Nay, human feet, as already suggested, have pressed even the top of Mont Blanc; and should we reach this summit of the Alps, we should stand upon the loftiest point of Europe, and behold a scene which but few eyes ever have, or ever will, rest upon. We should

> " breathe
> The difficult air of the iced mountain's top,
> Where the birds dare not build, nor insect's wing
> Flit o'er the herbless granite."

We should, in fact, have reached the climax of the sublime in natural scenery.

Thus far I have described, almost without exception, only what I have seen. But let us now venture into regions where we have only the description of others to guide us. Let us enter the region of ancient Armenia, a country composed of wide plains, bounded and intersected by precipitous mountains. As we journeyed south-easterly over one of these plains, a remarkable conical summit would arrest our attention, at the distance of sixty miles. Day after day, as we approached, it would creep up higher and higher above the horizon, developing its commanding features, and rivetting more intensely the attention upon it. As we came near its base, we should see that its top rose far into the region of eternal ice, whose glassy surface would reflect the light like a mirror, and whose lower edge had shot forth enormous glaciers as far as the heat would allow them to descend. In the plain below, we should be sweltering in a tropical heat; but the same sun that melted us would make no impression upon the wintry crown of the mountain. We could not keep our eyes or thoughts turned away from an object so sublime. And it would deepen the impression to learn that this gigantic cone, shooting up three and a half miles, was once a volcano; and still more would it deepen our interest to learn that this is the mountain which universal tradition in that region regards as the Mount Ararat, the resting-place of the ark. It would strike us forcibly to realize that what seems to us now to be a pillar of heaven, was the patriarch's stepping-stone from the antediluvian into the postdiluvian world.

One more example may suffice. Go with me to the Sandwich Islands, and we shall get an impressive glimpse of the principal agency by which the earth's crust has been ridged, furrowed, and dislocated. As we land upon Hawaii, we perceive it to be composed mainly of lava of no very ancient date. We ascend a lofty *plateau*, and many a league in advance of us we see a column of smoke rising from a vast plain. Directing our course thither, while yet some miles from it, we descend a steep slope to a broad terrace, and then another slope to a second terrace. These slopes and terraces extend circularly around the pillar of smoke like the seats of a vast amphitheatre.

Coming near to this column, our steps are arrested on the margin of a vast gulf, fifteen hundred feet deep, and from eight to ten miles in circumference, whose bottom is the seat of the most remarkable volcano on the globe; — I mean Kilauea. Wait here till night closes around us, and we shall witness a scene of awful sublimity. Over the immense area of that gulf will the volcanic agency beneath be **exerted**. Ever and anon, and mingling in strange discord, will hissings and groanings, mutterings and thunderings, be heard rolling from side to side, and making the earth tremble around. Then from one and another volcanic cone — perhaps from fifty — will the glowing lava burst forth ; red-hot stones will be driven furiously upward ; vapor, and smoke, and flames will be poured out, and the dark and jagged sides of that vast furnace will glow with unearthly splendor ; and here and there will lakes of liquid lava appear, one or two miles in extent, heaving up their billows, and dashing their fiery spray high into the air.   O, there is not on earth a livelier emblem of the world of despair ; and yet we know it is not the lake which burneth with fire and brimstone, nor the abode of lost spirits.   We know it to be only one of the safety-valves of our globe, and an exhibition of that mighty agency within the globe which has heaved and dislocated its crust ; and, therefore, as we gaze upon the scene, and forget our fatigue and sleep, we experience only the emotions of awful sublimity, which can hardly fail to rise into adoration of that infinite Being who can say, even to this agency, Thus far shalt thou go, and no farther.

These are samples only of those delightful emotions which he experiences, who possesses a taste for natural scenery.   And kindred emotions will be awakened within him, wherever he wanders among the works of God.   They form some of the purest and most satisfying pleasures which this world affords.   They constitute pleasant oases along the dreary journey of life ; and so deeply does memory engrave them on her tablet, that no change of time or circumstances can hide them from our view.   Now, it is obvious that if the Author of nature and of the human soul had

17 *

been malevolent, instead of making every thing which man meets in creation "beauty to his eye, and music to his ear," he would have made all offensive and painful. Instead of the delightful emotions of beauty and sublimity which now rise within us as we open our eyes upon nature, feelings of aversion and fear would haunt us. Every sound would have been discordant, and every sight terrific. He could not have been even indifferent to our happiness, when he commissioned those desolating agencies of nature, fire and water, to ridge up and furrow out the earth's surface as the groundwork of the future landscape. For he has taken care that the result should be a scene productive of pleasure only to the soul that is in a healthy state. Benevolence only, infinite benevolence, could have done this.

My third argument in favor of the divine benevolence is founded on the arrangements for the distribution of water on the globe.

We should expect on so uneven a surface as the earth presents, that this element, which forms the liquid nourishment of all organic life, and which in many other ways seems indispensable, must be very unequally distributed, and fail entirely in many places ; and yet we find it in almost every spot where man erects his habitation. And those places where there is a deficiency are usually extended plains ; not, as we should expect, the mountainous regions. The latter are usually well watered ; and this is accomplished in three ways. In the first place, in most mountainous countries, the strata are so much tilted up, as to prevent the water from running off. In the second place, the pervious strata are frequently interrupted by faults sometimes filled by impervious matter. In the third place, the comminuted materials that cover the rocks as soils, are often so fine, or of such a nature, as to prevent the passage of water; and thus much of the water that falls upon elevated land remains there, while enough percolates through the pervious materials to water the valleys and supply the streams. These carry it to the lakes and the ocean, where it is returned by evaporation in the form of clouds, and thus an admirable system of circulation is kept up, whereby this essential element is purified, and conveyed to every part of the surface where man or beast require it.

There is one recent discovery, which deserves notice here, because it depends upon the geological structure of the earth. When pervious and impervious strata alternate, and are considerably inclined, water may be brought from great depths by hydrostatic pressure, if the impervious stratum be bored through and the water-bearing deposit be reached. A perpetual fountain may thus be produced, and water be obtained in a region naturally deficient in it. An Artesian fountain of this description, in the suburbs of Paris, has been brought from the enormous depth of eighteen hundred feet! *

Now, just consider that to deprive the earth of water is to deprive it of inhabitants, and you cannot but see in the means by which it is so widely, nay, almost universally, diffused, and made to circulate for purification, — the most decided marks of divine benevolence. Why is it not as striking as the curious means by which the blood and the sap of animals and plants are sent to every part of the system to supply its waste, and give it greater development?

---

* In September, 1850, I visited this well, and found the water running still, at the rate of six hundred and sixty gallons per minute at the surface, and half that amount at the top of a tube one hundred and twelve feet high, from whence it could be carried to any part of Paris; and, in fact, does supply some of the streets. I tasted the water, and found it pleasant, though warm, (84 deg. Fahrenheit.)

I derive a fourth geological argument for the benevolence of the Deity, from the manner in which the metallic ores are distributed through the earth's crust.

It can hardly be doubted, by the geologist, that nearly every part of the earth's crust, and its interior too, have been some time or other in a melted state. Now, as the metals and their ores are usually heavier than other rocks, we should expect that they would have accumulated at the centre of the globe, and have been enveloped by the rocks so as to have been forever inaccessible to man. And the very great weight of the central parts of the earth — almost twice that of granite — leads naturally to the conclusion that the heavier metals may be accumulated there, though this is by no means a certain conclusion; since at the depth of thirty-four miles air would be so condensed by the pressure of the superincumbent mass as to be as heavy as water; water at the depth of three hundred and sixty-two miles would become as heavy as quicksilver; and at the centre steel would be compressed into one fourth, and stone into one eighth, of its bulk at the surface. Still it is most probable that the materials naturally the heaviest would first seek the centre. And yet, by means of sublimation, and expansion by internal heat, or the segregating power of galvanic action, or of some other agents, enough of the metals is protruded towards the surface, and diffused through the rocks in beds, or veins, so as to be accessible to human industry. Here, then, we find divine benevolence, apparently in opposition to gravity, providing for human comfort.

I have said that these metals were accessible to human industry. And it does require a great deal of labor, and calls into exercise man's highest ingenuity to obtain them. They might have been spread in immense masses over the surface :

they might all have been reduced to a metallic state in the great furnace, which we have reason to suppose is always in blast, within the earth. But then there would have been no requisition upon the exertion and energy of man. And to have these called into exercise is an object of greater importance to society than to supply it with the metals. God, therefore, has so distributed the ores as to stimulate man to explore and reduce them, while he has placed so many difficulties in the way as to demand much mental and physical effort for their removal. Man now, therefore, receives a double benefit. While the metals themselves are of immense service, the discipline of body and mind requisite for obtaining them is of still greater value. This is the combined result of infinite wisdom and benevolence.

If I mistake not, there is such a relation between the amount of useful metals and the wants of society as could have resulted only from divine benevolence. The metal most widely diffused, and the only one occurring in all the rock formations, from the oldest to the newest, is iron ; — the metal by far the most important to civilized society. This is also by far the most abundant, and easily obtained. It often forms extensive beds, or even mountain masses upon the surface. All the other metals are confined almost exclusively to the older rocks. Among them, lead, copper, and zinc are probably most needed, and accordingly they are next in quantity and in the facility with which they may be explored. Manganese, mercury, chrome, antimony, cobalt, arsenic, and bismuth are more difficult to obtain ; but the supply is always equal to the demand. In the case of tin, silver, platinum, and gold, we find some interesting properties to compensate in a great measure for their scarcity. Gold and platinum possess a remarkable power of resisting those powerful agents of chemical change which destroy every thing else. They are never oxidized in the earth, and with a very few exceptions, the most powerful reagents leave them untouched, while platinum will not yield in the most powerful heat of the furnace. Gold, silver, and tin are capable of an astonishing extension, whereby they may be spread over the surface of the more abundant metals to protect and adorn them ; and since the discovery of the galvanic mode of accomplishing this, so easily is it done, that I know not but a gold or silver surface is to become as common as metallic articles.

My fifth geological argument for the divine benevolence is derived from the joint and desolating effects of ice and water upon the earth's surface, both before and after man's creation.

In northern countries, and perhaps in high southern latitudes, it seems that after the deposition of the tertiary rocks, and after the surface had assumed essentially its present shape, it was subjected for a long time to a powerful agency, whereby the rough and salient parts were worn down and rounded, the rocks in place smoothed and furrowed, valleys scooped out, huge blocks of stone transported far from the parent bed, piled up, and thick accumulations of bowlders, sand, and gravel, strewn promiscuously over the surface. At the commencement of this process, the ocean, probably loaded with ice, stood above a large part of the present continents. It soon began to subside, or the land to rise, and a more quiet action succeeded. The joint action of the ocean and the glaciers on the land ground down into sand, clay, and loam, the coarser drift, and sorted it in the form of beaches, terraces, and alluvial deposits. All this while, both the land and the water seem to have been, for the most part, destitute of inhabitants. But these were the very processes needed for man and his contemporary races, who were to appear during the latter part of the pleistocene period. In other words, the soils were thus got ready for nourishing the vegetation necessary to sustain the new creation, which would convert these desolate and deserted sea-beds into regions of fertility and happiness to teeming millions.

Now, just consider what must have been the effect of these mighty aqueous and glacial agencies upon the earth's surface. Over the level regions they strewed the finer materials; and where the rocks had been thrown up into ridges and displaced by numerous fissures, or subsequently worn into bluffs and precipices by the ocean, it needed just such an agency to smooth down those irregularities, to fill up those gulfs, to give to the hills and valleys a graceful outline, and to cover all the surface with those comminuted materials that would need only cultivation to make them a fertile soil. Some rocks do, indeed, decompose and form soils; but this process would be too slow, unless in moist and warm regions, where it is easier to find a footing for plants than in climes more uncongenial to their growth. We cannot then hesitate to regard this tremendous agency of ice and water in northern and high southern regions as decidedly beneficial in its influence. It must, indeed, have spread terrible destruction over those regions. But it seems that a time was chosen for its operation when the globe was almost destitute of organic life, and not long before the time when a new and nobler creation than those previously occupying the earth was to be placed upon it. Desolating as this agency must have appeared, and actually was, at the time, yet who can doubt, when we see the ultimate fruits of it, that its origin was divine benevolence?

In the ultimate results of aqueous inundations at the present day, we can trace the same benevolent design. Those floods do, indeed, produce partial evils; nay, life, as well as property, often falls a prey to them. But they produce those alluvial soils which are more prolific of vegetation than any other on the globe. Who has not heard of the fertility of the banks of the Nile, the Niger, the Ganges, the Amazon, and the Mississippi? all of them the fruit of inundations. Truly, such floods as these may be said *to clap their hands* in praise of the divine goodness.

My sixth geological argument for the divine benevolence is derived from the existence of volcanoes.

The first impression made on the mind by the history of volcanic action is, that its effects are examples rather of vindictive justice than of benevolence. And such is the light in which they are regarded by Mr. Gisborne, an able English divine, in his "Testimony of Natural to Revealed Religion." He looks, indeed, upon all the disturbances that have taken place in the earth's crust as evidence of a fallen condition of the world, as mementoes of a former penal infliction upon a guilty race. And aside from the light which geology casts upon the subject, this would be a not improbable conclusion. Take for an example the case of volcanoes and earthquakes.

A volcano is an opening made in the earth's crust by internal heat, which has forced melted or heated matter through the vent. An earthquake is the effect of the confined gases and vapors, produced by the heat upon the crust. When the volcano, therefore, gets vent, the earthquake always ceases. But the latter has generally been more destructive of life and property than the former. Where one city has been destroyed by lava, like Herculaneum, Pompeii, and Stabiæ, twenty have been shaken down by the rocking and heaving of earthquakes. The records of ancient as well as modern times abound with examples of these tremendous catastrophes. Preëminent on the list is the city of Antioch. Imagine the inhabitants of that great city, crowded with strangers on a festival occasion, suddenly arrested on a calm day, by the earth heaving and rocking beneath their feet; and in a few moments two hundred and fifty thousand of them are buried by falling houses, or the earth opening and swallowing them up. Such was the scene which that city presented in the year 526; and several times before and since that period has the like calamity fallen upon it; and twenty, forty, and sixty thousand of its inhabitants have been destroyed at each time. In the year 17 after Christ, no less than thirteen cities of Asia Minor were in like manner overwhelmed in a single night. Think of the terrible destruction that came upon Lisbon in 1755. The sun had just dissipated the fog in a warm, calm morning, when suddenly the subterranean thundering and heaving began; and in six minutes the city was a heap of ruins, and sixty thousand of the inhabitants were numbered among the dead. Hundreds had crowded upon a new quay surrounded by vessels. In a moment the earth opened beneath them, and the wharf, the vessels, and the crowd went down into its bosom; the gulf closed, the sea rolled over the spot, and no vestige of wharf, vessels, or man ever floated to the surface. How thrilling is the account left us by Kircher, who was near, of the destruction of Euphemia, in Calabria, a city of about five thousand inhabitants, in the year 1638! " After some time," says he, " the violent paroxysm of the earthquake ceasing, I stood up, and, turning my eyes to look for Euphemia, saw only a frightful black cloud. We waited till it had passed away, when nothing but a dismal and putrid lake was to be seen where the city once stood." In like manner did Port Royal, in the West Indies, sink beneath the waters, with nearly all its inhabitants, in less than one minute, in the year 1692.

Still more awful, though usually less destructive, is often

18

the scene presented by a volcanic eruption. Imagine yourselves, for instance, upon one of the wide, elevated plains of
Mexico, far from the fear of volcanoes. The earth begins to
quake under your feet, and the most alarming subterranean
noises admonish you of a mighty power within the earth that
must soon have vent. You flee to the surrounding mountains
in time to look back and see ten square miles of the plain
swell up, like a bladder, to the height of five hundred feet, while
numerous smaller cones rise from the surface still higher, and
emit smoke ; and in their midst, six mountains are thrown up
to the height, some of them at least, of sixteen hundred feet,
and pour forth melted lava, turning rivers out of their course,
and spreading terrific desolation over a late fertile plain, and
forever excluding its former inhabitants. Such was the eruption, by which Jorullo, in Mexico, was suddenly thrown up,
in 1759.

Still more terrific have been some of the eruptions in Ice-
land. In 1783, earthquakes of tremendous power shook the
whole island, and flames burst forth from the ocean. In June
these ceased, and Skaptar Jokul opened its mouth ; nor did it
close till it had poured forth two streams of lava, one sixty
miles long, twelve miles broad, and the other forty miles long,
and seven broad, and both with an average thickness of one
hundred feet. During that summer the inhabitants saw the
sun no more, and all Europe was covered with a haze.

Around the Papandayang, one of the loftiest mountains in
Java, no less than forty villages were reposing in peace.
But in August, 1772, a remarkable luminous cloud enveloping
its top aroused them from their security. But it was too late.
For at once the mountain began to sink into the earth, and
soon it had disappeared with the forty villages, and most of
the inhabitants, over a space fifteen miles long and six broad.

Still more extraordinary — the most remarkable on record — was an eruption in Sumbawa, one of the Molucca Islands, in 1815. It began on the fifth day of April, and did not cease till July. The explosions were heard in one direction nine hundred and seventy miles, and in another seven hundred and twenty miles. So heavy was the fall of ashes at the distance of forty miles that houses were crushed and destroyed. The floating cinders in the ocean, hundreds of miles distant, were two feet thick, and vessels were forced through them with difficulty. The darkness in Java, three hundred miles distant, was deeper than the blackest night; and finally, out of the twelve thousand inhabitants of the island, only twenty-six survived the catastrophe.

Now, if we confine our views to such facts as these, we can hardly avoid the conclusion that earthquakes and volcanoes are terrific exhibitions of God's displeasure towards a fallen and guilty world. But if it can be shown that the volcanic agency exerts a salutary influence in preserving the globe from ruin, nay, is essential to such preservation, we must regard its incidental destruction of property and life as no evidence of a vindictive infliction, nor of the want of benevolence in its operation. And the remarkable proofs which modern geology has presented of vast accumulations of heated and melted matter beneath the earth's crust, do make such an agent as volcanoes essential to the preservation of the globe. In order to make out this position, I shall not contend that all the earth's interior, beneath fifty or one hundred miles, is in a state of fusion. For even the most able and decided of those geologists who object to such an inference, admit that oceans of melted matter do exist beneath the surface. And if so, how liable would vast accumulations of heat be, if there were no safety-valves through the crust, to rend asunder even a whole continent? Volcanoes are those safety-valves, and more than two hundred of them are scattered over the earth's surface, forming vent-holes into the heated interior. Most of them, indeed, have the valves loaded, and the effort of the confined gases and vapors to lift the load produces the terrific phenomena of earthquakes and volcanoes. But if no such passages into the interior existed, what could prevent the pent-up gases from accumulating till they had gained strength enough to rend a whole continent, and perhaps the whole globe, into fragments? Is it not, then, benevolence by which this agency prevents so dreadful a catastrophe, even by means that bring some incidental evils along with them?

Some able writers do, indeed, object to the idea that volcanoes are safety-valves to the globe, deriving their objections from certain facts respecting the position of volcanic craters in the Sandwich Islands, if I do not misrecollect. Without going into the details of that case, for want of time and space, it seems to me that the facts respecting the connection between earthquakes and volcanoes, admitted by all, will justify such a view of the latter as is expressed by the term "safety-valves." For earthquakes are but the incipient effects of the volcanic force within the globe; and if these effects have been so terrible at the beginning, what must be the full exhibition of that force, if not able to find a passage for the struggling gases and lava through the strata above them? Who can say that it might not rend a continent asunder, and, if deep enough seated, even the whole globe?

The question will undoubtedly be asked by every reflecting mind, why infinite wisdom and benevolence could not have devised a plan for securing the good resulting from volcanoes and earthquakes without the attendant evils. The same question meets us at almost every step of our examination of the present system of the world. For we every where meet with evil, incidentally connected with agencies whose predominant effects are beneficial. I incline to the opinion, that the true answer to this question is, that the evil is permitted that thereby greater good may be secured to the universe. Still the subject of the origin of evil is one whose full solution can hardly be expected in the present world, because we cannot here master all its elements. When it can be solved, we can tell why so much desolation and suffering are permitted to accompany the earthquake and the volcano. But if we can show that benefits far outweighing the evil are the result of this terrific agency, we gather from it decided evidence of the divine benevolence ; — the same evidence which we gain from any other operations of nature; for in them all there is only a preponderance of good, not unmixed good. The desolation of this fair world by volcanic agency, and especially the destruction of life, do, indeed, teach us that this present system of nature is adapted to a state of probation and death, instead of a state of rewards and immortal life. It is adapted to sinful and fallen beings, rather than to those who are perfect in holiness and in happiness. In short, it is earth, not heaven. It is not such a world as heaven must be, to secure unalloyed and eternal happiness. Nevertheless, benevolence decidedly predominates in the arrangements of the present system, even in the desolating agency under consideration. I do not deny that God may sometimes employ this agency, as he may every other in nature, for the punishment of the guilty. But before we infer that this is the general use and design of volcanoes and earthquakes, we should ponder well the questions put by our Savior *to some that told him of the Galileans, whose blood*

18 *

Pilate had mingled with their sacrifices. Suppose ye, answered the Savior, *that these Galileans were sinners above all the Galileans, because they suffered such things ?   I tell you nay. Or those eighteen, upon whom the tower of Siloam fell and slew them, think ye that they were sinners above all men that dwelt in Jerusalem ?   I tell you nay.* Let us follow the example of Jesus Christ, and take a more enlarged view of these startling and distressing events.   Let us inquire whether they are not the incidental effects of agencies essential to the permanence and happiness of the great system of the universe.   This is certainly the case in regard to volcanoes. We have strong reason to believe that they are essential to the preservation of the globe ; and of how much higher consequence is this than the comparatively small amount of property and life which they destroy!   If we can only rise to these higher views, and not suffer our judgment to be warped by the immediate terrors of the earthquake and the volcano, we shall see the smile of infinite benevolence where most men see only the wrath of an offended Deity.

My seventh geological argument for the divine benevolence is derived from the manner in which coal, rock salt, marble, gypsum, and other valuable materials were prepared for the use of man, long before his existence.

If a created and intelligent being from some other sphere had alighted on this globe during that remote period when the vegetation now dug out of the coal formation covered the surface with its gigantic growth, he might have felt as if here was a waste of creative power.   Vast forests of sigillaria, lepidodendra, coniferæ, cycadeæ, and tree ferns would have waved over his head, with their imposing though sombre foliage, while the lesser tribes of calamites and equisetaceæ would have filled the intervening spaces ; but no vertebral animal would have been there to enjoy and enliven the almost universal solitude. Why, then, he must have inquired, is there such a profusion of vegetable forms, and such a colossal development of individual plants ? To what use can such vast forests be applied ? But let ages roll by, and that same being revisit our world at the present time. Let him traverse the little Island of Britain, and see there fifteen thousand steam engines moved by coal dug out of the earth, and produced by these same ancient forests. Let him see these engines performing the work of two millions of men, and moving machinery which accomplishes what would require the unaided labors of three or four hundred millions of men, and he could not doubt but such a result was one of the objects of that rank vegetation which covered the earth ere it was fit for the residence of such natures as now dwell upon it. Let him go to the coal fields of other countries, and especially those of the United States, stretching over one hundred and fifty thousand square miles, containing a quantity absolutely inexhaustible, and already imparting comfort to millions of the inhabitants, and giving life and energy to every variety of manufacture through the almost entire length of this country, and destined to pour out their wealth through all coming time, long after the forests shall all have been levelled, — and irresistible must be the conviction upon his mind, that here is a beautiful example of prospective benevolence on the part of the Deity. In those remote ages, while yet the earth was unfitted for the higher races of animals that now dwell upon it, it was eminently adapted to nourish that gigantic flora which would produce the future fuel of the human race, when that crown of all God's works should be placed upon the earth. Ere that time, those forests must sink beneath the ocean, be buried beneath deposits of rock

thousands of feet thick.   But during all that period, all those
chemical changes which are essential to convert them into
coal would be accomplished, and, at last, man would find
access, by his ingenuity and industry, to the deep-seated beds
whence his fuel might be drawn.   Nor would these vast
repositories fail him till the consummation of all things.
Surely there was no waste, but there was a far-reaching plan
of benevolence in the profusion of vegetable life in the earlier
periods of our planet.

Essentially the same remark will apply to the limestone,
gypsum, rock salt, and several other mineral products of the
earth, which are almost indispensable to man in a civilized
state.   For these, too, were produced by slow processes, during those vast periods of duration that preceded man's existence.   Limestone has been chiefly elaborated by the organs
of animals, many of them of microscopic littleness.   Yet
lofty ranges of mountains and immense deposits in the intervening valleys have been the result.   Nearly one seventh
part of the crust of the globe, it has been said, is thus constituted of the works or remains of animals.   And can we doubt
but that these rocks are thus spread over the surface of the
globe because they are needed by all mankind, like air and
water ?   It must have been benevolence that so arranged the
agencies by which they were produced, during the revolution
of primeval ages, that they have this wide diffusion.   Gypsum
and fossil salt are more sparingly diffused ; but still enough
is always to be found to meet the demand.   Nor is it reasonable to doubt that the same prospective goodness which provided for coal and limestone, commissioned other agencies to
lay up a store of gypsum, salt, bitumen, clay, and other substances dug out of the earth for man's benefit.

My eighth geological argument for the divine benevolence

is based upon the perfect adaptation of the natures of ani-
mals and plants to the varying condition of the globe through
all the periods of its past history.

The very slight changes in climate, situation, and food, that will destroy most species of animals and plants, is hard to be realized by man, whose nature will sustain very great changes of this kind. So will most of the animals and plants that have been domesticated by man, and which accompany him into every soil and climate. But the great mass of animals and plants would perish by such a transplantation. They are adapted to a particular region, often of narrow limits; and to remove them from thence, even to one slightly diverse, is to cause their deterioration and final destruction. In other words, their natures are exactly adapted to the place of habitation assigned them. And it must have required infinite wisdom thus to fit the delicate machinery of animal and vegetable organization to the great variety of circumstances on the globe in which it is placed. But we find that same wisdom to have been manifested in all the vast periods of organic life. We have the most unequivocal evidence that the condition of the earth has undergone important changes. We cannot examine the remarkable flora and fauna of the older rocks, the gigantic sauroid fishes, the huge orthoceratites and ammonites, the heteroclitic trilobites, and the strange sigillaria and lepidodendra, calamites and aster-ophyllites, the lofty coniferæ, and the anomalous cycadeæ, — we cannot examine these without realizing that a state of the globe very different from the present must have existed when they had possession of it. And when we contemplate also the enormous saurians and batrachians of the middle secondary rocks, and the colossal quadrupeds of the tertiary strata, we cannot doubt that a tropical or an ultra-tropical climate must have prevailed in high northern latitudes during their existence. We perceive that there has been a gradual decrease of temperature on the surface from the earliest times. In each successive race of organized beings which have been placed on the globe, there must have been, therefore, some change of constitution to adapt them to the altered state of the climate and productions of the earth. And we find this alteration to have been always made with consummate skill, so as to secure the most complete development of organic beings, and the greatest enjoyment to sensitive natures. Malevolence would not have done this; for it might with infinite knowledge at command, have filled each successive period of the world with natures unadapted to the mutable condition of things, capable, indeed, of a prolonged existence, not to enjoy, but only to suffer. But infinite benevolence was fitting up this world by slow secondary agencies for the elevated races which now occupy it, especially for one species, rational and immortal; and it lavished its kindness and wisdom by filling the world, during those preparatory ages, with multitudes of happy beings, fitted exactly to each altered condition of the air, the water, and the soil.

My ninth and last geological argument for the divine benevolence is founded upon the permanence and security of the world, in spite of the mighty changes it has undergone, and the powerful agencies to which it is now subject.

When we learn from the records of geology, as they are inscribed upon the rocks, how numerous and thorough have been the revolutions of the surface and the crust of the globe in past ages; how often and how long the present dry land has been alternately above and beneath the ocean; how frequently the crust of the globe has been fractured, bent, and dislocated, — now lifted upward, and now thrown downward, and now folded by lateral pressure; how frequently melted matter has been forced through its strata and through its fissures to the surface; in short, how every particle of the accessible portions of the globe has undergone entire metamorphoses; and especially when we recollect what strong evidence there is that oceans of liquid matter exist beneath the solid crust, and that probably the whole interior of the earth is in that condition, with expansive energy sufficient to rend the globe into fragments, — when we review all these facts, we cannot but feel that the condition of the surface of the globe must be one of great insecurity and liability to change. But it is not so. On the contrary, the present state of the globe is one of permanent uniformity and entire security, except those comparatively slight catastrophes which result from earthquakes, volcanoes, and local deluges. Even the climate has experienced no general change within historic times, and the profound mathematical researches of Baron Fourier have demonstrated that, even though the internal parts of the globe are in an incandescent state, beneath a crust thirty or forty miles, the temperature at the surface has long since ceased to be affected by the melted central mass; that it is not now more than one seventeenth of a degree higher than it would be if the interior were ice; and that hundreds of thousands of years will not see it lowered, from this cause, more than the seventeenth part of a degree. And as to the apprehension that the entire crust of the globe may be broken through, and fall into the melted matter beneath, just reflect what solidity and strength there must be in a mass of hard rock from fifty to one hundred miles in thickness, and your fears of such a catastrophe will probably vanish.

Now, such a uniformity of climate and security from general ruin are essential to the comfort and existence of animal

nature. But it must have required infinite wisdom and benevolence so to arrange and balance the mighty elements of
change and ruin which exist in the earth, that they should
hold one another in check, and make the world a quiet, unchanged, and secure dwelling-place for so many thousands
of years. Surely that wisdom must have been guided by
infinite benevolence. And it would seem from geology that
the same union of wisdom and benevolence have always
arranged the past conditions of the earth. For, during each
of the periods of organic existence, uniformity and security
seem to have prevailed so long as the purposes of the Deity
required. In early times, indeed, when animals were mostly
confined to the waters, it was not necessary that the dry land
should be as exempt as at present from catastrophes ; and
probably they were then more frequent ; and it may be that,
while there were uniformity and security in one portion of the
globe, or in one element, there might have been disturbance
and desolation in others. And it is doubtful whether such
general quiet has ever prevailed for so long a time as
during the present, or historic period. We see a reason
for this in the fact that never before were so many animals in existence, with a structure so delicate and complicated.

Such are the evidences of divine benevolence, drawn from
a field at first view most unpromising. And yet, when we
come to look beyond the surface, where do we find more decisive or more numerous indications of God's beneficence ?
They are not like many hasty generalizations, which superficial examination has often brought from natural phenomena
in proof of this same truth, but which, although beautiful at
first view, must be abandoned upon careful research. But

these, though repulsive at first, gain solidity and beauty by examination. And they are the more interesting because they come from an unexpected quarter. Men have been accustomed to search among the drift piled up by water and ice, among dislocated and rent strata of rocks, among mountains overturned and fields made desolate by volcanic eruptions, for the mementoes of penal inflictions; but they have not imagined that divine benevolence might be seen among these disturbances and desolations; and that simply because they confined their views to the immediate effect of geological agencies, and did not enlarge their views to take in their connection with the great system of the universe. But now that we find the stamp of benevolence even here, we learn an instructive lesson. Every reflecting mind is aware that the doctrine of divine benevolence lies at the foundation of all natural and revealed religion, and that until this be established we labor in vain to erect a superstructure. It is well known, also, that the existence of natural and moral evil has been considered a strong objection to this great truth. Now, geology furnishes us with many examples, in which agencies, often fraught with terrific evils, are nevertheless eminently beneficial when the whole extent of their operation is taken into account. Why is it not a fair inference that, in all other cases where evils stand out prominently, they are only incidental results of some wide system of operations, of which our limited vision embraces only a part, but whose tendencies as a whole are eminently salutary, and whose incidental evils do, in fact, increase the salutary effects? If so, what reason have we to believe that, when the light of eternity shall clarify our mental eye, and enlarge our knowledge of the present system of the universe, we shall find all

19

" partial evil to be universal good," and that our narrow views alone threw obscurity and difficulty over this subject in this life ?   O, if even here so many rays of divine love find their way into our narrow prison-house, what will be their brightness when they pour in upon us from the unveiled glories of the heavenly world !

LECTURE VII.

DIVINE BENEVOLENCE AS EXHIBITED IN A FALLEN WORLD.

The geological proofs of the divine benevolence considered in the last lecture present only a partial view of that glorious characteristic of Jehovah. I am tempted, therefore, to exhibit it in its more general aspect and broader relations. This will necessarily bring into view other important religious truths respecting man's fallen condition and character, and, as a consequence, the modified aspect of the divine goodness in such a world.

To those destitute of a revelation this world has, indeed, ever seemed an inextricable maze, an enigma too dark for human wisdom to solve. Nor have those favored with the Bible agreed in their modes of clearing up the mystery. Having endeavored to explain all by following out some leading and favorite idea, their theories have varied as these predominant conceptions differed. One, for instance, fixes his gaze so intently upon the divine benevolence that he is blind to every manifestation of Jehovah's sterner attributes. Another, deeply impressed with the story of man's original apostasy, sees only vindictive justice, and penal infliction, and disordered action, in all the movements of nature and the trials and sufferings of man. A third, captivated by the discoveries of modern geology, relative to the existence of suffering and death in the world before man's creation, and learning, moreover, from physiology, that death is a general law of all organized natures, vegetable as well as animal, is led to doubt whether the disorders of the world have any important connection with man's apostasy.

Now, it were easy to show that our views on these subjects have a most important bearing upon our entire system of theology; and, therefore, they deserve our most thorough and candid examination. To such an examination I now invite your serious attention.

It is not my object to appeal to the Scriptures to prove the divine benevolence. That were an easy task. So, were this an unfallen world, every object and event would be redolent of God's goodness. But where sin and death abound, that goodness must assume a different aspect, since its unmixed manifestation would work mischief. Now, the point aimed at in this lecture is to ascertain whether natural religion can point out decisive evidence of divine benevolence. We can conceive it quite possible that in a fallen world God might find it necessary so to mingle displays of justice with those of goodness, that man might be in doubt which predominated.

There is another reason for considering this subject apart from scriptural evidence. We need to establish the doctrine of divine benevolence as a basis on which to rest the evidences of inspiration; or, rather, we want to be able to assume God's benevolence, in arguing for the truth of the Bible, and in judging of its contents. This doctrine, therefore, is one of the most important, as it is certainly the most difficult, in natural theology.

Obviously the first step in this investigation must be to ascertain what is the real state of this world, as a manifestation of the benevolence and justice of God. In other words, we need to ascertain what exhibitions of these attributes are presented to us in nature, and in the economy of Providence, and how much of the evil in the world is to be imputed to man's perversion of the gifts of God. I shall proceed, therefore, to state the main points on this subject which fair and candid reasoning seems to me to sustain. When these points are before us, with a summary of the evidence by which they are supported, we shall be prepared to deduce important conclusions respecting God's character and dispensations, and man's position and destiny.

In the first place, then, I maintain that benevolence decidedly predominates in the present system of the world.

Let this proposition be fully understood. It does not mean that there is no mixture of evil in the operations of nature, but only that good decidedly overbalances the evil. And by the operations of nature I mean those processes resulting from natural laws, which are uninfluenced by the perverseness of man. How much of evil may be imputed to his perversion of the gifts of Providence will be considered in another place, as will also those cases in which evil seems inseparable from the original arrangements of the world. All that I am now concerned to prove is, that, in a vast majority of instances, we see the marks of benevolent design and benevolent operation in the arrangements of nature.

This position is established, in the first place, by the fact that the design of every natural contrivance is to produce happiness.

To show that such is the case, by an appeal to facts, would be, in truth, to write the history of every natural process, and show its design. But it will be sufficient to consider only such cases as appear most decidedly to militate against my

19 *

position, and to show that even these are not designed to cause evil or suffering.

How does it happen, then, you may inquire, that evil is the result of a multitude of contrivances and processes in nature? It is an incidental effect, I answer; that is, an effect happening aside from the main design of the contrivance. Take a few illustrations.

No one can doubt that the law of gravity is essential to the preservation and comfort of the world, and to the harmonious motions of the heavenly bodies. Yet how often does it give rise to frightful accidents to men and animals! But when they are crushed by falling bodies, or by falling themselves, who imagines this to be the design of gravitation? How clear that its real object is beneficial, and that the evil resulting from it is unavoidable in a world constituted like ours! Why the world is not constituted differently, is an inquiry which men may try to answer; but an answer is not important to my present object.

Take an example from the organic world. Every one is aware that without a nervous system in animals there would be no sensibility, nor sensation, and, of course, no enjoyment; and without these, animals would be unconscious of danger, and would not guard against it, nor withdraw from it. We are sure, therefore, that these two objects are the grand design of the nervous system, and, of course, it is a benevolent design. But the nervous system causes a great deal of suffering as well as pleasure. Obviously, however, this is only an incidental effect, which could not be prevented without a miracle; while the main design is to produce happiness and guard against evil.

It may be asked, however, by what principle we can determine what is the design of a contrivance, and what the incidental effect. Why select a part of the effects, and call them the object aimed at by the contriver, while we regard others as incidental, and merely permitted, not intended ?

The principle on which we make this distinction is very clear. We judge of the design of a contrivance by its predominant tendencies and effects. If evil as often results as good, misery as often as happiness, we could not decide whether the design was benevolent or malevolent, or an indifference to both. But the benevolent tendency and effects of every natural contrivance are so obvious, and so immensely outweigh all its evil results, that we are compelled to admit the design of the Author of nature to be benevolent. And, therefore, when we see evil occasionally result from such contrivances, we are authorized to say that this is only an incidental effect; not, indeed, wholly undesigned, for we cannot doubt that God has a design in the permission of all evil. But for each particular arrangement and movement in nature we can discover a predominant and benevolent object.

Take another example from the human frame. In that frame we find a multitude of organs, nearly all of which are obviously adapted to a particular use. Now, the anatomist cannot lay his finger upon one of them, and say, This was intended to produce derangement and suffering in the system. Here is a muscle contrived to clog the operations of its neighbors ; here a blood-vessel adapted to corrupt the blood and produce disease ; here a gland whose object is to secrete a poisonous fluid, to contaminate the whole system; here a nerve made to produce pain ; here a plexus of vessels suited to bring on disease. On the contrary, this anatomist perceives at once that all the organs of the animal system, and their collocation, are fitted in the best possible manner to produce health. It is obvious at a glance that this is their design.

But if such be the fact, how happens it that so few persons pass through life without disease ? Is it all to be imputed to an abuse and perversion of the organs and powers
of life ? Not so, in my opinion. But those organs are all
liable to disease ; and when we see how delicate and complicated they are, we ought not to wonder that even the unavoidable causes of derangement should often bring it on.
Yet, after all, health is the rule and the object, and disease
only the exception. But I shall say more on this subject in
another part of the argument.

Some one, however, who hears me, has doubtless ere this
had his thoughts recur to the organs of carnivorous animals,
the poisonous fangs of serpents, and the organs of the scorpion, the tarantula, and of insects, for the generation and
protrusion of deadly poison. Here we have organs expressly
provided for the destruction of other animals. That such is
their design, no physiologist can doubt ; and hence they are
intended to produce suffering, and not happiness.

Is this an exactly correct statement of the case ? True,
suffering is the result of such organs ; but the arrangement
is intended to accomplish still higher purposes. The leading
one is to procure food for sustenance, the other is self-defence.
Both of these are essential to the animal's continued existence. That suffering should be incidentally connected with
instruments or organs so important, is no more difficult to explain than is the existence of evil any where. The object
even of these contrivances, then, is beneficial. And if so, I
know of no other example in nature so seemingly adverse to
the position I have laid down, that the main object of every
natural contrivance is benevolent in its origin and results. If
this be so, how clearly does it indicate the character of the
contriver to be benevolent !

My second argument is derived from the fact that the organic functions often produce pleasure where suffering was just as consistent with their most perfect action ; or I might say that such are the arrangements of the natural world, that pleasure often results to sentient beings from its operations, when they might have been as perfectly performed with the production of pain. A few illustrations will render the meaning of this position obvious.

As we look abroad upon nature, one of the most striking traits we discover is its unbounded variety. With the Psalmist we involuntarily exclaim, *O Lord, how manifold are thy works !* It is not merely variety as to form, texture, attitude, and arrangement ; but who can describe the countless tints of coloring which are spread over the heavens and the earth? Now, there is in the human soul an aptitude to be pleased with variety ; nay, there is a craving for it. Nor can there be a more terrible infliction than unvarying monotony and sameness of appearance, arrangement, and action. If, therefore, the Creator had been malevolent, or indifferent to the happiness of man and other sentient beings, he might have gratified this disposition most perfectly by giving to the human soul its present love of variety, and then spreading over the face of nature a dead uniformity of figure, position, arrangement, and coloring ; forming every thing upon the same model. And this might have been done without impairing at all the perfect operation of all her laws that are essential. Every thing might have been as systematic and harmonious as it now is ; but sentient beings would have been miserable ; and this must have been supremely gratifying to infinite malevolence. He might also have so constructed the organs of hearing, sight, and smell, that every sound might have been ungrateful and grating, every odor repulsive, and every prospect disgusting. While hunger would have urged animals, as it now does, to seek food, its reception might have been painful, or utterly void of gustatory enjoyment. So in regard to social enjoyments; we might have been irresistibly drawn towards our fellow-men, and yet their society might have been hateful in the extreme.

Had such a state of things existed, how very clearly we should have inferred the malevolence of the Author of nature! Or if such a state had been witnessed about as often as its opposite, we might reasonably have said that he was indifferent to the happiness of his creatures. Why, then, may we not, with equal reason, infer his benevolence, when we find, in a vast majority of cases, — nay, for aught I know, universally, — that pleasure is superadded to animal enjoyment where it was wholly unnecessary to the perfect operation of nature's laws?

The fact is, God has made all nature " beauty to our eye and music to our ear," when it was wholly unnecessary for the perfect operation of her laws; and the inference is irresistible, that he delights in the happiness of his creatures. Nor can the fact that evil exists in the world destroy the force of this argument, unless that evil is so general as to be obviously the design of the Creator in devising and arranging the system of the world. While we admit its existence, we say that it is only incidental, and that pleasure is so often superadded unnecessarily, as to prove happiness to be the design, and evil the exception.

The two arguments above presented are the evidence on which Dr. Paley relies to prove the divine benevolence. They are, indeed, as it seems to me, unanswerable. But if I mistake not, they do by no means exhaust the storehouse of nature's proofs of this fundamental principle of natural and revealed religion. I derive a third argument for the predominance of benevolence in the works of nature from the variety of means often provided for the performance of important functions; so that animals and plants can adapt themselves to different circumstances, and prolong their existence.

The examples which I have in mind to illustrate this argument are all derived from the organic world. I refer, for instance, to the fact that nearly all our muscles, and many other important organs, as the hands, the feet, the eyes, and the lungs, are in pairs, so that if one meets with an injury, or is destroyed, the other can, to some extent, perform the office of both. The brain has two hemispheres, and one of them may be seriously wounded without destroying the healthy action of the other.

But perhaps the most appropriate example is in the blood-vessels, whose inosculations are so numerous that even though large arteries and veins be tied, the blood will find its way through the smaller ones, which ultimately will so enlarge as to keep up the circulation nearly as well as before the injury. And, in fact, almost every one of the large blood-vessels has been tied by the surgeon with little ultimate injury to the patient.

In the process of deglutition, or swallowing the nourishment essential to the existence of all the more perfect animals, — since the food and the air for respiration pass for a time through a common opening, the pharynx, — it is extremely important that the passage to the lungs should be most vigilantly guarded; since strangulation would follow the introduction there of any thing but air. Accordingly, the entrance of the glottis is so sensitive, that the approach of the food causes it to close. But lest this security should sometimes fail, we have an additional guard in the epiglottis, which shuts down like a valve upon the orifice. Even with this double precaution, strangulation sometimes follows the act of deglutition. How much oftener would it occur, had not benevolence thus multiplied its vigilant sentinels at the point of danger!

Another illustration of this argument lies in the fact, that many of the organs of animals and plants possess the power, when an exigency requires it, of greatly increasing their action. When, for instance, an unusual quantity of osseous matter is requisite to repair a broken bone, the glands, whose office it is to elaborate that matter, are capable of secreting an extraordinary quantity, until the injury is repaired.

Of an analogous character is the sympathy existing between the different organs, so that when one has an unusual amount of labor to perform, the rest impart of their nervous energy to sustain their overtasked companion. Thus, and thus only, could animals be carried through many of the severe exigencies of their existence. Their organs help one another, just as if they were conscious of one another's necessities, and were prompted by benevolence to aid the weakest.

In like manner, some of the organs possess the power of vicarious secretion; that is, of producing, in peculiar circumstances, secretions that are usually made by other glands. How they can do this, and how they can know when to do it, are among the mysteries of physiology. Nevertheless, the object of this arrangement is most obvious, viz., the continuance of health and life in spite of accidents, which would otherwise prove fatal.

The same vicarious system is manifest in the well-known examples, where the loss of one or more of the senses gives

increased acuteness to the rest. The sense of touch, for instance, in the blind man, has sometimes proved no mean
substitute for eyes; and, indeed, any of the senses by
cultivation, in peculiar exigencies, may be prodigiously
strengthened.

Now, in all these cases, where the vicarious principle is
brought into operation, or sympathy concentrates the power
of many organs in one, or the loss of one organ or sense
quickens the sensibility of the rest, do we not recognize the
prospective care and kindness of infinite benevolence? Do
you say that it merely shows infinite wisdom, which adjusts
means to ends with consummate skill, in order to be sure of
success in its designs? Why, then, I inquire, should these
provisions for trying exigencies in the animal system always
tend to the happiness of the creature? Surely there were
other means at the command of infinite wisdom for securing
the existence of the animal, which would bring misery upon
it instead of happiness. The benevolent tendency of the
design, therefore, proves the benevolent feelings of the
designer.

The extraordinary provisions that are made in some cases
for the multiplication of animals and plants, in order to prevent the extinction of any races, and to give life and happiness to as many animals as can be sustained, is another indication of benevolent care on the part of the Creator. Not
less than five modes of reproduction are known to exist, viz.,
the viviparous, the ovo-viviparous, the oviparous, the gemmiparous, and the fissiparous; and among the lowest families of
animals several of these modes exist in the same species, so
that their extinction, or even deficient multiplication, is
scarcely possible.

The same benevolence is manifested in the power possessed
20

by animals and plants to adapt themselves to different circumstances. Often are they thrown into conditions widely
diverse as to food, temperature, and exposure to chemical
and mechanical agencies, with no possibility on their part of
avoiding them. This is eminently true of man; and were
not animals able to adapt themselves to these various states,
they must perish. True, there are limits to this adaptation;
but they are wide enough to accomplish the great purposes
of existence, and to make us comfortable and happy amid
great changes in our condition. Nor is this power of adaptation among animals limited to their physical nature. Their
mental habits admit of an oscillation equally wide, so that,
ere long, we become happy in a condition which at first was
painful in the extreme. New habits take the place of the old
ones so gradually that we scarcely realize the change.

Now, if this power were not possessed in such a world as
ours, could organic natures not bend at all to circumstances,
constant suffering and premature dissolution would be the
result. The power of adaptation, therefore, looks like the
benevolent provision of a kind Father, who wishes to make
his creatures as happy as he can in the circumstances in
which his wisdom has placed them. Certainly, malevolence,
or indifference to their happiness, would not have introduced
this power of adaptation into their natures; for it is certain
that their continued existence might have been secured in
some other way, had no reference been had to their happiness.

I base my fourth argument for the predominance of benev-
lence, in the arrangements of nature, upon the aggregate
results of the most destructive and terrific agencies which
she employs.

The immediate effects of these agencies are often so

appalling and so unmixed with good, that men view them only
as penal inflictions; or, when the sufferers are unconscious
of guilt, as mysterious dispensations of evil, which need the
light of another world to reconcile with infinite benevolence.
When the tornado or sirocco's hot breath sweeps over the
devoted land ; when the river overflows its banks, and ingulfs
the defenceless inhabitants along its course, or the giant waves
of the ocean roll in upon the devoted shore ; when the heaving earthquake overturns in a moment vast cities, and the
earth swallows them in its bosom ; or when the volcano pours
out its suffocating smoke and its scorching lava, and obliterates from earth the defenceless town, as once Herculaneum
and Pompeii were converted into petrified cities, — in the
midst of such desolating agencies, where can we discover a
gleam of benevolence ?   Not surely in the immediate effects.
But suppose the tornado, the flood, the earthquake, and the
volcano are essential to the preservation of the earth from a
far wider ruin, so that, in fact, while they destroy some property and life, they preserve a far greater amount, and are
essential to such preservation, — why is it not benevolence
that gives a slight play to these terrific elements, while it
checks their wild war so soon as the requisite security has
been obtained ?   When the storm has sufficiently purified the
atmosphere, when the flood has enriched the wide alluvial
fields, and the earthquake and the volcano have given vent to
the pent-up fires in the earth, so that they no longer threaten
to rend a continent asunder, then a restraining power is put
upon them, and they are allowed no more range than is essential to the general good.   We may not, indeed, see why the
good could not be secured without the evil.   But this question
leads to the inquiry, whether the present system of the universe is the best possible ; and that it is so we have the

guaranty of the divine perfections. Those perfections admit the existence of evil; but at the same time they take care that the aggregate result of the greatest evils should be beneficial.

Nor would we limit this position to evils springing out of the nature or the changes of the inanimate world; for some of the severest evils are dependent upon the organization or operation of animate nature. Man, for instance, finds himself often grossly annoyed by some species of the inferior animals, in his comfort, property, and even life. And he wonders why infinite wisdom and benevolence should permit certain species to exist, when they seem fitted only to annoy the rest. But he knows not what he desires when he wishes their extinction. For such is the balance of organic nature, that to strike out even one species, is like removing a link from a chain. Once broken, every other link is affected, and the whole chain lies useless upon the ground. Or, to speak without a figure, if you blot out certain species of animals or plants, you disturb the balance of the whole system of organic nature; nor can you tell where the disturbance thus introduced will end. It may lead to the excessive multiplication of species still more injurious than those you have destroyed. At any rate, since the perfections of the Deity lead to the conclusion that the existing proportion between different species is the best, all things considered, and change in the balance must be injurious, we may conclude, that though noxious animals and plants may produce individual inconvenience and injury, the aggregate effects upon the whole of organic nature are salutary, and, therefore, indicative of benevolence.

Similar reasoning will, I think, apply to the existence of that large class of animals called carnivorous. These are evidently intended to prey upon other animals; and for this

purpose they are provided with weapons for seizing and destroying their prey. It is often extremely painful to a man
of kind feelings to witness the scenes of blood and havoc
which these flesh-eating animals produce. But we forget two
things. The first is, that in order to keep the numbers of animated beings full in the different tribes, it is necessary that
there should be a great excess of numbers created, to meet
all the casualties to which they are exposed ; and that excess
must in some way or other be removed from life. Secondly,
all the enjoyment of the carnivorous races is so much clear
gain to the sum of animal happiness ; for the excess of numbers in the tribes of vegetable feeders suffer no more in being
destroyed by the carnivorous races, than if they died in some
other way ; not so much, indeed, as if they perished by famine. We may safely conclude, then, that even this system
of mutual slaughter, when viewed in all its relations, is the
means, in such a world as ours, of increasing the amount of
enjoyment, and is, therefore, a benevolent provision.

This course of reasoning may be extended, as I judge, to
the greatest of all mortal evils, — I mean death. In the case
of the inferior animals, the amount of physical or mental suffering from this cause is comparatively small. And if they
survive the change of death, surely there is benevolence in so
easy a translation. Or, if they do not exist hereafter, the
stroke of death is a small deduction from the happiness of a
whole life. In man's case, we must not take into the account
the aggravations of death which his own misconduct produces. And aside from these, what a blessing it would be to be
transferred to a more exalted state of being, by an experience
no more painful than that of a Christian dying what may be
called a natural death, by mere decay ! Then, too, how
much greater happiness is the result of a succession of

20 *

beings on earth, than one undying race would enjoy, both because the successive races would be ever passing through novel scenes, which would soon become monotonous to a continuous race, and because, as we have already suggested, a succession of races admits of the existence, at any one time, of a far greater number of species! Then, too, we must not forget the salutary moral influence which man experiences from the expectation of death ; so great, indeed, that without it, it seems doubtful whether the world would be any thing better than a Pandemonium. In making indissoluble the connection between sin and death, therefore, in such a system as the present, benevolence presided with wisdom and justice in the councils of Jehovah.

But in the third lecture I have treated this whole subject so much more fully, that I need not add any thing further in this connection.

I base my fifth and last argument, to prove the predominance of benevolence in the present system of nature, on the fact that good so often results from evil as a natural consequence. Or, to state the argument in another form, good seems generally to be the object or final cause of evil, whereas evil flows only incidentally from good.

This argument scarcely differs from the last, except in the more general form of its statement. That brings forward certain prominent and appalling evils, and endeavors to show that, in striking the balance of their effects, the preponderance is on the side of benevolence. This advances a step farther, and attempts to show that the direct object of evil is to produce good.

It follows, hence, that the examples adduced and elucidated under the last argument are not inappropriate to sustain and illustrate the present. Yet others should be added.

Almost the entire history of medicine and surgery illustrates the manner in which physical evils result in physical good. Indeed, men never resort to the physician, or the surgeon, because their remedies and operations are desirable, but only because they are the necessary means of health and comfort. These means are, indeed, for the most part, of human invention, but not, therefore, the less indicative of the divine intention; for they are founded upon such a constitution in nature as makes it possible to discover remedies for disease and accidents. And the characteristics of nature's constitution are an index of the intentions of its Author.

The severe mental discipline through which the youth must pass, who would attain distinction in learning, affords us an example of intellectual evil resulting in intellectual wealth and happiness. The trial is too severe for many irresolute minds, and they give over the effort, and sink down into a state of indolence and neglect. But he who bears manfully the discipline will at length gather the golden fruit. And he will be satisfied, too, of the wisdom and benevolence of that law of mental progress, which makes it impossible ever to find a royal road to the temple of learning, and which shuts out from that temple all who shrink from the preparatory discipline.

Still more strikingly illustrative of this argument are the evils which men suffer as necessary precursors of moral good. These may be physical or mental; embracing all those experiences that take the name of trials, afflictions, and disappointments. These are often intensely bitter, and they constitute, indeed, the master evils of life. We shudder when we see them coming; and we often writhe in agony when in the furnace. But how many have come out of that furnace purified from base alloy, and ready for the service of God and the world! To do good is henceforth their delight; and they thank God for the severe discipline. When his heavy blows fell upon them, one after another, they felt as if they were the strokes of an incensed Deity. But now they see that they were only the necessary inflictions of infinite love. And they admire the wisdom that could thus educe so much good out of so great evil.

I do not contend that good is always educed from evil in this world, or could be ; but only that, in a plurality of cases, if men improve the evils they suffer as they might, such would be the effect. And if this be admitted, it is sufficient to estab- lish the general principle, that one of the direct objects of evil in this world is to produce individual benefit.

But the converse of this proposition cannot be maintained. We cannot, indeed, deny that evil sometimes results from good ; but never as the direct object of the latter. The effect is only incidental ; that is, not as the main object ; and so a few cases of this sort cannot invalidate the proposition which I defend.

I might multiply much more the arguments furnished by nature to prove a predominance of benevolence in the arrange- ments and operations of the present system of things. But I see no way of escaping the force of those presented, and can- not doubt that all will admit the conclusion. I advance, there- fore to a second proposition, and maintain that *the benevolence exhibited in the present system of nature is not unmixed.*

I mean, by this statement, that the divine benevolence ex- hibited in this world is modified by other perfections. While there is a predominance of benevolence, there are also indi- cations of God's displeasure ; or, at least, his dealings seem to be adapted to restrain and amend a wicked race, rather than to make an innocent and holy race happy ; so that the condition of the human family is far less happy than unmixed benevolence would confer.

In proof of this assertion, I maintain, first, that evil is incidental to every process and event in nature.

This is preëminently true of all those actions which we call vicious. Indeed, they are in themselves evils of the worst kind ; and not only so, but they are connected incidentally with scarcely any thing but evil, though sometimes, as theologians say, overruled for good.

Take next the common operations of nature, which, of course, have no moral character. Their leading design, as we have already seen, is to produce good to sentient beings ; but incidentally they bring much evil. Food is intended for gustatory enjoyment and for nourishment ; but it is often the occasion of severe suffering, and becomes an active poison. Gravity is intended to hold the material universe in a proper balance, and to attach every moving thing on earth to the surface ; but it occasions a vast number of accidents, and a vast amount of suffering. Water and fire are of immense direct benefit ; yet the first buries a vast amount of property and life in its bosom, and the latter is scarcely less injurious in its incidental effects. Indeed, what natural agency can be named, that is not armed with the power to do evil ?

But the same principle extends also to benevolent actions. With our views of divine benevolence, we might expect that virtuous conduct would never be coupled with evil. But this notion does not accord with facts ; for the incidental evils connected with benevolent action are often the most painful in life. Indeed, in how many instances has doing good been rewarded by the loss of life, and under all the aggravations of suffering which malignant ingenuity could invent! And the fact has been, that those whose motives in doing good were the purest have suffered the most. Witness the life and the death of Him who knew no sin, and yet was led as a lamb to the slaughter. Since wickedness in this world is sometimes allowed to have the power of annoying goodness we might expect that the more disinterested the latter, the more malignant and persecuting would be the former, because its own deformity is made more manifest.

But the incidental evils connected with benevolent action are not limited to those resulting from the malice of the wicked. If, for instance, some huge system of iniquity has become incorporated into the very texture of society, benevolence cannot root it out without producing many a severe laceration of individuals, who are incidentally connected with the system, but to whom no blame attaches. The history of the efforts that have been made to substitute Christianity for heathenism and other false religions, is full of examples illustrative of this principle, in conformity with the remarkable declaration of Christ, *Think not that I am come to send peace on earth ; I came not to send peace, but a sword.* Alike prolific of illustrations are all the great attempted reforms which the world has witnessed, whether for delivering religion from human corruptions, or eradicating slavery, or intemperance, or breaking the political yoke of the oppressor. In fine, no reasonable man ought to expect to do much good in this world, without suffering much himself and bringing some incidental suffering upon others.

Now, although the evils that have been described are incidental, they belong to the constitution of this world, and, therefore, show the feelings and intentions of its Author, as much as those effects of his works which appear to be their final causes. But do not such evils, incidental to every event, indicate a feeling in the divine mind different from unmixed benevolence ? Strictly speaking, these evils are not penal inflictions. But they certainly do not show in the Creator a simple desire to promote the happiness of men, by directly conferring it. They rather indicate a necessity, on account of some peculiarity in the character of man, of mingling severity with goodness in the divine conduct towards him.

In thus representing incidental effects as indicative of the feelings of the Deity, I may seem to contradict my reasoning under the first head, where I gave, as proof of God's benevolence, the fact that the direct object of every contrivance is beneficial, and evil only incidental. But I did not mean to intimate that the incidental effects of a contrivance are no index of the feelings of its author, but only that the direct effects show more clearly than the incidental what are his wishes and intentions, especially if the former are the most numerous, important, and striking. Still, incidental effects are never without an object; and where they are evil, as in the case supposed, they indicate other feelings towards men, in the divine mind, than unmixed benevolence. For it is a strange limitation of God's wisdom and power to say, as some do, that the evils could not be prevented.

It may be said, however, that if men only conform to the laws of nature, they will escape all the evils they suffer. On the other hand, I maintain, — and this constitutes my second argument to show that the divine benevolence is not unmixed, — I maintain that the highest virtue and the most consummate prudence cannot avoid all the evils of life.

Such prudence and virtue will not secure any one against many destructive natural agencies and operations to which he is exposed. Miasms productive of fatal disease may contaminate the atmosphere we breathe, unperceived by us; poison may exist in the food which we take as our necessary sustenance ; the mechanical violence of the elements, or of gravity, may crush us ; the lightning may smite us to the earth ; the wild beast may rush from his unnoticed lair as we pass ; or the deadly insect, or serpent, may inject its poison into our blood at an unexpected moment; or the floods may overwhelm, or the fire consume us.

Now, although prudence and virtue may defend us against many evils, they afford no security against such as I have named, in very many instances.   We are often ignorant of their existence or proximity till we become their victims, and suffering, often intense, is the consequence.   Indeed, the greatest of all physical evils — I mean death — is as sure to visit every son and daughter of Adam as any event can be ; and nothing but insanity, or its religious synonyme, fanaticism, has ever pretended to be proof against disease and death.   You cannot, indeed, point out any particular organ or agency, whose direct object is to produce disease and death ; but they are nevertheless the inevitable result of organic operations and agencies in such a world as this.

It will be said, perhaps, that the good resulting to the whole from even the most severe of these sufferings, overbalances the evil, and therefore they are indications of benevolence in such a world as ours.   True, as things are, this may be so. But the question is, Why is there such a constitution given to nature as made it necessary to introduce disease, accident, and death ?   Would not unmixed benevolence have conferred the good, but have withheld the evil ?   Had there not been something in man's character requiring the discipline of trials, would pure benevolence have sent them ?   At least, we should suppose that they might all have been avoided by prudence and virtue.   Why should benevolence make such severe drawbacks upon the happiness even of the virtuous,

if something were not radically wrong in the human constitution ?

Thirdly. The great sterility of so large a part of the earth,
and the necessity of severe bodily labor to secure sustenance
from it, show us that the benevolence exhibited in nature and
in man's condition is not unmixed. Though some limited
regions are exuberantly fertile, the larger part of the earth
yields up even a mere sustenance only after the severest
labor. And the vast majority of the race can do nothing
more than to obtain food for the body. The artificial state of
most societies does, indeed, keep the lower classes much more
depressed than a better state of the world would bring them
into ; but at the best, nature unites with revelation in attesting
the truth of the sentence passed upon man — *In the sweat of
thy face shalt thou eat thy bread.*

Nor is this necessity for severe labor confined to the cultivation of the earth, but extends to all kinds of human pursuits. Success, as a general fact, can be secured only by
vigorous industry ; and often, in spite of their most honest and
persevering efforts, men fail of securing even a competence
for the support of themselves and their dependants.

Some will say that all this arises from a necessity in the
very nature of the case. But does not such a view limit the
divine power and wisdom ? Could not God have prepared a
world more paradisiacal than the present, where the earth
should spontaneously yield her fruits, and pour out her hidden
treasures at man's feet ? Who will deny this ? Why, then,
has he not done it ? Because obviously a race so prone to
evil as man, so incapable of maintaining his integrity in the
lap of ease and indulgence, needs all this severe discipline to
keep him where he ought to be. Here, then, we see a reason
why God must mingle seeming severity with benevolence.

21

The same thing is seen, in the fourth place, in the confined and depressed condition of the human mind in this world, and in the multiplied obstacles in the way of its cultivation and enlargement.

What a clog to the intellect is a body governed by gross appetites, and often stopping the ingress of truth, or perverting its aspect, by disordered and imperfect senses! Nearly one third of the time must that intellect sink into oblivion, while sleep recruits the physical powers. And nearly another third of life must be given to the wants of the body ; and as we have seen, the great mass of men are obliged to devote nearly their whole time to serve the necessary wants of the body. What an incalculable waste of mind does the world exhibit! And even when all artificial and unnecessary obstructions are taken out of the way, what an immense waste must it always present, while in so gross a corporeal tenement! for were it free to exhibit its true nature, we cannot doubt its power of unwearied and incessant activity. And such might have been its condition here, had it pleased infinite wisdom and benevolence. But what unmixed benevolence would have prompted, perfect wisdom would not permit to fallen man.

I feel confident that my first two propositions are established, viz., that there is a predominance of benevolence in the arrangements and operations of the present world, and yet that it is not unmixed benevolence. I advance to a third proposition, which asserts that *the same mixed system of good and evil, which now exists, has always prevailed since the earth was inhabited.*

Geology shows us the true succession of events since the first appearance of organic beings on the globe, but no chronological dates are registered on the rocks. And it is only by observing processes in existing nature, analogous to those whose record is engraven on the solid strata, that we can infer that the years since life first appeared on the surface must have been very many. But however far back in the hoary past that event occurred, we have indisputable evidence that the same laws then controlled the operations of nature as now, and the result was the same mixture of good and evil.

In the crystalline structure, and in the perfect crystals of the older rocks, we learn the laws which predominated at their production. And we find that the same chemical, electrical, and electro-magnetical influences presided over their formation as are now exhibited in the laboratory of the chemist or the laboratory of nature. Now, these crystals conduct us back much farther than the dawn of terrestrial life, though similar ones, and produced by the same laws, are found through the whole series of rocks, from the oldest to the newest. And I might appeal to many other facts in the earth's history, which demonstrate an identity between the physical laws that have controlled nature's processes in every period of past time.

We have evidence, also, of the same identity in the laws of life, or organic laws. In the anatomical structure of the earliest animals and plants we find the same general type that pervades the present creation, modified only, as it now is, to meet peculiar circumstances. This is true not only of the osseous, but also of the muscular, circulatory, nervous, lymphatic, and nutritive organs. Hence, as we might expect, we have evidence of the prevalence of the same functional or physiological laws then, as now. Respiration was performed, as it now is, and with the same effects. Vegetable and animal food was then, as now, masticated, digested, and assimilated ; and since animals possessed the same senses, we infer that their habits were essentially the same. There is not, indeed, any evidence that ancient animals and plants exhibited any peculiarities of structure or function, save those necessary to adapt them to the circumstances, so unlike the present, in many respects, in which they lived.

We are sure, also, that death has ever reigned over all organic nature. It has always been produced by the same causes, and attended by the same suffering. And its ravages were repaired by the same system of reproduction as now exists. All this we might presume would be the case, upon the discovery of an identity of laws, mechanical, chemical, and organic ; but we have direct evidence, also, in the countless remains of animals and plants entombed in the rocks, more than twenty thousand species of which have been disinterred by naturalists and described.

I might multiply facts almost without number to sustain the position, that the same mixed system has ever prevailed upon the globe ; for geology is full of the details. But in a subsequent lecture, the subject will be more amply discussed.

Such are the facts respecting the divine benevolence, as they are presented in the volume of nature. Though benevolence decidedly predominates, it is modified by other divine attributes, and ever has been, since organic existence began upon the globe. Let us now, *in the fourth place, see what inferences are fairly deducible from the whole subject.* For those inferences, if I mistake not, will not only clear away every cloud from the divine benevolence, but throw much light upon man's condition.

In the first place, the subject shows us that the world is not in a state of retribution.

As a general fact, virtue is to some extent rewarded, and vice to some extent punished. But it is not always so. Indeed, the picture is sometimes reversed apparently; and the good are afflicted because they do good, and the wicked triumph because they do evil. Evil abounds, but it is not so distributed as righteous retribution would award it; neither is good. Since, therefore, God's justice must be infinitely perfect, there must be some other object for the prevalence of good and evil in the world besides righteous retribution.

Secondly. We learn from the subject that the world is in a fallen condition.

I mean, that man has fallen from holiness and happiness. For the world is evidently not such a world as infinite wisdom and benevolence would prepare for a being perfectly holy and happy. Philosophize as we may, we cannot discover any reason why the abode of such a being should be filled with evils of almost every name — evils which the most consummate prudence and the most elevated virtue cannot wholly avoid — evils which often come upon the good man because he is eminent for holiness. But if man has fallen from original holiness and happiness by transgression, we might expect just such a world to be fitted up for his residence, because evil is indissolubly linked to sin, perhaps in the very nature of things, certainly by divine appointment. We know that it brings a curse upon every thing with which it is connected; and here we see a reason for the blight that has marred some of the fairest features of nature, and introduced pain and suffering into the animal frame, and brought a cloud over man's noble intellect, and hebetude over his moral powers. Such a fallen condition will explain what no other supposition can, viz., the clouded, fettered, and depressed condition of all organic nature.

21 *

Yet, thirdly. We should not infer that man's condition was hopeless, but rather that mercy might be in store for him.

The very fact that the world is not in a state of retribution would seem to afford hope that God had other purposes than punishment in allowing evil to be introduced. And then the vast predominance of benevolence and happiness around us cannot but inspire hope for the fallen.

This will be still more manifest if we infer, and can show, fourthly, that the world is in a state of probation or trial.

By this I mean that men are placed in a condition for the trial and discipline of their characters, in order to fit them for a higher state. If fallen and depraved, they need to pass through such a discipline before they can be prepared for that higher condition. And surely no one can observe the scenes through which all pass, without being struck with their eminent adaptedness to train man to virtue and holiness. Until we have been pupils for a time in this school, we are not fit even for the successive states in this life into which we pass; much less for a higher condition. But there is a marvellous power in this discipline to prepare us for both, as vast multitudes have testified while they lived and when they died. Even death seems, so far as we can see, to be the only means by which a sinful being can be delivered from his stains; and the dread of this terrific evil is one of the most powerful restraints upon vice, and stimulants to virtue. There is, in fact, no condition in which man is placed, no good or evil that he meets, which is not eminently adapted, if rightly improved, to discipline and strengthen his virtue. Hence we cannot doubt that this is the grand object of the present arrangements of the world. True, if misimproved, the same means become only a discipline in vice. But this is only in conformity with a general principle of the divine government, that the things which rightly used are highly salutary, are proportionably injurious when perverted.

Fifthly. The subject shows us a reason why suffering and death prevailed in this world long before man's existence.

God foresaw — I will not say foreordained, though he certainly permitted it — that man would transgress; and, therefore, he made a world adapted to a sinful fallen being, rather than to one pure and holy. If he had adapted it to an unfallen being, and then changed it upon his apostasy, that change must have amounted to a new creation. For, as I have endeavored to show in a previous lecture, (Lecture III.,) the whole constitution of our world, and even its relations to other worlds, must have been altered to fit it for a being who had sinned. To have introduced such a one into a world fitted up for the perfectly holy, would have been a curse instead of a blessing. It was benevolence on the part of God to allow evil to abound in a world which was to be the residence of a sinful creature ; for the discipline of such a state was the only chance of his being rescued from the power of sin, and restored to the divine favor.

It may be thought, however, inconsistent with divine benevolence to place the inferior, irrational animals in a condition of suffering because man would transgress, and thus punish creatures incapable of sinning for his transgression.

Animals do, indeed, suffer in such a world as ours ; but not as a punishment for their own or man's sin. The only question is, Do they suffer so much that their existence is not a blessing ? Surely experience will decide, without inquiring as to their future existence, that their enjoyments, as a general fact, vastly outweigh their sufferings ; and hence their existence indicates benevolence. It should also be recollected that their natures are adapted to a world of sin and death, and they are doubtless more happy here than they would be in a different condition, which might be more favorable to unfallen accountable beings.

Finally. This subject harmonizes infinite and perfect benevolence in God with the existence of evil on earth.

This is the grand problem of theology; and though I would not say that our reasoning clears it of all difficulties, yet it does seem to me that, by letting the light of this subject fall upon the question, we come nearer to its solution than by viewing it in any other aspect. For this subject shows us that benevolence decidedly predominates in all the arrangements of the material universe, and then it assigns good reasons why this benevolence is not unmixed; in other words, why severity is sometimes mingled with goodness. It shows us that God, with a prospective view of man's sin, adapted the world to a fallen being; making it, instead of a place of unmingled happiness, a state of trial and discipline; not as a full punishment, (for that is reserved to a future state,) but as an essential means of delivering this immortal being from his ruin and misery, and of fitting him for future and endless holiness and happiness. Thus, instead of indicating indifference or malevolence in God, because he introduced evil into the world, it is a striking evidence of his benevolence. Such a plan is, in fact, the conjoint result of infinite wisdom and benevolence for rescuing the miserable and the lost. Had God placed such a being in a world adapted to one perfectly holy, his sufferings would have been vastly greater, and his rescue hopeless.

Thus far do both reason and revelation conduct us in a plain path; and that, probably, is as far as is necessary for all the purposes of religion. Up to this point, infinite benevolence pours its radiance upon the path, and we see good reasons for the evils incident to this life; nay, we see that they are the result of that same benevolence which strews the way with blessings; that, in fact, they are only necessary means of the greatest blessings. I am aware that there is a question lying farther back, in the outskirts of metaphysical theology, which still remains unanswered, and probably never can be settled in this world, because some of its elements are beyond our reach. The inquisitive mind asks why it was necessary for infinite wisdom and power to introduce evil, or allow it to be introduced, into any system of created things. Could not such natures have been bestowed upon creatures, that good only might have been their portion? A plausible answer is, that evil exists because it can ultimately be made subservient of greater good, taking the whole universe into account, than another system. Certainly to fallen man we have reason to believe natural evils are the grand means of his highest good; and hence we derive an argument for the same conclusion in respect to the whole system of evil. Indeed, such are the divine attributes, that it is absurd to suppose God would create any system which was not the best possible in existing circumstances. But even though we cannot solve these questions in their abstract form, and as applied to the whole creation, it is sufficient for every practical purpose of religion if we can show, as we have endeavored to do in this lecture, how the present system of the world for a fallen being illustrates, instead of disproving, the divine benevolence.

Here, then, is the resolution of some of the darkest enigmas of human existence, which philosophy, unaided by revelation, has never solved. Here we get hold of the thread that conducts us through the most crooked labyrinths of life,

and enables us to let into the deepest dungeons of despondency and doubt, the light of hope and of heaven.

Here, too, we find the powerful glass by which we can
pierce the clouds that have so long obscured the full-orbed
splendors of the divine benevolence. To some, indeed, —
and they sagacious philosophers, — that cloud has seemed
surcharged only with vengeance. And even to those who
have caught occasional glimpses of the noble orb behind, the
cloud over its face has always seemed to be tinged with
some angry rays. Indeed, so long as this is a sinful state,
justice will not allow all the glories of the divine goodness to
be revealed. And yet, through the glass which philosophy
and faith have put into our hands, we can see that the disk
is a full-orbed circle, and that no spots mar and darken its
clear surface. How gloriously, then, when all those clouds
shall have passed away, and the last taint of evil shall have
been blotted out by the final conflagration, shall that sun, in
the new heavens, send down its light and heat upon the new
earth, wherein dwelleth righteousness!

On the other hand, how sad the prospect which the analogies of this subject open before him who misimproves his
earthly probation, and goes out of the world unprepared for a
higher and purer state of existence! If we can see reasons
why on earth God should mingle goodness and severity in
this man's lot, we can also see reasons why the manifestations of benevolence should all be withdrawn when he passes
into a state of retribution. For if an individual can resist the
mighty influences for good which the present state of discipline affords, and only become worse under them all, his case
is utterly hopeless, and Heaven can do no more, consistently
with the eternal principles of the divine government, to save

nim.   Infinite benevolence gives him over, and no longer
nolds back the sword of retributive justice.   Nay, the justice
which inflicts the punishment is only benevolence in another
form.   And this it is that makes the infliction intolerable.
How much more terrible to the wayward child are the blows
inflicted by a weeping, affectionate father, than if received
from an enemy!   God is that affectionate Father; and he
punishes only because he loves the universe more than the
individual; and he has exhausted the stores of infinite mercy
in vain to save him.   Wicked men sometimes tell us that they
are not afraid to trust themselves in the hands of infinite benevolence ; whereas it is eminently this quality of the divine
character which, above all others, they have reason to fear.
For if, even in this world of probation and hope, God finds it
necessary to mingle so much severity with goodness, what
but a cup of unmingled bitterness shall be put into his hands
who goes into eternity unrenewed and unpardoned, and finds
that even infinite benevolence has become his eternal enemy!

LECTURE VIII.

UNITY OF THE DIVINE PLAN AND OPERATION IN ALL AGES OF THE WORLD'S HISTORY.

CONTRIVANCE, adaptation, and design are some of the most striking features of the natural world. They are obvious throughout the whole range of creation, in the minutest as well as in the most magnificent objects ; in the most complicated as well as in the most simple. So universally present are they, that whenever we meet with any thing in nature which seems imperfectly adapted to other objects, as the organ of an animal or plant, which exhibits malformation, it excites general attention, and the mere child need not be told that, in its want of adaptation to other objects, it is an exception in the natural world.

In order to illustrate what I mean by contrivance, adaptation, and design, let me refer to a familiar example — the human eye. Made up of three coats and three humors, of solids and fluids, of nerves, blood-vessels, and muscles, and rivalling the most perfect optical instrument, it must have required the most consummate contrivance to give the requisite quantity and position to parts so numerous and unlike, for producing the phenomena of vision. Yet how perfectly it is done ! How few, out of the hundreds of millions of eyes of men and other animals, fail of vision through any natural defect !

No less marvellous are the adaptations of the eye. In order to be adapted to the wonderful effect which we call light, its coats and humors must be transparent, and possess a certain density and opacity, that the rays may form an image on the retina. Yet to prevent confusion in the image, the transparency must be confined to the central parts of the eye, and a dark plexus of veins and muscles must be so situated as to absorb the scattering rays. In order to adapt the eye to different distances, and to the greater or less intensity of the light, delicate muscles must be so situated as to contract and dilate the pupil, and lengthen and shorten the axis. That the eye might be directed to different objects, strong muscles must be attached to its posterior surface; and that the eyelid might defend it from injuries in front, a very peculiar muscle must give it power to close. No less perfect is the adaptation of the eye to the atmosphere, or, rather, there is a mutual adaptation; and it is as proper to say that the atmosphere is adapted to the eye, as that the eye is adapted to the atmosphere. In like manner, there is a striking relation between the eye and the sun and other heavenly bodies, and between the eye and day and night; so that we cannot doubt but they were made for one another. We might, indeed, extend the relations of the eye to every object in the universe; and the same may be said of every organ of plants and animals. The adaptation between them is as wide as creation. And it is the wonderful harmony between so many millions of objects that makes us feel that infinite wisdom alone could have produced it.

The design of the multiplied contrivances and adaptations exhibited by the eye is too obvious to need a formal statement. Comparatively few understand the wonderful mechanism of the eye; but we should consider it proof of idiotism, or insanity, for the weakest mind to doubt what is the object of the eye. This is, to be sure, a striking example. But

22

out of the many organs of animals, how few are there of which we do not see the design ! And as the subject is more examined, the few excepted cases are made still fewer. They are more numerous in plants, because we cannot so well understand them, and because of their microscopic little-ness. They are so few, however, throughout all nature, that they never produce a doubt that, for every individual thing in creation, there is a distinct object. If we confine our views to the most simple parts of matter, we can see design in them. If we take a wider view, and examine those minor systems which are produced by the grouping of the elements of matter, we shall see design there ; and if we rise still higher in our examination, and compare systems still more extensive, until we group all material things, wise and beauti-ful design is still inscribed upon all. In fine, creation is but a series of harmonies, wheel within wheel, in countless vari-ety, yet all forming one vast and perfect machine. Examine nature as widely and as minutely as we may, we never find one part clashing with another part; no laws, governing one portion of creation, different from those governing the others. Amid nature's infinitely diversified productions and opera-tions we find but one original model or pattern. As Dr. Paley finely expresses it, " We never get amongst such origi-nal or totally different modes of existence as to indicate that we are come into the province of a different Creator, or under the direction of a different will." All appears to have been the work of one mighty mind, capable of devising and creat-ing the vast system so perfectly that every part shall beauti-fully harmonize with every other part ; a mind capable of holding in its capacious grasp at once the entire system, and seeing the relation and dependence of all its parts, from the minutest atom up to the mightiest world. In short, the unity

of design which pervades all creation is perfect, more so
than we witness in the most finished machine of human
construction ; for

> "In human works, though labored on with pain,
> A thousand movements scarce one object gain ;
> In God's, one single can its end produce,
> Yet serves to second too some other use."

Such are the wonderful contrivance, adaptation, and design
which the material world every where exhibits.   But the
geologist carries us back through periods of immense antiquity, and digs out from the deep strata evidences of other
systems of organic life, which have flourished and passed
away; other economies, which have existed on the globe
anterior to the present.   And how was it with these ?   Had
they any relation to the existing system ?   Were they governed by different laws, or are they all but parts of one great
and harmonious system, embracing the whole of the earth's
past duration ?   We could not decide these questions beforehand ; but geology brings to light unequivocal evidence that
the latter supposition is the true one ; that is, in the language
of the poet, —

> "All are but parts of one stupendous whole,
> Whose body nature is, and God the soul."

To present the evidence of this conclusion will be my object
in this lecture.

*In the first place, the laws of chemistry and crystallography,
electricity and magnetism, have ever been the same in all past
conditions of the earth.*

Chemistry has attained to such a degree of perfection that

the analyst can now determine the composition of the various vegetable, animal, and mineral substances which he meets, with an extreme degree of accuracy. In many instances, he can do this in two ways. He can always separate the elements which exist in a compound, and ascertain their relative quantity ; and this is called *analysis.* And sometimes he can take those elements and cause them to unite, so as to form a particular compound ; and this is called *synthesis.* By these methods he has ascertained that, amid the vast variety of substances in nature, there are only about sixty-four which cannot be reduced to a more simple form, and are therefore called *elements*, or simple substances. Now, the chemist finds that, when these elements unite to form compounds, certain fixed laws are invariably followed. They combine in definite quantities, which are always the same, or some multiple of the same weight ; so that each element has its peculiar and invariable combining weight ; and it cannot be made to combine in any other proportion. You may mix two or more elements together in any proportion, but it is only a certain definite quantity of each that will combine, while the rest will remain in excess. Hence the same compound substance, from whatever part of the world it comes, or under however diverse circumstances produced, consists of the same ingredients in the same proportion. These laws are followed with mathematical precision, and we have reason to believe that the same compound substance, produced in different parts of the world, never differs in its composition by the smallest conceivable particle. Indeed, with the exception of the planetary motions and crystallography, chemical combination is the most perfect example of practical mathematics to be found in nature.

Such are the laws which the chemist finds invariably to

regulate all the changes that now take place in the constitution
of bodies. What evidence is there that the same laws have
ever prevailed ? In the rocks we have chemical compounds,
produced in all ages of the world's history, since fire and
water began to form solid masses. Now, these may be, and
have been, analyzed ; and the same laws of definite proportion in the ingredients, which now operate, are found to have
controlled their formation. The oldest granite and gneiss,
which must have been the earliest rocks produced, are just as
invariable in their composition as the most recent salt formed
in the laboratory. And the same is true of the silicates, the
carbonates, the sulphates, the oxides, chlorides, fluorides, and
other compounds which constitute the rocks of different ages.
We never find any produced under the operation of different laws.

Now, the almost invariable opinion among chemists is, that
the reason why the elements unite thus definitely is, that they
are in different electrical states, and therefore attract one
another. Hence the most important laws of electricity have
been coeval with those of chemistry ; indeed, they are identical ; nor can we doubt, if such be the fact, that every other
electrical law has remained unchanged from the beginning.
And from the intimate connection, if not complete identity,
between electricity and magnetism, it is impossible to doubt
that the laws which regulate the latter are of equal antiquity
with those of the former. Indeed, we find evidence in all the
rocks, especially those which are prismatic and concretionary,
of the active influence of galvanism and electro-magnetism in
their production.

The reasoning is equally decisive to prove the unchanging
character of the laws which regulate the formation of crystals.
The chemist finds that the same substance, when it crystal-

22 *

lizes, invariably takes the same geometrical forms. The nucleus or primary form, with a few exceptions, of no importance in the present argument, to which all these secondary forms may be reduced by change, is one particular solid, with unvarying angles; and all the secondary forms, built upon the primary, correspond in their angles. In short, in crystallography we have another example of perfect practical mathematics, as perfect as the theory.

Now, the oldest rocks in the globe contain crystals, and so do the rocks of all ages, sometimes of the same kind as those produced in the chemist's laboratory. And they are found to correspond precisely. It matters not whether they were the produce of nature's laboratory countless ages ago, or of the skill of the nineteenth century, — the same mathematics ruled in their formation with a precision which infinite wisdom alone could secure.

In the second place, the laws of meteorology have ever been the same as at present.

Under meteorological laws I include all atmospheric phenomena. And although we have no direct proof from geology in respect to the more rare of these phenomena, such as the aurora borealis and australis, and transient meteors, yet in respect to the existence of clouds, wind, and rain, the evidence is quite striking. In several places in Europe, and in many in this country, are found, upon layers of the new red sandstone, the distinct impressions of rain drops, made when the rock was fine mud. They correspond precisely with the indentations which falling rain-drops now make upon mud, and they show us that the phenomena of clouds and storms existed in that remote period, and that the vapor was condensed as at present. In the fact that the animals entombed in the rocks of various ages are found to have had organs of

respiration, we also infer the existence of an atmosphere analogous to that which we now breathe. The rain-drops enable
us to proceed one step farther; for often they are elongated
in one direction, showing that they struck the ground obliquely,
doubtless in consequence of wind. In short, the facts stated
enable us to infer, with strong probability, that atmospheric
phenomena were then essentially the same as at present; and
analogy leads us to a similar conclusion as to all the past periods of the world's history, certainly since animals were placed
upon it. What a curious register do these rain-drops present
us! an engraving on stone of a shower that fell thousands
and thousands of ages ago! They often become, too, an
anemoscope, pointing out the direction of the wind, while the
petrified surface shows us just how many drops fell, quite as
accurately as the most delicate pluviameter. What events in
the earth's pre-Adamic history would seem less likely to come
down to us than the pattering of a shower?

*In the third place, the agents of geological change appear
to have been always the same on the earth.*

Whoever goes into a careful examination of the rocks will
soon become satisfied that no fragment of them all remains in
the condition in which it was originally created. Whatever
was the original form in which matter was produced, there is
no longer any example of it to be found. The evidence of
these changes is as strong almost as that constant changes are
going on in human society. And we find them constantly
progressing among the rocks, as well as among men; nor do
the agents by which they are produced appear to have been
ever different from those now in operation. The two most
important are heat and water; and it is doubtful whether there
is a single particle of the globe which has not experienced the
metamorphic action of the one or the other. Indeed, it is

nearly certain that every portion of the globe has been melted, if not volatilized. All the unstratified rocks have certainly been fused, and probably all the stratified rocks originated from the unstratified, and have been modified by water and heat. In many of these rocks, especially the oldest, we perceive evidence of the joint action of both these agents. Evidently they were once aqueous deposits; but they appear to have been subsequently subjected to powerful heat. As we ascend on the scale of the stratified rocks, the marks of fire diminish, and those of water multiply, so that the latest are mere mechanical or chemical depositions from water.

In these facts, then, we see proof that heat and water have been the chief agents of geological change since the first formation of a solid crust on the globe ; for some of the rocks now accessible, as already stated, date their origin at that early period. We might also trace back the agency of heat much farther, if the hypothesis adopted by not a few eminent geologists be true, which supposes the earth to have been once in a gaseous state from intense heat. But to press this point will add very little to my argument, even could I sustain it by plausible reasoning. I will only say, that, so far as we know any thing of the state of the earth previous to the consolidation of its crust, heat appears to have been the chief agent concerned in its geological changes.

Among other agencies of less importance, that have always operated geologically, is gravity. Its chief effect, at present is to bring the earth's surface nearer and nearer to a level, by causing the materials, which other agencies have loosened from its salient parts, to subside into its cavities and valleys It also condenses many substances from a gaseous to a liquid or solid state, especially those deep in the earth's crust, and thus brings the particles more within the reach of cohesive

attraction and chemical affinity, often changing the constitution, and always the solidity, of bodies. And in the position
of the ancient mechanical rocks, occupying as they do the
former basins of the surface, and in the superior consolidation of the earlier strata, we find proof of the action of gravity
in all past geological time.

Electricity too, in the form of galvanism, has never been
idle. We have reason to think that it operates at this moment
in accumulating metallic ores in veins; and this segregation
appears to have operated in all ages, not only in filling veins,
but also, probably, in giving a laminated character and jointed
structure to mountains of slate, as well as a concretionary
and prismatic form to others.

Last, though not least, we may reckon among the agents
of geological change the forces of cohesion and affinity.
When water and heat, gravity and galvanism, have brought
the atoms of bodies into a proper state, these agents are always ready to change their form and constitution; and they
have ever been at hand to operate by the same laws, and we
witness their effects in the oldest as well as the newest rocks
found in the earth's crust. This point, however, has been
sufficiently considered, when treating of the unvarying uniformity of the laws of chemistry and crystallography.

But though the nature of the agencies above considered has
never changed, the intensity or amount of their action has
varied; how much is a point not yet settled among geologists.
Some regard that intensity, as it has existed during the present
or alluvial period, as a standard for all preceding periods;
that is, the intensity of these forces has never varied more
during any period of the earth's history than it has since the
alluvial period commenced. Most geologists, however, regard
this as an extreme opinion, and think they see evidence in

geology of a far greater intensity in these agencies in past periods than exists at present. They think they have proof that the world was once only a molten mass of matter, and some evidence that previously it was in a state of vapor. They believe that vast mountains, and even continents, have sometimes been thrown up from the ocean's bed by a single mighty paroxysmal effort; and such effects they know to be far greater than the causes of change now in operation can produce, without a vast increase of their intensity. But this question need neither be discussed nor decided for the sake of my present argument, since my object is to prove an identity in the nature and laws, not in the intensity, of geological agencies.

In the fourth place, the laws of zoölogy and botany have always been the same on the globe.

An examination of the animals now living, amounting to some hundred thousand species, perhaps to one or two millions, shows that they may be arranged in four great classes. The first class embraces the vertebral animals, distinguished by having a vertebral column, or back-bone, a regular skeleton, and a regular nervous system. It comprehends all the quadrupeds and bipeds, with man at their head, and is much superior to all other classes in complexity of organization and strength of the mental powers. The second class embraces the mollusks, or animals inhabiting shells. They are destitute of a spinal marrow, and for the most part their muscles are attached to the external covering, called the shell, although this shell is sometimes internal. The third class are called articulated animals, having envelopes connected by annulated plates, or rings. It includes such animals as the lobster, bloodsucker, spider, and insects generally. The fourth class have a radiated structure, and often resemble plants, or their habitation is a stony structure.   Hence they are sometimes called zoöphytes, which means *animal plants ;* or lithophytes, which means *stony plants.*   They swarm in the ocean, and some of them build up those extensive stony structures called coral reefs.

Now, if we examine the descriptions of the organic remains in the rocks, we find that in all ages of the world these four great classes of animals have existed.   But in the earliest times, the three last classes — the mollusks, the articulated, and the radiated tribes — vastly preponderated, while the vertebral class had only a few representatives ; and it is not till we rise as high as the new red sandstone, that we meet with any, except fishes, save a few batrachians in the old red sandstone, and the carboniferous group, detected alone by their tracks.   Then the reptiles began to appear in abundance, with tortoises and enormous birds of a low organization, but no mammiferous animal is found, until we reach the oölite ; and scarcely any till we rise to the tertiary strata, when they became abundant ; but not so numerous as at present, though for the most part of larger size.   Thus we find that the more perfect animals have been developed gradually, becoming more and more complex as we rise on the scale of the rocks. But in the three other classes, there does not appear to have been much advance upon the original types, although in numbers and variety there has been a great increase.

The plants now growing upon the globe, amounting probably to nearly one hundred thousand species, are divided into two great classes, by a very decided character.   Some of them have distinct flowers, and others are destitute of them. The former are called phenogamian, or flowering plants ; and the latter cryptogamian, or flowerless plants.

At present, the flowering plants very much predominate in

the flora of every country. But in the earliest periods of organic existence, the reverse was the case. We find, indeed but very few flowering plants, and these of a character somewhat intermediate between flowering and flowerless; such as the coniferæ and cycadeæ, including the pine tribe. A few palms appeared almost as early, and some other monocotyledons. But most of the dicotyledons did not appear till the tertiary period, where more than two hundred species have been found. Of the three hundred species found in and beneath the carboniferous group, two thirds are tree ferns, or gigantic equisetaceæ. More than one third of the entire flora of the secondary formation consists of cycadeæ; whereas, this family of plants forms not more than the two thousandth part of the existing flora. In short, we find the more perfect plants as well as animals to be few in the earliest periods, and to have been gradually introduced up to the present time. But as to the flowerless plants, most of them seem to have been as perfect at first as they now are.

These facts teach us conclusively that the outlines of organic life on the globe have always been the same; that the great classes of animals and plants have always had their representatives, and that the variations which have been introduced, have been merely adaptations to the varying condition of the earth's surface. The higher and more complex natures, both of animals and plants, were not introduced at first, because the surface was not adapted to their existence; and they were brought in only as circumstances, favorable to their development, prepared the way.

There is another fact of great interest on this subject. Even a cursory examination of the animals and plants now on the globe, shows such a gradation of their characters that they form a sort of chain, extending from the most to the least per-

fect species.   But we see at once that the links of this chain
are of very unequal length ; or, rather, that there are in some
instances wide intervals between the nearest species, as if one
or more links had dropped out.   How remarkable that some
of these lost links should be found among the fossil species !
I will refer to a few examples.

Among existing animals no genera or tribes are more widely
separated than those with thick skins, denominated pachyder-
mata ; such as the rhinoceros and the elephant.   But among
the fossil animals of the tertiary strata, this tribe of animals
was much more common ; and many of them fill up the
blanks in the existing families, and thus render more perfect
and uniform the great chain of being which binds together
into one great system the present and past periods of organic
life.

A similar case occurs among fossil plants.   In tropical climates we find a few species — not much over twenty — of a
singular family of plants, the cycadeæ connecting the great families of coniferæ, or dicotyledons, with the palms, which are mo-
nocotyledonous, and the ferns, which are acotyledonous.   The
chasm, however, between those great and dissimilar classes
of plants is but imperfectly filled by the few living species of
cycadeæ.   But of the fossil species hitherto found above the
coal formation, almost one half are cycadeæ ; so that here,
too, the lost links of the chain are supplied.

" Facts like these," says Dr. Buckland, " are inestimably
precious to the natural theologian, for they identify, as it
were, the Artificer, by details of manipulation throughout his
works.   They appeal to the physiologist, in language more
commanding than human eloquence ; the voice of very stocks
and stones, that have been buried for countless ages in the
deep recesses of the earth, proclaiming the universal agency

23

of one all-directing, all-sustaining Creator, in whose will and power these harmonious systems originated, and by whose universal providence they are, and have at all times been, maintained." — *Bridgewater Treatise*, vol. i. p. 502.

One other fact, showing the identity of former zoölogical laws with those which now prevail, must not be omitted. I refer to the existence on the globe in all past periods of organic life of the two great classes of carnivorous and herbivorous animals; and they have always existed, too, in about the same proportion. To the harmony and happiness of the present system, we know that the existence and proper relative number of these different classes are indispensable. For in order that the greatest possible number of animals that live on vegetable food should exist, they must possess the power of rapid multiplication, so that there should be born a much larger number than is necessary to people the earth. But if there existed no carnivorous races to keep in check this redundancy of population, the world would soon become so filled with the herbivorous races that famine would be the consequence, and thus a much greater amount of suffering result than the sudden death inflicted by carnivorous races now produces. To preserve, then, a proper balance between the different species is, doubtless, the object of the creation of the carnivorous. This system has been aptly denominated " the police of nature." And we find it to have always existed. The earliest vertebral animals — the sauroid fishes and sharks — were of this description. The sharks have always lived, but the sauroid fishes became less numerous when other marine saurians were created; and when they both nearly disappeared, during the tertiary period, other predaceous families were introduced, more like those now in existence.

The history of the mollusks, or animals inhabiting shells,

furnishes us with an example still more striking.   These animals, as they now exist, are divisible into the two great classes of carnivorous and herbivorous species, being distinguished by their anatomical structure ; and so has it ever been.   In the fossiliferous rocks below the tertiary, we find immense numbers of nautili, ammonites, and other kindred genera of polythalamous shells, called cephalopods, which were all carnivorous.   And when they nearly disappeared with the cretaceous period, there was created another race with carnivorous propensities and organs, called trachelipods ; and those continue still to swarm in the ocean.   Had they not appeared when the cephalopods passed away, the herbivorous tribes would have multiplied to such an extent as ultimately to destroy marine vegetation, and bring on famine among themselves.

These examples are sufficient to prove the existence of the carnivorous and herbivorous races in all ages and in about the same relative numbers.   And it certainly furnishes most decisive evidence of the oneness of all these systems of organic life on the globe.

In the fifth place, the laws of anatomy have always been the same since organic structures began to exist.

It had long been known that the organs of animals were beautifully adapted to perform the functions for which they were intended.   But it was not till the investigations of Baron Cuvier, within the last half century, that it was known how mathematically exact is the relation between the different parts of the animal frame, nor how precise are the laws of variation in the different species, by which they are fitted to different elements, climates, and food.   It is now well known, that each animal structure contains a perfect system of correlation, and yet the whole forms a harmonious part of the entire animal system on the globe. But the language of Cuvier himself will best elucidate this subject, so far as it is capable of popular explanation.

"Every organized individual," says he, "forms an entire system of its own; all the parts of which mutually correspond, and concur to produce a certain definite purpose, by reciprocal reaction, or by combining towards the same end. Hence none of these separate parts can change their forms without a corresponding change in the other parts of the same animal, and consequently each of these parts, taken separately, indicates all the other parts to which it has belonged. Thus, if the viscera of any animal are so organized as only to be fitted for the digestion of recent flesh, it is also requisite that the jaws should be so constructed as to fit them for devouring prey; the claws must be constructed for seizing and tearing it to pieces; the teeth for cutting and dividing its flesh; the entire system of the limbs, or organs of motion, for pursuing and overtaking it; and the organs of sense, for discovering it at a distance. Nature, also, must have endowed the brain of the animal with instinct sufficient for concealing itself, and for laying plans to catch its necessary victims.

"In order that the jaw may be well adapted for laying hold of objects, it is necessary that its condyle should have a certain form; that the resistance, the moving power, and the fulcrum, should have a certain relative position with respect to each other, and that the temporal muscles should be of a certain size; the hollow, or depression, too, in which these muscles are lodged, must have a certain depth; and the zygomatic arch, under which they pass, must not only have a certain degree of convexity, but it must be sufficiently strong to support the action of the masseter.

"To enable the animal to carry off its prey when seized, a

corresponding force is requisite in the muscles which elevate the head ; and this necessarily gives rise to a determinate form of the vertebræ, to which these muscles are attached, and of the occiput into which they are inserted.

" In order that the teeth of a carnivorous animal may be able to cut the flesh, they require to be sharp, more or less so in proportion to the greater or less quantity of flesh which they have to cut. It is requisite that their roots should be solid and strong, in proportion to the greater quantity and size of the bones which they have to break to pieces. The whole of these circumstances must necessarily influence the development and form of all the parts which contribute to move the jaws.

" To enable the claws of a carnivorous animal to seize its prey, a considerable degree of mobility is necessary in their paws and toes, and a considerable strength in the claws themselves. From these circumstances, there necessarily result certain determinate forms in all the bones of their paws, and in the distribution of the muscles and tendons by which they are moved. The fore arm must possess a certain facility of moving in various directions, and consequently requires certain determinate forms in the bones of which it is composed. As the bones of the fore arm are articulated with the arm bone, or humerus, no change can take place in the form or structure of the former, without occasioning correspondent changes in the form of the latter. The shoulder-blade, also, or scapula, requires a correspondent degree of strength in all animals destined for catching prey, by which it likewise must necessarily have an appropriate form. The play and action of all these parts require certain proportions in the muscles which set them in motion, and the impressions formed by these muscles must still farther determine the form of all these bones.

23 *

" After these observations it will easily be seen that similar
conclusions may be drawn with respect to the hinder limbs
of carnivorous animals, which require particular conforma-
tions to fit them for rapidity of motion in general ; and that
similar considerations must influence the forms and connections of the vertebræ and other bones constituting the
trunk of the body, and to fit them for flexibility and readiness
of motion in all directions.   The bones, also, of the nose, of
the orbit, and of the ears, require certain forms and structures
to fit them for giving perfection to the senses of smell, sight,
and hearing, so necessary to animals of prey.   In short, the
shape and structure of the teeth regulate the forms of the
condyle, of the shoulder-blade, and the claws, in the same
manner as the equation of a curve regulates all its other
properties ; and as, in regard to a particular curve, all its
properties may be ascertained by assuming each separate
property as the foundation of a particular equation, in the
same manner a claw, a shoulder-blade, a condyle, a leg, an
arm bone, or any other bone, separately considered, enables
us to discover the description of teeth to which they have
belonged ; and so, also, reciprocally, we may determine the
form of the other bones from the teeth.   Thus commencing
our investigations by a careful survey of any one bone by
itself, a person who is sufficiently master of the laws of organic structure may, as it were, reconstruct the whole animal
to which that bone had belonged."

After applying the same principle to animals with hoofs,
Cuvier comes to a conclusion even more surprising. "Hence,"
says he, " any one who observes merely the print of a cloven
hoof, may conclude that it has been left by a ruminant animal, and regard the conclusion as equally certain with any
other in physics or in morals.   Consequently this single

footmark clearly indicates to the observer the forms of the teeth, of all the leg bones, thighs, shoulders, and of the trunk of the body of the animal which left the mark. It is much surer than all the marks of Zadig.

" By thus employing the method of observation, where theory is no longer able to direct our views, we procure astonishing results. The smallest fragment of bone, even the most apparently insignificant apophysis, possesses a fixed and determinate character relative to the class, order, genus, and species of the animal to which it belonged ; insomuch that when we find merely the extremity of a well-preserved bone, we are able, by a careful examination, assisted by analogy and exact comparison, to determine the species to which it once belonged, as certainly as if we had the entire animal before us. Before venturing to put entire confidence in this method of investigation, in regard to fossil bones, I have very frequently tried it with portions of bones belonging to well-known animals, and always with such complete success, that I now entertain no doubts with regard to the results which it affords."

The remarkable correlation between the parts of existing animals having been thus proved by the most rigid and satisfactory tests, we shall inquire with interest for the result, when Cuvier applied the same principles to the fossil animals. If the laws of anatomical structure were the same when these extinct races lived as they now are, these principles will apply equally well to the bones found in the rocks ; and though often only scattered fragments are brought to light, the anatomist will be able to reconstruct the whole animal, and present him to our view. Cuvier was the first who solved this problem. The quarries around Paris had furnished a vast number of bones of strange animals, and these were thrown promiscuously into the collections of that city. Well prepared by previous study, this distinguished anatomist went among them with the inquiry, *Can these bones live ?* The spirit of scientific prophecy was upon him, and, as he uttered his inspirations, *there was a noise, and behold a shaking, and the bones came together, bone to his bone. And the sinews and the flesh came upon them, and the skin covered them.* " I found myself," says he, " as if placed in a charnel-house, surrounded by mutilated fragments of many hundred skeletons of more than twenty kinds of animals, piled confusedly around me. The task assigned me was to restore them all to their original position. At the voice of comparative anatomy, every bone and fragment of a bone resumed its place. I cannot find words to express the pleasure I experienced in seeing, as I discovered one character, how all the consequences which I predicted from it were successively confirmed ; the feet were found in accordance with the characters announced by the teeth ; the teeth in harmony with those indicated beforehand by the feet ; the bones of the legs and thighs, and every connecting portion of the extremities, were found set together precisely as I had arranged them, before my conjectures were verified by the discovery of the parts entire ; in short, each species was, as it were, reconstructed from a single one of its component elements."

It is hardly necessary to say that, since this first successful experiment, the same principles have been more thoroughly investigated and extended with the same success into every department of fossil organic nature. The results which have crowned the labors of such men as Agassiz, Ehrenberg, Kaup, Goldfuss, Bronn, Blainville, Brongniart, Deshayes, and D'Orbigny, on the continent of Europe, and of Conybeare, Buckland, Mantell, Lindley, and Hutton, and eminently of

Owen, in Great Britain, although sustained by the most rigid principles of science, are nevertheless but little short of miraculous; and they demonstrate most clearly the identity of anatomical laws, in all ages, among animals and plants of every size and character, from the lofty lepidodendra and sigillaria to the humblest moss or sea-weed, and from the gigantic dinotherium, mastodon, megatherium, and iguanodon, to the infinitesimal infusoria.

In the sixth place, physiological laws have always been the same upon the globe.

That death has reigned in all past ages over all animated tribes, as it now reigns, so that in that war there has never been a discharge, I need not attempt formally to prove. For the preserved and petrified relics of all the former races, that now lie entombed in the rocks, furnish a silent but impressive demonstration of the former triumph of that great physiological law, which is stamped by the signet of Jehovah upon all existing organic natures — *Dust thou art, and unto dust shalt thou return.*

Scarcely more necessary is it to attempt to show that the same system of reproduction for filling the chasms which death occasions, and which is now universal in the animal and vegetable kingdoms, has always existed. Indeed, such a system is a necessary counterpart to a system of dissolution. And we find the same phases to this reproductive system in ancient and in modern periods. Organic remains clearly teach us that there have always been viviparous as well as oviparous creatures, and gemmiparous as well as fissiparous animals and plants. The second great physiological law of existing nature has, then, always been the same.

The character of the nourishment by which animals and plants have been sustained has never varied. The latter have ever been nourished by inorganic, and the former by organic, matter. Some animals have ever fed upon the flesh of other animals, as their petrified remains, enclosing the masticated and half-digested fragments of other animals, testify. Other tribes have fed only upon herbs or fruits; and some were omnivorous; just, in fact, as we find the habits of existing animals.

No less certain are we that the processes of digestion and assimilation have ever been unchanged. We find the same organs for these purposes as in existing animals, viz., the mouth, the stomach, the intestines, and the blood-vessels, as the coprolites and the cololites abundantly testify. We infer, therefore, with great confidence, the existence of gastric juice and bile for completing the transformation of the food into blood. Indeed, the discovery by a lady (Miss Mary Anning, of England) of that singular secretion from which the color called *India ink* is prepared, with the ink-bag of the sepia, or loligo, in a petrified state, shows that the process of secretion existed in these ancient animals; and when we find that in all respects their structure was like that of existing animals, although some of the softer vessels have not been preserved, we cannot doubt but the entire process of digestion, and the conversion of blood into bone, nerve, and muscle, was precisely the same as it now is.

In the fact, also, that we find in fossil specimens organs of respiration, such as lungs, gills, and trachea, we learn that the process of a circulation of blood, and its purification by means of the oxygen of the atmosphere, have never varied. Animal heat, too, dependent as it is essentially upon this oxygenating process, was always derived from the same source as at present.

The perfectly preserved minute vessels of vegetables

enable us, by means of the microscope, to identify them with the plants now alive; and they prove, too, incontestably, that the nourishment of vegetables has always been of the same kind, and has been converted into the various proximate principles of plants by the same processes.

Again. We have evidence that these ancient animals possessed the same senses as their congeneric races now on the globe. We have one good example in which that most delicate organ, the eye, is most perfectly preserved. It is well known that the visual organ of insects and of crustaceans is composed of a multitude — often several hundreds or thousands — of eyes, united into one, so as to serve the purpose of a multiplying glass; each eye producing a separate image of the object observed. Such an eye had the trilobite. Each contained at least four hundred nearly spherical lenses on the surface of the cornea, united into one organ; revealing to us the interesting fact, that the relations of light to animal organization were the same in that remote era as they now are.

But I need not multiply proof of the functional identity of organic nature in all ages. It may, however, be inquired, how this identity, as well as that of anatomical structure, is reconciled with the great anomalies, both in size and form, which have confessedly prevailed among ancient animals. Compare the plants and animals which now occupy the northern parts of the globe with those which flourished there in the remote periods of geological history, and can we believe them to be portions of one great system of organic nature?

Compare, for instance, the thirty or forty species of ferns now growing to the height of a few inches, or one or two feet, in Europe and this country, with the more than two hundred species already dug out of the coal mines, many of which were forty to forty-five feet in height; or the diminutive ground pines, and equiseta, now scarcely noticed in our forests, with the gigantic lepidodendron, sigillaria, calamites, and equiseta, of the carboniferous period; and who will not be struck with the great difference between them?

Or go to Germany, and imagine the bones of the dinotherium to start out of the soil, and become clothed with flesh and instinct with life. You have before you a quadruped eighteen feet in length, and of proportional height, much larger than the elephant, and with curved tusks reaching two or three feet below its lower jaw, while no other living animal would be found there larger than the ox, or the horse — mere pygmies by the side of such a monster, and evidently unfit to be his contemporaries.

Again. Let the megatherium be brought back to life on the pampas of South America, and you have an animal twelve feet long and eight feet high, with proportions perfectly colossal. Its fore feet were a yard long, its thigh bone three times thicker than that of the elephant, its width across the haunches five feet, its spinal marrow a foot in diameter, and its tail, where it was inserted into the body, two feet in diameter. What a giant in comparison with the sloth, the anteater, and the armadillo, to which it was allied by anatomical structure!

Still more unequal in size, as compared with living batrachians, was the labyrinthidon, once common in England and Germany, if, indeed, the tracks on sandstone were made by that animal. It was, in fact, a frog as large as an ox, and perhaps as large as an elephant. Think of such animals swarming in our morasses at the present day!

But coming back from Europe, and turning our thoughts to the animals that trod along the shores of the estuary that once washed the base of Mount Holyoke, in New England, we shall encounter an animal, probably of the batrachian family, of more gigantic proportions. It was the *Otozoum Moodii*, a biped, with feet twenty inches long, more than twice the size of those of the labyrinthidon ; yet its tracks on the imperishable sandstone show that such a giant once trod upon the muddy shore of that ancient estuary.

Along that same shore, also, enormous struthious birds moved in flocks, making strides from three to five feet long, with feet eighteen inches long, lifting their heads, it may be, from twelve to eighteen feet above the ground, surpassing, as it appears, even the gigantic dinornis of New Zealand, now that the feet of the latter have been discovered. I refer to the *Brontozoum giganteum*, whose tracks are so common on the new red sandstone of the Connecticut valley. What dwarfs are we in comparison, who now consider ourselves lords of that valley !

Still more remarkable for peculiarities of structure was the tribe of saurians, which were once so numerous in the northern parts of Europe and America. The ichthyosaurus, a carnivorous marine reptile, sometimes thirty feet long, had the snout of a porpoise, the teeth of a crocodile, the head of a lizard, the vertebræ of a fish, the sternum of an ornithorhynchus, and the paddles of a whale. Those paddles, corresponding to the fins of a fish, or the web feet of water birds, were composed, each of them, of more than one hundred bones. In short, we find in this animal a combination of mechanical contrivances, which are now found among three distinct classes of the animal kingdom. Its eye, also, having an orbital cavity, in one species, of fourteen inches in its longest diameter, was proportionally larger than that of any living animal.

The plesiosaurus had the general structure of the ichthyo-

24

saurus; but its neck was nearly as long as its whole body—longer, in proportion to its size, than even that of the swan.

The iguanodon was an herbivorous terrestrial reptile that formerly inhabited England. It approaches nearest in structure to the iguana, a reptile four or five feet long, inhabiting the marine parts of this continent. Yet the iguanodon was thirty feet long, with a thigh six feet, and a body fourteen feet in circumference. What an alarm would it now produce, to have such a monster start into life in the forests of England, where no analogous animal could be found more than half a foot in length! Surely this must have been one of the fabulous monsters of antiquity.

Still more heteroclitic and unlike existing nature was the pterodactyle, a small lizard, contemporary with the ichthyosaurus and plesiosaurus. At one time anatomists regarded it as a bird, at another as a bat, and finally as a reptile, having the head and neck of a bird, the body and tail of a quadruped, the wings of a bat, and the teeth of a saurian reptile. With its wings it could fly or swim; it could walk on two feet or four; with its claws it could climb or creep. "Thus," says Dr. Buckland, "like Milton's fiend, all qualified for all services, and all elements, the pterodactyle was a fit companion for the kindred reptiles that swarmed in the seas, or crawled on the shores of a turbulent planet."

> "The fiend,
> O'er bog, or steep, through straight, rough, dense, or rare,
> With head, hands, wings, or feet pursues his way,
> And swims, or sinks, or wades, or creeps, or flies."

Now, when the details of such facts are brought before us, it is very natural to feel that it is the history of monsters, and that the Centaurs, the Gorgons, and Chimeras of the ancients, are no more unlike existing animals than these resurrections from the rocks. But further examination rectifies our mistake, and we recognize them as parts of one great system. All the peculiarities of size, and structure, and form, which we meet, we find to be only wise and benevolent adaptations to the different circumstances in which animals have been placed. The gigantic size of many of them, compared with existing races, may be explained by the tropical, or even ultra tropical character of the climate ; and not a single anomaly of structure and form can be pointed out, which did not contribute to the convenience and happiness of the species, in the circumstances in which they were placed. It is our ignorance and narrow views alone that give any of them the aspect of monsters. Listen to the opinion of Sir Charles Bell, one of the ablest of modern anatomists. " The animals of the antediluvian world," says he, " were not monsters ; there is no *lusus*, or extravagance. Hideous as they appear to us, and like the phantoms of a dream, they were adapted to the condition of the earth when they existed." " Judging by these indications of the habits of the animals, we acquire a knowledge of the condition of the earth during their period of ex· istence ; that it was suited at one time to the scaly tribe of the lacertæ, with languid motion ; at another, to animals of higher organization, with more varied and lively habits ; and, finally, we learn that, at any period previous to man's creation, the surface of the earth would have been unsuitable to him." — *Bridgewater Treatise*, pp. 35 and 31.

A similar view is given of this subject by England's geological poet, (Rev. Mr. Wilks,) in whose playful verses we find more of true science and just inference than in many

a ponderous tome of grave prose. In one of his poems he
says, —

> " Seamy coal,
> Limestone, or oölite, and other sections,
> Give us strange tidings of our old connections ;
> Our arborescent ferns, of climate torrid,
> With unknown shapes of names and natures horrid ;
> Strange ichthyosaurus, or iguanodon,
> With many more I cannot verse upon, —
> Lost species and lost genera ; some whose bias
> Is chalk, marl, sandstone, gravel, or blue lias ;
> Birds, beasts, fish, insects, reptiles ; fresh, marine,
> Perfect as yesterday among us seen
> In rock or cave ; 'tis passing strange to me
> How such incongruous mixture e'er could be.
> And yet no medley was it : each its station
> Once occupied in wise and meet location.
> God is a God of order, though to scan
> His works may pose the feeble powers of man."

The facts and reasonings which have now been presented
will sustain the following important inferences : —

*In the first place, we learn that the notions which have so
widely prevailed, in ancient and modern times, respecting a
chaos, are without foundation.*

Among all heathen nations of antiquity, the belief in a
primeval chaos was almost universal ; and from the heathen
philosophers it was transmitted to the Christian world, and
incorporated with the Mosaic cosmogony. It is not, indeed,
easy to ascertain what is the precise idea which has been attached to a chaos. It is generally described, however, as " a
confused assemblage of elements," " an unformed and undi-
gested mass of heterogeneous matter ; " not, of course, subject
to those laws which now govern it, and which have arranged

it all in beautiful order, even if we leave out of the account vegetable and animal organization. Now, I have attempted to show that there never was a period on the globe when these laws, with the exception of the organic, did not operate as they now do. Nay, the geologist, when he examines the oldest rocks, finds the results of these laws at the supposed period when chaos reigned; that is, in the earliest times of our planet. And what are these results? The most splendid crystallizations which nature furnishes. The emerald, the topaz, the sapphire, and other kindred gems, were elaborated during the supposed chaotic state of the globe; for no earlier products have yet been discovered than these most perfect illustrations of crystallographical, chemical, and electrical laws. If, indeed, any should say, that by a chaos they mean only that state of the world when no animals or plants existed, — in other words, when no organic laws had been established, — to such a chaos I have no objection. And this is the chaos described in the Bible, where it is said that, before the creation of animals and plants, the earth was *without form and void.* The *tohu vau bohu* of Moses, which is thus translated in our English Bible, means, simply and literally, *invisible and unfurnished — invisible,* both because the ocean covered the present land, and darkness was upon the face of the deep; and *unfurnished,* because as yet no organic natures had been called into existence. This is the meaning which the old Jewish writers, as Philo and Josephus, attached to these words; and they have been followed by some of the ablest modern commentators. "It is wonderful," says Rosenmuller the elder, "that so many interpreters could have persuaded themselves that it was possible to detect a chaos in the words תֹהוּ וָבֹהוּ. That notion unquestionably derived its origin from the fictions of the Greek and Latin poets, which were transferred by

24 *

those interpreters to Moses. If we follow the practice of
the language, the Hebrew phrase has this signification : *The
earth was waste and desert*, or, as others prefer, *empty and
vacuous ;* that is, *uncultured and unfurnished* with those things
with which the Creator afterwards adorned it." — *Antiquiss.
Tell. Hist.* p. 19–23.

Upon the whole, there is no evidence whatever, either in
nature or revelation, that the earth has ever been in a state
corresponding to the common notions of a chaos ; while, on
the other hand, there is strong proof that the present laws of
nature have been in operation from the beginning. These
laws have varied in the intensity of their action, and we
have strong reason to believe that organic laws did not always
exist ; but none of these laws have ever been suspended, to
leave the elements to mix in wild disorder in a formless mass.
It is high time that religion was freed from the indescribable
incubus of a chaos.

*Finally, the most important conclusion to which the mind is
conducted by this subject is, that the present and past conditions of this world are only parts of one and the same great
system of infinite wisdom and benevolence.*

We have seen that the same wise and benevolent laws,
organic and inorganic, have always controlled, as they now
control, this lower world. It is true we find modified conditions of the globe in its past history ; but they were always
the foreseen result of the same laws, and in harmony with
the same great plan. And the modifications of organic structure, which were great in the successive economies, were
always in perfect correspondence with the earth's physical
changes. Nowhere do we meet with conflicting plans ; but
throughout all nature, from the earliest zoöphyte and sea-
weed of the silurian rocks to the young animals and plants that

came into existence to-day, and from the choice gems that
were produced when the earth was without form and void, to
the crystals which are now forming in the chemist's laboratory, one golden chain of harmony links all together, and
identifies all as the work of the same infinite mind.

"In all the numerous examples of design which we have
selected from the various animal and vegetable remains that
occur in a fossil state," says Dr. Buckland, "there is such a
never-failing identity in the fundamental principles of their
construction, and such uniform adoption of analogous means
to produce various ends, with so much only of departure from
one common type of mechanism as was requisite to adapt
each instrument to its own especial function, and to fit each
species to its peculiar place and office in the scale of created
beings, that we can scarcely fail to acknowledge in all these
facts a demonstration of the unity of the intelligence in
which such transcendent harmony originated; and we may
almost dare to assert that neither atheism nor polytheism
would ever have found acceptance in the world, had the evidences of high intelligence and unity of design which have
been disclosed by modern discoveries in physical science
been fully known to the authors or the abetters of systems
to which they are so diametrically opposed. It is the same
handwriting that we read, the same system and contrivance
that we trace, the same unity of object and relation to
final causes which we see maintained throughout, and constantly proclaiming the unity of the great divine original."
— *Bridgewater Treatise*, p. 584.

"The earth, from her deep foundations, unites with the
celestial orbs, that roll throughout boundless space, to declare
the glory and show forth the praise of their common Author
and Preserver; and the voice of natural religion accords har-

moniously with the testimonies of revelation, in ascribing the origin of the universe to the will of one eternal and dominant intelligence, the almighty Lord and supreme First Cause of all things that subsist ; *the same yesterday, to-day, and for-ever, before the mountains were brought forth, or ever the earth and the world were made, God from everlasting and without end.*" — *Bridgewater Treatise*, p. 596.

LECTURE IX.

THE HYPOTHESIS OF CREATION BY LAW.

In all ages of the world, where men have been enlightened enough to reason upon the causes of phenomena, a mysterious and a mighty power has been imputed to the laws of nature. A large portion of the most enlightened men have felt as if those laws not only explain, but possess an inherent potency to continue, the ordinary operations of nature. Most men of this description, however, have thought that to originate nature must have demanded the special exercise of an infinite and all-wise Being. But a few, in every age, have endeavored to exalt law into a Creator, as well as Controller, of the world. The hypothesis has assumed a great variety of forms, and until recently few have attempted to draw it out in all its details, and apply it to all nature. Among the ancient philosophers it was based on the eternity of matter, and made the foundation of a system of rank atheism. Starting with the position, as an axiom, that nothing produces nothing, — in other words, that creation out of nothing is impossible, — Democritus maintained that all existence was the result of two necessary and self-existent principles, viz., space, infinite in extent, and atoms, infinite in number. The latter have been eternally in motion, in directions varying from right lines; and their necessary collisions have produced the various forms of organic and inorganic nature. To produce animals and plants, it was only necessary that the atoms should be suitably arranged. The only animating principle was the rapid agitation of atoms.

In modern times, very few philosophers have ventured to solve the whole problem of the universe by any self-acting, self-producing power in nature. La Place limited himself to the mode in which the great bodies of the universe were produced by the vortical movements of nebulous matter; although his object, equally with that of Democritus and Epicurus, was to dispense with an intelligent, personal Deity. Lamarck, Geoffrey St. Hilaire, and Bory St. Vincent, assuming the existence of matter and its laws, have endeavored to show, by the inherent vitality of some parts of matter, how the first or lowest classes of animals and plants may have been produced; and how, from these, by the theory of development and the force of circumstances, all the higher families, with their instincts and intellects, may have been evolved. A still more recent, but anonymous, writer has had the boldness to unite these nebular hypotheses, with those of spontaneous generation and transmutation, into a single system, and to attempt to clothe it with the garb of philosophy; nay, to do this in consistency, not only with Theism, but with a belief in revelation. This theory is what I denominate the *hypothesis of creation by law*. And judging from its wide reception, we should be led to infer that it had strong probabilities in its favor. It should, therefore, at least receive a careful and candid examination. For though many of its statements and conclusions are absurd, and some of them are highly ridiculous, the hypothesis, at least in some of its parts, falls in with certain loose notions that have got possession of the public mind, and which nothing but cogent reasoning can eradicate.

Before entering upon such an examination, however, it

seems necessary to go somewhat more into detail in illustration of the nature of this hypothesis. It may conveniently be described under the heads of *cosmogony*, which attempts to account for the origin of the world; *zoögony*, which explains the origin of animals; and *zoönomy*, which describes the laws of animal life.*

The cosmogony of this theory is embraced in what is denominated the nebular hypothesis, propounded by the eminent mathematician La Place. He supposes that, originally, the whole solar system constituted only one vast mass of nebulous matter, being expanded into the thinnest vapor and gas by heat, and more than filling the space at present occupied by the planets. This vapor, he still further supposes, had a revolution from west to east on an axis. As the heat diminished by radiation, the nebulous matter must condense, and consequently the velocity of rotation must increase, and an exterior zone of vapor might be detached; since the central attraction might not be able to overcome the increased centrifugal force. This ring of vapor might sometimes retain its original form, as in the case of Saturn's ring; but the tendency would be, in general, to divide into several masses, which, by coalescing again, would form a single mass, having a revolution about the sun, and on its axis. This would constitute a planet in a state of vapor; and by the detachment of successive rings might all the planets be produced. As they went on contracting, by the same law, satellites might be formed to each; and the ultimate result would be solid planets and satellites, revolving around the sun in nearly the same plane, and in the same direction, and also on their axes.

* I adopt this division from an able American review of the "Vestiges."

Although this hypothesis has been regarded with favor by many philosophers, who were Theists, and even Christians, yet the object of La Place in proposing it was to sustain atheism. Sir Isaac Newton had expressed the conviction that " the admirable arrangement of the solar system cannot but be the work of an intelligent and most powerful Being." La Place declared that, in this statement, Newton " had deviated from the method of true philosophy," and brought forward these views to sustain his declaration. Whether they do sustain it, will be considered in another place. But since it is one of those modes in which men have attempted to account for the universe without a Deity, it is a proper subject of examination in this lecture, in which we are inquiring whether law alone will account for the creation and sustentation of the universe.

The zoögony of this hypothesis undertakes to show how animals and plants may be produced without any special exercise of creating power on the part of the Deity. It supposes matter to be endowed with certain laws, whose operation alone will determine life in brute matter, or, rather, whose operation constitutes life. Some would have it that a part of matter is essentially vital ; that is, endowed with inherent life ; and that this matter, like leaven, communicates life to dead matter arranged in a certain order. But the more modern view is, that life is produced by electrical agency. It is found that the fundamental form of organic beings is a globule, having another globule forming within it. It is also found that globules may be produced in albumen by electricity ; and if we could discover how nature produces albumen, it is thought that the whole process by which living organisms are produced would be distinctly before us. It seems to be simply the operation of electricity, and requires no intervention of special creating energy. If the question arises, Whence came such marvellous laws to exist in nature ? the atheist replies that matter and its laws are eternal, having neither beginning nor end ; while the Theist, who maintains this hypothesis, asserts that, when God created matter, he endowed it with such laws, having an inherent, self-executing power.

Having thus ascertained, as it supposes, how life and organization in the simplest forms may be produced, the next inquiry is, how the more perfect and complicated forms of organic beings may be developed by laws, without divine power. This constitutes the zoönomy of the subject. The French zoölogist, Lamarck, first drew out and formally defended this hypothesis, aided by others, as Geoffroy St. Hilaire and Bory St. Vincent. Their supposition was, that there is a power in nature, which they sometimes denominated the Deity, yet did not allow it to be intelligent and independent, but a mere blind, instrumental force. This power, they supposed, was able to produce what they called *monads*, or rough draughts of animals and plants. These monads were the simplest of all organic beings, mere aggregations of matter, some of them supposed to be inherently vital. And such monads are the only things ever produced directly by this blind deity. But in these monads there was supposed to reside an inherent tendency to progressive improvement. The wants of this living mass of jelly were supposed to produce such effects as would gradually form new organs, as the hands, the feet, and the mouth. These changes would be aided by another principle, which they called the *force of external circumstances*, by which they meant the influence upon its development of its peculiar condition ; as, for instance, a conatus for flying, produced by the internal principle,

25

would form wings in birds; a conatus for swimming in water would form the fins and tails of fishes; and a conatus for walking would form the feet and legs of quadrupeds. Thus the organs were not formed to meet the wants, but by the wants, of the animal and plant. Of course, new wants would produce new organs; and thus have animals been growing more and more complicated and perfect from the earliest periods of geological history. Man began his course as a monad, but, by the force of Lamarck's two principles, has reached the most elevated rank on the scale of animals. His last condition before his present was that of the monkey tribe, especially that of the orang-outang. The advocates of this hypothesis generally, however, suppose that there are from three to fifteen species of men, and that the different races are not mere varieties of one species. The most perfect species, the Caucasian, after leaving the monkey state, has gradually risen through the inferior species, and is still making progress; so that we cannot tell where they will stop. In general, the advocates of this hypothesis are materialists; that is, they do not suppose that there is a soul in man, distinct from the body, but that thought is one of the functions of the brain. They usually also regard moral qualities as mainly dependent upon organization, agreeably to the opinions of ultra phrenologists; and hence that they are more to be pitied than blamed for their deviations from rectitude.

Such is the hypothesis. Let us now, in the first place, assume it to be proved, and see what inferences follow.

I remark, first, that the occurrence of events according to law does not remove the necessity of a divine contriving, superintending, and sustaining Power.

That every event in the universe takes place according to fixed laws I am ready to admit. For what is a natural law?

Nothing more nor less than the uniform mode in which divine power acts. In the case of miracles, it may be that the ordinary laws of nature are suspended or counteracted; at least, they are increased or diminished in their power. Yet from what we know of the divine perfections, we must conclude that God has certain fixed rules by which he is regulated in the performance of miracles; and, of course, in the same circumstances we should expect the same miracles. So that we may reasonably admit that even miracles are regulated and controlled by law, like common events; though, from the infrequency of the former, men cannot understand the laws that regulate them.

Now, if the advocates of this hypothesis mean simply that every event is regulated by law, — in other words, that with like antecedents like consequents will be connected, — I have no controversy with them; and such is the precise statement of a modern anonymous popular writer on the subject.

He declares that his " purpose is, to show that the whole revelation of the works of God presented to our senses and reason is a system based on what we are compelled, for want of a better term, to call *law;* by which, however, is not meant a system independent or exclusive of the Deity, but one which only proposes *a certain mode of his working.*" — *Sequel to the Vestiges of Nat. Hist. of Creation,* p. 2. — But this is by no means all that is meant by this hypothesis. Nay, the grand object of the writer above quoted is, to show that there is no such thing as miraculous interference in the creation or preservation of the universe. He admits only the ordinary laws of nature, but denies all special and extraordinary laws; and says that it does not " appear necessary that God should exercise an immediately superintending power

over the mundane economy." — *Vestiges*, p. 273. — Nay, he
denies that the original creation of the universe and of animals
and plants required any thing but the operation of natural
laws; of such laws as we see and understand. The thought
does not seem to have occurred to him, that special and miraculous acts of the Deity may be as truly governed by law
as the motions of planets. Every thing of that sort he seems
to regard as a violation of law, — a stepping aside from fixed
principles, — a sort of afterthought with Jehovah, — a remedy
for some defect in his original plans. True, the law of miracles and of special providence is very different from the common course of nature ; and, therefore, the one may for a time
supersede the others. But this does not prove that the former
is not regulated by laws ; nor that it did not enter into the
original plan of the universe in the divine mind. It must have
been a part of that plan ; every thing was a part of it, and
there can be with him no afterthought, no improvement, no
alteration of his eternal designs.

Admitting that every event, miraculous as well as common,
is under law, it by no means renders a present directing and
energizing Deity unnecessary. This hypothesis admits that
organic life had a beginning, for its grand object is to show
how it began by law alone. Now, who gave to matter, in a
gaseous state, such wonderful laws that this fair world should
be the result of their operation ? If it would require infinite
wisdom as well as power to create the present universe at
once out of nothing, would it demand less of contrivance and
skill to impart such powers to brute matter? It was not
merely a power to produce organic natures, to form their
complicated organs, to give life, and instinct, and intellect ;
but to adapt each particle, each organ, each animal, and each

plant, most exactly and most wonderfully to its place in the
vast system, so that every single thing should most beautifully
harmonize with every other thing.

Again. What is a natural law without the presence and
energizing power of the lawgiver? How easily are men
bewildered by words! and none has led more astray than this
word *law*. We talk about its power to produce certain effects ; but who can point out any inherent power of this sort
which it possesses ? Who can show how a law operates but
through the energizing influence of the lawgiver? How unphilosophical then to separate a law of nature from the Deity,
and to imagine him to have withdrawn from his works! For
to do this would be to annihilate the law. He must be present
every moment, and direct every movement of the universe, just
as really as the mind of man must be in the body to produce
its movements. Take away God from the universe, or let
him cease to act mentally upon it, and every movement would
as instantly and certainly cease, as would every movement of
the human frame, were the mind to be withdrawn, or cease to
will. We realize the necessity of the divine presence and
energy to produce a miracle. But if miracles are performed
according to law, as much as common events, — and we
surely cannot prove they are not, — why is a present Deity
any more necessary in the one case than in the other ? The
Bible considers common and miraculous events exactly alike
in this respect. And true philosophy teaches the same.

I see not, then, why this law hypothesis does not require an
infinite Deity, just as much as the ordinary belief, which supposes that God originally created the universe by his fiat, and
sustains it constantly by his power, and from time to time
interferes with the regular sequence of cause and effect by
miracles. The only difference seems to be this : While the

25 *

common view represents God as always watching over his
works, and ready, whenever necessary, to make special interpositions, the law hypothesis introduces him only at the very
dawn of the universe, exerting his infinite wisdom and power
to devise and endow matter with exquisite laws, capable, by
their inherent self-executing power, of originating all organic
natures, and producing the infinite variety of nature, and keep-
ing in play her countless and unceasing agencies. It was
only necessary that he should impress attenuated matter with
these laws, and then put the machine in motion, and it would
go on forever, without any need of God's presence or agency;
so that he might henceforward give himself up to undisturbed
repose.

I know, indeed, that La Place, and some other advocates
of this latter hypóthesis, do not admit any necessity for a
Deity even to originate matter or its laws; and to prove this
was the object of the nebular hypothesis. But how evident
that in this he signally failed! For even though he could
show how nebulous matter, placed in a certain position, and
having a revolution, might be separated into sun and planets,
by merely mechanical laws, yet where, save in an infinite
Deity, lie the power and the wisdom to originate that matter,
and to bring it into such a condition, that, by blind laws alone,
it would produce such a universe — so harmonious, so varied,
so nicely adjusted in its parts and relations as the one we inhabit? Especially, how does this hypothesis show in what
manner these worlds could be peopled by countless myriads
of organic natures, most exquisitely contrived, and fitted to
their condition? The atheist may say that matter is eternal.
But if so, what but an infinite mind could in time begin the
work of organic creation? If the matter existed for eternal
ages without being brought into order, and into organic

structures, why did it not continue in the same state forever? Does the atheist say, All is the result of laws inherent in matter? But how could those laws remain dormant through all past eternity, — that is, through a period literally infinite, — and then at length be aroused into intense action? Besides, to impute the present wise arrangements and organic creations of the world to law, is to endow that law with all the attributes with which the Theist invests the Deity. Nothing short of intelligence, and wisdom, and benevolence, and power, infinitely above what man possesses, will account for the present world. If there is, then, a power inherent in matter adequate to the production of such effects, that power must be the same as the Deity; and, therefore, it is truly the Deity, by whatever name we call it. In short, the fact that La Place did not see that his hypothesis utterly failed to account for the universe without a Deity, strikingly shows us, that a man may be a giant in mathematics, while he is only a pygmy in moral reasoning; or, to make the statement more general, how a man, by an exclusive cultivation of one faculty of the soul, may shrivel all the rest into a nutshell.

From these views and reasonings, it is clear, I think, that the hypothesis of creation by law does not necessarily destroy the theory of religion. For if we admit that every thing in the world of matter and of mind, not excepting miracles and special providences, is regulated, if not produced, by law, it does not take away the necessity of a contriving, sustaining, and energizing Deity. Even though we admit that God has communicated to nature's laws, at the beginning, a power to execute themselves, (though the supposition is quite unphilosophical,) no event is any the less God's work, than if all were miraculous.

In consistency with this conclusion, we find that while some advocates of this hypothesis evidently intended it to sustain atheism, its most plausible advocate, as we have seen, fully admits, not only the divine existence, but the reality of reve-lation. It may, indeed, be doubted whether this anonymous writer has not virtually taken away the Deity, and even moral accountability, by his materialism and his ultra-phrenology ; yet we do not see but he may assert his law system without denying God's existence or attributes.

It must be admitted, however, that the influence of this hypothesis upon practical religion is disastrous. It does, apparently, so remove the Deity from all concern in the affairs of the world, and so foists law into his place, that practically there is no God. If his agency is acknowledged, as having put the vast machine in motion, in some indefinitely remote period of past duration, yet the feeling is, that since then he has given up the reins into the hands of law, so that man has nothing to do with him, but only with nature's laws ; that he has only to submit to these, and not expect any interposition for his relief, however earnestly he cry for it. Now, it is obviously the intention and desire of the advocates of this hypothesis thus to remove God away from his works, and from their thoughts ; else why should they so strenuously resist the notion of miracles ? For these may just as properly be referred to law as common events. Yet it is one of the most striking features of the hypothesis, that it opposes strongly the idea of any special oversight and interposition on the part of the Deity. True, when we look at the subject philosophically, we must acknowledge that an event is just as really the work of God, when brought about by laws which he ordains and energizes, as by miraculous interposition. Still the practical influence of these two views of Providence is quite different.

Whoever the author of the Vestiges may be, he has evidently lived in a religious community, and felt the influence of a religious atmosphere ; for he tries to conform his system as much as possible to the principles of Protestant Christianity. In other words, he feels so much the power of practical piety around him, that he does not suffer the influence of the system which he advocates to exhibit itself fully, nor to drive him into those extravagances of belief which naturally result from it. In order to see what is its natural tendency, we need to go to such a country as Germany, or Switzerland, where there is little to restrain the wildest vagaries of belief. In the works of Professor Lorenz Oken, of Zurich, we see fully developed the tendencies and results of this hypothesis of development by law, combined with the unintelligible idealism of Kant, Fichte, Schelling, &c. In his Physiophilosophy, translated by the Ray Society for the edification of sober, matter-of-fact Anglo-Saxons, we find a man, of strong mind and extensive knowledge, taking the most ridiculous positions with the stoutest dogmatism, and the most imperturbable gravity, yet whose blasphemy is equalled only by their absurdity. Let a few quotations illustrate and confirm this statement.

" The highest mathematical idea, or the fundamental principle of all mathematics, is the zero $= 0$.

" Zero is in itself nothing. Mathematics is based upon nothing, and consequently arises out of nothing.

" Real and ideal are no more different from each other than ice and water : both of these, as is well known, are essentially one and the same, and yet are different, the diversity consisting in the form. Every real is absolutely nothing else than a number.

' The Eternal is the nothing of nature.

" There is no other science than that which treats of nothing.

" There exists nothing but nothing — nothing but the Eternal.

" Every thing in the world is endowed with life ; the world itself is alive, and continues only, maintains itself by virtue of its life.

" Man is God wholly manifested. God has become man, zero has become $+$ —.   Man is the whole of arithmetic, compacted, however, out of all numbers ; he can, therefore, produce numbers out of himself.

" Animals are men who never imagine. They are beings who never attain to consciousness concerning themselves. They are single accounts; man is the whole of mathematics.

" Arithmetic is the truly absolute or divine science.   Theology is arithmetic personified.

"For God to become real, he must appear under the form of the sphere.   There is no other form for God.   God manifesting is an infinite sphere.

" God is a rotating globe ; the world is God rotating.

" The whole universe is material, is nothing but matter ; for it is the primary act repeating itself eternally in the centre.   The universe is a rotating globe of matter.

" There is no dead matter ; it is alive through its being, through the Eternal that is in it.   Matter has no existence in itself, but it is the Eternal only that exists in it.   Every thing is God that is there, and without God there is absolutely nothing.

" Every thing that is is material.   Now, however, there is nothing that is not ; consequently there is every where nothing immaterial.

" Fire is the totality of ether, is God manifested in his totality.

" Every thing that is has originated out of fire ; every thing is only cooled, rigidified fire.

" God being in himself is gravity ; acting, self-emergent light ; both together, or returning into himself, heat.

" God only is monocentral. The world is the bicentral God, God the monocentral world, which is the same with the monas and dyas. Self-consciousness is a living ellipse.

" God is a threefold trinity ; at first the eternal, then the ethereal, and finally the terrestrial, where it is completely divided.

" The symbolical doctrine of the colors is correct according to the philosophy of nature. Red is fire, love — Father. Blue is air, truth, and belief — Son. Green is water, formation, hope — Ghost. These are the three cardinal virtues. Yellow is earth, the immovable, inexorable falsity, the only vice — Satan. There are three virtues, but only one vice. A result obtained by physio-philosophy, whereof pneumato-philosophy as yet augurs nothing.

" The primary mucus, out of which every thing organic has been created, is the sea mucus.

" The whole sea is alive. It is a fluctuating, ever self-elevating, and ever self-depressing organism.

" If the organic fundamental substance consist of infusoria, so must the whole organic world originate from infusoria. Plants and animals can be only metamorphoses of infusoria. No organism has consequently been created of larger size than an infusorial point : whatever is larger has not been created, but developed.

" The mind, just as the body, must be developed out of these animals, (infusoria.) The human body has been formed by an extreme separation of the neuro-protoplasmic or mucous mass ; so must the human mind be a separation, a memberment

of infusorial sensation. The highest mind is an anatomized
or dismembered mesmerism, each member whereof has been
constituted independent in itself.

"The liver is the soul in a state of sleep, the brain is the
soul active and awakening.

"Circumspection and forethought appear to be the thoughts
of the bivalve mollusca, and snails.

"Gazing upon a snail, one believes that he finds the proph-
esying goddess sitting upon the tripod. What majesty is in
a creeping snail, what reflection, what earnestness, what
timidity, and yet at the same time what firm confidence!
Surely a snail is an exalted symbol of mind slumbering deeply within itself."

It is difficult for an Anglo-Saxon mind to believe that a
man who could write thus was not out of his senses. Yet
Oken is an eminent physiologist, and has made, it is said, important discoveries in respect to the cranial homologies, which
have been developed in Professor Owen's work on the Homologies of the Vertebrate Skeleton. Nay, Oken declares himself to have written his Physio-philosophy "in a kind of inspiration" — from what world the religious man might be in
doubt.

These extravagant notions show what is the natural tendency of the law hypothesis. Yet it does not necessarily
convert a man into an atheist. And if any of its advocates
declare themselves Theists, and even Christians, we need not
regard them as hypocrites, though we may consider them as
in an eminently dangerous position; and that, when they shall
act consistently, they will swing off into utter irreligion. But
my arguments against the hypothesis will be based on the position that *it is not sustained by facts;* and this is the second
position of my lecture.

The nebular hypothesis is a part of the foundation on which the doctrine of creation by law rests. And the high scientific reputation of its author, as well as its apparent coincidence with some of the deductions of geology respecting the earliest condition of the earth, have made philosophers look upon it with considerable favor. Yet very few have been ready to give it implicit credence. And of late the most plausible evidence in its favor seems to be fast vanishing away. The ablest mechanicians are unable to see how a rotary motion should be produced in nebulous matter by refrigeration; or, if this be assumed, how the successive portions, detached by superior centrifugal force, should form spherical masses. But a still more formidable objection lies in the fact that, as improvements are made in telescopes, one and another of the nebulæ, on which the hypothesis rests, have been resolved into stars; and the presumption hence arising is very strong that all are resolvable. In the present aspect of the subject, no sagacious philosopher would dare to rest even an hypothesis upon the unresolved nebulæ. If, however, the nebular hypothesis were shown to be true, it would prove nothing in regard to the production of animals and plants by mere law, without the special agency of the Deity.

The essential and inherent vitality of some kinds of matter is another doctrine on which this hypothesis rests. " In vain," says Bory St. Vincent, " has matter been considered as eminently brute. Many observations prove that, if it is not all active, by its very nature, a part of it is essentially so; and the presence of this, operating according to certain laws, is able to produce life in an agglomeration of the molecules; and since these laws will always be imperfectly known, it will at least be rash to maintain that an infinite intelligence did not impose them; since they are manifested by their

26

results." — *Dictionnaire Classique d'Histoire Naturelle*, art. *Materie*.

The " observations " to which this writer refers to sustain his hypothesis are those which had been made upon certain vegetable infusions, which, in certain circumstances, exhibited minute particles in motion, apparently by vital forces. These were called *monads*, and were not supposed to be distinct animals, but only atoms, ready to be organized. The more modern and accurate researches of Ehrenberg and others, however, have shown, beyond all doubt, that these monads are true animals, the minutest of all living beings hitherto discovered. Not less than twenty-six species of them have been described and figured by microscopists, the smallest of which never exceeds the twelve thousandth of an inch in diameter.

The vegetable physiologists have described certain peculiar motions in the minute vessels of plants, that might readily be regarded as matter essentially vital. I refer to what they call *rotation* and *cyclosis*. But these are never seen save in the living plant; and, therefore, seem dependent on the general life of the vegetable.

There is, however, danger of mistaking certain motions of the particles of matter, by chemical agency, for the effect of vitality. A curious example is thus described by Ehrenberg, which was discovered by Professor Bornsdorff. " If a solution of the chloride of aluminum be dropped into a solution of potassa, by the alternate precipitation and solution of the aluminum, in the excess of the alkali, an appearance will be given to the drop of aluminate matter, by the chemical changes and reactions which take place, as if the *Amœba diffluens* were actually present, both as to its form and evolutions, and will seem to be alive. Such appearance is considered by its able discoverer as bearing the same relationship to the real animalcule as a doll, or a figure moved by mechanism, does to a living child."

We see, then, that the supports on which rests the doctrine of the essential vitality of matter, give way before better instruments and more careful research. Another statement, however, of much higher pretensions, has lately been made, and on no mean authority. Able electricians declare that, by passing currents of galvanism through solutions of silicate or ferrocyanate of potassa, or some analogous substance, after a time, sometimes several years, numerous small insects have been developed, belonging to the *acari* family.

These experiments appear to have been conducted with fairness and skill; and that the insects showed themselves at the pole of the battery, around which the gelatinous silex collected, cannot be doubted. It is true, however, that, when the solution was exposed to the atmosphere, the insects appeared much sooner and more numerous than when care was taken to exclude every thing but oxygen enough to sustain life. This fact leads to the suspicion that the ova of the insect might have been communicated through the air, and that, even when an attempt was made to exclude the atmosphere, some ova were still present. This conclusion is rendered still more probable by some experiments made by Professor Schulz, of Berlin, on the production of infusoria. Having first boiled the vegetable and animal infusions, so as to destroy all germs of organic life, and expelled all the atmosphere, he attached an apparatus in such a manner that, whatever air entered afterwards, must pass through sulphuric acid, or a solution of potash. The result was, that no infusoria or vegetable forms appeared during two months; but in the same infusion, placed in the open air, and exposed to the same light

and heat as that enclosed in the glass vessel, numerous animalcula and fungi appeared in a day or two. It will need,
therefore, very long and patient experiments to establish the
assertion that galvanism alone can produce living animals
without the presence of germs.

Not many years since, the equivocal or casual production
of animalcula, without any other parentage than law, was
thought to be made out by a multitude of facts. For these minute
creatures appeared almost every where, and in places where
it seemed impossible that their ova should be found.   But the
researches of Ehrenberg have cleared up the difficulties of
their origination in the ordinary modes of reproduction, in
nearly every instance, and the advocates of the law hypothesis have been fairly driven from this stronghold of their argument.   In describing the various modes of reproduction with
which nature has provided the infusoria, Professor Owen
says, " Thus each leaves, by the last act of its life, the means
of perpetuating and diffusing its species by thousands of fertile germs. When once the thickly-tenanted pool is dried
up, and its bottom converted into a layer of dust, these inconceivably minute and light ova will be raised with the dust by
the first puff of wind, diffused through the atmosphere, and
may there remain long suspended ; forming, perhaps, their
share of the particles which we see flickering in the sunbeam,
ready to fall into any collection of water, beaten down by
every summer shower into the streams or pools which receive
or may be formed by such showers, and, by virtue of their
tenacity of life, ready to develop themselves whenever they
may find the requisite conditions of their existence. The
possibility, or, rather, the high probability, that such is the
design of the oviparous generation of the infusoria, and such
the common mode of the diffusion of their ova, renders the

hypothesis of equivocal generation, which has been so frequently invoked to explain their origin in new-formed natural
or artificial infusions, quite gratuitous." — *Lectures on Comp.
Anat.* vol. ii. p. 31.

No longer able to maintain a foothold among the animalcula, the defenders of this hypothesis have of late attempted
to take a stand among animals of a somewhat higher grade,
viz., the entozoa, or animals inhabiting other animals. These
being considerably larger than the infusoria, their ova could
not float in the atmosphere ; but they possess a wonderful
tenacity of life ; some of them exhibiting signs of life after
having been in boiling water for an hour ; others have revived
after having been packed for a long time in ice, and frozen ;
others have revived after lying in a dried state for six or
seven years. Their power of reproduction, in the ordinary
modes, is also prodigious, exceeding even that of the infusoria. It will, then, demand very strong evidence to prove that
such animals possess also the power of spontaneous production, without parentage, or that their existence within other
animals cannot be explained without such a supposition. For,
if capable of being produced without parentage, why should
such extraordinary care have been taken for their multiplication, in almost all the ordinary modes in which animals are
reproduced ?

The extraordinary facts that have been discovered by Professors Steenstrup, Owen, and others, within a few years,
respecting what they call *alternate generation*, or *parthenogenesis*, have been thought favorable to the hypothesis of development. Among the mollusca, the polyparia, the entozoa,
and infusoria, it is found that, in some species, the result of
sexual union is the production of a larva without sex, and,
therefore, incapable of propagating in the usual way. Yet

26 *

that larva can of itself produce another larva quite different from itself, and this larva another, and so on, sometimes for eight or ten generations, when the spermatic force seems to be exhausted, and a progeny exactly like the original parents that started the series is produced, capable of giving rise to another and a similar series. . Here, then, we find a succession of progeny for several generations, and all quite unlike one another, yet without any immediate parental agency. Why is it not an example of spontaneous generation ? and why may not new species be produced in this manner ?

There are two facts prominent on this subject which afford a full answer to such questions. One is, that these generations of larvæ always begin with the spermatozoon and the ovum of parents; the other is, that the series always closes, if allowed to run its natural course, in individuals with sex, exactly identical with those that started it; so that the species always remains entire. The whole process is simply one of the infinitely varied modes which nature employs to preserve and perfect the species. The process never stops with any of the larvæ intervening between the fertile parents at the beginning, and the fertile individuals at the end of the series. Professor Owen supposes — certainly with much plausibility — that some of the original germ-cells, not wanted for the production of the first larva, pass on to form the successive generations, till the series is complete; so that, after all, the case is not an exception to the general law of reproduction by parental agency; and instead of sustaining, it certainly goes against, the notion of spontaneous generation and of transmutation of species; because it shows how far parental influence may reach, and how tenacious nature is of specific distinctions. For the same reasons, the case affords a presumption against other alleged cases of equivocal generation and metamorphoses of species.*

Appeal has also been made to the vegetable kingdom for examples of the production of organic beings, viz., plants without seeds. Who has not observed, for instance, how the clearing up and burning over of a piece of land will often cause an entirely new tribe of plants to spring up and flourish? Whence came the seeds? We have seen, for instance, (in Richmond, Virginia,) a thick growth of pines upon a spot where from six to ten feet of soil had been removed a few years previously.

It is very possible, in some cases of this kind, that the soil, having been produced. by aqueous agencies, may contain seeds to a considerable depth, and that their vitality may have been preserved for centuries; for we know that seeds three thousand years old, taken from Egyptian catacombs, have germinated, in favorable circumstances. In most cases of this sort, however, the winds have probably supplied the seed, it may be, long before. We were one day wandering over Mount Holyoke, where a spot recently cleared was covered with the fire-weed, a species of senecio; and as we were musing upon its origin, a strong blast of wind swept over the plants, just ready to throw off their seeds. Sustained by their light egrets, they floated away on the air in numbers sufficient to cover half the mountain with the plant, when it should be cleared and burnt over. Yet their existence would never be suspected till those circumstances should be devel-

* For the details of this remarkable subject, see the "Parthenogenesis" of Professor Owen, p. 76, (London, 1849;) Steenstrup's "Alternation of Generations," published by the Ray Society in 1845, and Sedgwick's "Discourse on the Studies of the University," Supplement, p. 193, (London, 1850.)

oped.   At least, until we can prove that the soil contains no seeds by the most careful examination, it will be premature to infer the equivocal production of the plants growing upon it.

Vegetable physiology furnishes another fact, which seems to me to look still more favorable to this law hypothesis than the preceding, although it has not been noticed, so far as I know, by the advocates of that hypothesis.   Speaking of the matter of which certain flowerless plants are composed, Dr. Lindlay says, " It is even uncertain whether this matter will produce its like, and whether it is not a mere representation of the vital principle of vegetation, capable of being called into action, either as a fungus, or algæ, or lichen, according to the particular conditions of heat, light, and moisture, and the medium in which it is placed ; producing fungi upon dead or putrid organic beings, lichens upon living vegetables, earth, or stones, and algæ where water is the medium in which it is developed."   Again, in speaking of that green slime which often covers the soil, rocks, walls, and glass in damp places, he says, " The slime resembles a layer of albumen, spread with a brush ; it exfoliates in drying, and finally becomes visible by the manner in which it colors green or deep brown.   One might call it a provisional creation, waiting to be organized, and then assuming different forms according to the nature of the corpuscles which penetrate it, or develop among it.   It may further be said to be the origin of two very distinct existences, the one certainly animal, the other purely vegetable." — *Natural System*, pp. 326, 328, 334.

Now, admitting all the facts that have been detailed respecting the production of infusoria, entozoa, acari, and cryptogamian plants to be true, although most of them are far from being proved, it seems to me that they do not show us how vitality is produced by mere law, without the special agency of the Deity. Writers on the subject seem to overlook the distinction between organization and life. The first may be present in its highest perfection without the latter, as it is in animals and plants recently killed. The organization is merely a preparation to receive the mysterious principles which we call *life* and *intellect*. Light, heat, and electricity may be the essential agents in producing the organization, but they do not explain the nature, or account for the presence, of life. That must, so far as we know, come from some other and a higher source. Galvanism may bring gelatinous matter into the form of an insect, or infusoria, or entozoa; but there is no evidence that it can impart life, however exquisite the organization. It may be, and we have reason to suppose it is, the divine will to bestow life whenever a certain organization exists; but this does not show that his special agency is not concerned in it. He may will that the peculiar life of a lichen shall be given to the same elementary matter which, in another situation, he constitutes an alga, or a fungus, or even an animal. But this would not prove that natural law alone could produce life. There is nowhere any evidence that sensibility, contractility, and especially intellect and volition, are the result of any natural operations. In their properties they are so entirely diverse from all known physical effects, that we must impute them to some other than a natural cause. We must call in the power of a supreme intelligent Being. The laws of affinity, light, heat, and electricity, of endosmose and exosmose, may prepare the organization, but their power ends there; and hence true philosophy requires us to impute the phenomena of life and intellect to an extraneous and infinitely higher cause.

The case, then, stands thus : In ninety-nine cases out of a

hundred, we are certain that organization requires the previous existence and agency of a being similarly organized, which we call the parent. But suppose that, in a very few cases, the laws of nature can produce the organization. It still demands another and a higher power — not a blind impulse, but an intelligent cause — to bestow life and intellect. To prove the existence of a natural cause for the arrangement of the atoms into an organic structure, does by no means prove the same for those higher and mysterious principles that make that structure a living, thinking being.

Such, however, are the strongest arguments by which the advocates of the law hypothesis sustain their views of the origin of organism, life, and intellect. The next step in their reasoning is to show how animals and plants may be transmuted from one species, or genus, or family, to another; so that the existing vast variety can be traced to a few original germs. They maintain that these developments of the more from the less perfect have proceeded along certain parallel lines; one series of developments, for instance, taking the line of the fishes, another of the reptiles, another of the birds, another of quadrupeds, and so on.

To prove these developments or transmutations, they appeal first to the physiological history of the mammalian embryo. In its earliest stages, it can hardly be distinguished, except in size, from the unborn polygastric infusoria. The brain of a human embryo appears at first like that of an invertebrate animal; next like that of a fish; then successively like that of a reptile, a bird, a rodent mammal, a ruminant, and a monkey. So the heart, at an early stage, looks like that of an insect; then it has two chambers, like that of a fish; then it becomes three chambered, like that of a reptile; and finally, four chambered, as in the mammalia. The inference which these theorists would draw from such facts is, that man actually begins his existence as an animalcule, and passes successively through the mould or condition of other animals, before he reaches the highest. And the reasons why he does become a man, rather than an echinoderm, or a fish, or a monkey, is only some slightly modifying circumstance, as, for instance, a longer gestation. It appears to me, however, that the inferences sound philosophy should derive from such facts are, first, that, while there is a seeming resemblance between the human embryo and that of lower animals, there is, in fact, a real and a wide diversity; so that the one infallibly becomes an inferior animal, and the other a man. Could a single example be produced in which a human embryo stopped at and became an insect, or a fish, or a monkey, there might be some plausibility in the supposition. But it is as certain to become a man as the sun is to rise and set; and, therefore, the human condition results from laws as fixed as those that regulate the movements of the heavenly bodies. That is a very superficial philosophy which infers identity of nature from mere external resemblance.

The phenomena of hybridity furnish another ground of argument in favor of the transmutation of species, and of course in favor of the law hypothesis; for that hybrids are sometimes the result of the union of different species will not be denied. There is, however, a natural repugnance to union between different species; and in a state of nature this can very rarely be overcome. But domestication changes and almost obliterates many natural instincts, and hence hybridity is far more common among domesticated animals and plants. As a general fact, also, the hybrid offspring is incapable of propagating its own race, without union with one of the original species by which it was produced ; and this inability to continue this mixed race has been generally regarded among naturalists as the best characteristic of species. Some, however, attempt to show that some hybrid races do continue from generation to generation to propagate their kind. But in most cases the hybrid race ere long runs out, and there is always a strong tendency to revert to the original stock ; and were it not for the influence of man, probably such a thing as hybridity would scarcely ever have been heard of. Nature seems to have established strong barriers around species, so that an identity should be preserved ; and even if we admit the possibility of their coalescence in some cases, yet we have evidence that almost always they are preserved distinct from century to century ; and the same is true even of the more prominent varieties, for we find not only the same species, but the same varieties of animals and plants, preserved some three thousand years in the Egyptian catacombs, that are now alive in the same country. How idle, then, to suppose that the laws of hybridity will account for such radical and entire transmutations as this hypothesis supposes ! To accomplish this, it would need as strong a tendency in nature to a union of species, genera, and families, as now exists against it.

But a special appeal has been made on this subject to geology. The history of organic remains, it is thought, corresponds to what we might expect, if the hypothesis of development is true. In the oldest rocks we find chiefly the more simple invertebrate animals, and the vertebrated tribes appear at first in the form of fish, then of reptiles, then of birds, then of mammals, and last of all of man. What better confirmation could we wish than this gradually expanding series ? True, all the great classes of organic beings, vegetable and animal, are found nearly at the earliest epoch, and continue through the entire series of rocks. But we have only to suppose a distinct stirps for each of the classes, and that the developments took place along parallel lines, in order to harmonize the facts with the hypothesis.

Such a general view of the subject of organic remains seems to give plausibility to the hypothesis of organic development. But the tables are turned when we descend to particulars. The idea of a distinct stirps or germ for each great class of animals and plants seems to me to destroy an essential feature of the hypothesis. It supposes that law produces at once a vertebral animal and a flowering plant; for the first, certainly, we find in the very lowest of the fossiliferous rocks. "The lower silurian," says Sir Roderick Murchison, in 1847, "is no longer to be viewed as an invertebrate period, for the onchus (a genus of fish) has been found in the Llandeilo Flags, and in the lower silurian rocks of Bala."

It is also a most important fact, that this fish of the oldest rock was not, as the development scheme would require, of a low organization, but quite high on the scale of fishes. The same is true of all the earliest species of this class. "All our most ancient fossil fishes," says Professor Sedgwick, "belong to a high organic type; and the very oldest species that are well determined fall naturally into an order of fishes which Owen and Müller place, not at the bottom, but at the top of the whole class." — *Discourse on the Studies of the University,* &c. 5th edit. p. lxiv. pref.

This point has been fully and ably discussed by Hugh Miller, Esq., in his late work, "The Footprints of the Creator, or the Asterolepis of Stromness." The asterolepis was one of these fishes found in the old red sandstone, sometimes over twenty feet long; yet, says Mr. Miller, "instead of being, as the development hypothesis would require, a fish low in its

27

organization, it seems to have ranged on the level of the highest ichthyic-reptilian families ever called into existence."

Another point which Mr. Miller has labored hard to establish, and of which there seems to be no reasonable doubt, is, that in many families of animals, not only were the first species that appeared of high organization, but there was a gradual degradation among those that were created afterwards. Of the fishes generally, he says, that " the progress of the race, as a whole, though it still retains not a few of the higher forms, has been a progress, not of development from the low to the high, but of degradation from the high to the low." Again he says, " We know, as geologists, that the dynasty of the fish was succeeded by that of the reptile ; that the dynasty of the reptile was succeeded by that of the mammiferous quadruped ; and that the dynasty of the mammiferous quadruped was succeeded by that of man, as man now exists — a creature of a mixed character, and subject, in all conditions, to wide alternations of enjoyment and suffering.   We know further, — so far, at least, as we have succeeded in deciphering the record, — that the several dynasties were introduced, not in their lower, but in their higher forms ; that, in short, in the imposing programme of creation, it was arranged as a general rule, that in each of the great divisions of the procession the magnates should walk first.   We recognize yet further the fact of degradation specially exemplified in the fish and the reptile."   " Among these degraded races, that of the footless serpent, which *goeth upon its belly*, has long been noted by the theologian as a race typical, in its condition and nature, of an order of hopelessly degraded beings, borne down to the dust by a clinging curse ; and curiously enough, when the first comparative anatomists in the world give *their* readiest and most prominent instance of degradation among the divisions of the natural world, it is this very order of footless reptiles that they select."

Among the invertebrate animals are numerous examples of the deterioration of a race. M. Alcide D'Orbigny, one of the most accomplished of living paleontologists, in his *Cours Elementaire de Paleontologie et de Geologie*, speaks as follows of the cephalopods found in the oldest rocks : " See, then, the result ; the cephalopods, the most perfect of the mollusks, which lived in the early period of the world, show a progress of degradation in their generic forms. We insist on this fact relative to the cephalopods, which we shall hereafter compare with the less perfect classes of mollusks, since it must lead to the conclusion that the mollusks, as to their classes, have certainly retrograded from the compound to the simple, or from the more to the less perfect."

Such facts as these are absolutely fatal to the hypothesis of development ; and geology abounds with them. Indeed, through all her archives, we search in vain for facts that show any thing like a passage of one species, genus, or family, into another. Certain distinct types characterize the different formations up to a certain period, when there is a sudden change ; and in the subsequent strata we find animals and plants entirely different from those that have disappeared. The new races are, indeed, often of a higher grade than those that preceded them, but could not have sprung from them.

The true theory of animal and vegetable existence on our globe appears to be this : Such natures were placed upon the earth as were adapted to its varying condition. When the earliest group was created, such were the climate, the atmosphere, the waters, and the means of subsistence, that the lower tribes were best adapted to the condition of things. That group occupied the earth till such changes had occurred as to

make it unsuited to their natures, and consequently they died
out, and new races were brought in ; not by mere law, but by
divine benevolence, power, and wisdom.   These tribes also
passed away, when the condition of things was so changed as
to be uncongenial to their natures, to give place to a third
group, and these again to a fourth, and so on to the present
races, which, in their turn, perhaps, are destined to become
extinct.   From the first, however, the changes which the earth
has undergone, as to temperature, soil, and climate, have been
an improvement of its condition ; so that each successive
group of animals and plants could be more and more complicated and perfect ; and therefore we find an increase and
development of flowering plants and vertebral animals.   And
yet, from the beginning, all the great classes seem to have
existed, so that the changes have been only in the proportion
of the more and less perfect at different periods.   In short, we
have only to suppose that the Creator exactly adapted organic
natures to the several geological periods, and we perfectly
explain the phenomena of organic remains.   But the doctrine
of development by law corresponds only in a loose and general way to the facts, and cannot be reconciled to the details.
If that hypothesis cannot get a better foothold somewhere
else, it will soon find its way into the limbo of things abortive
and forgotten.

I have now noticed, I believe, the principal sources of evidence in which the law hypothesis rests ; and at the best, we
find only a possibility, but rarely, if ever, a probability, that
such a power exists in nature.   I turn now, for a few moments, to the arguments on the other side ; that is, against the
hypothesis.

And first, it cannot explain the wonderful adaptation of ani-
mals and plants to their condition and to one another.

There is not a more striking thing in nature than that adaptation; and geology shows us that it has always been so. Now, if any thing requires the exercise of infinite wisdom and power, it is this feature of creation. But according to this hypothesis, the laws of nature may be so arranged as to create every animal and plant just at the right time, and place them in the right spot, and adjust every thing around them to their nature and wants. In other words, it supposes law capable of doing what only infinite wisdom and power can do. What is this but ascribing infinite perfection to law, and imputing to it effects which only an infinite intelligence could bring about? In other words, it is making a Deity of the laws which he ordains. Theoretically it may be of little importance by what name men call the Deity; but practically to impute natural effects to law, as an independent power, is to put a blind, unintelligent agency in the place of Jehovah.

In the second place, where one fact in nature looks favorable to this hypothesis, a thousand facts teach the contrary.

Take for example the reproduction of animals. Out of every thousand individuals we have certain evidence that nine hundred and ninety-nine are brought into existence by the ordinary modes of generation; that is, they depend upon progenitors. Still, if in the thousandth case the animal's existence was clearly casual, if we could see an elephant, or an ox, start into life without parental agency, that single case would prove the hypothesis. But never do its advocates pretend that any of the larger animals are produced in this way. Nor is it till they get among the smaller and obscure animals, whose habits are very difficult to trace out, that we find any examples where a suspicion even can exist of the communication of vitality irrespective of parental agency. Is not a strong presumption hence produced that further and more

27 *

scrutinizing observation will show the few excepted cases not
to be real exceptions ?   Does not sound philosophy demand
that the proof of the casual production of the thousandth case
shall be as decided as that of the normal generation of the
nine hundred and ninety-nine ?   But no one, it seems to me,
will pretend that any thing like such certainty exists in a single
example throughout all nature.   The presumption, then, is
really more than a thousand to one against the hypothesis.

Take an example from hybridity.   While a thousand species retain from age to age their individuality, not more than
one coalesces with its neighbor, and loses its identity.   And
even here, all admit that there is a constant tendency in the
hybrid race to revert to the original stock ; and there is strong
reason to believe that this will sooner or later take place, and
that it would speedily occur in every case, were it not for the
influence of domestication.   Such facts make the presump
tion very strong, that species are permanent, and any exten
sive metamorphosis impossible.   Hybridity appears to be in a
measure unnatural ; and the old proverb true in respect to
it —

> " Si furca naturam expellas,
>   Usque recurret."

By the hypothesis under consideration, we ought to expec·
at least a few examples of the formation of new organs in
animals, in the efforts of nature to advance towards a more
perfect state.   It has usually been said that the time since
animals were first described is too short for such development.   But we have examples, from the catacombs of Egypt,
of animals and plants that lived in that country three thousand
years ago ; and yet, according to Cuvier, — and who is a better
judge ? — they are precisely like the living species.   Strange
that this great length of time should not have produced even

one new organ, or the marks of a conatus to produce one. We are, indeed, pointed to the different varieties of the human species, as examples of this progress. But these diversities, also, can be shown to be the same now as at the earliest date of historical records ; and where, then, is the evidence that they ever have undergone, or ever will undergo, any change of importance ? There may indeed be examples of amalgamation, but under favorable circumstances the original varieties are again developed.

In the third place, geology contradicts this hypothesis.

We have seen that it offers no satisfactory explanation of the gradual increase of the more perfect animals and plants, as we rise higher in the rocks. That fact is most perfectly explained by supposing that divine wisdom and benevolence adapted the new species, which from time to time were created, to the changing and improving condition of the earth. A multitude of species have been dug from the rocks ; but not one exhibits evidence of the development of new organs in the manner described by this hypothesis. New species often appear, but they differ as decidedly from the previous ones as species now do ; and at the beginning of each formation there is often a very decided advance in the organic beings from those found in the top of the subjacent formation. How can this hypothesis explain such sudden changes, when its essential principle is, that the progress of the development is uniform ? Nothing can explain them surely but special creating interposition.

Geology also shows us that for a vast period the world existed without inhabitants. Now, what was it that gave the laws of nature power, after so long an operation unproductive of vitality, to produce organic natures ? Who can conceive of any inherent force that should thus enable them, all at once, to do what true philosophy shows to have demanded infinite skill?

In short, of all the sciences, geology most clearly shows special divine interference to explain its phenomena. It presents us with such stupendous changes, after long periods of repose, such sudden exhibitions of life, springing forth from the bosom of universal death, that nothing but divine, special, miraculous agency can explain the results. And of all the vast domains of nature, it seems to me no part is so barren of facts to sustain this hypothesis as the rocks; nor so full of facts for its refutation. These, however, have been so fully detailed in a previous part of this lecture that they need not be here repeated.

In the fourth place, the prodigious increase of the power and the means of reproduction, which we find among the lower tribes of animals, affords a strong presumption against this hypothesis.

The animals highest on the scale, and most perfect in their organization, have only one mode of reproduction, viz., the viviparous. Descending a little lower, we come to the oviparous and ovoviviparous tribes. Passing to the invertebrate animals, we meet with two other modes of reproduction, the gemmiparous and fissiparous. In the first mode, the animal is propagated by buds, like some plants, as the tiger lily; by the second mode, a spontaneous division of the animal takes place.

Now, in some of the lowest of the invertebrate tribes, we find most of the modes of propagation that have been enumerated in operation; so that the same individual in one set of circumstances is oviparous, in another gemmiparous or fissiparous. The consequence is, a power of multiplication inconceivably great. Mr. Owen calculates that the *ascaris lumbricoides,* the most common intestinal worm, is capable of producing sixty-four millions of young ; and Ehrenberg asserts that the *hydatina senta,* one of the infusoria, increased in twelve days to sixteen millions, and another species, in four days, to one hundred and seventy billions.

Why, now, are these astonishing powers of reproduction given to these minute animals, if it be true that they can also be produced without parentage, and by mere law ?   This latter mode would supersede the necessity of the former ; and, therefore, the care taken by Providence to provide the former is a strong presumption that the latter does not exist.

In the fifth place, it is an instructive fact on this subject that, as instruments have been improved, and observations have become more searching, the supposed cases of spontaneous generation have diminished, until it is not pretended now that it takes place except in a very few tribes, and those the most obscure and difficult to observe of all living things. A hundred years ago, naturalists, and especially other men, might easily have been made to believe that many of the smaller insects had a casual origin.   But long since, save in the matter of the acari, the entomological field has been abandoned by the advocates of the law hypothesis, and they have been driven from one tribe after another, till at length some of the obscure hiding-places of the entozoa and infusoria are now the only spots where the light is not too strong for the large-pupiled eyes of this hypothesis.   Is not the presumption hence arising very strong that it will need only a little further improvement in instruments and care in observation to carry daylight into these recesses, and demonstrate the parentage and normal development of all organic beings ?

Finally. The gross materialism inseparable from this hypothesis is a strong argument against it.

I am not aware that any one, except Oken, perhaps, has ever attempted to show that mind, as a spiritual essence, distinct from matter, has been created by natural laws; in other words, that there is in nature a power to produce mind. All such maintain that intellect is material, or, rather, the result of organization, the mere function of the brain, as are also life and instinct. Generally, also, they contend — and, indeed, consistency seems to require it — that the moral powers depend chiefly upon different developments of the brain; so that a disposition to do wrong results more from organization than from punishable mental obliquity; indeed, the worst of criminals are often, on this account, more to be pitied than blamed, and the physician is of more importance than the moralist and the divine for their reformation.

Now, if this system of materialism is true, we ought to embrace it, without any fear of ultimate bad effects. But a philosopher will hesitate long before he adopts a system which thus seems to degrade man from his lofty standing as a spiritual, accountable, and immortal being, and makes his intellectual and moral powers dependent upon the structure of the brain, and, therefore, destined to perish with the material organization, with no hope of future existence, unless God chooses to recreate the man. Nay, if there be no distinct spirit in man, what evidence have we that there is one in Jehovah? A true philosopher, I say, will demand very strong evidence before he adopts any hypothesis that leads a logical mind to such conclusions; and I see not how the one under consideration can terminate in any thing else.

Such are the reasons that lead me to reject the hypothesis of creation by law. I have endeavored to treat the subject in a candid and philosophical manner, not charging atheism upon its advocates when they declare themselves Theists and

Christians. Neither have I called in the aid of ridicule, as might easily be done, and as, in fact, has been done by almost every opponent of the system who has written upon it. I have endeavored to show that the hypothesis, tried in the balances of sound philosophy, is found wanting; because, in the first place, the facts adduced to sustain it are insufficient; and secondly, because, where one fact seems to favor it, a thousand testify against it. Is not the conclusion a fair one, that the hypothesis has no solid foundation? Is not the evidence against it overwhelming? Yet it has many advocates, and I must think — I hope not uncharitably — that these are the reasons: First, because men do not like the idea of a personal, present, overruling Deity; and secondly, because there is very little profound and thorough knowledge of natural history in the community. It is just such an hypothesis as chimes in with the taste of that part of the world who have a smattering of science, and who do not wish to live without some form of religion, but who still desire to free themselves from the inspection of a holy God, and from the responsibility which his existence and presence would impose. Depend upon it, gentlemen, you will meet these delusions not unfrequently among the cultivated classes of society, where they have already done immense mischief. You will, indeed, find all the eminent comparative anatomists and physiologists, such as Cuvier and Owen; such chemists as Liebig; such zoölogists as Agassiz and Edward Forbes; such botanists as Hooker, Henslow, Lindley, Torrey, and Gray; and such geologists as De la Beche, Lyell, Murchison, Sedgwick, D'Orbigny, Buckland, and Miller, decided in their rejection of these views. But when even educated men obtain only a smattering of natural science, they find something very fascinating in this hypothesis; and this is just the religion, or,

rather, the irreligion, that suits the superficial, selfish, and
pleasure-seeking exquisites of fashionable drawing-rooms,
theatres, and watering-places. You will find, therefore, the
need of thoroughly studying this subject, or you will not be
able, as you would wish, to vindicate the cause of true science
and true religion.

I cannot terminate this discussion without referring to an
ingenious analogy, suggested by Hugh Miller, in his " Footprints of the Creator," and drawn from the facts he had stated
respecting the degradation of species. No one who has
thoroughly studied Bishop Butler's Analogy of Natural and
Revealed Religion to the Course of Nature will venture to
say that Mr. Miller's suggestions are mere fancy. As the ideas
are entirely original with him, I give them .n his own words.

Having spoken of the several dynasties of animals that have
succeeded one another on the globe, in a passage which we
have already quoted, he says, " Passing on to the revealed
record, we learn that the dynasty of man in the mixed state
and character is not the final one ; but that there is to be yet
another creation, or, more properly, re-creation, known theo-
logically as the resurrection, which shall be connected in its
physical components, by bonds of mysterious paternity, with
the dynasty which now reigns, and be bound to it mentally
by the chain of identity, conscious and actual ; but which, in
all that constitutes superiority, shall be as vastly its superior
as the dynasty of responsible man is superior to even the
lowest of the preliminary dynasties. We are further taught
that, at the commencement of this last of the dynasties, there
will be a re-creation of not only elevated, but also of degraded
beings — a re-creation of the lost. We are taught yet further that, though the present dynasty be that of a lapsed race,
which at their first introduction were placed on higher ground

than that on which they now stand, and sank by their own act, it was yet part of the original design, from the beginning of all things, that they should occupy the existing platform; and that redemption is thus no afterthought, rendered necessary by the fall, but, on the contrary, part of a general scheme, for which provision had been made from the beginning; so that the divine Man, through whom the work of restoration has been effected, was in reality, in reference to the purposes of the Eternal, what he is designated in the remarkable text, *the Lamb slain from the foundation of the world.* Slain from the foundation of the world! Could the assertors of the stony science ask for language more express? By piecing the two records together, — that revealed in Scripture and that revealed in the rocks, — records which, however widely geologists may mistake the one, or commentators misunderstand the other, have emanated from the same great Author, — we learn that in slow and solemn majesty has period succeeded period, each in succession, ushering in a higher and yet higher scene of existence; that fish, reptiles, mammiferous quadrupeds, have reigned in turn; that responsible man, 'made in the image of God,' and with dominion over all creatures, ultimately entered into a world ripened for his reception; but, further, that this passing scene, in which he forms the prominent figure, is not the final one in the long series, but merely the last of the *preliminary* scenes; and that that period to which the by-gone ages, incalculable in amount, with all their well-proportioned gradations of being, form the imposing vestibule, shall have perfection for its occupant and eternity for its duration. I know not how it may appear to others, but for my own part I cannot avoid thinking that there would be a lack of proportion in the series of being, were the period of perfect and glorified humanity abruptly con-

28

nected, without the introduction of an intermediate creation of *responsible* imperfection with that of the dying, irresponsible brute. That scene of things in which God became man, and suffered, *seems*, as it no doubt *is*, a necessary link in the chain."

A single concluding thought. forces itself upon my mind. It is this : How ingenious and persevering men are in deluding themselves on the subject of religion ! Since the time of Christ, what countless devices have they framed to escape from the lofty truths and spiritual piety of his gospel ! Nor are they satisfied with this ; for the gospel has shed so much light upon the religion of nature, that even this is more than men like ; and, therefore, every science is ransacked for facts to neutralize all religion. Men's consciences do not permit them to throw off all the forms of religion ; and, therefore, they are satisfied if they can only tear cut its heart. They like to preserve and to embalm its external covering, as the naturalist does the skin of an animal for his cabinet. And as the latter fills his specimen with straw and arsenic, and fits glass eyes into it, so do men fill up their religious specimen with error and vain speculation, and fit into its head the eyes of false philosophy, and then claim for it intellectual worship. It is the business of educated men to show that such caricatures are neither science nor religion. May you, gentlemen, have your full share in this most useful and noble work.*

* The subject of this lecture has been ably discussed, within a few years, in most of the leading periodicals in Europe and America, though I must say not always with the candor calculated to do the most good. The two most able volumes that have fallen into my hands, on the subject, are Professor Sedgwick's "Discourse on the Studies of the University," &c., (fifth ed., London, 1850,) and Hugh Miller's "Footprints of the Creator," now republished in this country.

LECTURE X.

SPECIAL AND MIRACULOUS PROVIDENCE.

NEXT in importance to the question whether the Deity exists, is the inquiry whether he exerts any direct agency in upholding the universe and in controlling its events. This point has been discussed in all ages in which there have been philosophers or theologians, and the current of opinion has fallen principally into three channels.

In the first place, some have removed the Deity entirely from his works into a fancied extra-mundane sphere, where in solitude he might enjoy the blessedness of his own infinite nature, without the trouble of directing the events of the universe, or watching over the works of his hand. Forgetful of the great principle, that the intellectual powers produce happiness only when called into exercise, they have fancied that the care of the universe must be a burden to its Creator, and that it would derogate from his dignity. It is supposed, therefore, that the world has been given up to the rule of fate or chance.

In the second place, a more numerous class have maintained that the Supreme Being, after creating the world, committed its preservation and government either to a subordinate agent, or to the laws which he impressed upon matter and mind, which possess an inherent power to execute themselves; so that, in fact, God exercises no direct and immediate agency in natural operations. The learned and usually profound

Cudworth adopted the hypothesis of a *plastic nature,* as he terms it, by which he means a vital, spiritual, and unintelligent, yet subordinate agent, by whose agency the world is governed and its operations carried on. At first view, this hypothesis would seem to lead inevitably to atheism; but such was not the intention of its author. Still, it is obviously so clumsy, that had it not been the product of a great mind, it never would have received so much notice, or called forth such mighty efforts for its refutation, as have been bestowed upon it.

Two varieties of opinion exist among those who believe the world governed and sustained by natural laws, established by the Deity. Some maintain that these laws are general, not particular; not extending to minor events, but only the more important; not providing for species, but only for families. Hence they suppose that these general cases may interfere with one another, and produce results apparently repugnant to the intention of their Author. Others, shocked at the absurdity of such conclusions, believe the laws of nature to extend to every event, and never to interfere with one another, and always to act in accordance with the divine will and appointment, but without any direct agency exerted by the Deity. They suppose these laws — in other words, secondary agencies — to have the power of producing all natural phenomena.

In the third place, there are others who believe that a law can have no efficiency without the presence and agency of the lawgiver. They, therefore, suppose every event in the natural world to be the result of the direct and immediate agency of God. What we call laws are only the uniform mode of his operation. They agree with the advocates of the last-named theory in supposing the laws of nature to

extend to every event, and to be in accordance with the ordination of the Deity ; but they differ in maintaining that the
presence and direct efficiency of a lawgiver are essential to
the operation of natural laws.

I should then define a Special Providence to be an event
brought about apparently by natural laws, yet, in fact, the
result of a special agency, on the part of the Deity, to meet a
particular exigency, either by an original arrangement of
natural laws, or by a modification of second causes, out of
sight at the time.

The doctrine, which supposes the Deity to exercise a superintendence and direction over all the affairs of the universe,
in any of the modes that have been mentioned, whether by a
subordinate agent, or by laws, general or particular, with
inherent self-executing power, or by the direct efficiency of
the divine will, is called the doctrine of divine providence.
If the superintendence extend only to general laws, it is called
a general providence. If those laws reach every possible case,
it is called a particular or universal providence.

By a *Miraculous Providence* is meant a superintendence
over the world that interferes, when desirable, with the regular operations of nature, and brings about events, either in
opposition to natural laws, or by giving them a less or greater
power than usual. In either of these cases, the events
cannot be explained by natural laws ; they are above, or
contrary to, nature, and, therefore, are called miracles, or
prodigies.

There may be, and, as I believe, there is, another class of
occurrences, intermediate between miracles and events strictly
natural. These take place in perfect accordance with the
natural laws within human view, and appear to us to be
perfectly accounted for by those laws ; and yet, in some way

28 *

or other, we learn that they required some special exercise of divine power, out of human view, for their production. Thus, according to the views of most Christian denominations, conversion takes place in the human heart in perfect accordance with the laws of mind, and could be philosophically explained by them ; yet revelation assures that it *is not of blood*, [natural descent,] *nor of the will of the flesh, nor of the will of man, but of God.* Divine power, therefore, is essential to the change, although we see only the operation of natural causes. So a storm may appear to us to be perfectly accounted for by natural laws; and yet divine efficiency might have produced a change in some of those laws out of our sight, and thus meet a particular exigency. Such events I call *special providence ;* and I maintain that we cannot tell how frequently they may occur.

It is chiefly the bearings of science, especially of geology, upon the doctrine of miraculous and special providence, which I wish to consider. But it may form a useful introduction, to state the evidence, which goes to show that the agency of the Deity, in the ordinary operations of nature, is a direct efficiency ; or, in other words, that the laws of nature are only the modes in which divine agency operates.

In the first place, if we suppose ever so many secondary causes to be concerned in natural events, the efficiency must, after all, be referred to God.

What is a secondary cause ? or, in other words, what is a law of nature considered as a cause ? It is simply a uniform mode of operation. We find that heavy bodies uniformly tend towards the earth's centre, and that we call the law of gravity; but if those bodies sometimes ascended, and sometimes moved horizontally, under the same circumstances, we could not infer the existence of such a law.

Now, there must be some cause for uniformity of operation in nature. There must be some foreign power, which gives the uniformity, since it is certain that the law itself can possess no efficiency. We may, indeed, find one law dependent upon a second law, and this upon a third, and so on. But the inquiry still arises, What gives the efficiency to this second and third law? and still the answer must be, Something out of itself. So that if we run back on the chain of causes ever so far, we must still resort to the power of the Deity to find any efficiency that will produce the final result. In most cases, we can trace back only one or two links on the chain. For instance, we account for the falling of all bodies by the law of gravity. But philosophers have wearied themselves in vain to find any cause for gravity, except in the will of God. The failure of every other hypothesis, though invented by such men as Newton and Le Sage, has been signal. Sound philosophy, then, requires us to infer that gravity owes its efficiency to the direct exertion of divine power. And so in all cases, when we can no longer discover second causes for any phenomenon, why should we imagine their existence, rather than refer it to the agency of God? For go back as far as we may, and discover a thousand intervening causes, the efficiency resides alone in God. We have no evidence that even infinite power can communicate that efficiency to the laws of nature, so that they can act without the presence and agency of God. The common idea, which endows those laws with independent power, will not bear examination.

In the second place, if natural operations do not depend upon the exercise of divine power, no other efficient cause can be assigned for their production.

We have seen that in the laws of nature, independently of the Deity, there is no efficiency; and I know not where else we can resort for any agency to carry forward the operations of nature, except to the same infinite Being. The fate and chance of the ancients, the plastic nature of Cudworth, the delegated nature of Lamarck, are indeed names invented by men to designate a certain imaginary efficiency residing somewhere, independent of the Deity, by which the phenomena of nature have been supposed to be produced. But the moment they are described, they are found to be mere imaginary agencies, meaning nothing more than the course of nature, or the laws of nature, which we have seen possess no independent efficiency. To a divine agency, therefore, we must resort, or be left without any adequate cause for the complicated and wonderful processes of nature.

In the third place, this view of the subject is strongly confirmed by the Christian Scriptures.

How universal is the divine agency represented in the well-known passage — *for of him, and through him, and to him, are all things.* Equally vivid is Paul's statement on Mars Hill — *In him we live, and move, and have our being.* How graphic a description is the 147th Psalm of God's agency in the natural world! Not only is all good ascribed to God, but evil also. By the mouth of Isaiah he says, *I form light and create darkness; I make peace and create evil; I the Lord do all these things.* In short, no event in the material or spiritual world is by the sacred writers ascribed to chance, or to nature, or the laws of nature, as it is among men; but to the direct efficiency of God. Nor is there any difference in this respect between miracles and common events. The one class is represented as originating in the agency of God, just as much as the other.

Finally. It will hardly be thought strange, in view of the preceding considerations, that a large proportion of the most acute and philosophical minds in modern times have preferred this view of divine providence to any other.

Sir Isaac Newton declares that the various parts of the world, organic and inorganic, " can be the effect of nothing else than the wisdom and skill of a powerful, ever-living Agent, who, being in all places, is more able by his will to move the bodies within his boundless, uniform *sensorium*, thereby to form and reform the parts of the universe, than we are by our will to move the parts of our own bodies."

Says Dr. Clarke, the friend and disciple of Newton, " All things which we commonly say are the effects of the natural powers of matter, and laws of motion, are, indeed, if we will speak strictly and properly, the effects of God's action upon matter continually, and at every moment, either immediately by himself, or mediately by some created, intelligent being. Consequently there is no such thing as the course of nature, or the power of nature, independent of the effects produced by the will of God."

In speaking of the principle of vegetable life, Sir James Edward Smith, the eminent botanist, says, " I humbly conceive that, if the human understanding can in any case flatter itself with obtaining, in the natural world, a glimpse of the *immediate agency* of the Deity, it is in the contemplation of this *vital principle*, which seems independent of material organization, and an impulse of his own divine energy." — *Introduction to Botany*, p. 26, (Boston edition.)

" We would no way be understood," says Sir John Herschel, " to deny the constant exercise of this [God's] direct power in maintaining the system of nature, or the ultimate emanation of every energy, which material agents exert, from his immediate will, acting in conformity with his own laws." — *Discourse on Nat. Philosophy.*

" A law," says Professor Whewell, " supposes an agent
and a power ; for it is the mode according to which the agent
proceeds, the order according to which the power acts.
Without the presence of such an agent, of such a power,
conscious of the relations on which the law depends, producing the effects which the law prescribes, the law can have
no efficiency, no existence.   Hence we infer that the intelligence by which the law is ordained, the power by which it is
put in action, must be present at all times and in all places
where the effects of the law occur ; that thus the knowledge
and the agency of the divine Being pervades every portion
of the universe, producing all action and passion, all permanence and change.   The laws of nature are the laws which
He, in his wisdom, prescribes to his own acts ; his universal
presence is the necessary condition of any course of events ;
his universal agency the only origin of any efficient force."
— *Bridgewater Treatise*, p. 270.

" The student in natural philosophy," observes the Bishop
of London, " will find rest from all those perplexities, which
are occasioned by the obscurity of causation, in the proposition which, although it was discredited by the patronage of
Malebranche and the Cartesians, has been adopted by Clarke
and Dugald Stewart, and which is by far the most simple and
sublime account of the matter — that all events which are
continually taking place in the different parts of the material
universe are the *immediate* effects of the divine agency." —
Whewell's Bridgewater Treatise, p. 273.

" Jonathan Edwards," says M'Cosh in his Method of the
Divine Government, " somewhere illustrates the manner in
which God upholds the universe, by the way in which an
image is upheld in a mirror.   That image is maintained by a
continual flow of rays of light, each succeeding pencil of

which does not differ from that by which the image was first
produced. He conceives that the universe is, in every part
of it, supported in a similar way by a continual succession
of acts of the divine will, and these not differing from that
which at first caused the world to spring into existence. Now,
it may be safely said of this theory that it cannot be disproved. Several considerations may be urged in support
of it."

Which of the views respecting divine providence that have
been stated has the best practical tendency, seems hardly to
admit of doubt. If we believe that God has submitted the
direction and government of this world to a subordinate
agent, a plastic nature ; or if we suppose he has impressed
matter and mind with certain general laws, which have the
power of executing themselves without his agency, and
especially if in their operation they do sometimes actually
clash with one another, or even if those laws extend to every
movement of matter and mind, — still, if they do not require
divine efficiency, men cannot but feel that God is removed
from his works, and that the laws of nature, and not his
agency, are their security. But if they believe that every
movement of matter or mind requires a direct exercise of divine power or efficiency, just as much as if every event was
a miracle, it cannot but bring God near to us, and make us
realize his presence.

If we obtain a timepiece from London or Paris, which
contains all the springs and wheels requisite to keep it in operation, by occasionally winding it up, how little do we think
of the artist who constructed it, except, perhaps, occasionally
to admire his ingenuity ! But if it had been necessary for
that artist to accompany the chronometer, and actually to put
forth the strength of his own arm every moment to keep it in

motion, how much more should we think of him and realize his presence ! The same effect, in a greater or less degree, will attend the belief that God must be not only virtually, but substantially, present every where, and be constantly exercising his power to keep in operation the vast machine of the universe. It cannot but deeply impress the heart, and exert a most salutary influence upon the affections, to realize that every event around us is brought about by the immediate agency of the supreme Being.

But notwithstanding the salutary influence of this view of Providence upon our moral feelings, and though philosophy pronounces it decidedly the most reasonable, still it meets with strong opposition. I need not stop to notice the objections, that it makes God the author of evil as well as good, and that it represents man as a mere machine in the hands of the Deity, and therefore takes away human responsibility. I say I need not stop to answer such objections, because they lie equally strong against any system which makes God the original author of the universe. But a more plausible objection is, that it makes all events miraculous. This objection is based on the supposition that every event which takes place through the direct and immediate agency of God is a miracle. But is this the true meaning of a miracle? Is the term ever applied to any but extraordinary events? It may or it may not imply a contravention of the laws of nature. But it does always imply something which the laws of nature cannot produce, and which, of course, they cannot explain. It is always the result of some new force coming in to the aid of the laws of nature, or in the place of them, or even sometimes, perhaps, in opposition to them; as when the *sun stood still upon Gibeon, and the moon in the valley of Ajalon.* Hence an event may take place through the direct and immediate agency of God, and yet not be a miracle. If it be neither above, nor independent of, nor in opposition to the laws of nature, then it forms a part of the ordinary providence of God ; it is a part of the usual, the fixed and uniform course of nature, and can be explained by known and unalterable laws. The nature of the event is not affected at all by the question whether it is produced by the direct efficiency of God, or by a power inherent in those laws. We, who believe that the direct efficiency of God is necessary to the operation, and even to the existence, of the laws of nature, are just as firm believers in the constancy of those laws as he who supposes them possessed of inherent powers. When that constancy is interrupted in any way, we call it a miracle. Hence it appears that our views of the nature of a miracle are the same as his, viz., an event which takes place out of the ordinary course of nature ; and, therefore, our system is no more liable to the objection that all events are made miracles than his system.

The way is now prepared for inquiring what geology teaches respecting the ordinary and extraordinary providence of God over this world.

The evidences of ordinary providence, which are common to geology and other sources of proof, I shall pass by ; both because they are familiar to all, and because I have, in a former lecture, shown the existence and operation of the present laws of nature in all past ages. But there is one feature of the past condition of the world taught by geology to which I would call your attention, as exhibiting a more impressive view of the wisdom and skill of ordinary providence than almost any other department of nature presents. When the heavenly bodies are once put under the control of the two great forces that guide them, viz., the centrifugal and cen tripetal, we see no reason why they may not move on forever in their accustomed paths. But the two great agents of geological change, fire and water, have an aspect of great irregularity and violence, and are apparently less under the control of mathematical laws. In the mighty intensity of their action in early times, we can hardly see how there could have been much of security or permanence in the state of the globe, without the constant restraining energy of Jehovah. We feel as if the earth's crust must have been constantly liable to be torn in pieces by volcanic fires, or drenched by sweeping deluges. And yet the various economies of life on the globe, that have preceded the present, have all been seasons of profound repose and uniformity. The truth is, these mighty agencies have been just as much under the divine control as those which regulate the heavenly bodies; and I doubt not but the laws that regulate their action are as fixed and mathematical as those which guide the sun, moon, and planets. Still, it must have required infinite wisdom and power so to arrange the agencies of nature that the desolating action of fire and water should take place only at those epochs when every thing was in readiness for the ruin of an old economy and the introduction of a new one. Geological agencies differ from astronomical in this — that the former must be allowed an irregular action within certain limits; bereas the latter act with unvarying uniformity in all circumstances. If the former had not some room for irregular action, they would not act at all; but if allowed too much liberty, they will destroy what they were intended to preserve. And God does restrain, and always has restrained them, just at the point where desolation would be the result of their more powerful operation. I do not, indeed, contend that it requires more power or wisdom to bind those mighty agencies within proper limits than to control the heavenly bodies. But to our limited faculties it certainly seems a more difficult work; and, therefore, the geological history of the globe gives us a more impressive idea of the ordinary providence of God than we see in the calm and uniform movements of nature around us.

In the second place, geology furnishes us with some very striking examples of miraculous providence.

In disproving the eternity of the organic world, in a former lecture, I adduced and illustrated these examples so fully, that I shall do little more in this place than give a recapitulation of that argument.

If we suppose the earth originally to have been merely a diffused mass of vapor, like comets, or nebulæ, I can conceive how, by the operation of such natural laws as now exist, it might have been condensed into a solid globe; into a melted state, indeed, from the amount of heat extricated in the condensation. Those same laws might subsequently form over the molten mass a solid crust, which, at length, might be ridged and furrowed by the action of internal heat, so as to form the basis of continents and the beds of oceans. In due time, the vapors might condense, so as to fill those basins with water; and, by the mutual and alternate action of the waters above and the heat beneath, the rocks might be comminuted, so as to form the basis of soils. So far might the arrangements of the world have proceeded by natural laws; in other words, by the ordinary providence of God. But at this point we must bring in an extraordinary agency of the Deity, or the world would have remained, in the expressive language of revelation, *without form and void;* that is, invisible and unfurnished. You have, indeed, the framework of a world, but the most difficult and complicated part of the work,

the creation of plants and animals, remains yet to be performed.   Here, then, is the precise point where you must
call in the miraculous agency of the Deity, or the earth would
forever remain an uninhabited waste. For if it does not
require miraculous agency to bring into existence animals
and plants, I know not what can require it, or prove its operation.   I can almost as easily conceive how matter might
spring from nothing fortuitously, certainly I can as easily
conceive of its eternity, as that organism and life can result
from the ordinary laws of nature.

It may be, however, that I shall here be met by the statement, that some distinguished geologists maintain the probable
existence of organized beings on the globe at an indefinitely
earlier period than that in which their remains first appear in
the rocks.   They contend that the extreme heat which has
melted the older rocks has obliterated all traces of organic
existence below a certain line.   Now, in order to meet this
difficulty, it is not necessary to show this opinion to be erroneous.   We have only to advance another step in our general
argument, which brings us upon ground admitted to be good
by the geologists above alluded to.   They all of them believe
that many new animals and plants have from time to time
appeared on the globe ; that, in fact, there have been several
almost entire changes in its inhabitants.   Most of them suppose these new races to have been introduced in large numbers at particular epochs, though some prefer the theory
which supposes the new species to have been introduced one
by one, as the old ones became extinct.   But even this supposition does not essentially affect my argument ; because
they all allow that these successive species were really new,
and could not have been the result of any metamorphosis of
the old species.   And it is the fact that new organic beings

nave, from time to time, been created, that is alone essential to my argument. Whether they were created by groups or singly, is an interesting geological question ; but, in either case, miraculous power must have been put forth as really and as efficiently to call into existence a single new species of animalcula, or sea-weed, as to introduce an entirely new race. The successive economies of organic life that have existed on the earth, and passed from it, do most unequivocally demonstrate the extraordinary or miraculous providence of God.

But we might abandon even this strong ground of our argument, and still geology would afford us a most unequivocal example of the creative agency of the Deity. That science shows, beyond all question, that man, and most of his contemporary races of animals and plants, have not always occupied this globe ; and, indeed, that they were not placed upon it till nearly every form buried in the rocks had passed away. And since those races which now inhabit the globe have among them a larger proportion of highly organized and more complicated species than have ever before been contemporaries, — especially since man is among them, confessedly the most perfect in organization and in intellect of all the beings that ever occupied this planet, — we can here point to the highest exercise of creative power ever exhibited in this lower world, as a certain memento of God's extraordinary or miraculous providence. Indeed, who, that has any adequate idea of the wonders of man's intellectual, moral, and immortal nature, and of the strange extremes that meet and harmonize in his physical and intellectual constitution, will believe that any loftier miracle has ever been exhibited on this globe than his creation ?

But I have already dwelt so long upon this whole argu-

29 *

ment in a former lecture, that I will add no more in this place. If the facts which I have stated do not prove the miraculous agency of the Deity in past ages, I know not how it can be proved. But assuming this position to be established, and several inferences of importance will follow.

In the first place, this subject removes all philosophical presumption against a special revelation from heaven.

If we can prove that the Deity has often so interfered with the course of nature as to introduce new species, nay, whole races of animals and plants upon the globe, — if, in a comparatively recent period, he has created a moral and immortal being, endowed with all the powers of a free and an accountable agent, — it would surely be no more wonderful if he should communicate to that being his will by a written revelation. Indeed, the benevolence of the Deity, as we learn it from nature, would create a presumption that such a revelation would be given, if it appear, as we know it does, that no sufficient knowledge is inherent in his nature to guide him in the path of duty ; since such a revelation would be no greater miracle than to people the world, originally destitute of life, and then to repeople it again and again, with so vast a variety of organic natures. Philosophy has sometimes been disinclined to admit the claims of revelation, because it implies a supernatural agency of the Deity ; and, until recently, revelation seemed to be a solitary example of special interference on the part of Jehovah. But geology adds other examples, long anterior to revelation — examples registered, like the laws of Sinai, on tables of stone. And the admission of the geological evidence of special interference with the regular sequence of nature's operations ought to predispose the mind for listening to the appropriate proofs of a moral communication to ignorant and erring man.

In the second place, the subject shows us how groundless is the famous objection to the miracles recorded in Scripture, founded on the position that they are contrary to experience.

" It is," says Mr. Hume, " a maxim worthy of our attention, that no testimony is sufficient to establish a miracle, unless the testimony be of such a kind, that its falsehood would be more miraculous than the fact which it endeavors to establish." Hence he asserts, that " the evidence of testimony, when applied to a miracle, carries falsehood on the very face of it, and is more properly a subject of derision than of argument, " and that whoever believes the Christian religion is conscious of a continued miracle in his own person, which subverts all the principles of his understanding, and gives him a determination to believe what is most contrary to custom and experience."

At the time when Mr. Hume wrote, and with his great skill in weaving together metaphysical subtilties, such an argument might deceive superficial minds ; for then a miracle was supposed to be contrary to all experience. But geology has disclosed many new chapters in the world's history, and shown the existence of miracles earlier than chronological dates. Even Mr. Hume would hardly deny that the creation of whole series of animals and plants was miraculous ; and yet, in proof of that creation, we need not depend upon testimony ; for we can read it with our own eyes upon the solid rocks. Such proof appeals directly to our common sense ; nor can any ingenious quibble, concerning the nature of human testimony, weaken its influence in producing conviction.

And if God has wrought stupendous miracles of creation in order to people the world, who does not see that it is still more probable he would perform other miracles when they were needed to substantiate a revelation of his will to those moral and accountable beings, who needed its special teachings to make them acquainted with their God, their duty, and their destiny?

Finally. The subject removes all presumption against the exercise of a special and miraculous providence in the divine government of the world.

In all ages of the world, philosophers, and even many theologians, have been strenuous opposers of special and miraculous providence. If they have admitted, as most of the latter class have done, that some miracles were performed in ancient times, they have strenuously maintained that the doctrine of special providence in these days is absurd, and that God cannot, without a miracle, bestow any special favors upon the virtuous in answer to their prayers, or inflict any special punishments upon the wicked; and that it is fanaticism to expect any other retributions than such as the ordinary and unmodified course of nature brings along with it.

The unvarying constancy of nature, in consequence of being governed by fixed laws, is the grand argument which they adduce in opposition to any supposed special providence. *Since the fathers fell asleep,* say they, *all things continue as they were from the beginning.* God has subjected the world to the government of laws, and he will not interfere with, counteract, set aside, or give a supernatural force to those laws, to meet particular exigencies. For the adjustment of all apparent inequalities of good and evil, suffering and enjoyment here, we must wait for the disclosure of eternity, when strict retributive Justice will hold her even scales. When natural evils come upon us, therefore, it is idle to expect their removal, except so far as they may be mitigated or overcome by natural means; and hence it is useless to pray for their removal, or to expect God will deliver us from them in any other way. When the heavens over us become brass, and the earth under our feet iron, and the rain of our land is powder and dust, and want, and famine, as the consequence, stalk forth among the inhabitants, of what use to pray to God for rain, since to give it would require a miracle, and the age of miracles has passed? When the pestilence is scouring through the land, and our neighbors and nearest friends are within its grasp, and we may next become its victims, — nay, when we, too, are on the borders of the grave, — why should we expect relief by prayer, since sickness is the result of natural causes, and God will not interpose to save us from the effects of natural evils, because that would be contrary to a fixed rule of his government? When dangers cluster around the good man in the discharge of trying duties, it would be enthusiasm in him to expect any special protection against his enemies, though he pray ever so fervently, and trust in divine deliverance with ever so much confidence. He must look to another world for his reward, if called to suffer here. Nor has the daringly wicked man any reason to fear that God will punish his violations of the divine law by any unusual display of his power; not in any way, indeed, but by the evils which naturally flow from a wicked life. In short, it will be useless to pray for any blessing that requires the least interference with natural laws, or for the removal of any evil which depends upon those laws. And since our minds are controlled as much by laws as the functions of our bodies, we are not to expect any blessings in our souls, which require the least infringement of intellectual laws. In fine, the effect of prayer is limited almost entirely to its influence upon our own hearts, in preparing them to receive with a proper spirit natural blessings, and to bear aright natural evils; to stimulate us to use with more diligence the means of avoiding or removing the latter, and securing the former.

Not a few philosophers of distinction, and some theologians, have adopted these views. Even Dr. Thomas Brown uses the following language : " It is quite evident that even Omnipotence, which cannot do what is contradictory, cannot combine both advantages — the advantage of regular order in the sequences of nature, and the advantages of a uniform adaptation of the particular circumstances of the individual. We may take our choice, but we cannot think of a combination of both; and if, as is very obvious, the greater advantage be that of uniformity of operation, we must not complain of the evils to which that very uniformity which we cannot fail to prefer — if the option had been allowed us — has been the very circumstance that gave rise." — *Lecture* 94.

" Science," says George Combe, " has banished from the minds of profound thinkers belief in the exercise by the Deity, in our day, of special acts of supernatural power, as a means of influencing human affairs ; and it has presented a systematic order of nature, which man may study, comprehend, and follow, as a guide to his practical conduct. Many educated laymen, and also a number of the clergy, have declined to recognize fasts, humiliations, and prayers, as means adapted, according to their views, to avert the recurrence of the evil, [the potato blight.] Indeed, these observances, inasmuch as they mislead the public mind with respect to its causes, are regarded by such persons as positive evils."

" The most irreligious of all religious notions, as it seems to us," says the North American Review, " is a belief in special providences ; for if the doctrine has any weight at all, it is gained at the expense of a general providence. To assume to

detect God as nearer to us on some occasions is to put him
farther off from us on other occasions. To have him in special
incidents is to forget him in the common tenor of events.
The doctrine of special providences evidently has no other
foundation than this, that men *think they can detect* God's
purpose and presence more signally in some incidents than
in others ; so that the doctrine, after all, is only a compli-
ment to man's power of detection, instead of an acknowledgment of God's special presence."

Such views and reasonings seem, upon a superficial examination, to be very plausible. But when we look into the
Bible, we cannot but see that the main drift of it is directly
opposed to such notions. That book does encourage man to
pray to God for the removal of evils of every kind ; evils as
much dependent upon natural laws as the daily course of the
sun through the heavens. It does teach us to look to God in
every trying situation for deliverance, if it is best for us to be
delivered. It does represent the wicked man as in danger
of special punishment. It exhibits a multitude of examples,
in which God has thus delivered those who trusted in him,
and punished those who violated his laws.

In every age, too, the most devotedly pious men have testified, that they have found deliverance and support in circumstances in which mere natural laws could afford them no
relief. Moreover, when men are brought into great peril or
suffering of any kind, they involuntarily cry to God for help.
When the vessel founders in the fury of the storm, the hardened sailor employs that breath in ardent prayer which just
before had been poured out in blasphemies. And when the
widowed mother hears the tempest howling around her dwelling at night, she cannot but pray for the protection of her
child upon the treacherous sea. When violent disease racks

the frame, and we feel ourselves rapidly sinking into the grave, it is scarcely in human nature to omit crying to God with a feeling that he can save us. In short, it is a dictate of nature to call upon God in times of trouble. Our reasoning about the constancy of nature, which appears to us while in safety so clearly to show prayer for the removal of natural evils to be useless, loses its power, and the feelings of the heart triumph. It now becomes, therefore, an important practical question, which of these views of the providence of God is correct. Is it those which our reasoning derives from the constancy of nature, or those inspired by piety and the Bible? I have already said, that the subject of this lecture removes all presumption against the latter view ; and I now proceed to show how God can exercise a special providence over the world, so as to meet the case of every individual, whether for blessing or punishment, and that, too, without miracles.

Whoever believes that geology discloses stupendous miracles of creation, at various epochs, will not doubt that all presumption against miraculous agency at any other time is thus removed. For we are thus shown that the law of miracles forms a part of the divine plan in the government of the world. But this does not prove the same to be the fact in respect to a law of special providence.

It is indeed true that geology gives us no distinct examples of special providence, in the sense which we have attached to that term in the present lecture. But it does furnish a multitude of instances in which changes of physical condition in the earth were met by most wisely adapted changes of organic nature. And even though these changes were the result of miraculous agency, they disclose this principle of the divine government, viz., that peculiarities of condition are to be met by special arrangements, so that every exigency shall be provided for in the manner infinite wisdom sees to be best. Now, this principle constitutes the essence of special providence; and, therefore, geology, in showing its past operation in the world's early organic history, affords a presumption that the same unchanging God may still employ it in his natural and moral government.

But does not this principle of special adaptation to individual exigencies demand miraculous agency in all cases? Can the wants of individuals be met in any other way than by miracles, or by the ordinary and settled laws of nature? I maintain that there are other modes in which this can be done; in which, in fact, every case requiring special interference can be met exactly and fully.

This can be done, in the first place, by a divine influence exerted upon the human mind, unperceived by the individual.

If it were perceived, it would constitute a miracle. But can we doubt that the Author of mind should be able to influence it directly and indirectly, unperceived by the man so acted upon? Even man can do this to his fellow; and shall such a power be denied to God?

Now, in many cases, — I do not say all, — it only needs that the minds of others should be inclined to do so and so towards a man, in order to place him in circumstances most unlike those that would have surrounded him without such an influence. Even the very elements, being to some extent under human control, can thus be made subservient, or adverse, to an individual; and, indeed, by a change in the feelings and conduct of others towards us, by an unseen influence upon their minds, our whole outward condition may be changed. In this way, therefore, can God, in many instances, confer blessings on the virtuous, or execute punishment upon the wicked, or give special answers to special prayer; and

30

yet there shall be no miracle about it, nor even the slightest violation of a law of matter or of mind. The result may seem to us only the natural effect of those laws, and yet the divine influence may have modified the effect to any extent.

In the second place, God can so modify the second causes of events out of our sight, as to change wholly, or in part, the final result, and yet not disturb the usual order of nature within sight, so that there shall be no miracle.

A miracle requires that the usual order of nature, as man sees it, be interrupted, or some force superadded to her agency. But if such change take place out of our sight, it might not disturb that order within sight; and, therefore, to us it would be no miracle.

The mode in which this can be done depends upon the fact that in nature we often find several causes, essential to produce an effect, connected together, as it were, in a chain; so that each link depends upon that which precedes it. Thus the power of vision depends upon the optic nerve, in the bottom of the eye. But this would be useless, were not the coats and humors of the eye of a certain consistence and curvature, in order to bring the rays together to form an image on the retina. Again, these coats and humors depend upon light, and light depends for its transmission, probably, upon that exceedingly elastic medium called the *luminiferous ether*. This is as far back as we can trace the series of causes concerned in producing vision. And yet this elastic ether may depend upon something else, and this cause of the movement of the ether upon another cause; and we know not how long the chain may be before we reach the great First Cause. Now, if any one of this series of second causes be modified, the effect will be a modification of the final result. This supposed modification may take place in that part of the chain of causes within our view, or in that part concealed from us. If it took place within sight, it would constitute a miracle ; because the regular sequence of cause and effect would be broken off, or an unnatural power be imparted to the cause producing the ultimate effect. If the modification took place in that part of the chain of second causes out of our sight, the final effect would be no miracle ; because it would be brought about by natural laws, and these would perfectly explain it. Nevertheless, this ultimate effect would be different from what it would be if God had not touched and modified that link of causation which lies out of our sight, back among the secret agencies of his will. And I see not but in this way he might modify the ultimate effect as much as he pleased, and still preserve the unvarying constancy of nature. For in all these cases we should see only the links of the chain of causes nearest to us; and, provided they operated in their usual order, how could we know that any change had taken place in the region beyond our knowledge ? If the whole chain of causation were open to our inspection, then, indeed, would the transaction be an obvious miracle ; but now we see nothing but the unchanging operation of natural laws.

To illustrate this principle, let us imagine a few examples. Suppose the land visited by drought, and its pious inhabitants assemble to pray for rain. We know very well that the causes on which a storm of rain depend are very complicated. How easy for the divine Being, in answer to those prayers, to modify one or more of these secret agencies of meteorological change, that are concealed from our sight, so as to bring together the vapors over the land and condense them into rain ! And yet that storm shall have nothing about it unusual, and it results from the same laws which we have before seen to be in operation. Still, it may have been the result of a special agency exerted by Jehovah in answer to prayer, yet in such a manner that no known law of nature is infringed upon, or even rendered more powerful in its action.

Equally intricate and complicated are the causes of disease, and especially of those pestilences that sometimes march over a whole continent, with the angel of death in their train; and alike easy is it for God, in answer to earnest prayer, to avert their progress, or to cripple their power, or turn them aside from a particular district, without the least interference with the visible connection of cause and effect.

The beloved father of a family lies upon a bed of sickness, and disease is fast gaining upon the powers of life. His numerous and desolate family, in spite of the cold suggestion that it will be of no avail, will earnestly beseech the Being in whose hands is the power of disease, to arrest the fatal malady. And could not their Father in heaven, in the way I have pointed out, give them their request, and yet their parent's recovery be the natural result of careful nursing and medical skill? imposing, however, upon that family as great an obligation as if a manifest miracle had been wrought to save him.

The widow's only son, in spite of her counsels and entreaties, becomes a vagabond upon the seas, and, at length, one of the crew of the battle ship. The perils of the deep and of vicious companions are enough to make that widow a daily and most earnest suppliant at the mercy-seat of her heavenly Father, for his protection and salvation. But, at length, war breaks out, and the perils of battle render his fate more doubtful. Still, faith in God buoys up her heart, and she cannot abandon the hope of yet seeing her son returned, reformed, and becoming a useful man. And at length, rescued from the storm and shipwreck, and the carnage of battle, and the yet more dangerous snares of sin, that youth returns, a renovated man, and cheers that mother's setting sun by an eminently useful life. Now, all this may have happened simply by the operation of natural laws. But it may also have been the result of divine interference in answer to prayer; and hard will you find it to convince that rejoicing mother that the hand of God's extraordinary providence was not in it.

The devoted missionary, at the promptings of a voice within, quits a land of safety and peace, and finds himself in the midst of dangers and sufferings of almost every name ; *in perils of waters, in perils of robbers, in perils in the city, in perils in the wilderness, in weariness, in watchings often, in hunger and thirst, in fastings often, in cold and nakedness.* The furnace of persecution is heated, and he performs his duties with his life constantly in his hand. But he uses no weapon save faith and prayer. He feels that " he is immortal till his work is done." And, in fact, he outlives all his dangers, and, in venerable old age, surrounded by the fruits of his labor, — a reformed and affectionate people, — he passes quietly into the abodes of the blessed. Here, again, why should we hesitate to refer his protection and deliverance to the special interposition of his heavenly Father, in the manner I have pointed out ?

On the other hand, the history of dreadfully wicked men is full of terrible examples of calamity and suffering, as the consequence of their sins. True, the evil came upon them apparently by the operation of natural laws ; but shall we hence infer that God in no case has so modified these laws, by an agency among the hidden causes of events, as to make

30 *

the result certain? He certainly could do this; and to say that he never has done it, is to remove one of the most powerful restraints that operate upon the wicked.

In several examples recorded in the Bible, both of deliverance for the virtuous and of punishment for the wicked, so many natural agencies are concerned, that we are left in doubt whether the events are to be regarded as miraculous or not. Let the deluge, the destruction of Sodom, and the passage of the Israelites through the Red Sea, serve as examples. In the first, we find the flood imputed to a forty days' rain and the overflowing of the ocean; and its reduction to a wind. In the destruction of the cities of the plain, the phenomena described correspond very well with the effects of volcanic agency; and we find accordingly that the region where those cities stood shows marks of that agency. In the passage of the Red Sea, the removal of the waters, to allow the Israelites to pass, is imputed to a strong east wind all night. Nevertheless, the pillar of a cloud by day and the pillar of fire by night were a manifest and standing miracle in this transaction.

Now, may it not be that, in all these cases, so far as natural agencies were concerned, they were made to conspire with the miraculous in the manner which I have described, viz., by such a modification of some of the remote causes by which they were brought into action, as exactly to answer the divine purpose in the catastrophe of the deluge, of Sodom, and in the passage of the Red Sea?

A third mode by which the purposes of special providence can be brought about without miracles is by such an adjustment of the direct and lateral influences on which events depend, that the time and manner of their occurrence shall exactly meet every exigency.

Although it expresses a truth to represent the second causes of events as constituting the links of a chain, it is not the whole truth. For, in fact, those causes are connected together in the form of a network, or, more exactly still, by a sphere filled with interlocked meshes; or, to speak more mathematically, the forces by which events are produced are both direct and indirect. It would be easy to calculate the effect of a single direct force; but if, in its progress, it meets with a multitude of oblique impulses, striking it at every possible angle, what human mathematics can make out the final resultant? Yet, in fact, such is the history of almost every event. The lateral influences, which meet and modify the direct force, are so numerous, and unexpected often, that men are amazed at the result, sometimes as unexpected as a miracle. "When an individual," says Isaac Taylor, "receives an answer to his prayer, the interposition may be made, not in the line which he himself is describing, but in one of those which are to meet him on his path; and at a point, therefore, where, even though the visible constancy of nature should be violated, yet, as being at the time beyond the sphere of his observation, it is a violation not visible to him." "And herein is especially manifested the perfection of divine wisdom, that the most surprising conjunctions of events are brought about by the simplest means, and in a manner that is perfectly in harmony with the ordinary course of human affairs. This is, in fact, the great miracle of providence, that no miracles are needed to accomplish its purposes." — *Nat. History of Enthusiasm*, p. 128.

This complication of causes does not merely give variety to the works and operations of nature, but it enables God to produce effects which could never have resulted from each law acting singly; nor is there a scarcely conceivable limit to

these modifications. Indeed, in this way can Providence
accomplish all his beneficent purposes, and meet every individual case, just as infinite wisdom would have it met. "By
this agency," says M'Cosh, "God can at one time increase,
and at another time lessen, or completely nullify, the spontaneous efforts of the fixed properties of matter. Now he can
make the most powerful agents in nature — such as wind,
fire, and disease — coincide and coöperate to produce effects
of such a tremendous magnitude as none of them separately
could accomplish ; and again, he can arrest their influence
by counteracting agencies, or, rather, by making them counteract each other. He can, for instance, by a concurrence
of natural laws, bring a person, who is in the enjoyment of
health at present, to the very borders of death, an hour or an
instant hence ; and he can, by a like means, suddenly restore
the same or another individual to health, after he has been on
the very verge of the grave. By the confluence of two or
more streams, he can bring agencies of tremendous potency
to bear upon the production of a given effect, such as a war,
a pestilence, or a revolution ; and, on the other hand, by
drawing aside the stream into another channel, he can arrest,
at any given instant, the awful effects that would otherwise
follow from these agencies, and save an individual, a family,
or a nation, from the evils which seem ready to burst upon
them.

"Guided by these principles and guarded by sound sense,
the inquiring mind will discover many and wonderful designed
connections between the various events of divine providence.
Read in the spirit of faith, striking coincidences will every
where manifest themselves. What singular unions of two
streams at the proper place to help on the exertions of the
great and good ! What curious intersections of cords to

catch the wicked as in a net, when they are prowling as wild
beasts ! By strange but most apposite correspondences,
human strength, when set against the will of God, is made to
waste away under God's indignation burning against it, as, in
heathen story, Meleager wasted away as the stick burned
which his mother held in the fire." — *Method of the Divine
Government*, pp. 176, 203.

In many cases, the lateral streams of influence that flow in
and bring unexpected relief to the pious man, and unexpected punishment to the wicked, or a marked answer to prayer,
seem to the individuals little short of miraculous. Yet, after
all, they can see no violation of the natural order of cause
and effect. But the wonder is, how the modifying influence
should come in just at the right moment. It may, indeed, have
received a commission to do this very thing from the immediate impulse of Jehovah; yet, being unperceived by us, it is
no miracle. Or the whole plan may have been so arranged
at the beginning that its development will meet every case
of special providence exactly. Which of these views may
be most accordant with truth, may admit of discussion. Yet
we think that all the modes that have been pointed out, by
which miraculous and special providences are brought about,
may be referred to one general proposition, which we now
proceed to state.

*In the fourth place, the plan of the universe in the divine
mind, at the beginning, must have embraced every case of
miracles and of special providence.*

From the nature of the divine attributes we infer with certainty that every event occurring in the universe must have
entered into the original plan of creation in the mind of God.
Surely no one will deny that he must have foreseen the

operation of every law which he established, and, consequently, every event which it would produce. But there must be some ground for foreknowledge to rest upon; otherwise it is conjecture, not knowledge. And what could that basis be but the divine plan?

Equally clear is it that, whatever plans existed in the mind of God, when he brought the universe into existence, must always have been there. For to suppose that there was a point of duration when the plan was first conceived, would imply new knowledge in one confessedly omniscient; and that destroys the idea of omniscience.

Similar reasoning from the nature of the divine attributes leads us to the conclusion that God always acts according to law. That he does this in the ordinary operations of nature, all admit. But even when he introduces a miracle, — perhaps by a counteraction of ordinary laws, — he may still act by some rule; so that, were precisely the same circumstances to occur again, the same miracle would be repeated. Beforehand, we could not say whether God would conduct the affairs of the universe by one unvarying system of natural laws, or occasionally interfere with the regular sequence of cause and effect by miracle. But though the latter course should be adopted, as we have reason to think it is, even the special interference must be according to law; so that, in fact, there is a law of miracles as well as of common events. Again, if God sometimes alters one or more of the links out of sight, in a chain of second causes, in order to meet a providential exigency, or if he modifies for the same purpose some of the oblique influences by which events are affected, all this must be done by rule; that is, by law. Indeed, to suppose him ever to act without law, is to represent him as less wise than men, who, if judicious, are always governed by settled principles, which produce the same conduct in the same circumstances.

From this reasoning we may safely infer two things : first, that the laws regulating miracles and special providences are as fixed and certain as those of ordinary events ; and secondly, that those laws must have formed a part of the plan of creation originally existing in the divine mind. And hence, thirdly, we must admit that every case of miracle and special providence must have entered into that plan.

When he formed it, he foresaw every possible event that would result from its operation to the end of the world. He saw distinctly the condition of every individual of the human family, from the beginning to the close of life ; all his dangers and trials, his sufferings and his sins ; and he knew just when and where every prayer would be offered up. Nor can it be any more doubtful that, with infinite wisdom to guide him, and infinite power to execute his will, God could so have arranged and constituted the laws of nature, as to meet exactly every case that should ever occur, just in the way he would wish to have it met. Those laws might have been so framed and disposed that, after running on in one unvarying course for ages, a new one might come in, or the old ones be modified, and at once produce effects quite different, and then the first laws resume again their usual course. And the new or modified law might be made to produce its extraordinary or peculiar effects just at the moment when some miracle or special providence would be needed. Thus what would be to us a special or miraculous interposition of divine power, might be the foreseen and foreordained result of God's original purpose. And if we can conceive how such an effect could be produced once, we cannot doubt that infinite wisdom and power could in like manner meet every possible case in which what we call special and miraculous providence would be needed. With our limited powers, we are obliged, after constructing a complicated machine, to put it into operation before we can judge certainly of its effects; and then, if our wishes are not met, we must alter the parts, or in some other way meet the new cases that occur; and hence we find it difficult to conceive how it can be otherwise with God. But he saw the operation of the vast machine of the universe just as clearly at the beginning as at any subsequent period. He, therefore, can do at the beginning what we can do only after experience, viz., adapt the parts to every variety of circumstances.

If I mistake not, we are indebted to Bishop Butler for the germ of these views; but Professor Babbage has illustrated them by reference to an extraordinary machine of his own invention, called "The Calculating Engine." It is adapted to perform the most extensive and complicated numerical calculations, of course with absolute certainty, because its parts are arranged by certain laws. And he finds that precisely such effects, on a small scale, can be produced by this machine, as have been imputed above to the divine agency in creation. It is moved by a weight and a wheel which turns at a short interval around its axis, and prints a series of natural numbers, — 1, 2, 3, 4, 5, &c., — each exceeding its antecedent by unity. "Now, reader, let me ask you," says Professor Babbage, "how long you will have counted before you are firmly convinced that the engine, supposing its adjustments to remain unaltered, will continue, whilst its motion is maintained, to produce the same series of natural numbers. Some minds, perhaps, are so constituted that, after passing the first hundred terms, they will be satisfied that they are acquainted with the law. After seeing five hundred terms, few will doubt; and after the fifty thousandth term, the propensity to believe the succeeding term will be fifty thousand and one, will be almost irresistible. That term will be fifty thousand and one; the same regular succession will continue; the five millionth and the fifty millionth term will appear in their expected order, and one unbroken chain of numbers will pass before you, from one up to one hundred millions. True to the vast induction which has thus been made, the next succeeding term will be one hundred millions and one; but after that, the next number presented by the rim of the wheel, instead of being one hundred millions and two, is one hundred millions ten thousand and two.

"The law which seemed to govern this series fails at the one hundred million and second term. That term is larger than we expected by ten thousand. The next term is larger than was anticipated by thirty thousand. If we still continue to observe the numbers presented by the wheel, we shall find that for a hundred, or even for a thousand terms, they continue to follow the new law relating to the triangular numbers; but after watching them for twenty-seven hundred and sixty-one terms, we find that this law fails in the case of the twenty-seven hundred and sixty-second term. If we continue to observe, another law then comes into action. This will continue through fourteen hundred and thirty terms, when a new law is again introduced, which extends over about nine hundred and fifty terms; and this, too, like all its predecessors, fails, and gives place to other laws, which appear at different intervals. It is also possible so to arrange the engine, that at any periods, however remote, the first law shall be interrupted for one or more times, and be superseded by any

31

other laws, after which the original law shall be again produced, and no other deviation shall ever take place.

"Now, it must be remarked that the law that each number presented by the engine is greater by unity than the preceding number, which law the observer had deduced from an induction of a hundred million of instances, was not the true law that regulated its action; and that the occurrence of the number one hundred million ten thousand and two at the one hundred million and second term was as necessary a consequence of the original adjustment as was the regular succession of any one of the intermediate numbers to its immediate antecedent. The same remark applies to the next apparent deviation from the new law, which was founded on an induction of two thousand seven hundred and sixty-one terms; and to all the succeeding laws, with this limitation only, that whilst their consecutive introduction at various definite intervals is a necessary consequence of the mechanical structure of the engine, our knowledge of analysis does not yet enable us to predict the periods at which the more distant laws will be introduced." — *Ninth Bridgewater Treatise.*

The application of these statements to the doctrine of special as well as of miraculous providence is very obvious. If human ingenuity can construct a machine which shall exhibit the introduction of new laws, after the old ones had been established by an induction of a hundred million of examples, and these new ones be succeeded by others, how much easier for the infinite God to construct the vast and more complicated machine of the universe, so that new laws, or modifications of the old ones, shall be introduced at various periods of its history, to meet every exigency! How easy for him so to adjust this machine at the beginning, that the new laws and new modes of action should be introduced, precisely at those points where a special providence would be desirable, to reward the virtuous and to punish the wicked, and then the old law again assume its dominion ! And how easily, in this way, could the case of every individual be met, from the beginning to the end of the world ! I mean, how easy would this work be to infinite wisdom and power !

But if all events, miraculous as well as common, may depend upon unbending law, how does such a view differ from the one I am now opposing, viz., that the constancy of nature's laws precludes the idea of any special interference on the part of God, in human affairs ? The main point of difference, I reply, is, that the advocates of the latter view will not admit any such thing at the present day as special interference, on the part of the Deity, with nature. They admit only uniform and ordinary laws, which they suppose are never interrupted. This I deny ; and endeavor to show, not only that the contrary may be a fact, but that God purposed it originally, and determined the laws by which it might be accomplished. The fact that he did this beforehand, even from eternity, no more precludes his agency, than the special interference of a father to help his child through a dangerous pass is disproved, because he foresaw the danger and provided the means of defence even before the child was born. If the father was actually with the child, as he went through the danger, and held out to him the requisite help, what difference could it make, though the father purposed to do so a long time previously ? And if we admit that God's efficiency alone gives power to the ordinary laws of nature, we shall admit that in every special law he is as really present with his energy, as a father who should lead his child by the hand through the dangerous path. So that, practically at least, the difference between these two views of the subject is very great; the one removing God far away, and putting law in his place; and the other bringing him near, and making him the actual and constant agent in every event. The one view is practical atheism, although often adopted by religious men; the other is practical Christianity.

By the principles of physical science, then, the scriptural doctrines of miraculous and special providence are proved to be in accordance with philosophy. The miracles of revelation are shown to have been preceded by the miracles of geology; and are, therefore, in conformity with the principles of the divine government. The modifications which God can make in the causes of events out of human view, or the changes which he can produce by lateral influences upon the final result, — all, it may be, in conformity to an eternal plan, reaching the minutest of human affairs, — enable him to execute every purpose of special providence so as to satisfy every exigency.

The sceptic may say, that we cannot prove by facts that God does so modify and arrange the laws and operations of nature as to adapt his dealings to the case of individuals. But, on the other hand, neither can he show that God does not thus interfere with nature's uniformity. It is enough to show that he can do it without a miracle, in order to establish the doctrine of special providence. How often he exercises this power, we cannot know; but we may be sure as often as is desirable.

A most important application of these principles may be made to the subject of prayer. For in answering prayer, God is, in fact, merely executing some of the purposes of his special providence; and it is gratifying to the pious heart to see how he can give an answer to the humblest petitioner. No matter though all the laws of nature seem in the way of an answer, — God can so modify their action as to conform them to the case of every petitioner. War, famine, and pestilence may all be upon us, yet humble prayer may turn them all aside, and every other physical evil ; and that without a miracle, if best for us and for the universe. Tell a man that the only effect of prayer is its reflex influence upon himself, in leading him to conform more strictly to nature's laws, and you send a paralysis and a death chill into all his moral sensibilities. Indeed, he cannot pray ; but tell him that God will be influenced, as is any earthly friend, by his supplications, and his heart beats full and strong, the current of life goes bounding through his whole system, the glow of health mantles his cheek, and all his senses are roused into intense and delightful action.

The sad influence of a perversion and misunderstanding of the doctrine of nature's constancy upon the youthful mind is well exhibited by a late able writer. " Early trained to it under the domestic roof," says M'Cosh, " the person regularly engaged in prayer during childhood and opening manhood. But as he became introduced to general society, and began to feel his independence of the guardians of his youth, he was tempted to look upon the father's commands, in this respect, as proceeding from sourness and sternness, and the mother's advice as originating in an amiable weakness and timidity. He is now careless in the performance of acts which in time past had been punctually attended to. How short, how hurried, how cold are the prayers which he now utters ! Then there come to be mornings on which he is snatched away to some very important or enticing work without engaging in his customary devotions. There are evenings, too, following days of mad excitement or sinful pleasure, in which he feels utterly indisposed to go into the presence of

31 *

God, and to be left alone with him. He feels that there is an utter incongruity between the ball-room, or the theatre, which he has just left, and the throne of grace, to which he should now go. What can he say to God, when he would pray to him? Confess his sins? No; he does not at present feel the act to be sinful. Thank God for giving him access to such follies? He has his doubts whether God approves of all that has been done. But he may ask God's blessing? No; he is scarcely disposed to acknowledge that he needs a blessing, or he doubts whether the blessing would be given. The practical conclusion to which he comes is, that it may be as consistent in him to betake himself to sleep without offering to God what he feels would only be a mockery. What is he to do the following morning? It is a critical time. Confess his error? No; cherishing as he does the recollection of the gay scene in which he mingled, and with the taste and relish of it yet upon his palate, he is not prepared to acknowledge his folly. Morning and evening now go and return, and bring new gifts from God, and new manifestations of his goodness; but no acknowledgment of the divine bounty on the part of him who is yet ever receiving it. No doubt there are times when he is prompted to prayer by powerful feelings, called up by outward trials or inward convictions; but ever when the storms of human life would drive him to the shore, there is a tide beating him back. His course continues to be a very vacillating one — now seeming to approach to God, and anon driven farther from him, till he obtains from books, or from lectures, a smattering of half-understood science. He now learns that all things are governed by laws, regular and fixed, over which the breath of prayer can exert as little influence, as they move on in their allotted course, as the passing breeze of the earth over the sun in his circuit. False philosophy has now come to the aid of guilty feelings, and hardens their cold waters into an icicle lying at his very heart, cooling all his ardor, and damping all his enthusiasm. He looks back, at times, no doubt, to the simple faith of his childhood with a sigh; but it is as to a pleasing dream, or illusion, from which he has been awakened, and into which, the spell being broken, he can never again fall." — *Method of the Divine Government*, p. 224.

O, what a change would this world exhibit, were the whole Christian church to exercise full faith in God's ability to answer prayer without a miracle, only to the extent pointed out by philosophy, to say nothing of the Bible; for, in fact, a large proportion of that church, confounded by the specious argument derived from nature's constancy, have virtually yielded this most important principle to the demands of scepticism. When natural evils, such as war, famine, drought, and pestilence, came upon our forefathers, they, taking the Bible for their guide, observed days of fasting and prayer for their removal. But how seldom do their descendants follow their example! And yet even physical science testifies that the fathers acted in conformity to the true principles of philosophy. Would that the Christian church would consent to be led back to the Bible doctrine on this subject by philosophy.

That same philosophy, also, should lead the good man, when struggling through difficulties, to exercise unshaken confidence in the divine protection, even though all nature's laws seem arrayed against him; for at the unseen touch of God's efficiency, the iron bars of law shall melt away like wax, and deliverance be given in the midst of appalling dangers, if best for the man and for the universe; and if not best, he will not desire it.

Science, too, bids the wicked man not to fancy that the

constancy of nature will shield him from the infliction of merited and special punishment, should God choose to make bare the rod of his justice; for the blow may come as certainly in the course of nature as against it.

Let modern Christian theology, then, receive meekly the rebuke administered on this important point by physical science. For how lame and halting a defence of the Scripture doctrine of special providence and prayer has that theology been able to make ! How few of our systems of theology contain a manful vindication of truths so important ! Let not the Christian divine, therefore, refuse the aid thus offered by physical science. Let him no longer indulge groundless jealousies against true philosophy, as if adverse to religion. Especially let him not spurn the aid of geology, which alone, of all the sciences, discloses stupendous miracles of creation in early times, and thus removes all presumption against the miracles of Christianity and special providence at any time.

It is, indeed, an instructive fact, that a science which has been thought so full of danger to Christianity should thus early be found vindicating some of the most peculiar and long-contested doctrines of revelation. And yet it ought not to surprise us, for geology is as really the work of God as revelation. And though, when ill understood and perverted, she may have seemed recreant to her celestial origin, yet the more fully her proportions are developed, and her features brought into daylight, the more clearly do we recognize her alliance to every thing pure and noble in the universe. " And surely," says a late writer, " it must be gratifying thus to see a science, formerly classed, and not perhaps unjustly, amongst the most pernicious to faith, once more become her handmaid ; to see her now, after so many years of wandering from theory to theory, or rather from vision to vision, return once

more to the home where she was born, and to the altar at
which she made her first simple offerings ; no longer, as she
first went forth, a wilful, dreamy, empty-handed child, but
with a matronly dignity, and a priest-like step, and a bosom
full of well-earned gifts, to pile upon its sacred hearth.   For
it was religion which gave geology birth, and to the sanctuary
she hath once more returned." — *Wiseman's Lectures on
Science and Revealed Religion*, p. 192, Am. ed.

LECTURE XI.

THE FUTURE CONDITION AND DESTINY OF THE EARTH.

MAN has a stronger desire to penetrate the future than the past. And yet the details of most future events are wisely concealed from him. There are two, and only two, sources of evidence from which he can obtain some glimpses of what will be hereafter. The one is revelation, the other analogy. So far as God has thought proper to reveal the future, our information is precise and certain. But it does not embrace a multitude of events about which we have strong curiosity. By analogy is meant a prediction of the future from the past. On the principle that nature is constant, we infer what will be from what has been. If, however, new laws are hereafter to come into operation, or if present agencies will then operate very differently from what they now do, it is obvious that analogy can be only an imperfect guide Still, in respect to many important events, its conclusions are infallible. Judging, for instance, from the past, we are absolutely certain that no living thing will escape the great law of dissolution, which, thus far, apart from the few exceptions made known to us by revelation, has been universal.

The future changes in the condition of the earth, as they are taught us by revelation and analogy, or, rather, by geology, will form the subject of my present lecture. And my first object will be, to ascertain, if possible, precisely what the Bible teaches us concerning these changes.

We find in the Scriptures several descriptions, more or less definite, of the changes which this globe will hereafter undergo. Some of them, however, are couched in the figurative language of prophecy, and others are incidental allusions; and concerning the precise meaning of such descriptions, there will, of course, be a diversity of opinion.

There are, however, some passages on this subject as literal and as precise in their meaning as language can be. Now, it is one of the rules for interpreting language, that, where a work contains several accounts of the same event, the description which is most simple and literal ought to be made the index for obtaining the meaning of those passages which are figurative, or, on any account, obscure. I shall, therefore, select the passage of Scripture which all acknowledge to be most plain and definite, respecting the future destruction of the earth, and the new heavens and earth that are to succeed, and first inquire into its precise meaning; after which, we shall be better prepared to ascertain what modification of that meaning other passages of sacred writ demand.

It needs but a cursory examination of the Bible to convince any one that the description in the Second Epistle of Peter of the future destruction and renovation of the earth and heavens, is eminently the passage first to be examined, because the fullest and clearest on this subject. It is the apostle's object directly and literally to describe these great changes, apart from all embellishments of language.

There shall come, says he, *in the last days, scoffers, walking after their own lusts, and saying, Where is the promise of his coming? for since the fathers fell asleep, all things*

continue as they were from the beginning of the creation
For this they willingly are ignorant of, that by the word of
God the heavens were of old, and the earth standing out of
the water and in the water ; whereby the world that then
was, being overflowed with water, perished.   But the heavens
and the earth, which are now, by the same word are kept in
store, reserved unto fire, against the day of judgment and
perdition of ungodly men.   But, beloved, be not ignorant of
this one thing, that one day is with the Lord as a thousand
years, and a thousand years as one day.   The Lord is not
slack concerning his promise, as some men count slackness,
but is long suffering to us-ward, not willing that any should
perish, but that all should come to repentance.   But the day
of the Lord will come as a thief in the night, in the which
the heavens shall pass away with a great noise, and the ele-
ments shall melt with fervent heat ; the earth, also, and the
works that are therein, shall be burned up.   Seeing, then,
that all these things shall be dissolved, what manner of per-
sons ought ye to be in all holy conversation and godliness ?
Looking for, and hasting unto the coming of the day of God,
wherein the heavens, being on fire, shall be dissolved, and the
elements shall melt with fervent heat.   Nevertheless, we, ac-
cording to his promise, look for new heavens, and a new
earth, wherein dwelleth righteousness.

It would require too much time, and, moreover, is not
necessary to the object I have in view, to enter into minute
verbal criticism upon this passage. I will only remark that
the phrase translated *the earth and the works that are therein*,
might with equal propriety be rendered "the earth and the
works that are *thereon ;*" and yet the difference of meaning
between the two modes of expression is of no great importance. Again, by the term *heavens*, in this passage, we are

evidently to understand the atmosphere, or region immediately surrounding the earth; as in the first chapter of Genesis, where it is said that *God called the firmament heavens ;* the plural form being used in the Hebrew, though not in the English translation.

What, now, by a fair exegesis, is taught in this passage concerning the destruction and renovation of the world? The following train of remark may conduct us to the true answer to this inquiry : —

In the first place, this passage is to be understood literally. It would seem as if it could hardly be necessary to present any formal proof of this position to any person of common sense, who had read the passage. But the fact is, that men of no mean reputation as commentators have maintained that the whole of it is only a vivid figurative prophecy of the destruction of Jerusalem. Others suppose the new heavens and new earth here described to exist before the conflagration of the world. But these new heavens and earth are represented as the residence of the righteous, after the burning and melting of the earth, which, according to other parts of Scripture, is to take place at the end of the world, or at the general judgment. How strange that, in order to sustain a favorite theory, able men should thus invert the obvious order of these great events, so clearly described in the Bible ! Still more absurd is it to attempt to fasten a figurative character upon this most simple statement of inspiration. It is, indeed, true, that the prophets have sometimes set forth great political and moral changes, the downfall of empires, or of distinguished men, by the destruction of the heavens and the earth, and the growing pale and darkening of the sun and moon. But in all these cases the figurative character of the description is most obvious; while in the passage from Peter

32

its literal character is equally obvious. Take, for example, this statement — *By the word of God the heavens were of old, and the earth, standing out of the water and in the water ; whereby the world that then was, being overflowed with water, perished. But the heavens and the earth, which are now, by the same word are kept in store, reserved unto fire, against the day of judgment and perdition of ungodly men.*

I believe no one has ever doubted that the destruction of the world by water, here described, refers to Noah's deluge. Now, how absurd to admit that this is a literal description of that event, and then to maintain the remainder of the sentence, which declares the future destruction of that same world by fire, to be figurative in the highest degree ! For if this destruction mean only the destruction of Jerusalem, or any other great political or moral revolution, the language is one of the boldest figures which can be framed. Who, that knows any thing of the laws of language, does not see the supreme absurdity of thus coupling in the same sentence the most simple and certain literality with the strongest of all figures ? What mark is given us, by which we may know where the boundary is between the literal and the metaphorical sense ? From what part of the Bible, or from what uninspired author, can a parallel example be adduced ? What but the strongest necessity, the most decided *exigentia loci*, would justify such an anomalous interpretation of any author ? Nay, I do not believe any necessity could justify it. It would be more reasonable to infer that the passage had no meaning, or an absurd one. But surely no such necessity exists in the present case. Understood literally, the passage teaches only what is often expressed, though less fully, in many other parts of Scripture ; and even though some of these other passages should be involved in a degree of obscurity, — and

I am not disposed to deny that some obscurity rests upon one or two of them, — it would be no good reason for transforming so plain a description into a highly-wrought figurative representation; especially when by no ingenuity can we thus alter more than one part of the sentence. I conclude, therefore, that, if any part of the Bible is literal, we are thus to consider this chapter of Peter.

In the second place, this passage does not teach that the earth will be annihilated.

The prevailing opinion in this country, probably, has been, and still is, that the destruction of the world described by Peter will amount to annihilation — that the matter of the globe will cease to be. But in all ages there have been many who believe that the destruction will be only the ruin of the present economy of the world, but not its utter extinction. And surely Peter's description does not imply annihilation of the matter of the globe. He makes fire the agent of the destruction, and, in order to ascertain the extent of the ruin that will follow, we have only to inquire what effect combustion will have upon matter. The common opinion is, that intense combustion actually destroys or annihilates matter, because it is thereby dissipated. But the chemist knows that not one particle of matter has ever been thus deprived of existence; that fire only changes the form of matter, but never annihilates it. When solid matter is changed into gas, as in most cases of combustion, it seems to be annihilated, because it disappears; but it has only assumed a new form, and exists as really as before. Since, therefore, biblical and scientific truth must agree, we may be sure that the apostle never meant to teach that the matter of the globe would cease to be, through the action of fire upon it; nor is there any thing in his language that implies such a result, but most obviously the reverse.

If these things be so, then, in the third place, we may infer that Peter did not mean to teach that the matter of the globe would be in the least diminished by the final conflagration. I doubt not the sufficiency of divine power partially or wholly to annihilate the material universe. But heat, however intense, has no tendency to do this; it only gives matter a new form. And heat is the only agency which the apostle represents as employed. In short, we have no evidence, either from science or revelation, that the minutest atom of matter has ever been destroyed since the original creation; nor have we any more evidence that any of it ever will be reduced to the nothingness from which it sprang. The prevalent ideas upon this subject all result from erroneous notions of the effect of intense heat.

In the fourth place, the passage under consideration teaches us that whatever upon or within the earth is capable of combustion will undergo that change, and that the entire globe will be melted.

The language of Peter has always seemed to me extremely interesting. He says that *the heavens* [or atmosphere] *will pass away with a great noise, and the elements shall melt with fervent heat ; the earth, also, and the works that are therein, shall be burned up ; looking for, and hasting unto the coming of the day of God, wherein the heavens, being on fire, shall be dissolved, and the elements shall melt with fervent heat.*

This language approaches nearer to an anticipation of the scientific discoveries of modern times than any other part of Scripture. And yet, at the time it was written, it would not have enabled any one to understand the chemistry of the great changes which it describes. But, now that their chemistry is understood, we perceive that the language is adapted to it, in a manner which no uninspired writer would have done. The atmosphere is represented as passing away with a great noise — an effect which the chemist would predict by the union of its oxygen with the hydrogen and other gases liberated by the intense heat. Yet what uninspired writer of the first century would have imagined such a result?

Again, when we consider the notions which then prevailed, and which are still widely diffused, why should the apostle add to the simple statement that the earth would be burnt up, the declaration that its elements would be melted? For the impression was, that the combustion would entirely destroy the matter of the globe. But the chemist finds that the greater part of the earth has already been oxidized, or burnt, and on this matter the only effect of the heat, unless intense enough to dissipate it, would be to melt it. If, therefore, the apostle had said only that the world would be burnt up, the sceptical chemist would have inferred that he had made a mistake through ignorance of chemistry. But he cannot now draw such an inference; for the apostle's language clearly implies that only the combustible matter of the globe will be burnt, while the elements, or first principles of things, will be melted; so that the final result will be an entire liquid, fiery globe. Such a wonderful adaptation of his description to modern science could not surely have resulted from human sagacity, but must be the fruit of divine inspiration.

And this adaptation is the more wonderful when we find it running through the whole Bible wherever the sacred writers come in contact with scientific subjects. In this respect, the Bible differs from every other system of religion professedly from heaven.

Whenever other systems have treated of the works of nature, they have sanctioned some error, and thus put into

32 *

the hands of modern science the means of detecting the imposture. The Vedas of India adopt the absurd notions of an ignorant and polytheistic age respecting astronomy, and the Koran adopts as infallible truth the absurdities of the Ptolemaic system. But hitherto the Bible has never been proved to come into collision with any scientific discovery, although many of its books were written in the rudest and most ignorant ages. It does not, indeed, anticipate scientific discovery. But the remarkable adaptation of its language to such discoveries, when they are made, seems to me a more striking mark of its divine origin than if it had contained a revelation of the whole system of modern science.

In the fifth place, the passage under consideration teaches that this earth will be renovated by the final conflagration, and become the abode of the righteous. After describing the day of God, *wherein the heavens, being on fire, shall be dissolved, and the elements shall melt with fervent heat,* Peter adds, *Nevertheless, we, according to his promise, look for new heavens and a new earth, wherein dwelleth righteousness.* Now, the apostle does not here, in so many words, declare that the new heavens and earth will be the present world and its atmosphere, purified and renovated by fire. But it is certainly a natural inference that such was his meaning. For if he intended some other remote and quite different place, why should he call it *earth,* and, especially, why should he surround it with an atmosphere ? The natural and most obvious meaning of the passage surely is, that the future residence of the righteous will be this present terraqueous globe, after its entire organic and combustible matter shall have been destroyed, and its whole mass reduced by heat to a liquid state, and then a new economy reared up on its surface, not adapted to sinful, but to sinless beings, and,

therefore, quite different from its present condition — probably
more perfect, but still the same earth and surrounding heavens.

There are, indeed, some difficulties in the way of such a
meaning to this passage, and objections to a material heaven ;
and these I shall notice in the proper place. But I have
given what seems to me the natural and obvious meaning of
the passage.

Such, as I conceive, are the fair inferences from the apostle's description of the end of the world.   Let us now inquire
whether any other passages of Scripture require us to modify
this meaning.

The idea of a future destruction of the world by fire is
recognized in various places, both in the Old and New Testaments.   Christ speaks more than once of heaven and earth
as passing away.   Paul speaks of Christ as descending, at the
end of the world, in flaming fire.   And the Psalmist describes
the destruction of the heavens and the earth as a renovation.
They shall perish, says he, *but thou* [God] *shalt endure ; yea,
all of them shall wax old like a garment, and as a vesture
shalt thou change them, and they shall be changed.*   In Revelation, after the apostle had given a vivid description of the
final judgment and its retributions, he says, *And I saw a new
heaven and a new earth ; for the first heaven and the first
earth were passed away, and there was no more sea.*   He then
proceeds to give a minute and glowing description of what
he calls the New Jerusalem, coming down from God, out of
heaven.   It is scarcely possible to understand the whole of
this description as literally true.   We must rather regard it
as a figurative representation of the heavenly state.   And hence
the first verse, which speaks of the new heavens and the new
earth, in almost the same language which Peter uses, may
be also figurative, indicating merely a more exalted condition

than the present world.   Hence, I would not use this passage
to sustain the interpretation given of the literal description by
Peter.   And yet it is by no means improbable that the figurative language of John may have for its basis the same truths
which are taught by Peter.   Nor ought we to infer, because
a figure is built upon that basis in the apocalyptic vision, that
the simple statements of Peter are metaphorical.

In the passage quoted from Peter, it is said, *Nevertheless,
we, according to his promise, look for new heavens and a new
earth, wherein dwelleth righteousness.*   Most writers have
supposed the apostle to refer either to the promise made to
Abraham, that his seed should inherit the land, or to a prophecy in Isaiah, which says, *Behold, I create new heavens, and a
new earth, and the former shall not be remembered, or come
into mind.   But be you glad and rejoice forever in that which
I create ; for behold, I create Jerusalem a rejoicing, and her
people a joy.   And I will rejoice in Jerusalem, and joy in my
people; and the voice of weeping shall be no more heard in
her, nor the voice of crying.   There shall be no more thence
an infant of days, nor an old man that hath not filled his
days; for the child shall die a hundred years old ; but the
sinner, being a hundred years old, shall be accursed.   And
they shall build houses, and inhabit them ; and they shall
plant vineyards, and eat the fruit of them.   They shall not
build, and another inhabit ; they shall not plant, and another
eat ; for as the days of a tree are the days of my people, and
mine elect shall long enjoy the works of their hands.   The
wolf and the lamb shall feed together, and the lion shall eat
straw like the bullock ; and dust shall be the serpent's meat.
They shall not hurt nor destroy in all my holy mountain,
saith the Lord.*

Now, it seems highly probable that the new heavens and

earth, here described, represent a state of things on the present earth before the day of judgment, and not a heavenly and immortal state ; for sin and death are spoken of as existing in it ; both which, we are assured, will be excluded from heaven.   Hence able biblical writers refer this prophecy to the millennial state, or the period when there will be a general prevalence of Christianity.   In this they are probably correct.   But some of these writers, as Low and Whitby, proceed a step farther, and infer that Peter's description of the new heavens and new earth belong also to the millennial period ; first, because they presume that the apostle referred to this promise in Isaiah ; and secondly, because he uses the same terms, namely, " new heavens and new earth."   But are these grounds sufficient to justify so important a conclusion ? How common it is to find the same words and phrases in the Bible applied by different writers to different subjects, especially by the prophets !   Even if we can suppose Peter to place the new heavens and the new earth before the judgment, in despite of his plain declaration to the contrary, yet there are few who will doubt that the new heavens and earth described in revelation are subsequent to the judgment day, so vividly described in the verses immediately preceding.

And as to the promise referred to by Peter, if he really describes the heavenly state, surely it may be found in a multitude of places ; wherever, indeed, immortal life and blessedness are offered to faith and obedience.   Isaiah, therefore, may be giving a figurative description of a glorious state of the church in this world, under the terms " new heavens and new earth," emblematical of those real new heavens and new earth beyond the grave, described by Peter.   And hence, it seems to me, the language of the prophet should not be allowed to set aside, or modify, the plain meaning of the apostle.

I shall quote only one other passage of the Bible on this subject. I refer to that difficult text in Romans, which represents the whole creation as groaning and travailing together in pain until now ; and that it will be delivered from the bondage of corruption into the glorious liberty of the children of God.

I have stated in a former lecture, that Tholuck, the distinguished German theologian, considers this a description of the present bound and fettered condition of all nature, and that the deliverance refers to the future renovation of the earth. Such an exposition chimes in perfectly with the views on this subject which have long and extensively prevailed in Germany. And it certainly does give a consistent meaning to a passage which has been to commentators a perfect labyrinth of difficulties. If this be not its meaning, then I may safely say that its meaning has not yet been found out.

In view, then, of all the important passages of Scripture concerning the future destruction and renovation of the earth, I think we may fairly conclude that none of them require us to modify the natural and obvious meaning of Peter which has been given. In general, they all coincide with the views presented by that apostle ; or if, in any case, there is a slight apparent difference, the figurative character of all other statements besides his require us to receive his views as the true standard, and to modify the meaning of the others. We may, therefore, conclude that the Bible does plainly and distinctly teach us that this earth will hereafter be burned up ; in other words, that all upon or within it, capable of combustion, will be consumed, and the entire mass, the elements, without the loss of one particle of the matter now existing, will be melted ; and then, that the world, thus purified from the contamination of sin, and surrounded by a new atmosphere, or heavens, and adapted in all respects to the nature and wants of spiritual and sinless beings, will become the residence of the righteous. Of the precise nature of that new dispensation, and of the mode of existence there, the Scriptures are indeed silent. But that, like the present world, it will be material, — that there will be a solid globe, and a transparent expanse around it, — seems most clearly indicated in the sacred record.

The wide-spread opinion that heaven will be a sort of airy Elysium, where the present laws of nature will be unknown, and where matter, if it exist, can exist only in its most attenuated form, is a notion to which the Bible is a stranger.

The resurrection of the body, as well as the language of Peter, most clearly show us that the future world will be a solid, material world, purified indeed, and beautified, but retaining its materialism.

Let us now see whether, in coming to these conclusions from Scripture language, we are influenced by scientific considerations, or whether many discerning minds have not, in all ages, attached a similar meaning to the inspired record.

Among all nations, the history of whose opinions have come down to us, and especially among the Greeks, the belief has prevailed that a catastrophe by fire awaited the earth, corresponding to, or rather the counterpart of, a previous destruction by water. These catastrophes they denominated the *cataclysm*, or destruction by water, and the *ecpyrosis*, or destruction by fire. The ruin was supposed to be followed, in each case, by the regeneration of the earth in an improved form, which gradually deteriorated; the first age after the catastrophe, constituting the golden age; the next, the silver age; and so on to the iron age, which preceded another cataclysm, or ecpyrosis. The intervals between these convulsions were regarded as of various lengths, but all of them of great duration.

These opinions the Greeks derived from the Egyptians.

The belief in the future conflagration of the world also prevailed among the ancient Jews. Philo says that "the earth, after this purification, shall appear new again, even as it was after its first creation." — *De Vita Mosis*, tom. ii. — Among the Jews, these ideas may have been, in part, derived from the Old Testament; though its language, as we have seen, is far less explicit on this subject than the New Testament. That distinguished Christian writers, in all ages since the advent of Christ, have understood the language of Peter as we have explained it, would be easy to show. I have room, however, to quote only the opinions of a few distinguished modern writers.

Dr. Knapp, one of the most scientific and judicious of theologians, thus remarks upon the passage of Peter already examined: "It cannot be thought that what is here said respecting the burning of the world is to be understood figuratively, as Wettstein supposes; because the fire is here too directly opposed to the literal water of the flood to be so understood. It is the object of Peter to refute the boast of scoffers, that all things had remained unchanged from the beginning, and that, therefore, no day of judgment and no end of the world could be expected. And so he says that originally, at the time of the creation, the whole earth was covered and overflowed with water, (Gen. i.,) and that from hence the dry land appeared; and the same was true at the time of Noah's flood. But there is yet to come a great fire revolution. The heavens and the earth (the earth with its atmosphere) are reserved, or kept in store, for the fire, until the day of judgment, (v. 10.) At that time the heavens will pass away with a great noise, and the elements will be dissolved by fervent heat, and every thing upon the earth will be burnt up. The same thing is taught in verse **12**. But in verse **13** Peter gives the design of this revolution. It will not be annihilation, but we expect a new heavens and a new earth, wherein dwelleth righteousness, *i. e.*, an entirely new, altered, and beautiful abode for man, to be built from the ruins of his former dwelling-place, as the future habitation of the pious, (Rev. xxi. 1.) This will be very much in the same way as a more perfect and an immortal body will be reared from the body which we now possess." — *Theology*, vol. ii. p. 649.

From Dr. Chalmers my extracts will be longer than are necessary to show his opinion upon this subject, because he felicitously refutes certain erroneous ideas, widely prevalent, respecting matter and spirit. " We know historically," says he, " that earth, that a solid, material earth, may form the dwelling of sinless creatures, in full converse and friendship with the Being who made them." " Man, at the first, had for his place this world, and, at the same time, for his privilege an unclouded fellowship with God, and for his prospect an immortality, which death was neither to intercept nor put an end to. He was terrestrial in respect to condition, and yet celestial, both in respect of character and enjoyments.

" The common imagination that we have of paradise on the other side of death, is that of a lofty aerial region, where the inmates float in ether, or are mysteriously suspended upon nothing ; where all the warm and sensible accompaniments, which give such an expression of strength, and life, and coloring to our present habitation, are attenuated into a sort of spiritual element, that is meagre and imperceptible, and utterly uninviting to the eye of mortals here below ; where every vestige of materialism is done away, and nothing left but certain unearthly scenes, that have no power of

33

allurement, and certain unearthly ecstasies with which it is felt impossible to sympathize. The holders of this imagination forget all the while that there is no necessary connection between materialism and sin; that the world which we now inhabit had all the solidity and amplitude of its present materialism before sin entered into it; that God, so far, on that account, from looking slightly upon it, after it had received the last touch of his creating hand, reviewed the earth, and the waters, and the firmament, and all the green herbage, with the living creatures, and the man whom he had raised in dominion over them, and *he saw every thing that he had made, and behold, it was all very good.* They forget that, on the birth of materialism, when it stood out in the freshness of those glories which the great Architect of nature had impressed upon it, that *the morning stars sang together, and all the sons of God shouted for joy.* They forget the appeals that are every where made in the Bible to his material workmanship, and how, from the face of these visible heavens, and the garniture of this earth which we tread upon, the greatness and goodness of God are reflected on the view of his worshippers. No, my brethren, the object of the administration we sit under is to extirpate sin, but it is not to sweep away materialism. By the convulsions of the last day it may be shaken and broken down from its present arrangement, and thrown into such fitful agitations as that the whole of its existing framework shall fall to pieces; and with a heat so fervent as to melt the most solid elements, may it be utterly dissolved. And thus may the earth again become without form and void, but without one particle of its substance going into annihilation. Out of the ruins of this second chaos may another heaven and another earth be made to arise, and a new materialism, with other aspects of magnificence and beauty, emerge from the wreck of this mighty transformation, and the world be peopled, as before, with the varieties of material loveliness, and space be again lighted up into a firmament of material splendor.

" It is, indeed, a homage to that materialism, which many are for expunging from the future state of the universe altogether, that, ere the immaterial soul of man has reached the ultimate glory and blessedness designed for it, it must return and knock at the very grave where lie the mouldered remains of the body which it wore, and there inquisition must be made for the flesh, and the sinews, and the bones which the power of corruption has, perhaps centuries before, assimilated to the earth around them, and then the minute atoms must be reassembled into a structure that bears upon it the form, and lineaments, and general aspect of a man, and the soul passes into this material framework, which is hereafter to be its lodging-place forever ; and that not as its prison, but as its pleasant and befitting habitation; not to be trammelled, as some would have it, in a hold of materialism, but to be therein equipped for the services of eternity ; to walk embodied among the bowers of our second paradise ; to stand embodied in the presence of our God."

" The glorification of the visible creation," says Tholuck, the distinguished German divine, " is more definitely declared in Rev. xxi. 1, although it must be borne in mind that a prophetic vision is there described. Still more definitely do we find the belief of a transformation of the material world declared in 2 Peter, iii. 7–12. The idea that the perfected kingdom of Christ is to be transferred to heaven, is properly a modern notion. According to Paul and the Revelation of John, the kingdom of God is placed upon the earth, in so far as this itself has part in the universal transformation. This exposition has been adopted and defended by most of the oldest commentators; *e. g.*, Chrysostom, Theodoret, Hieronymus, Augustine, Luther, Koppe, and others. Luther says, in his lively way, ' God will make, not the earth only, but the heavens also, much more beautiful than they are at present. At present, we see the world in its working clothes; but hereafter it will be arrayed in its Easter and Whitsuntide robes.' "

" I cannot but feel astonishment," says Dr. John Pye Smith, " that any serious and intelligent man should have his mind fettered with the common, I might call it the vulgar, notion of a proper destruction of the earth; and some seem to extend the notion to the whole solar system, and even the entire material universe; applying the idea of an extinction of being, a reducing to nothingness. This notion has, indeed, been often used to aid impassioned description in sermons and poetry; and thus it has gained so strong a hold upon the feelings of many pious persons, that they have made it an article of their faith. But I confess myself unable to find any evidence for it in nature, reason, or Scripture. We can discover nothing like destruction in the matter of the universe as subjected to our senses. Masses are disintegrated, forms are changed, compounds are decomposed; but not an atom is annihilated. Neither have we the shadow of reason to assert that mind, the seat of intelligence, ever was, or ever will be, in a single instance, destroyed. The declaration in Scripture that *the heavens and the earth shall flee away, and no more place be found for them*, is undoubtedly figurative, and denotes the most momentous changes in the scenes of the divine moral government. If it be the purpose of God that the earth shall be subjected to a total conflagration, we perfectly well know that the instruments of such an event lie close at hand, and wait only the divine volition to burst out in a moment. But that would not be a destruction ; it would be a mere change of form, and, no doubt, would be subservient to the most glorious results. *We, according to his promise, look for new heavens and a new earth, wherein dwelleth right-eousness.*" — *Lectures on Geology and Revelation*, p. 161, (4th London edition.)

Says Dr. Griffin, one of the ablest of the American divines, " A question here arises, whether the new heavens and new earth will be created out of the ruins of the old ; that is, whether the old will be renovated and restored in a more glorious form, or whether the old will be annihilated, and the new made out of nothing. The idea of the annihilation of so many immense and glorious bodies, organized with inim-itable skill, and declarative of infinite wisdom, is gloomy and forbidding. Indeed, it is scarcely credible that God should annihilate any of his works, much less so many and so glori-ous works. It ought not to be believed without the most de-cisive proof. On the other hand, it is a most animating thought that this visible creation, which sin has marred, which the polluted breath of men and devils has defiled, and which by sin will be reduced to utter ruin, will be restored by our Jesus, will arise from its ruins in tenfold splendor, and shine with more illustrious glory than before it was defaced by sin.

" After a laborious and anxious search on this interesting subject, I must pronounce the latter to be my decided opin-ion. And the same, I find, has been the more common opin-ion of the Christian fathers, of the divines of the reforma-tion, and of the critics and annotators who have since flourished. I could produce on this side a catalogue of names which would convince you that this has certainly been

33 *

the common opinion of the Christian church in every age, as it was also of the Jewish.

" The words which are employed to express the destruction of the world do not necessarily imply annihilation. Is it said that the world shall perish? The same word is used to express the ancient destruction of the world by the flood, when certainly it was not annihilated. Is it said that the world shall have an end, and be no more? This may be understood only of the present form and organization of the visible system? Is it said that the heavens and the earth shall be dissolved by fire? But the natural power of fire is not to annihilate, but only to dissolve the composition and change the form of substances." — *Sermons*, vol. ii. p. 450.

We have now examined the most important testimony respecting the future destruction and renovation of the earth; for inspiration only can certainly determine its future condition. But science may throw some light upon the changes through which it is to pass. And I now proceed to inquire whether geology affords us any glimpses of its future condition.

In the first place, geology shows us that the earth contains within itself all the agencies necessary for its future destruction in the manner pointed out in the Bible.

Some author has remarked that, from the earliest times, there has been a loud cry of fire. We have seen that it began with the ancient Egyptians, and was continued by the Greeks. But in recent times it has waxed louder and far more distinct. The ancient notions about the existence of fire within the earth were almost entirely conjectural, but within the present century the matter has been put to the test of experiment. Wherever, in Europe and America, the temperature of the air, the waters, and the rocks in deep excavations has been ascertained, it has been found higher than the mean temperature of the climate at the surface; and the experiment has been made in hundreds of places. It is found, too, that the heat increases rapidly as we descend below that point in the earth's crust to which the sun's heat extends. The mean rate of increase has been stated by the British Association to be one degree of Fahrenheit for every forty-five feet. At this rate, all known rocks would be melted at the depth of about sixty miles. Shall we hence conclude that all the matter of the globe below this thickness (or, rather, for the sake of round numbers, below one hundred miles) is actually in a melted state? Most geologists have not seen how such a conclusion is to be avoided. And yet this would leave only about one eight hundredth part of the earth's diameter, and about one fourteenth of its contents, or bulk, in a solid state. How easy, then, should God give permission, for this vast internal fiery ocean to break through its envelope, and so to bury the solid crust that it should all be burnt up and melted! It is conceivable that such a result might take place even by natural operations. And certainly it would be easy for a special divine agency to accomplish it.

It may be thought, however, that the igneous fluidity of the internal part of the globe is too mighty and improbable a conclusion to be based upon the increase of temperature, observed only to the depth of two or three thousand feet. But this is not the only evidence of such a condition of the earth's interior. Three hundred active volcanoes, and still more numerous extinct ones, have opened their mouths and poured forth their molten contents from a great depth, to bear witness to the existence of vast masses of melted rock beneath the earth's crust. The globe, too, is flattened at the poles, just to the amount it would be by rotation on its axis, had it been a liquid mass; and, therefore, there is every probability that it was once liquid; and if so once, its interior is probably still so, because the period for cooling it, when once surrounded by a solid crust, must be incalculably long. That this solid crust has once been liquid from heat, is most obvious to all who carefully examine it. For the unstratified rocks have certainly once been melted, and most of the stratified series were derived from the unstratified. Again, the organic remains dug out from the deep-seated strata prove that, when they were alive, the surface, even in high latitudes, must have been subject to a tropical, or even an ultra-tropical heat; thus showing us that the temperature of the globe has gradually diminished, as we should expect from the theory of original igneous fluidity. And, finally, no other hypothesis but the gradual cooling of the earth's crust, and the powerful volcanic agency that must from time to time have torn and ridged up that crust, will account for the present fractured and overturned condition of the strata, and the elevation of our continent from the ocean's bed. But this supposition does most satisfactorily explain all these phenomena, and also those of earthquakes and volcanoes.

I must acknowledge, however, that all these arguments fail of convincing a few geologists of the doctrine of internal igneous fluidity, to the extent above described. But they all admit that the facts do prove the existence of vast oceans of melted matter beneath the earth's crust. Nor do even these geologists doubt but the globe contains within itself the agencies requisite for a universal conflagration. Mr. Lyell says that "there must exist below enormous masses of matter, intensely heated, and in many instances in a constant state of fusion." He says, also, "When we consider the combustible nature of the elements of the earth, so far as they are known to us, the facility with which their compounds may be decomposed and made to enter into new combinations, the quantity of heat which they evolve during those processes ; when we recollect the expansive power of steam, and that water itself is composed of two gases, which, by their union, produce intense heat ; when we call to mind the number of explosive and detonating compounds which have been already discovered, — we may be allowed to share the astonishment of Pliny, that a single day should pass without a general conflagration. ' *Excedit profecto omnia miracula, ullum diem fuisse quo non cuncta conflagrarent.*' " — Lyell's *Principles of Geology*, b. ii. chap. xx. vol. ii.

" As a consequence of the refrigeration of the centre and crust of the globe," says D'Orbigny, " the withdrawment of matter has produced elevations and depressions on the consolidated crust ; to which movements, in connection with those of the waters, we must impute the complete destruction of the existing fauna. These dislocations have brought about at each epoch changes of level in the consolidated beds and in the seas. And after a period of agitation, more or less prolonged, after each of these geological revolutions, different beings have been created to cover anew and enliven the surface of the earth. — *Cours Elementaire Paleontologie*, p. 148.

All geologists, then, agree that the elements of the earth's final conflagration are contained within its bosom or upon its surface. At present, these elements are so bound down by counteracting agencies, that all is quiet and security. But let the fiat of the Almighty go forth for their liberation, and the scenes of the last day, as described in the Bible, will commence. The ploughshare of ruin will be driven onward, until this fair world is all ingulfed, and no trace of organic life remains. Yet to him who realizes that the destruction is only a necessary preparation for a brighter world, which will emerge from the ruins of the present; that, when the matter of the globe has been purified, its surface shall be covered with new and lovelier forms of beauty, surrounded by a still more bland and balmy atmosphere, and inhabited by sinless and immortal beings, — to him who realizes all this, the desolation will put on the aspect of a glorious transformation.

In the second place, still deeper will be this impression, when we recollect that similar transmutations have already been experienced by the earth with an improvement of its condition. There is no evidence that the entire surface of the earth has ever undergone a complete fusion since organic life first appeared upon it. But we have reason to think that, frequently, at least, when one race of animals and plants has disappeared from the earth, it has been the result of violent catastrophes, proceeding from the elevation or subsidence of continents or chains of mountains. Says Agassiz, " A very remarkable, and perhaps the most surprising fact is, that the appearance of the chains of mountains, and the inequalities of the surface resulting from it, seem to have coincided generally with the epochs of the renewal of organized beings. — *Ed. Journal of Science*, Oct. 1842, p. 394. — These vertical movements of such large portions of the earth's crust could have resulted only from the direct or indirect agency of volcanic power, though the destruction of organic life, which must have been the consequence, may have resulted as often from aqueous as igneous inundations. But usually both agencies were probably concerned, and the predominance of one or the other of these agencies is of little consequence to the argument; for if such wide-spread ruin has already repeatedly passed over the earth, a still wider desolation may be presumed possible, if only a little wider play shall be given to the agents of destruction. Already have the changes of this sort which the earth, or portions of it, have undergone, resulted in an improved condition of its surface. In other words, at each successive epoch, animals and plants of a higher and more perfect organization have appeared, because the temperature, the air, and the earth's general condition have been better adapted to their happy existence. The amount of limestone seems to have been constantly increasing, and, as a consequence, the fertility of the soil; probably, also, the amount of carbonic acid has diminished in the atmosphere, as animals with lungs have been multiplied. In short, there is a prodigious increase, among the present inhabitants of the globe, of animals and plants possessing complicated and delicate organization and loftier intellectual powers, over all former conditions of the globe. But we have reason to believe, from the Christian Scriptures, that the next economy of life which shall be placed upon the globe will far transcend all those that have gone before. Every vestige of sin, suffering, decay, and death will disappear. Says the Bible, *There shall be no more death, neither sorrow nor crying, neither shall there be any more pain, for the former things are passed away. And there shall in no wise enter it any thing that defileth, neither whatsoever worketh abomination, or maketh a lie.* In short, the change is no other than the conversion of this world into heaven. Reasonably, therefore, might we anticipate a most thorough destruction of the present world, to prepare the way for the introduction of such a glorious state. The Scriptures describe that state by the most splendid imagery that can be derived from existing nature. It is represented, figuratively, no doubt, as a splendid city, prepared of God, and let down to the earth. Its twelve foundations are all precious stones, its gates pearls, its wall jasper, and its streets pure gold, as it were, transparent glass. The Lord God Almighty and the Lamb are the temple of that city. Instead of the sun and the moon, the glory of God enlightens it, and the Lamb is the light thereof. From out of their throne proceeds the water of life, clear as crystal, and along its banks grows the tree of life, with its twelve manner of fruits, yielding its fruit every month.

Here, then, we have the most splendid and enchanting objects in nature brought before us as representatives of the new heavens and the new earth. Yet we cannot learn from the Bible, or science, what material dress nature will then put on. We are taught only that it will far exceed, in splendor and perfection, the drapery which she now wears. We may be assured that it will be eminently adapted to a spirit that is henceforth to be perfectly holy, happy, incorruptible, and immortal. Both revelation and geology agree in assuring us that the new earth, which will emerge from the ruins of the present, will be improved in its condition; but the particulars of that condition are not described — probably because we could not, in our present state, understand them.

Such are the views concerning the earth's future destruction and renovation, which appear to me to be taught by a fair interpretation of Scripture, and which harmonize with the teachings of geology. But we are met here by two formidable difficulties. In the first place, if the present earth is to be burnt up and melted at the last day, it must require thousands of years before another solid crust shall be formed upon its surface, capable of sustaining organic natures which are material. But the Bible represents the righteous, at the day of judgment, as reunited to their bodies, which they left in the grave, and entering at once into their residence upon the new earth. Where, then, can we find the thousands of years which, by this theory, are essential to prepare this residence for their reception? Into what intermediate place, what new Hades, shall they pass, until verdure shall clothe the new earth, and more than the primeval beauty of Eden take the place of the volcanic desolation which must reign over a world just beginning to cool from incandescent heat?

I freely acknowledge that this is a serious objection to my theory; and perhaps it is insuperable, unless we resort to miraculous interference. It were easy to say, that God can, in a moment, convert a globe of fire into a paradise of beauty, and make its landscapes smile with charms transcending the bowers of paradise lost. Indeed, the Scriptures represent the New Jerusalem as prepared by God's own hands, and let down at once upon the earth to form the metropolitan abode of the righteous.

But, after all, I am unwilling thus to dispose of the difficulty. For it is a clumsy way to meet objections, when we undertake to philosophize upon events, either past, present, or future, to foist in a miracle, in order to eke out our hypothesis. We thus make an image of as incoherent parts as that in Nebuchadnezzar's dream, and as easily broken in pieces.

There is a second mode by which the difficulty under consideration can be completely obviated, could we only admit the theory on which it rests. Some theological writers have maintained that the day of judgment will occupy a long period, — thousands and tens of thousands of years perhaps, — in order that every individual may experience a literal trial before the universe for all his conduct on earth, so that the conscience of every one in that vast assembly shall approve the final sentence. They appeal to various texts of Scripture,

34

where it is strongly stated that rigid inquisition will be made on that solemn day into the conduct and motives of every individual. And it may be, indeed, that such descriptions are to have a literal fulfilment; and if so, we should have a period long enough for the new earth to be recovered by natural means from its volcanic desolation, and to be covered over with new forms of beauty. But I confess the theory of such a long period of judgment does not seem to me to be sustained by the most approved rules of exegesis, and therefore I am unwilling to rest upon it to sustain my own hypothesis.

But is it not possible that our difficulty of conceiving how the spiritual body can enter at once upon its residence in the new heavens and earth, while yet the globe is only a shoreless ocean of fire, results from a mistaken conception of the nature of the spiritual body ? Do we not judge of it by our own present bodies, and imagine that it must necessarily possess such an organization as would be destroyed by the extremes of heat and cold ? And are we authorized to draw such an inference ? The Scriptures have, indeed, left us very much in the dark as to the specific nature of the future glorified body, which Paul calls a spiritual body. He does not mean that it is composed of spirit, for then it would not differ from the soul itself, by which it is to be animated. He certainly means that it is composed of matter; unless, indeed, there be in the universe a third substance, distinct both from matter and spirit. But of the existence of such a substance we have no positive evidence ; and, therefore, must conclude the spiritual body to be matter; called spiritual, probably, because eminently adapted to form the immortal residence of pure spirit.

Yet we learn from the apostle's description that it is not composed of flesh and blood, which, he says, cannot inherit the kingdom of God ; neither is it capable of decay, like our present bodies. Indeed, the illustration which he derives from the decay and germination of a kernel of wheat shows us that the future body will be as much unlike the present as a stalk of wheat is different from the seed whence it sprang ; and, in appearance, scarcely any two things are more unlike. Hence we may suppose the resurrection body of the righteous to be as different from that which the soul now animates as matter can be, in its most diverse forms.

Now, the question arises, Do we know of any form of matter in the present world which remains the same at all temperatures, and in all circumstances, which no chemical or mechanical agencies can alter ? — a substance which remains unchanged in the very heart of the ice around the poles, and in the focus of a volcano ; which remains untouched by the most powerful reagents which the chemist can apply, and by the mightiest forces which the mechanician can bring to bear upon it ? It seems to me that modern science does render the existence of such a substance probable, though not cognizable by the senses. It is the luminiferous ether, that attenuated medium by which light, and heat, and electricity are transmitted from one part of the universe to another, by undulations of inconceivable velocity. This strange fluid, whose existence and action seems all but demonstrated by the phenomena of light, heat, and electricity, and perhaps, too, by the resistance experienced by Encke's, Biela's, and Halley's comets, must possess the extraordinary characteristic above pointed out. It must exist and act wherever we find light, heat, or electricity ; and where do we not find them ? They penetrate through what has been called empty space ; and, therefore, this ether exists there, propagating its undulations at the astonishing rate of two hundred thousand miles per second. They emanate in constant succession from every intensely heated focus, such as the sun, the volcano, and the chemical furnace ; and, therefore, this strange medium is neither dissipated nor affected by the strongest known heat. Both light and heat are transmitted through ice ; and, therefore, this ether cannot be congealed. The same is true of glass, and every transparent substance, however dense ; and even the most solid metals convey heat and electricity with remarkable facility ; and, therefore, this ether exists and acts with equal facility in the most solid masses as in a vacuum. In short, it seems to be independent of chemical or mechanical changes, and to act unobstructed in all possible modifications of matter. And, though too evanescent to be cognizable by the senses, or the most delicate chemical and mechanical tests, it possesses, nevertheless, a most astonishing activity.

Now, I am not going to assert that the spiritual body will be composed of this luminiferous ether. But, since we know not the composition of that body, it is lawful to suppose that such may be its constitution. This is surely possible, and that is all which is essential to my present argument.

Admitting its truth, the following interesting conclusions follow : —

In the first place, the spiritual body would be unaffected by all possible changes of temperature. It might exist as well in the midst of fire, or of ice, as in any intermediate temperature. Hence it might pass from one extreme of temperature to another, and be at home in them all ; and this is what we might hope for in a future world. Some, indeed, have imagined that the sun will be the future heaven of the righteous ; and on this supposition there is no absurdity in the theory. Nor would there be in the hypothesis which should locate heaven in solid ice, or in the centre of the earth.

In the second place, on this supposition, the spiritual body would be unharmed by those chemical and mechanical agencies which matter in no other form can resist.

The question has often arisen, how the glorified body, if material, would be able to escape all sources of injury, so as to be immortal as the soul. In this hypothesis, we see how it is possible ; for though the whole globe should change its chemical constitution, though worlds should dash upon worlds, the spiritual body, though present at the very point where the terrible collision took place, would feel no injury ; and safe in its immortal habitation, the soul might smile amid " the wreck of matter and the crush of worlds."

In the third place, on this supposition, the soul might communicate its thoughts and receive a knowledge of events and of other minds, through distances inconceivably great, with the speed of lightning. If we suppose the soul, in such a tenement, could transmit its thoughts and desires, and receive impressions, through the luminiferous ether, with only the same velocity as light, it might communicate with other beings upon the sun, at the distance of one hundred million miles, in eight minutes ; and such a power we may reasonably expect the soul will hereafter possess, whether derived from this or some other agency. We cannot believe that, in another world, the soul's communication with the rest of the universe will be as limited as in the present state. On this supposition, she need not wander through the universe to learn the events transpiring in other spheres, for the intelligence would be borne on the morning's ray or the lightning's wing.

Finally, on this supposition, the germ of the future spiritual body may, even in this world, be attached to the soul; and it may be this which she will come seeking after on the resurrection morning.

34 *

I know not but this wonderful medium, in some unknown form, may attach itself to the sleeping dust ; and though that dust be scattered upon the winds, or diffused in the waters of the ocean, and transformed into other animal bodies, still that germ may not be lost. The chemist has often been perplexed, when he thinks how the bodies of men are decomposed after death, and how every particle must, in some cases, pass into other bodies ; he has been perplexed, I say, to see how the resurrection body should be identified, and especially how those particles could become a part of different bodies. Perhaps the hypothesis under consideration may relieve the difficulty. Perhaps, too, it may teach us how the soul exists and acts, when separated from the body. It may act through this universal medium, though in a manner less perfect than after it has united itself to the spiritual body raised from the grave.*

But I fear I am venturing too far into the region of conjecture. My only object is, to show that we do know of a substance which might form a spiritual body which should be in its element upon the new earth, even though it were in the condition of a fiery ocean. It could not, indeed, be an organic body of such a kind as heat would destroy ; though I see no reason why it may not possess an organism far more delicate and wonderful than that of our present bodies, and yet be unaffected by heat or cold, or mechanical or chemical agencies. I do not feel, therefore, that the objection which I am considering is insuperable. It results, I apprehend, from

---

* This subject has been treated more fully, and I hope more satisfactorily, in a little work of mine, which has just reached its second edition, entitled Religious Lectures on Peculiar Phenomena in the Four Seasons, (Amherst, 1851.) See the first Lecture, on the Resurrections of Spring.

the false assumption that the spiritual body will be subject to those influences by which our present comparatively gross bodies are so powerfully affected.

Shall I be pardoned if I say that, in the experiments of an incipient and maltreated science, we have, perhaps, a glimpse of the manner in which the soul will act in the future spiritual body ? for if those experiments be not all delusion, — and how can we reasonably infer that experiments so multiplied, so various, and in many cases, when not in the hands of itinerant jugglers, so fairly performed, — I say, how can we regard all these as mere trickery ? and if not, they are best explained by supposing the soul to act independently of the bodily organs, and through the same medium which we have supposed to constitute the future spiritual body. In this view, mesmerism assumes a most interesting aspect, forming, as it were, a link between the present and the future world. The theory which I have advanced does not, indeed, fall to the ground, though mesmerism should be found a delusion ; yet it is but justice to say, that it first came under my eye in that most classical, philosophical, and attractive work, Townsend's " Facts in Mesmerism." A similar view, however, was presented several years earlier, in a work by Isaac Taylor, no less ingenious and profound, the " Physical Theory of Another Life," a work, however, which makes not the slightest allusion to mesmerism. The author supposes such a state of things as I have imagined in another life to be in existence even now. " The sensation of light," says he, " is now believed to result from the vibrations, not the emanations, of an elastic fluid, or ether ; but this same element may be capable of another species of vibrations ; or the electric or the magnetic fluids may be susceptible of some such vibrations ; or an element as universally diffused as light through the universe may be the medium of sonorous undulations, equally rapid and distinct, and serving to connect the most remote regions of the universe by the conveyance of sounds, just as the most remote are actually connected by the passage of light. Yet the sonorous vibrations of this supposed element may be far too delicate to awaken the ear of man, or, in fact, of a kind not perceptible by the human auditory nerve." " We refuse to allow that a conjecture of this sort is extravagant, or destitute of philosophical probability ; on the contrary, consider it as borne out, in a positive sense, by the discoveries of modern science. Might we then rest for a moment upon an animating conception (aided by the actual analogy of light) such as this, viz., that the field of the visible universe is the theatre of a vast social economy, holding rational intercourse at great distances ? Let us claim leave to indulge the belief, when we contemplate the starry heavens, that speech, inquiry and response, commands and petitions, debate and instruction, are passing to and fro ; or shall the imagination catch the pealing anthems of praise, at stated seasons, arising from worshippers in all quarters, and flowing on with thundering power, like the noise of many waters, until it meet and shake the courts of the central heavens ? " — *Physical Theory of Another Life*, p. 202, 3d Am. ed.

The second objection to the view which I have presented of the future destruction and renovation of the earth, as an abode of the righteous, may be thus stated : Heaven is an unchanging state ; but a world which has been burned up and melted, even if we might suppose spiritual beings to dwell upon it, must undergo still further change. The radiation of its heat would form a crust over its surface ; the waters, dissipated into vapor, would be recondensed ; volcanic agency would ridge up the crust into mountains and valleys ; and, in

short, geological agencies would at length form such a surface, so far as rocks and soil are concerned, as we now
tread upon. And even though organic beings should not be
again placed upon it, those changes would proceed, till, perhaps, another and another great catastrophe by fire might pass
over it ; nor can we say where these mutations would end.
Can we believe such a world to be heaven ?

Here, again, as in the last objection, it appears to me, the
main difficulty lies in our judging of the future spiritual body
by that organism which we now inhabit. Heaven is, indeed,
an unchanging state of happiness and holiness. But does it,
therefore, follow that there can be no change in its material
form and aspect ? I have already shown that the spiritual
body may be of such a composition that no change of temperature, of place or constitution, in surrounding bodies, can
at all affect it. If the soul could be happy in one set of
physical circumstances while in such a tenement, it might
be happy in any other circumstances with which we are acquainted. But it does not follow that the happiness of the
soul might not be increased by the changes of the material
world around it. What is it on earth that affords the greatest
amount of happiness derived from the external world ? It is
the immense variety of creation, produced chiefly by chemical and mechanical agencies. These changes afford us the
most striking exhibitions of the wisdom, power, and benevolence of the Deity, within our knowledge ; and why may not
analogous, or still more wonderful changes, and greater variety,
give still higher conceptions of the divine character to the
inhabitants of heaven, and excite a purer and a stronger love ?
And to study that character will form, I doubt not, the grand
employment of heaven. Who can tell what depths of knowledge may there be laid open into the internal constitution of

matter, and its combinations, and especially its union with spirit! And what surer means of bringing out these developments than change, constant and everlasting change? For who can set limits to those mutations which an infinite God can produce upon the matter of this vast universe? It is easy to see that they may be literally infinite.

Once more. We have seen that the geological changes which our world has hitherto undergone have been an improvement of its condition, and that each successive economy has been a brighter exhibition of divine wisdom and benevolence. Shall this progress be arrested when the present economy closes? We know that the righteous will forever advance in holiness and happiness. Why may not a part of that increase depend upon their introduction into higher and higher economies through eternal ages? May not this be one of the modes in which new developments of the character of God will open upon them in the world of bliss?

The Scriptures represent the material aspect of the new heavens and the new earth, when first the righteous enter upon them, to be one of surpassing glory. But why may not other developments await them in the round of eternal ages, as their expanding faculties are able to understand and appreciate them?

The greater the variety of new scenes in the material world which shall be presented to the mind, such as an infinite Deity shall devise, the more intense the happiness of their contemplations; and who can set limits to the permutations which such a being can produce, even upon matter? I can form no conjecture as to the nature of those new developments; nor do I believe they could be understood in our present state. I feel as if those formed too low an estimate of the new heavens and the new earth, who imagine a repetition there of the

most curious organic structures, the most splendid flowers and
fruits, and the most enchanting landscapes of the present
world.   I fancy that scenes far more enchanting, and objects
far more glorious, will meet the soul at its first entrance upon
the new earth, even though to mortal vision it should present
only an ocean of fire.   I imagine a thousand new inlets into
the soul — nay, I think of it as all eye, all ear, all sensation ;
now plunging deeper into the infinitesimal parts of matter
than the microscope can carry us, and now soaring away,
perhaps on the waves of the mysterious ether, far beyond the
ken of the telescope.   And if such is the first entrance into
heaven, who can conjecture what new fields and new glories
shall open before the mind, and fill it with ecstasy, as it flies
onward without end!   But I dare not indulge further in these
hypothetical, yet fascinating thoughts ; yet let us never forget, that in a very short time, far shorter than we imagine,
all the scenes of futurity will be to us a thrilling reality.   We
shall then know in a moment how much of truth there is in
these speculations.   But if they all prove false, fully confident am I that the scenes which will open upon us will surpass our liveliest conceptions.   The glass through which we
now see darkly will be removed, and face to face shall we
meet eternal glories.   Then shall we learn that our present
bodily organs, however admirably adapted to our condition
here, were in fact clogs upon the soul, intended to fetter its
free range, that we might the more richly enjoy the liberty
of the sons of God, and expatiate in the spiritual body, *the
building of God, the house not made with hands, eternal in
the heavens.*

Let us, then, live continually under the influence of the
scenes that await us beyond the grave.   They will thus become familiar to us. and we shall appreciate their infinite

superiority to the objects that so deeply interest us on earth. We shall be led to look forward even with strong desire, in spite of the repulsive aspect of death, to that state where the soul will be freed from her prison-house of flesh and blood, and can range in untiring freedom through the boundless fields of knowledge and happiness that are in prospect. Then shall we learn to despise the low aims and contracted views of the sensualist, the demagogue, and the worldling. High and noble thoughts and aspirations will lift our souls above the murky atmosphere of this world, and, while yet in the body, we shall begin to breathe the empyreal air of the new heavens, and to gather the fruits of the tree of life in the new earth, where righteousness only shall forever dwell.

LECTURE XII.

THE TELEGRAPHIC SYSTEM OF THE UNIVERSE.

In order to impress some important truth or transaction, men have sometimes represented surrounding inanimate objects as looking on and witnessing the scene, or listening to the words, and ready ever afterwards to open their mouth to testify to the facts, should man deny them. I know of no writings from which to derive so striking an illustration of these strong figurative representations as the sacred Scriptures.

Take, for a first example, the solemn covenant entered into between Jehovah and the Israelites, in the time of Joshua. To fix the transaction as firmly as possible in the minds of the fickle people, he *took a great stone and set it up there under an oak that was by the sanctuary of the Lord. And Joshua said unto all the people, Behold, this stone shall be a witness unto us. For it hath heard all the words of the Lord which he spake unto us. It shall, therefore, be a witness unto you, lest ye deny your God.*

In a second example, the prophet Habakkuk describes the insatiable wickedness of the Chaldeans ; and addressing the nation as an individual, he says, *Thou hast consulted shame to thy house by cutting off many people, and hast sinned against thy soul. For the stone shall cry out of the wall, and the beam out of the timber shall answer it.* Such abominations had aroused even the most insensible part of creation, the very timber and the stone, to life and indignation.

35

In a third example, the whole multitude of Jews had just spread their garments upon the ground for Christ to ride over, they meanwhile crying out, *Blessed be the King that cometh in the name of the Lord. Peace in heaven and glory in the highest.* But some of the Pharisees said, *Master, rebuke thy disciples ; and he answered and said unto them, If these should hold their peace, the stones would immediately cry out.* If man refused to do homage to the King of glory, when he came among them, the rocks, more sensible, would break forth in his praises.

The discoveries of modern science, however, show us that there is a literal sense in which the material creation receives an impression from all our words and actions that can never be effaced ; and that nature, through all time, is ever ready to bear testimony of what we have said and done. Men fancy that the wave of oblivion passes over the greater part of their actions. But physical science shows us that those actions have been transfused into the very texture of the universe, so that no waters can wash them out, and no erosions, comminution, or metamorphoses, can obliterate them.

The principle which I advance in its naked form is this : *Our words, our actions, and even our thoughts, make an indelible impression on the universe.* Thrown into a poetic form, this principle converts creation

> Into a vast sounding gallery ;
> Into a vast picture gallery ;
> And into a universal telegraph.

This proposition I shall endeavor to sustain by an appeal to well-established principles of science. Yet, since some of these principles are not the most common and familiar, and have not been applied, except in part, to this subject, I must be more technical in their explanation than I could wish, and more minute in the details.

The grand point, however, on which the whole subject turns, is the doctrine of reaction. By this is meant the mutual or reciprocal action of different things upon one another. Thus, if a body fall to the earth, the earth reacts upon it, and stops it, or throws it back. If sulphuric acid be poured upon limestone, a mutual action ensues; the acid acts on the stone, and the stone reacts upon the acid, and a new compound is produced. If light fall upon a solid body, the body reacts upon the light, which it sends back to the eye with an image of itself. These are examples of what is meant by reaction, or the reciprocal action of different substances upon one another. But it is not every kind of reaction that will prove a permanent impression to be made upon the universe by our conduct. Hence we must be more specific.

In the first place, the principle is proved and illustrated by the doctrine of mechanical reaction.

From the principle, long since settled in mechanics, that action and reaction are equal, it will follow that every impression which man makes by his words, or his movements, upon the air, the waters, or the solid earth, will produce a series of changes in each of those elements which will never end. The word which is now going out of my mouth causes pulsations or waves in the air, and these, though invisible to human eyes, expand in every direction until they have passed around the whole globe, and produced a change in the whole atmosphere; nor will a single circumgyration complete the effect; but the sentence which I am now uttering shall alter the whole atmosphere through all future time. So that, as Professor Babbage remarks, to whom we are indebted for the first moral application of this mechanical principle, " the air is one vast library, on whose pages are forever written all that man has ever said, or woman whispered." Not a word has ever escaped from mortal lips, whether for the defence of virtue or the perversion of the truth, not a cry of agony has ever been uttered by the oppressed, not a mandate of cruelty by the oppressor, not a false and flattering word by the deceiver, but it is registered indelibly upon the atmosphere we breathe. And could man command the mathematics of superior minds, every particle of air thus set in motion could be traced through all its changes, with as much precision as the astronomer can point out the path of the heavenly bodies. No matter how many storms have raised the atmosphere into wild commotion, and whirled it into countless forms; no matter how many conflicting waves have mixed and crossed one another; the path of each pulsation is definite, and subject to the laws of mathematics. To follow it requires, indeed, a power of analysis superior to human; but we can conceive it to be far inferior to the divine.

The same thing is true of the waters. No wave has ever been raised on their bosom, no keel has ever ploughed their surface, which has not sent an influence and a change into every ocean, and modified every wave, that has rolled in upon the farthest shores. As the vessel crosses the deep, the parted waves close in, and every trace of disturbance soon disappears from human vision. Nevertheless, it is certain that every track thus furrowed in the waters has sent an influence through their entire mass, such as is calculable by distinct formulæ; and it may be that glorified minds, by the principles of celestial mathematics, can as easily trace out the paths of the unnumbered vessels that have crossed the waters, as the astronomer can the paths of the planets or the comets.

The solid earth, too, is alike tenacious of every impression we make upon it; not a footprint of man or beast is marked upon its surface, that does not permanently change the whole globe. Every one of its countless atoms will retain and exhibit an infinitesimal, but a real, effect through all coming time. It is too minute, indeed, for the cognizance of the human senses. But in a higher sphere there may be inlets of perception acute enough to trace it through all its bearings, and thus render every atom of the globe a living witness to the actions of every living being.

In view of these facts, we cannot regard the glowing language of Babbage an exaggeration, when he says, " The soul of the negro, whose fettered body, surviving the living charnel-house of his infected prison, was thrown into the sea to lighten the ship, that his Christian master might escape the limited justice at length assigned by civilized man to crimes whose profit had long gilded their atrocity, will need, at the last great day of human accounts, no living witness of his earthly agony : when man and all his race shall have disappeared from the face of our planet, ask every particle of air still floating over the unpeopled earth, and it will record the cruel mandate of the tyrant. Interrogate every wave which breaks unimpeded on ten thousand desolate shores, and it will give evidence of the last gurgle of the waters which closed over the head of his dying victim. Confront the murderer with every corporeal atom of his immolated slave, and in its still quivering movements he will read the prophet's denunciation of the prophet king."

The distinguished mathematical professor from whom I have just quoted limits the effects of this mathematical reaction to this globe and its atmosphere. But if, as the philosophers now generally admit, there is a subtile and extremely

35 *

elastic medium pervading all space, why must they not extend to other worlds, yea, to the whole universe? Without an accurate acquaintance with the facts, indeed, it will seem a mere extravagant imagination to say that our most trivial word or action sends a thrill throughout the whole material universe; but I see not why sober and legitimate science does not conduct us to this conclusion. Nay, still further, it teaches us that the vibrations and changes which our words and actions produce upon the universe shall never cease their action and reaction till materialism be no more.

We venture, then, to push this thought of the ingenious mathematician into another sphere, which he did not enter. The majority, probably, of the ablest expounders of the Bible have maintained, as previously shown, that the apostle Peter most unequivocally teaches us that the new heavens, or atmosphere, and the new earth, wherein dwelleth righteousness, are merely our present earth and atmosphere, melted and burnt by the fires of the last day, and fitted up anew, — a second and a lovelier paradise, — to be the everlasting abode of holiness and happiness. Indeed, to attempt to fix any other meaning upon Peter's language makes of it a most absurd jumble of literal and figurative expressions, and produces an inversion of chronological events. But, admitting the literal meaning of the apostle to be the true one, then those reactions, produced by our words and conduct upon the present world, shall not be destroyed by the fires of the last day, but reappear in the new economy, and modify the pulsations of the new heavens and the new earth through all eternity.

But even though heaven should be in some other part of the universe, and not this earth refitted, yet, if it be a material residence, why, on the principles already explained, should it not be reached and affected by those vibrations which the laws of mathematics assure us are now spreading from each individual, as a centre, through the whole universe? The conflagration of the earth will alter its chemical constitution, and convert matter into new forms; but the mechanical character of the atoms will not be destroyed; and when they emerge from the final catastrophe, in new and brighter forms, they may still bear and exhibit the impress of every word and every action which they now receive.

Such representations as these, I am aware, will, upon first thought, seem to most minds little better than the dreams of fancy, although founded upon the laws of mathematics. For how soon does every trace disappear from the earth of the most terrible convulsions and the mightiest human efforts! The shout of countless multitudes, the thunder and the crash of battle, and even the volcano's bellowing, are soon succeeded by unbroken silence; and we cannot discover a trace of any of those countless scenes of noise and convulsion that have been acted upon the world's busy stage. How practically absurd, then, to imagine that any influence goes out from the feeble efforts of individuals, that can be recognized, either now or hereafter, on the wide field of the universe!

Such objections as these, however, are based upon the impression, of which it is hard to divest ourselves, that our present means of distinguishing the effects of physical forces are as perfect as we can hope for in eternity. And yet, who will doubt that, when our present gross bodies shall be laid aside, the soul, looking forth from a spiritual body, with quickened powers and unobstructed vision, shall penetrate a new world in the infinitesimal parts of creation? What absurdity in the supposition that then the minutest movement among the atoms, which can now be discovered only by the mathematics of quantities infinitely small, may then stand out as distinctly to our inspection as do now the features of the landscape? What absurdity in the supposition that, even now, there are finite minds in the universe who possess this quickened power of perception, and, though in distant worlds, do actually know what is passing here by the vibrations which our words and actions produce upon elastic matter?

Thus far I have spoken of the influence of our words and actions only upon the material universe, although the principle with which I started includes thoughts also. But are not actions merely the external manifestation of thoughts and purposes? and, therefore, is not thought the efficient agency that impresses the universe? I shall also attempt to show that there are other modes in which the intellect may do this, aside from ordinary words and actions.

But I proceed to the second proof of the general principle. *And I derive it from what may be called optical reactions; that is, the reaction of light and the substances on which it impinges.* These exert such an influence upon it, that, when it is thrown back from them, and enters the organs of vision, or even a transparent lens, with a screen behind it, it produces an image of those objects; in other words, what we call vision.

Now, it is this fact, in connection with the progressive motion of light, that forms the basis of this branch of the argument. Though light moves with such immense velocity, that, for all practical purposes on earth, it is instantaneous, yet, in fact, it does occupy a little more than a second for every two hundred thousand miles which it passes over. Hence a flash of lightning occurring on earth would not be visible on the moon till a second and a quarter afterwards; on the sun, till eight minutes; at the planet Jupiter, when at its greatest distance from us, till fifty-two minutes; on Uranus, till two hours; on Neptune, till four hours and a quarter; on the star of Vega, of the first magnitude, till forty-five years; on a star of the eighth magnitude, till one hundred and eighty years; and on a star of the twelfth magnitude, till four thousand years; and stars of this magnitude are visible through telescopes; nor can we doubt that, with better instruments, stars of far less magnitude might be seen; so that we may confidently say that this flash of lightning would not reach the remotest heavenly body till more than six thousand years — a period equal to that which has elapsed since man's creation.

Now, suppose that, on these different heavenly bodies, beings exist with organs of vision sufficiently acute to discern a flash of lightning on earth, or, rather, to see all the scenes on that hemisphere of our world that is turned towards them; it is obvious that, on the remotest star, the earth would be seen, at this moment, just coming forth from the Creator's hand, in all the freshness of Eden's glories, with our first parents in the beauty of innocence and happiness, and all the beasts of the field and the fowls of the air playing around them. On a star of the twelfth magnitude would be seen the world as it showed itself four thousand years ago; on a star of the eighth magnitude, as it appeared one hundred and eighty years ago; and so on to the moon, where would be seen the occurrences of the present moment. And since there are ten thousand times ten thousand worlds, scattered through these extremes of distance, is it not clear that, taking them all together, they do at this moment contain a vast panorama of the world's entire history, since the hour when the morning stars sang together, and the sons of God shouted for joy on creation's morning?

' Thus," says the unknown author of a little work entitled

" The Stars and the Earth," in which these ideas were first developed — thus the universe encloses the *pictures* of the past, like an indestructible and incorruptible record, containing the purest and the clearest truth; and as sound propagates itself in the air, wave after wave, or, to take a still clearer example, as thunder and lightning are in reality simultaneous, but in the storm the distant thunder follows at the interval of minutes [seconds?] after the flash, so, in like manner, according to our ideas, the pictures of every occurrence propagate themselves into the distant ether, upon the wings of the ray of light; and although they become weaker and smaller, yet, in immeasurable distance, they still have color and form; and as every thing possessing color and form is visible, so must these pictures also be said to be visible, however impossible it may be for the human eye to perceive it with the hitherto discovered optical instruments."

This last statement of the writer every one will acknowledge is true when applied to God; for who will doubt that his eye can take in at a glance that universe which he has made? And to do that is to have before him the entire daily history of our globe; nay, probably, also, of every other world. Indeed, such a supposition affords us a lively conception of the divine omniscience, since we have only to suppose this panorama of the indefinite past to extend indefinitely into the future, and the infinite picture will also be present at this moment before the divine mind.

But is the supposition an absurdity, that there may be in the universe created beings, with powers of vision acute enough to take in all these pictures of our world's history, as they make the circuit of the numberless suns and planets that lie embosomed in boundless space? Suppose such a being at this moment upon a star of the twelfth magnitude, with an

eye turned toward the earth.   He might see the deluge of
Noah, just sweeping over the surface.   Advancing to a nearer
star, he would see the patriarch Abraham going out, not
knowing whither he went.   Coming still nearer, the vision of
the crucified Redeemer would meet his gaze.   Coming nearer
still, he might alight upon worlds where all the revolutions
and convulsions of modern times would fall upon his eye.
Indeed, there are worlds enough and at the right distances,
in the vast empyrean, to show him every event in human
history.

We may proceed a step farther, and inquire whether such
an exaltation of vision as we have supposed may not be hereafter enjoyed by the glorified human mind when it passes into
the spiritual body.   We can hardly believe such a transformation possible.   But suppose an individual born blind to
grow up to manhood and intelligence without ever having
been told any thing about vision.   Then suppose the oculist
to attempt an operation for the restoration of his sight, and, to
prepare him for the transition, let the wonders of human vision
be described to him, and he be told that, by a few moments
of suffering, he can be put in possession of this astonishing
faculty ; would it not appear as improbable to him as it now
does to us, to imagine that our vision can be so clarified and
exalted, that we can discern the events which are passing in
distant worlds as easily as we now do those immediately
around us.

But if such a power of reading human history, from its
panorama spread out on the face of the universe, be now possessed by unfallen beings in other spheres, what idea must
they form of the character of man ?   At one time, they must
regard the race as given up to hopeless rebellion, and the
inflictions of vindictive justice.   And then, anon, they would

see the sceptre of mercy stretched out, and a few faithful soldiers marching under the banner of virtue and fighting the battles of the Lord. Surely they would need a revelation to understand the anomalies and solve the paradoxes which passed under their eyes. They would wonder why a world so filled with tokens of divine goodness, yet so disfigured by wickedness in every form, had not long since been struck from its orbit by the hand of divine justice.

Thus far, in the present argument, I have been following, for the most part, in the track marked out by others. But I now venture to advance into regions hitherto untrodden for any such purpose ; yet I trust that the light which we may find to guide our steps may not prove the bewildering gleam of an *ignis fatuus*, but the lamp of true science.

My third argument is based upon electric reactions.

Whatever may be the true nature of electricity, it is convenient, and probably leads to no error, to speak of it as a fluid, or rather two fluids. For we find two kinds of electricity, denominated positive and negative ; and it is a general fact, that, when a body is brought into one electrical state, it throws other bodies around it into the opposite state, by a power called induction. Those bodies, whose electrical condition has been thus altered, will act on others lying in a remoter circle, and these upon others, and so on, we cannot tell how widely, for we have reason to suppose that electricity is a power that extends through all nature. It can hardly be doubted that i is the force which constitutes what we call chemical affinity by which the constituent parts of all compound bodies are held together ; and in those stony and metallic masses, that occasionally fall from the heavens, we have proof that this same power holds sway in other worlds ; for the most reasonable supposition is, that these meteors move like the planets

through the regions of celestial space, and give us some idea
of the constitution of planetary worlds. If so, the same chemical laws, and, of course, the same chemical forces, prevail
there as in our planet. Indeed, the uniformity of nature would
lead us to such a conclusion were there no facts like those of
meteors to teach it directly. It follows, from these principles, that, whenever we change the electrical condition of
bodies around us, we start a movement to whose onward
march we can assign no limits but the material universe.
These waves of influence consist of a series of attractions and
repulsions, and are independent of the mechanical reactions
already considered, which are produced by onward impulses
alone.

Now, a change in the electric condition of bodies is produced often by the slightest mechanical, chemical, thermal,
physiological, and probably even mental change in man. The
usual way of exciting currents of electricity is by friction.
But chemical action, as in the galvanic battery, produces a
still more energetic and uninterrupted current. The slightest
change of temperature, also, may disturb the electric equilibrium perceptibly. It has been of late ascertained, likewise,
that a change of physiological condition — that is, a change as
to healthy and normal action — affects the electricity of the
parts of the system, and consequently of surrounding bodies.
Substitute a man in the place of a galvanic battery, making
his two hands the electrodes, and there will go out from him
an electric current, that shall sensibly deflect the needle of a
galvanometer, an instrument employed for showing the presence of small portions of electricity.

Nay, further, it seems to be most probably established as
a fact in science, that a man, in the condition above specified,
by a simple act of his will upon his muscles, by which those

36

of one arm only shall be braced, will thereby send an electrical current of one sort through the galvanometer, while a like volition, which shall brace the muscles of the other arm, will set in motion an opposite current.

It is also ascertained, that of the two sorts of nerves which supply every muscle, the nerve of sensibility is a positive pole of a Voltaic circuit, while the nerve of motion, or the muscle into which it passes, is a negative pole. So that the sensor nerves act as electric telegraphs to carry the sensations to the brain, and inform it what is needed, while the motor nerves bring back the volition to the muscles — the brain acting as a galvanic battery, very much like the electric organs of certain fishes.

From these statements it clearly follows, that, besides the mechanical effects produced by our actions, there is also an electric influence excited and propagated by almost every muscular effort, every chemical change within us, every variation in the state of health, or vigor, and especially by every mental effort; for no thought, probably, can pass through the mind which does not alter the physiological, chemical, and electric condition of the brain, and consequently of the whole system. The stronger the emotion, the greater the change; so that those great mental efforts, and those great decisions of the will, which bring along important moral effects, do also make the strongest impression upon the material universe. We cannot say how widely, by means of electric force, they reach; but if so subtile a power does, as we have reason to suppose, permeate all space, and all solid matter, there may be no spot in the whole universe where the knowledge of our most secret thoughts and purposes, as well as our most trivial outward act, may not be transmitted on the lightning's wing; and it may be, that, out of this darkened world, there may not be found any spot where beings do not exist with sensibilities keen enough to learn, through electric changes, what we are doing and thinking.

If there be no absurdity in supposing that even the mechanical influence of our actions may be felt throughout the universe, still less is it absurd to infer the same results from electric agencies.

It would seem, from recent discoveries, that electricity has a more intimate connection with mental operations than any other physical force. If not identical with the nervous influence, it seems to be employed by the mind to accompany that influence to every part of the system ; and the greater the mental excitement, the more energetic the electric movement. It seems to us a marvellous discovery, which enables man to convey and register his thoughts at the distance of thousands of miles by the electric wires. Should it excite any higher wonder to be told, that, by means of this same power, all our thoughts are transmitted to every part of the universe, and can be read there by the acuter perceptions of other beings as easily as we can read the types or hieroglyphics of the electric telegraph? Yet what a startling thought is it, that the most secret workings of our minds and hearts are momentarily spread out in legible characters over the whole material universe ! nay, that they are so woven into the texture of the universe, that they will constitute a part of its web and woof forever ! To believe and realize this is difficult ; to deny it is to go in the face of physical science. How many things we do believe that are sustained by evidence far less substantial !

My fourth argument in support of the general principle is based upon odylic reaction.

And what is odylic reaction? What is odyle? you will

doubtless inquire. It is, indeed, a branch of science emphatically new. I know of no account of it, save what appears in a late work, of nearly five hundred pages, by Baron Reichenbach, of Vienna, entitled " Researches on Magnetism, Electricity, Heat, Light, Crystallization, and Chemical Attraction, in their Relations to the Vital Force," translated by William Gregory, professor of chemistry in the University of Edinburgh. This writer endeavors to show, by a great number of experiments, that there exists in all bodies, and throughout the universe, a peculiar principle, analogous to magnetism, electricity, light, and heat, yet distinct from them all, to which he gives the name of *odyle*. It is most manifest in powerful magnets ; next in crystals, and exists in the human body, the sun, moon, stars, heat, electricity, chemical action, and, in fact, the whole material universe. Those who are most sensitive to this influence are persons of feeble health, especially somnambulists ; but it is found that about one third of individuals, taken promiscuously, and many in good health, are sensible of it ; and it was by a series of observations on persons of all classes and conditions for years, that the facts have been elicited. The inquiry seems to have been conducted with great fairness and scientific skill, and the author has the confidence of several of the most distinguished scientific men in Europe. If there be no mistake in the results, they promise to explain philosophically many popular superstitions, and also the phenomena of mesmerism, without a resort to superhuman agency, either satanic or angelic. They yield, also, an interesting support to the principle of this lecture. Says Baron Reichenbach, " There is nothing in these observations [which he had just detailed] that, after the contents of the preceding treatises, can much surprise us ; but they are certainly a fine additional confirmation of what has been stated in regard to the sun and moon, and also of the fact that the whole material universe, even beyond our earth, acts on us with the very same kind of influence which resides in all terrestrial objects ; and lastly, it shows that we stand in a connection of mutual influence, hitherto unsuspected, with the universe ; so that, in fact, the stars are not altogether devoid of action on our sublunary, perhaps even on our practical, world, and on the mental processes of some heads." — P. 162.

By the experiments here referred to by this author, he had endeavored to show, that even the light of the stars exerted an odylic influence upon the human system ; that is, certain effects independent altogether of their light; and if there be no mistake in the experiments, they certainly do show this. Such a fact almost realizes the suggestions already made, that beings in other spheres may possess such an exaltation of sensibilities as to be able to learn what is going on in this world, and that it is easy to conceive how our sensorium may be raised to the same exalted pitch.

My fifth argument, illustrative of the general principle, is based upon chemical reaction.

Mechanical reaction changes the form and position of bodies ; chemical reaction alters their constitution. By the decomposition of some compounds, the elements are obtained for forming others ; and such changes are going on around us and within us in great numbers unperceived. In the worlds above us, and in the earth beneath us, from its circumference to its centre, the transmutations of chemistry are in progress, and many of them are modified by the agency of man ; so that here is another channel through which human actions exert an influence upon the material universe, and to an extent which we cannot measure. Let us look at some of the modes in which this is done.

36 *

Take, in the first place, the facts respecting photography, or the art of obtaining sketches of objects by means of the action of light. This is strictly a chemical process. In a beam of light, that comes to us from the sun, we find not only rays of light and heat, but chemical rays, which act upon some bodies to change their constitution. When these rays are reflected from a human countenance, and fall upon a silvered plate, that has been coated with iodine and bromine, they leave an impression, which is fixed and brought out as a portrait by the vapor of mercury and some other agents. Here the chemical changes produced by these rays are exceedingly perfect ; but they produce effects upon many other substances, artificially or naturally prepared ; such as paper, for instance, immersed in a solution of bichromate of potash, or upon vegetation, whose green color is probably the result of this action, (as is obvious from the fact that plants growing in the dark are destitute of color.)   Indeed, a large part of the changes of color in nature depend upon these invisible rays.

It seems, then, that this photographic influence pervades all nature ; nor can we say where it stops. We do not know but it may imprint upon the world around us our features, as they are modified by various passions, and thus fill nature with daguerreotype impressions of all our actions that are performed in daylight. It may be, too, that there are tests by which nature, more skilfully than any human photographist, can bring out and fix those portraits, so that acuter senses than ours shall see them, as on a great canvas, spread over the material universe. Perhaps, too, they may never fade from that canvas, but become specimens in the great picture gallery of eternity.

The thought may perhaps cross some mind, that, though

those human actions which are performed in sunlight may be imprinted upon the universe, yet no deed of darkness can thus reveal its author, and remain an eternal stigma upon his name. But there is another phase to this subject. What is the evidence that the chemical rays of a sunbeam are rays of light? We know that they are unequally diffused through the spectrum, being most energetic at its violet extremity; but there is no proof that they are visible. They may, like heat, exert their appropriate influence, which seems to be mainly that of deoxidation, and yet not be colorific. If so, we might expect them to operate in the dark; and experiment proves that they do. An engraving on paper, placed between an iodized silver plate and an amalgamated copper plate, was left in the dark for fifteen hours. On exposing the amalgamated plate to the vapor of mercury, " a very nice impression of the engraving was brought out — it having been effected through the thickness of the paper." — Mr. Hunt, " *On the Changes which Bodies are capable of undergoing in Darkness*," *Phil. Mag.* vol. xxii. p. 277. — Many like experiments prove the existence, among bodies, of a power analogous to, if not identical with, that which accompanies light, and is the basis of the photographic process. Some philosophers do not regard them as identical. But this is of little consequence in my present argument. For all agree that there is a power in nature capable of impressing the outlines of some objects upon others in total darkness.

In respect to such cases, there are one or two facts deserving of special notice. And, first. We must not infer, because man has yet been able to bring out to human view but a few examples of this sort, that they are, therefore, few in nature. Rather should the discovery of a few lead to the conclusion that nature may be full of them, and that a more delicate and refined chemistry may yet disclose them. For the few known cases give us a glimpse of a recondite law of nature, which most likely pervades creation. Some regard these dark rays as neither light, nor heat, nor chemical rays, but a new element; but, whatever its nature, no reason can be given why it should operate only in a few cases, and those of artificial preparation. More probably, through this influence, all bodies brought into contact, or proximity, impress their images upon one another; and the time may come, when, touched by a more subtile chemistry than man now wields, these images shall take a place among obvious and permanent things in the universe, to the honor and glory of some, but to the amazement and everlasting contempt of more.

Of more, I say; for wickedness has oftener sought the concealment of darkness than modest virtue. The foulest enormities of human conduct have always striven to cover themselves with the shroud of night. The thief, the counterfeiter, the assassin, the robber, the murderer, and the seducer, feel comparatively safe in the midnight darkness, because no human eye can scrutinize their actions. But what if it should turn out that sable night, to speak paradoxically, is an unerring photographist! What if wicked men, as they open their eyes from the sleep of death, in another world, should find the universe hung round with faithful pictures of their earthly enormities, which they had supposed forever lost in the oblivion of night! What scenes for them to gaze at forever! They may now, indeed, smile incredulously at such a suggestion; but the disclosures of chemistry may well make them tremble. Analogy does make it a scientific probability that every action of man, however deep the darkness in which it was performed, has imprinted its image upon nature, and that there may be tests which shall draw it into daylight, and make it permanent so long as materialism endures.

There is another chemical principle, called *catalysis*, through which human actions may make powerful and permanent impressions on the universe, and that, too, unperceived by man. In some cases, the mere presence of a certain agent, in a small quantity, will produce extensive changes of constitution in other bodies, while the agent itself remains unaltered. Thus a strip of platinum will determine the union of oxygen and hydrogen in the platinum lamp; and sulphuric acid, in a solution of starch, will change it first into gum, and then into sugar; while neither the platinum nor the acid experiences any change. These are called *catalytic* changes. More often, however, the catalytic agent is itself in the process of change, and it produces an analogous change in other bodies. A familiar example is yeast, or ferment. This substance contains a principle called *diastase*, one part of which is capable of converting two thousand parts of starch into sugar; and this is what is done in the familiar process of fermentation, when we always see verified the scriptural declaration, *A little leaven leaveneth the whole lump*.

The precise manner in which the diastase operates in these cases we may not be able to explain. The particles of the diastase, being themselves in motion, possess the power of putting in motion the particles of other bodies; and these, again, operate upon others, and so on, often to an astonishing extent. In the case of the platinum and the acid, however, no change takes place in their molecules, and we can only state it, as an unexplained fact, that they do produce changes in other bodies.

We have other examples of catalytic influences in nature,

exhibiting an agency still more subtile and energetic.   I refer to contagious and epidemic diseases in animals and plants. An influence goes abroad, and seems to be propagated through the atmosphere, traversing whole continents, and crossing wide oceans, powerful and deadly in its effects, yet inappreciable by the most delicate mechanical or chemical tests.   But the phenomena admit of explanation by supposing a movement, either in the particles of the atmosphere, or of the still more subtile and elastic medium that pervades all space ; a movement started at a particular spot, as the chol-era in India, and the small-pox or some epidemic from some focus, and communicating an unhealthy movement from atom to atom, till it has encircled the earth and mowed down its hecatombs.

Now, when we look at such facts, who can suppose it im-probable that man, who can hardly lift a finger without pro-ducing some chemical change, should start some of these movements, that may reach far beyond his imagination ? And here, as in the cases that have preceded, we must not estimate the actual change in the constitution of bodies by the apparent ; for we know that multitudes of such changes are passing within us and around us, without our cognizance ; and yet there may be chemical eyes in the universe quick enough to see them all, and to follow them onward to the final result ; for there must be a final resultant of all such forces ; nor can we doubt that, some time or other, and to some beings, if not to ourselves, it will be manifest.   Here, then, is another mode in which a chemical influence may go forth from us, reaching the utmost limits of matter and of time ; nay, perhaps extending into eternity, and revealing our ac-tions to the finer sensibilities of exalted beings.

I derive my sixth argument in support of the general prin-ciple from organic reaction.

Few persons, save the zoölogist and comparative anatomist, have any idea of the great nicety and delicacy of the
relations that exist between all the species of animals and
plants, so that what affects one affects all the rest. Perhaps the subject may be illustrated by supposing all the species of organic beings to be distributed at different distances
through a hollow sphere, while between them all there is a
mutual repulsion, and the whole are retained in the form of a
sphere by an attracting force directed to the centre. By
such an arrangement, if one species be taken out of the
sphere, or its repellency become stronger or weaker, the relative position of all the rest would be altered. No matter
how many millions of species there are, the movements of
one will cause a reaction among all the rest.

Now, this illustration, although an approximation, falls
short of representing the actual state of things in nature. It
is no exaggeration to say that a relation similar to tne supposed one exists throughout the vast dominions of animate
beings; so that you cannot obliterate or change one species
without affecting all the rest. Often the change is effected so
slowly and indirectly that the beings experiencing it are unconscious of it ; or they may realize some slight disturbance
of the balance in organic nature, and yet be unconscious of
the cause. By the illustration above given, when one or more
species is removed from the supposed sphere, or its repellent
force weakened or strengthened, although an influence will
reach all the other species, yet a new equilibrium will soon be
established, and no permanently bad effects seem to follow.
But not so in nature. There the balance originally fixed between different beings by infinite wisdom is the best possible ;
and every change, not intended by Providence, must be for
the worse. It was intended, for instance, that man should

subdue forests and extirpate noxious plants, as well as ferocious and noxious animals; and, therefore, such a change
operates to his advantage, but to the injury of the inferior animals.   Yet often he pushes this exterminating process so far
as to injure himself also.   Thus the farmer wages a relentless
war against certain birds, because of some slight evils which
they occasion.   But when they are extirpated, opportunity is
given for noxious insects to multiply, and to bring upon the
farmer evils much greater than those he thus escapes.

To prevent an excessive multiplication of some species is
one of the grand objects of the present balance established
among the whole.   Such an increase is an inevitable effect
of the extinction of a species, and it often occasions great
mischief.   The carnivorous species, especially, were intended
to act as nature's police, to prevent a too great increase of the
herbivorous races, which are rendered excessively fruitful to
keep the world full.   If, then, a carnivorous species become
extinct, the species on which it has fed will so multiply as to
prove great nuisances, and to produce wide disorder among
many species, not only of animals, but of plants.   And often
has man, in this way, by the extermination of species, in particular districts, unwittingly brought a powerful reaction on
himself.

On the Island of New Zealand, within one or two hundred
years past, eight or ten species of gigantic birds — the dinor·
nis and palapteryx — have become extinct, probably through
the persecution of man.   The natives, without doubt, hunted
them down for food, until all disappeared; and as no quadruped of much size inhabits the island, we think there is no
little plausibility in the suggestion of Professor Owen, that
when the birds were all gone, or nearly gone, the natives were
tempted to the practice of cannibalism, as the only means of

gratifying their passion for meat. What a terrible retribution for disturbing the equilibrium of organic nature !

The records of zoölogy and botany afford endless illustration of this subject. But the great truth which they all teach is, that so intimately are we related to other beings, that almost every action of ours reacts upon them for good or evil ; for good, upon the whole, when we conform to the laws which God has established ; and for evil, when by their violation we disturb the equilibrium of organized nature, and produce irregular action. In this latter case, we cannot tell where the disturbance, thus introduced, will end ; for it is not a periodical oscillation, like the perturbations of the heavenly bodies, nor a mere change of position and intensity by mechanical forces.

But does not this law of mutual influence between organic beings extend to other worlds ? Why should it not be transmitted by means of the luminiferous ether to the limits of the universe ? Who knows but a blow struck upon a single link of organic beings here may be felt through the whole circle of animate existence in all worlds ? That is a narrow view of God's work, which isolates the organic races on this globe from the rest of the universe. The more philosophical view throws the golden chain of influence around the whole animal creation, whether small or great, near or remote.

Reverting to the reasoning which we employed in tracing out the extent of mechanical reaction, we shall see that organic reaction may extend not only to other worlds, but also into eternity. For if the matter of the universe is to survive the conflagration of the last day, the future economy of life must have some connection with the present, whether this earth or some other part of the universe be the theatre of its development.

I speak here not of moral influences, which we know will

37

pass over from time into eternity, but of a physical reaction, which may also reach beyond the same gulf. For at least a part of those creatures, who in this world have felt the modifying power of other beings, will survive the world's final catastrophe, and occupy material, though spiritual bodies, whose germ is represented as derived from their bodies on earth. We have reason, then, to suppose some connection and modifying influence between them. And we might show, also, that moral causes, which so affect the physical character here, may exert a like power in eternity. But time will not permit the argument to be followed out.

The conclusion, then, from this argument also, is, that probably every action of ours on earth modifies the condition and destiny of every other created being in this and other worlds through time and eternity. What though human experience, dependent on the bluntness of mortal sensibilities, cannot demonstrate such an influence? Shall the gross perceptions of this disordered world be made the standard of all that exists? Rather let us listen to the suggestions of science, which tell us of the possibility of senses far more acute in other worlds, and in a future state of being — senses that can trace out and feel the vibrations of the delicate web of organic influence that binds together the great and the small, the past, the present, and the future, throughout the universe.

My seventh argument in support of the general principle depends upon mental reaction.

Mental reaction operates in two ways — indirectly and directly; indirectly through matter, directly by the influence of mind upon mind, without an intervening medium. When describing electric reactions, I have shown how our thoughts and volitions change the electric, chemical, and even mechanical condition of the body, and, through these media, that of all the material universe ; and I need not repeat that argument. But to modify the inanimate world through these agencies necessarily affects all other intellects, which are connected with matter ; and since man in a future world is to assume a spiritual body, we may reasonably suppose that all created beings are in some way connected with matter ; and, therefore, by means of materialism, through the subtile agencies that have been named, we may be sure that an influence goes out from every thought and volition of ours, and reaches every other intellect in the wide creation. I know not whether, in other worlds, their inhabitants possess sensibilities acute enough to be conscious of this influence ; certainly, in this world, it is only to a limited extent that men are conscious of it. Yet we must admit that it exists and acts, or deny the demonstrated verities of science.

But is there not evidence that mind sometimes acts directly upon other minds, without any gross, intervening media ? It may, indeed, be doubted whether any created intellect operates, except in connection with some form of matter. Yet there are certain facts in the history of individuals in an abnormal state, which show that one mind acts upon another, independent of the senses, or any other material means of intercommunication discoverable by the senses. Take the details of sleep-waking, or somnambulism ; and do not they present us with numerous cases in which impressions are made by one mind upon another, even when separated beyond the sphere of the senses ? Take the facts respecting double consciousness, and those where the power was possessed of reading the thoughts of others, or the facts relating to prevision ; and surely they cannot be explained but by the supposition of a direct influence of one mind upon another.

Still more decided in this respect are the most familiar facts of artificial somnambulism, called mesmerism. Whatever may be our views of this unsettled branch of knowledge as a whole, it would seem as if we could not doubt that its facts prove the action of mind upon mind, independently of bodily organization, without rejecting evidence which would prove any thing else.

Now, if we admit that mind does operate upon other minds while we are in the body, independent of the body, can we tell how far the influence extends? If electricity, or some other subtile agent, be essential to this action, it would indeed transfer this example to electric reaction, but it would still be real. Yet, in the absence of all certain proof of the electric power in this case, and with certain proof of the existence of such an influence, we may place it among those marvellous means by which man makes an impression, wide beyond our present knowledge, upon the universe, material and mental; and it ought to make us feel that our lightest thoughts and feeblest volitions may reach the outer limit of intellectual life, and its consequences meet us in distant worlds, and far down the track of eternity.

Finally. I derive an argument in support of the general principle from geological reaction.

By this expression, I mean those reactions of whose existence geology furnishes the proof. They are, in fact, the reactions already considered; but geology proves that they have actually operated in past time in many instances, by evidence registered on the rocks, and thus tends to confirm our reasoning derived from other sources. I do not mean that the proof is before us of precisely such an action as our reasoning has supposed, but so analogous to that supposed as to lend it confirmation. A few examples will illustrate the argument.

The effects of mechanical reaction are, perhaps, most frequent and striking in the rocks, especially those deposited from water. Here we have, for instance, the *ripple marks*, which present us with a faithful register of the slightest movement of the waters, and also of the motions of the atmosphere, or of the currents in it, that agitated the waters. In the almost impalpable powder that sometimes constitutes the rocks, we can trace the slightest erosion and comminution of the strata from which the deposit was worn. In the petrified rain drops we find an indelible trace of the most gentle shower. And here, too, we can see the direction of the wind. Such facts, also, imply the operation of electricity and gravity, of heat and cold, collecting and condensing the rain, and bringing it down ; and so similar to present meteorological phenomena do these ancient showers appear to have been, that we may conclude that electrical reactions, in all respects, were the same as at present.

The preservation of the tracks of numerous animals in some of the sandstones shows us how deep and permanent an impression the most trivial action of a living being may make. In these footmarks we sometimes notice a change in the direction of the animal along the surface ; and, of course, an impression deeper or more shallow than usual, of parts of the foot, by the action of the muscles employed in changing the animal's course. Here, then, we have the register of so slight an action as an increased or diminished action of a particular muscle of the leg. Nay, further, such a movement affords us an infallible register of an act of the animal's will, since that must have preceded the change ; and that implies an electric current, first inward along the sensor nerves, and then outward along the motor nerves.

Geology lays open before us a map of the changes in organic

37 *

nature from the apparent commencement of life on the globe, and thus enables us to see examples of this kind of reaction. We find different economies of life to have appeared, but all of them most wisely adapted to existing circumstances. In each economy we perceive the balance between the different tribes provided for. If, for instance, one race of carnivorous species died out, new races were created to occupy their place, so that the herbivorous species should not overrun the globe. Thus, when the early sauroid fishes diminished, the gigantic and carnivorous marine saurian reptiles were introduced. And when the chambered shells, whose occupants were carnivorous, disappeared with the secondary period, numerous univalve mollusks were created to feed on other animals; although previously that family were herbivorous. It would seem, however, as if each successive economy of organic life had contained within itself the seeds of extinction. It was, indeed, mainly a change of climate which first caused some species to disappear. But their destruction so disturbed the balance of creation that others followed, until total extinction was the result, which, however, was often hastened by catastrophes.

Thus we have in the stony volume of the earth's history actual examples of effects resulting from the acts, and even volitions, of the inferior animals, which can never be erased while the rocks endure.

If, therefore, with our imperfect senses, we can see these results so distinctly, we may safely infer that human conduct, and thought, and volition impress upon the globe, nay, upon the universe, marks which nothing can obliterate.

The thoughts which press upon the mind, in view of such a conclusion, are numerous and interesting. A few we can hardly help noticing.

In the first place, what a centre of influence does man occupy !

It is just as if the universe were a tremulous mass of jelly which every movement of his made to vibrate from the centre to the circumference. It is as if the universe were one vast picture gallery, in some part of which the entire history of this world, and of each individual, is shown on canvas, sketched by countless artists, with unerring skill. It is as if each man had his foot upon the point where ten thousand telegraphic wires meet from every part of the universe, and he were able, with each volition, to send abroad an influence along these wires, so as to reach every created being in heaven and in earth. It is as if we had the more than Gorgon power of transmuting every object around us into forms beautiful or hideous, and of sending that transmuting process forward through time and through eternity. It is as if we were linked to every created being by a golden chain, and every pulsation of our heart or movement of our mind modified the pulsation of every other heart and the movements of every other intellect. Wonderful, wonderful is the position man occupies, and the part he acts ! And yet it is not a dream, but the deliberate conclusion of true science.

Secondly. We see in this subject the probability that our minutest actions, and perhaps our thoughts, from day to day, are known throughout the universe.

I speak not here of the divine omniscience, which we know reaches every thought and action ; but I refer to created beings. Science shows us how, in a variety of modes, such knowledge may be conveyed to them by natural agencies ; and we have only to suppose them to be possessed of far more acute sensibilities than man's, in order to be affected by these agencies as we are by more powerful impressions.

And when we consider how fettered and depressed a condition this world obviously is in, because of its sinfulness, who will doubt but the unfallen beings of other spheres may enjoy those keener perceptions that will bring our whole history distinctly before them, day by day? The thought is, indeed, startling, but not unphilosophical.

If this suggestion be true, then may we indulge the thought as highly probable that our friends, who have gone before us into the eternal world, may be as familiar with our conduct, our words, and even our thoughts, as we are ourselves. If we are acting as we ought, and so as will please them, this must be an animating idea; but if we are not, let it serve to stimulate us to our duty, if a sense of the divine omniscience is not sufficient.

We infer from this subject, thirdly, the probability that, in a future state, the power of reading the past history of the world, and of individuals, may be possessed by man.

The nature of the future spiritual body, and of the heavenly state and employments, impresses the mind with the belief that it will be a condition far more exalted than the present, and that the inlets to the soul will be cleared of all obstructions; so that no impression made on such a sensorium shall fail to give the mind a distinct perception. In heaven, such extreme sensibility might become a source of richest pleasure; in the world of despair, an instrument of severe punishment; yet in both cases it might be the natural result of a man's earthly course. Now, such an indefinite exaltation of the perceptions in futurity scarcely any one will doubt. Why should we doubt any more that it may rise so high that man will be able to read, through the agencies we have pointed out, the minutest action and thought in human experience? If, as we have reason to suppose, angels can do it now, the Bible informs us that we shall be like the angels.

If this view be admitted, then it may be that the present world is the only spot in the universe where deeds of wickedness can be concealed. In a sinful world we can see reasons why the power of concealment should exist to some extent. For though no man should do or think any thing which he is ashamed to have known, yet, if all the plans of men for the promotion of good objects were fully known from their inception, the wicked could generally defeat them. But in a world of perfect holiness no such necessity would exist, since the universal desire would be to promote every worthy object; and, therefore, it may be that every soul will lie perfectly open to the inspection of all other souls — an arrange ment that seems appropriate to such a world.

In what an aspect does this principle present the conduct of the suicide ! Tired of earthly scenes, he rushes unbidden into eternity to escape them. But instead of escaping them, he goes where every one of these mortal evils — yea, and multiplied, too, a thousand fold — shall start up in his path with a distinctness of which he had no conception. And henceforth he can never find, as in this world, even a partial deliverance from their terrible vividness. It is as if, to avoid the moonlight, because too bright, a man should plunge into the sun.

Again, if this principle be true, how annoying will it be, to the man who has not acted well his part in this world, to meet in eternity the ever-recurring mementoes of his evil deeds ! He will hardly be able to open his eyes without seeing some plague-spot on creation as the result of his conduct; and although infinite wisdom and power have stayed the plague, no thanks are due to him. The tendencies of his conduct on earth will be most distressing to look upon; and these shall not cease to lie open before him till the last sand in the glass of eternity is run out.

But, on the other hand, how does this principle strew the path of eternity with flowers to that man who, in this world, finds his highest pleasure in doing good! Not merely his highest and noblest deeds of benevolence here shall loom up in bright perspective there, but a thousand acts of private beneficence, unknown to the world and forgotten by himself, shall stand out distinctly on the moving panorama of that better world; and he will be amazed to see what a wide and blessed influence they have exerted, and will exert, as the catalytic influence moves on and widens in its endless march. It might have ruined him to see these fruits in this world, by exciting pride and vain glory; but it will awaken there only gratitude and love to the grace that enabled him thus, in time, to sow the seeds which should fill eternity with flowers, and fragrance, and golden fruit.

Finally. What new and astonishing avenues of knowledge does this subject show us will probably open upon the soul in eternity!

I do not now speak of the new knowledge of the divine character which will then astonish and delight the soul by direct intuition, but rather of those new channels that will be thrown open, through which a knowledge of other worlds, and of other created beings, can be conveyed to the soul almost illimitably. And just consider what a field that will be. At present we know nothing of the inhabitants of other worlds, and it is only by analogy that we make their existence probable. Nor, with our present senses, could we learn any thing respecting them but by an actual visit to each world. But let the suggestions to which our reasonings have

conducted us prove true, — let our sensorium be so modified
and spiritualized that every thought, word, and action in those
worlds shall come to us through pulsations falling upon the
organ of vision, or by an electric current through the nerve
of sensation, or by some transmitted chemical change, — and
on what vantage ground should we be placed! Without
leaving the spot of our residence, supposing the universe constituted as it now is, we might study out the character and
constitution of the countless inhabitants of at least one hundred millions of worlds, which we know to exist; nay, of ten
thousand times that number, which probably exist. Every
movement of matter around us, however infinitesimal, would
be freighted with new knowledge, perhaps from distant
spheres. Every ray of light that met our gaze from the
broad heavens above us would print an image upon our visual
organs of events transpiring in distant worlds, while every
electrical flash might convey some idea to our mind never
before thought of. Every chemical ray, too, might inform us
of scenes far off in the regions of night; and then who can
calculate what organic and mental influences might be transmitted to us from beings of all ranks and scattered through
all worlds? To speak of organs, indeed, as the medium of
perceptions in another world, may be absurd; but we mean
only, by that term, whatever may be substituted for our present organs; and we assume that the properties of matter will
exist forever; and, therefore, we may presume that light, and
electricity, and chemical affinity, and corporeal and mental
influences will, under modified forms, be the modes by which
knowledge shall ever be transmitted. At least, assuming that
they will be, and the magnificent conceptions we have now
traced out may be hereafter realized. And surely, if they be
only slightly probable, the anticipation is full of thrilling

interest, and the moral effect of dwelling upon it must be salutary. It spreads out before us fields of knowledge which eternity can never exhaust, and attractive so immeasurably above all the knowledge of earth that we almost wait impatiently for the summons to break from our prison-house below, and to rise on our new pinions to celestial scenes.

If such rich means of knowledge of created things be enjoyed by celestial minds, and they can drink it in to the full measure of their faculties, then one inevitable effect must be to make them unite, ever and anon, in adoration and praise to the infinite Being who created and sustains all, and whose glory is illustrated by all his works. And we can conceive that there may be stated periods, when, from every part of the universe, the anthem of praise comes rolling onwards towards some central spot, where the divine presence is most felt. O, how gladly will each happy soul, animated by every new accession of knowledge, join in the swelling pæan as it mounts up to the third heavens! Who knows but this is the hour when the peal is beginning? O, let not this world be the only spot in the universe where it shall be unheard and unheeded. Surely we see enough of the divine glory here to begin the song, which we hope to pour forth in loftier notes on high, *unto the King eternal, immortal, invisible, the only wise God ; to whom be honor and glory, forever and ever. Amen.*

LECTURE XIII.

THE VAST PLANS OF JEHOVAH.

It is interesting and instructive to trace the history of man's progress in the knowledge of the existence, character, and plans of Jehovah. We shall find that progress to have been marked by epochs, rather than continuous advancement. Some new revelation from heaven, or some new discovery in science, has given a sudden expansion to his views of the Deity, which have then remained in a good degree stationary for a long period. My chief object in this lecture is to show what accessions to our knowledge of the divine plans have been derived from science, especially from geology. But it will give greater distinctness and impressiveness to the subject to take a review of the principal steps by which the human mind has reached its present accurate spiritual and enlarged views of the Deity.

We will first look at man in the rudest condition in society, in which he has any idea of the existence of beings superior to himself.

For there is a state of his being in which no such ideas exist in his mind; tribes of men, and especially individuals, who have lived in a wild state, away from all human intercourse, have been found with no idea of a superior being of any sort. Other tribes have existed a little more elevated above the irrational animals, and these have an impression, derived perhaps from their moral sense, or growing out of

38

their superstitious fears, that some power exists in the universe greater than themselves. But having never entertained an abstract idea on any other subject, and depending alone upon their senses for their knowledge, they identify God with the most remarkable objects of nature. They listen to his voice in the wind and the thunder, in the ocean's roar, and the volcano's bellowing ; and they see him in the sun, moon, and stars. They feel that he must be superior to themselves ; but how much superior, they know not. They never think of him as infinite; because the idea of infinity on any subject never enters their mind. They conceive of the earth only as a plain of considerable extent, bounded by a circle, beyond which their thoughts never wander ; and they look up to the heavens as a dome, perhaps solid, studded by luminous bodies, it may be a few feet or yards in diameter. They suppose that, somehow or other, this superior Being has the control of their destinies; but the idea of any thing like worship is too spiritual to be conceived of, except, perhaps, some superstitious rite, performed to deprecate the divine displeasure. In short, every thing in their notion of God is indefinite, gross, and confined to the narrow sphere of the senses.

In the second place, polytheism, especially among nations somewhat civilized, is an advance in man's conceptions of the Supreme Being.

Polytheism probably originated in the deification of distinguished men. Superior minds, who had been the leaders or the benefactors of mankind, were suddenly torn from an admiring world by death. Their bodies were left behind, but the animating principle, the immortal mind, had vanished in a moment ; and it was a most natural inquiry, even among the most ignorant, whether some undying principle had not escaped and gone to a higher sphere ; for it would be difficult to conceive how so much intelligence and virtue should be quenched in a moment in eternal night. It would be a most natural and gratifying conclusion with survivors, that their departed leaders and benefactors still lived, and were in some way concerned in watching over their interests, and in controlling their destinies. Conjectures of this sort would, in a few generations, settle into positive belief. Now, this would be a most important advance upon the gross materialism, and indefinite ideas, which identified divinity with striking objects of nature; for if distinguished warriors and statesmen were still alive after their bodies were laid in the grave, there must have escaped, at the moment of death, some principle too subtile to be cognizable by the senses, or by chemical, mechanical, or electrical agencies; and which, therefore, may have been immaterial. At least, by such a belief, men would be led insensibly to form an idea of the human soul as an extremely tenuous, if not immaterial, principle. Especially would educated men — those devoted to philosophical pursuits — come at length to have a clear conception of a spiritual being, neither visible by the senses, nor dependent upon the senses for the exercise of its faculties. Very soon would the imagination fill the universe with such beings, and conceive them as holding intercourse with one another, and as presiding over all the objects of this lower world, and directing all its destinies. It would be very natural, however, to endow these superior beings with human characteristics, and to suppose them actuated by human passions; and thus would the celestial society be represented as a counterpart of that on earth, deformed by the same vices and crimes. This would lead to the idea of a gradation in rank, power, and intellect among the gods, and to the conception of one as supreme. In the popular mythology, however, even Jupiter was represented as acting under the influence of selfishness, pride, lust, and passion ; and as sometimes brought into peril by his powerful inferiors. Some of the philosophers of Greece and Rome did, indeed, give descriptions of their supreme divinity not unworthy the biblical views of Jehovah. It may be that they got the clew to these just and elevated conceptions from the Bible. But it is not difficult to conceive that, in the manner which I have described, they might, by reasoning, with, perhaps, some hints derived from revelation, have gradually attained to these just and noble conceptions of the supreme divinity. Yet it ought not to be forgotten that these exalted views of the philosophers were not shared at all by the common people, and that even the philosophers themselves were for the most part polytheists.

The next step in man's knowledge of God was an immeasurable advance upon polytheism. *I refer to the revelation which God made of himself to the Jews in the Old Testament.* Most of this revelation did, indeed, precede the writings of the Greek and Roman philosophers, but it was confined to a rude and almost unknown people, until the days of their glory had gone by, and did not spread over the globe till an opportunity had been afforded to prove that *the world by wisdom knew not God.* You may, indeed, find, in the writings of a few philosophers, passages descriptive of the natural attributes of the Deity that will compare favorably with those of the Old Testament. But his moral attributes, his benevolence, mercy, justice, and holiness, are brought out in the Old Testament in a far more distinct and impressive manner than in all other ancient writings. Another point, and a vital one, with the writers of the Old Testament, in which that inspired volume goes infinitely beyond the philosophers, is the unity of God. They teach, as a fundamental principle, and with all the earnestness which inspiration can bestow, not only that Jehovah is supreme, but that he is God alone, and that no other gods exist. You may, indeed, find statements to this effect in the works of the philosophers; but the conduct of Socrates, the most enlightened of them all, — in his dying moments, — in directing a sacrifice to be made to Æsculapius, is a good practical commentary upon their doctrine of the divine unity. It shows that, with some correct notions of the supreme divinity, they believed in the existence of inferior deities; or, at least, they did not regard the popular error on this subject of importance enough to require them boldly to testify against it. But such testimony constitutes the burden of the Old Testament, as if all other religious truths were of little importance without it. And so far as these inspired books succeeded in fixing this doctrine in the minds of the Jews, they performed an immense service for religion. They swept at once from the universe the thirty thousand divinities of Greece and Rome, and placed Jehovah only on the throne. But, for some reason or other, polytheism has always been a doctrine most congenial to human nature; especially to the uncultivated mind; and the probability is, that the great mass of the Jews, while they believed in the supremacy of Jehovah, still supposed that the gods of the heathen had a real exist- ence. This certainly was the case before the Babylonish exile, though doubtless the patriarchs had more correct no- tions. This fact explains the otherwise unaccountable dispo- sition of the Jews to fall away to idolatry, in spite of all which Jehovah did to preserve among them his true worship.

On the subject, also, of the divine spirituality, we have evi- dence that the notions of the great mass of the Jewish nation were low and confused. They distinguished, it is true, very clearly between the body and the soul. But they probably

38 *

conceived of the latter as a very subtile, invisible, corporeal essence, and not that pure, immaterial substance which is understood by that term in metaphysics. The abstract ideas attached to the soul in the nineteenth century probably never entered their minds ; and though in strict language they might be called materialists, they were by no means such materialists as modern times have produced, who understandingly deny the existence of the soul, and regard it as a function of the brain. The Jews thought of God as the most subtile essence of which they could form any idea ; but whether he were material, or immaterial, probably they never inquired. And it cannot escape the notice of a reader of the Old Testament how frequently God is represented by figures derived from material objects. This was in accommodation to the rude and uncultivated state of most minds in those early days. Purely abstract truths would have conveyed no ideas to minds which had never been accustomed to abstractions. Hence it is, that we meet in the Bible with so many descriptions of the Deity, which theologians and philosophers denominate *anthropopathic* and *anthropomorphic*. It was in accommodation to the uncultivated state of common minds, which could form no conceptions of God that were not founded on some property belonging to man. The language of the sacred writers does, indeed, when correctly interpreted, convey the idea of the most perfectly simple, spiritual, and immaterial substance as constituting the divine essence ; and minds accustomed to abstract ideas find no difficulty in enucleating the spiritual meaning of Scripture. But had the divine Being been described by abstract terms, the great mass of men, even at the present day, would receive no impressive conception of the Godhead. God, therefore, in the Old Testament, revealed as much concerning himself and his plans, as men would understand. But other revelations and developments would follow, when the human mind should be prepared to receive and appreciate them.

The revelations of Christianity have brought to light so much respecting the moral character and moral government of Jehovah, as to leave little further to be desired or expected in this world.

The natural attributes of the Deity have a more spiritual and less anthropopathic aspect in the New Testament than in the Old. We are told in the former distinctly, that *God is a spirit, and those who worship him must worship him in spirit and in truth.* But God's moral character, as developed in the New Testament, in the plan of redemption and salvation, presents us with a perfection and a glory unknown in all previous revelations. We have, it is true, in the Old Testament intimations and predictions of the plan, which is fully developed and exemplified in the new dispensation. But these were only shadows of Jesus Christ and him crucified. When he appeared, and by his sufferings, as a substitute for man, reconciled divine justice and mercy, and made a clear exposition of the moral law, and a disclosure of a future state of retributions, a flood of light was thrown upon God's moral character. Every cloud that had rested upon it was cleared away, and immaculate holiness covered it with unapproachable splendor. In short, the human mind is incapable of forming a more correct estimate of moral excellence than is exhibited in the scriptural plan of salvation. The more it is meditated upon, and the more we experience its practical influence, the higher will be our conceptions of the moral glory of the divine character; nor have we reason to suppose that any further revelations would increase our apprehensions of it. For benevolence, mercy, justice, and grace are here exhibited in

unlimited, that is, in infinite, glory and perfection, and therefore can never be exceeded.

But though the exhibitions of the divine character and plans
contained in the Bible are thus perfect and excellent, they are
not the only exhibitions which the universe contains, and
which man is capable of understanding. *Lo, these are a part
of his ways.* The Bible has left the wonders of the natural
world where it found them, to be examined and developed by
philosophy. Some have thought that it has anticipated a few
scientific discoveries; but if it had done this in one instance,
it must have carried the same plan through the whole circle
of science; else how could readers determine when the sacred
writers were describing phenomena according to appearances
and general belief, and when according to real scientific truth?
But the fact is, scientific discoveries are left to man's ingenuity; and as they are made from time to time, they bring out
new and splendid illustrations of the character and plans of
Jehovah. Let us now recur to some of these discoveries, that
have opened the widest vistas into the arcana of nature.

*The discoveries in modern astronomy constitute the fifth
step in man's knowledge of God.*

In order to see how much man's conceptions of the universe
have been enlarged by these discoveries, compare the opinions
which prevailed before the introduction of the Copernican
system with what is now certain knowledge, founded upon
physico-mathematics, respecting the extent of the universe.
Then this earth was thought to be the centre and the principal body of the creation, immovably fixed, with the heavenly
bodies, generally thought to be of diminutive size, revolving
around it every twenty-four hours. The earth, too, except in
the opinion of a few sagacious philosophers, was not imagined
to be that vast globe which we now understand it to be, but a

flat surface, perhaps a few hundred or thousand miles in extent, bounded by a circle, and resting on an imaginary foundation. The heavenly bodies were looked upon as little more
than shining points, or at most a few yards, or by the most
daring fancies a few miles, in extent. What a change have
the telescope, the quadrant, and the transit instrument, aided
by profound mathematics, and the talismanic power of the
Newtonian theory of gravitation, produced! Every schoolboy now knows that this globe, enormous though it be compared with what the eye can take in from the loftiest emi-
nence, is but a mere speck in creation, and, with the
exception of the moon, appearing from other worlds only as
one of the smallest stars in their heavens; so small that its
extinction would not be noticed. To the ignorant mind, distances and magnitudes exceeding a hundred miles are conceived of only with great difficulty. But the astronomer,
when he conceives of magnitudes, must make a thousand
miles his shortest unit, and a million of miles when he conceives of distances in the solar system. And when he
attempts to go beyond the sun and the planets, the shortest
division on his measuring line must be the diameter of the
earth's orbit; and even then he will be borne onward so far,
not on the wings of imagination, but of mathematics, that this
enormous distance has vanished to a point. Even then he
has only reached the nearest fixed star, and, of course, has
only just entered upon the outer limit of creation. He must
prepare himself for a still loftier flight. He must give up the
diameter of the earth's orbit as the unit of his measurements,
because too short, and take as his standard the passage of
light, at the rate of two hundred thousand miles per second.
With that speed can he go on, until his mind has reckoned up
six thousand years of seconds, and he will reach fixed stars

whose light has not yet arrived at the earth, because it did not commence its journey till the time of man's creation.

But it is not merely in respect to distance and magnitude that astronomy has enlarged our knowledge of the universe. Numerically it has opened a field equally wide. Think of two thousand worlds rolling nightly around us, visible to the naked eye. Take the telescope, and see those two thousand multiply to fifty or one hundred millions, and then recollect how very improbable it is that the keenest optics of earth can reach more than an infinitesimal part of creation. Surely the mind is as much confounded and lost, when it attempts to conceive of the number of the worlds in the universe, as when it contemplates their distances and magnitudes. In respect to number and distance, at least, we find no resting-place but in infinity.

Now, when we turn our thoughts to the Author of such a universe, our conceptions of his power, wisdom, and benevolence cannot but enlarge in the same ratio as our views of his works. They must, therefore, experience a prodigious expansion. And, indeed, the merest child in a Christian land, in the nineteenth century, has a far wider and nobler conception of the perfections of Jehovah than the wisest philosopher who lived before astronomy had gone forth on her circumnavigation of the universe. From the fact, also, which astronomy discloses, that worlds are in widely different chemical and geological conditions, some gaseous and transparent, some solid and opaque, and some liquid and incandescent, the mind can hardly avoid the inference that they are fulfilling the vast and varied plans of Jehovah.

The sixth step in man's knowledge of Jehovah has been made by the microscope.

To give any correct idea of the boundless field which that

instrument has opened into the infinitesimal parts of creation, it would be necessary to go into details too extended for the present occasion. Perhaps the animalcula or infusoria furnish the best example. " In the clearest waters," says an able writer, " and also in the strongly-troubled acid and salt fluids of the various zones of the earth ; in springs, rivers, lakes, and seas ; in the internal moisture of living plants and animal bodies; and probably, at times, carried about in the vapor and dust of the whole atmosphere of the earth, exists a world, by the common senses of mankind unperceived, of very minute living beings, which have been called, for the last seventy years, *infusoria*. In the ordinary pursuits of life, this mysterious and infinite kingdom of living creatures is passed by without our knowledge of, or interest in, its wonders. But to the quiet observer how astonishing do these become, when he brings to his aid those optical powers by which his faculty of vision is so much strengthened ! In every drop of dirty, stagnant water, we are generally, if not always, able to perceive, by means of the microscope, moving bodies, of from one eleven hundred and fiftieth to one twenty-five thousandth of an inch in diameter, and which often lie packed so closely together that the space between each individual scarcely equals that of their diameter." — Prichard, *History of Infusoria*, p. 2, 1841.

Again says he, " It is hardly conceivable that, within the narrow space, [of a grain of mustard-seed,] eight millions of living, active creatures can exist, all richly endowed with the organs and faculties of animal life. Such, however, is the astonishing fact." — *Ib.* p. 3.

In short, whoever will thoroughly study this subject will be satisfied that Dr. Ehrenberg does not exceed the truth when he asserts, as the result of his inquiries, that " experience shows an unfathomableness of organic creations, when attention is directed to the smallest space, as it does of stars, when revealing the most immense." — *Prichard*, p. 8.

He who follows out the revelations of the telescope, as it penetrates deeper and deeper into space, will feel, when he has seen the remotest object which its power discloses, that there must certainly be a vast unknown region beyond, infinitely exceeding that one over which he has passed. Just so is it with the microscope. It penetrates to an astonishing distance into the infinitesimal forms of organic and inorganic matter; but every improvement in the instrument reaches a new and equally interesting field; and the conclusion forces itself upon the mind that there are regions beyond of indefinite extent, teeming with countless millions even of organic beings, of a size much more diminutive than those yet discovered, and with inorganic forms too minute for the imagination to conceive. Indeed, we can no more set limits to creation in the direction pointed out by the microscope than in that laid open by the telescope. We hence get a most impressive conception of divine wisdom and benevolence, which could thus bestow exquisite organization and life upon atoms minute beyond the power of the imagination to conceive. Indeed, it seems to me that the lesson is even more striking than the contemplation of vast worlds in rapid and harmonious motion; because the latter seem to demand only infinite power, but the former requires infinite wisdom to direct infinite power.

In the seventh and last place, geology has given great enlargement to our knowledge of the divine plans and operations in the universe, and in the following particulars : —

1. It expands our ideas of the time in which the material universe has been in existence as much as astronomy does in regard to its extent.

To those not familiar with the details of geology, this will probably seem a startling and extravagant assertion. There has been, and still is, an extreme sensitiveness in the minds of intelligent men on this subject. And I highly respect the ground from which their apprehensions spring, viz., a fear that to admit the great antiquity of the globe would bring discredit upon revelation. And yet I believe the most candid and able theologians of the present day do not fear that to admit the existence of the matter of the world previous to the six days' work of creation, is inconsistent with the Mosaic statement. But if we allow any period between its creation and the six demiurgic days, it is no more derogatory to Scripture to make that period ten millions of years than ten years. For if the sacred writer would pass over ten years in silence, he could, with the same propriety, pass over ten millions. Now, the longer I study geology, the nearer do my ideas approximate to the latter number as a measure of the earth's duration. Let us contemplate a few facts. We are able to trace the geological changes that have taken place on the earth since man's existence upon it with a good deal of accuracy. For since his remains are found only in alluvium, we must regard all changes that took place previous to the deposition of that formation to have been of an earlier date than his creation. Now, what are the changes which the last six thousand years have witnessed? In some places, the agency of rivers and other causes have made an accumulation of alluvial matter to the depth of not more than one or two hundred feet, although in particular places it is several hundred feet. These deposits have been pushed forward at the mouths of some large rivers, so as to cover hundreds, and even thousands, of square miles. Oceanic currents have also made deposits in the bottom of wide seas of considerable extent; and in some limited spots

39

these deposits have been consolidated into rock. The action
of frost and gravity, also, has crumbled from precipitous
ledges angular fragments enough to form a slope of detritus
sometimes a hundred feet high. The polyparia, or coral
builders, have advanced their work only a few feet in thickness during this period, and soils have accumulated in some
places about as much. Volcanic action has occasionally
thrown up a new island from the ocean's bed; but only a few
of them have been permanent. Some tracts of country, in
no case more than a few hundred miles in extent, have, by
the same agency, been raised a few feet, or sunk down the
same amount. But after all, the earth's surface remains essentially the same as when man was placed upon it.

Now, compare these slight changes with those which have
preceded it, through the operation of the same agencies,
since the first existence of animals upon the globe. I will
not contend, with some distinguished geologists, that these
same changes have always operated with the same intensity
as at present. But there are several circumstances which
show that the depositions from water could not have been
essentially different in ancient and modern times. Now, just
compare six or eight miles in thickness of the fossiliferous
deposits of the previous periods with the two hundred feet of
alluvium accumulated during the historic period; and, after
you have made all reasonable allowance for the greater intensity of action in former times, you will still find yourselves
confounded by the incalculable time requisite to pile up such
an immense thickness of materials, and then to harden most
of them into stone; especially when you call to mind the numerous changes of organic life, and the vast amount of
animal remains which they exhibit. A superficial observer
might lump such a work, and crowd it into a few thousand

years. But the more its details are studied, the longer does
the period appear that is requisite for its production. Each
successive investigation discovers new evidence of changes
in composition, or organic contents, or of vertical movements
effected by extremely slow agencies, so as to make the whole
work immeasurably long.

But when we have gone back to the commencement of
animal existence on the globe, we have taken but one step in
our review of its early history. The next backward step
embraces that wide period during which the stratified, non-
fossiliferous rocks — far thicker than the fossiliferous — were
deposited; probably by the agency of fire and water. Or if
we adopt the metamorphic theory of Mr. Lyell, we shall be
still more deeply impressed by the length of that period,
during which these rocks were in a course of deposition, consolidation, and metamorphosis. For he supposes them originally deposited from water, just as mud, sand, and gravel
now are accumulating in the ocean's bed, and to have enveloped organic beings, as similar materials now do. Next the
whole were consolidated, so as to form the exact prototype of
the existing fossiliferous rocks; and finally it underwent almost
complete fusion, by the slow propagation of internal heat
upwards, until all the organic contents were obliterated, and
a crystalline structure was substituted. Nay, according to
this theory, other systems of rocks, of an analogous character, may have preceded the present primary stratified ones,
and have been at length entirely melted into the unstratified;
so that we cannot say when organic life first began on the
globe. But I will not press this theory, because most of the
ablest geologists reject it, at least in its full extent. And we
have a period long enough to confound the imagination, if we
take the common view, which supposes the non-fossiliferous

rocks to have been deposited from water, at a temperature too high to admit the existence of organic beings.

We have now gone back to that point in the earth's history when a crust had begun to form over the shoreless ocean of melted matter, of which we have reason to suppose it was then composed. Shall we attempt to trace back that history any farther? The light does, indeed, grow dim, and the clew more and more uncertain, the farther we recede along the track of the earth's existence. Still there are some scattered rays that seem to recall to us a condition of the earth still earlier than that in which it constituted a molten globe. It may have been dissipated into vapor, like a comet, or a nebula; and subsequently, by the slow radiation of its heat, have been condensed into an opaque, though a melted, incandescent mass. Several analogies certainly throw an air of plausibility over this hypothesis. And if such was, indeed, the earliest condition of the earth, the time requisite to condense it into melted matter must have been longer than any other period of its history.

Who, now, at all familiar with the dynamics of geological agencies, shall undertake to give an arithmetical expression to the periods that make up the world's entire history? Not only does the reasoning faculty fail to grasp the entire sum, but even imagination, as she flies backwards through period after period, tires in the effort, and brings back not even a conjectural result. The same feeling does, in fact, come over the mind, which she experiences when astronomy has hurried her from world to world, from sun to sun, from system to system, from nebula to nebula, and yet she seems no nearer to the limits of creation than when she started. We know certainly that there are limits; because matter cannot be infinite. But we cannot conjecture where they are fixed. We know, also that there was a time when this world did not exist, an epoch when its entire mass was spoken into existence by the fiat of Jehovah ; because the Bible expressly declares it. But that epoch is unrevealed. If there is any truth in geology, it was certainly more than six thousand years ago. Nay, that science carries us as far back into the arcana of time as astronomy does into the arcana of space. Neither the distance in the one case, nor the duration in the other, can be estimated. But there is a sublime inspiration in the effort to grasp the subject ; and I see not why there is not as much grandeur and high gratification in the idea of vast duration as of vast expansion. And I see not why we do not gain as much enlargement of our conceptions of the plans of Jehovah respecting the universe in the one case as in the other. We cannot but infer, from the pre-Adamic state of our world, that it must have subserved other purposes than to sustain its present inhabitants.

2. In the second place, geology gives us impressive examples of the extent of organic life on the globe since its creation.

I shall not contend, with some geologists, that even the primary crystalline rocks may once have been filled with organic remains, which have been obliterated by heat ; and that, in this way, there may have been a number of creations of organized beings on the globe, of which no trace now remains. I take as the basis of my argument only the relics of animals and plants actually found in the rocks. And when one sees mountain masses, often of small shells, and spread over wide areas, he is amazed to learn how prolific nature has been. What a countless number of vegetables, too, must have been required to produce beds of coal from one to fifty feet thick, and extending over thousands of square miles, and alternating several times with sandstone in the same basin !

39 *

There is reason to believe, too, that the number of animals preserved in the strata bears only a small proportion to those which have been utterly destroyed and decomposed into their original elements. For example, in the sandstone along Connecticut River, the tracks of more than forty species of bipeds and quadrupeds have been found most distinctly marked. Some of these bipeds must have been of colossal size — as much as twelve or fifteen feet in height. And yet scarcely any other vestige of their existence has been discovered. They were the giant rulers of that valley for centuries ; but they have all vanished. How numerous, then, may have been the softer animals of the ancient world, which have not left even a footmark to certify their existence to coming generations !

But the facts recently brought to light respecting infusoria and polythalamia fill us with the greatest admiration of the extent of organic life upon the globe. We have already seen that some of these animals are so minute that eight millions of them are found in a space not larger than a mustard-seed ; and yet they had skeletons of silex, lime, and iron ; and, of course, these skeletons have been preserved ; and, though of the smallest size, it requires not less than forty-one billions to make a single cubic inch ; yet deposits of them, or of species not much larger, occur, several feet in thickness, and extending over several square miles. Nay, the chalk of Northern Europe, and also of Western Asia, where it constitutes most of Mount Lebanon, and extends southerly through Palestine into Arabia and Egypt, and also deposits in North and South America, thousands of miles in extent, — this rock, I say, is nearly half composed of microscopic shells. The oölite, also, contains them ; and, indeed, infusorial remains occur in flint and opal ; and, as instruments and observations are perfected, more and more of the solid rocks are found to have once constituted the framework of animals. It is hardly to be doubted that such was the fact with nearly all the limestone on the globe, occupying at least a seventh part of its surface. In fact, we seem fast coming to regard as sober truth the ancient adage, apparently so extravagant — *Omnis calx e vermibus ; omne ferrum e vermibus ; omnis silex e vermibus.* Indeed, it is the opinion of so competent a geologist as Dr. Mantell that " probably there is not an atom of the solid materials of the globe which has not passed through the complex and wonderful laboratory of life." — *Wond. of Geology,* vol. ii. p. 670. — What a vast field here opens before us to contemplate the far-reaching plans, the benevolence, and the wisdom of the Deity !

In the third place, geology shows us that the present system of organic life on the globe is but one link of a series, extending very far backward and infinitely forward.

Revelation describes only the existing species, leaving to science the task and the privilege to lift up the veil that hangs over the past, and to disclose other economies that have passed away. How many of them have existed we do not certainly know. If, with Agassiz, we characterize them by their predominant tribes, we might say that all the period previous to the new red sandstone constituted the reign of fishes ; from thence to the chalk, the reign of reptiles ; from thence to the drift, the reign of mammifera. But this is a less philosophical view than that of Deshayes, who finds five great groups of animals, specifically independent of one another. But who will attempt to fix the chronological limits of these systems ? We can only say that they must have been exceedingly long, if we can place any dependence upon existing analogies ; and we know that each one of them is made up of numerous subdivisions, or minor groups, widely, though not entirely, different in composition and organic contents. We know that the more we examine the whole series, the deeper does our conviction become that its commencement runs back far, very far, into the depths of past eternity. We know, also, from the joint testimony of Scripture and geology, that another change is to pass over the world, to prepare it for inhabitants far more elevated than those now living upon it, and in possession of perfect holiness and perfect happiness. And it may be it will experience far greater changes, adapting it for higher and higher grades of being, through periods of duration to which we can assign no limits. O, what a vast chain of being is here spread out before the imagination, reaching immeasurably far into the depths of the eternity which is past, and into the eternity which is to come! What a field for the display of God's infinite perfections! What a vista does it open to us into the vast plans and purposes of Jehovah!

In the fourth place, geology reveals to us a curious series of improvements in the condition of worlds, as they pass through successive changes.

If the earth began its existence in the state of vapor, we can hardly imagine it in that state capable of sustaining any organic natures, formed upon the general type of those now existing. Nor, when the vapor was condensed into a molten globe, could such natures inhabit it, till a crust had formed over its surface, and the heat had been so reduced as not to decompose animals and plants. Even then, the natures placed upon it must have been of a peculiar and low type of organization, capable of enduring the high temperature and catastrophes which would destroy those of more delicate and complicated organization. But gradually did the temperature diminish, while aqueous and atmospheric agencies were accumulating a deeper and a richer soil, so that the next change of inhabitants would allow natures of a higher organization and a denser population to occupy the surface. Their remains, buried in the earth, would increase the quantity of carbonate of lime in a form available for the use of animals and plants ; that is, lime would gradually be eliminated, by plants and animals, from its more concealed combinations in the crystalline rocks, and be converted into carbonates, sulphates, and humates. A larger amount of organic matter would also be converted into humus. Now, limestone soils are of all others most favorable to vegetation, when there is a sufficient supply of organic matter. Hence every successive change becomes more and more adapted for animals and plants, because the lime and the organic matter in a state favorable for their support have been increasing ; and the present state of the surface is more favorable than any conditions which have preceded it, and accordingly it is peopled with more perfect and more numerous organic natures. Can we doubt but that, if another change passes over the earth, this same great principle of progressive improvement will be manifested in the renovated world ? I am not prepared to maintain, however, that this future change will be, like the past ones, an improvement as to soil and climate ; for the change, as Scripture teaches, will be accomplished by fire ; and so different will be the state of existence in the new earth, wherein dwelleth righteousness, that we cannot say how far the present system of nature will be introduced. But that it will be an improved condition, we can hardly doubt, if we infer any thing from the splendid figures by which it is described in the Bible, and from the character of those who are to be its denizens.

Some of the facts of modern astronomy impress us with the

idea that this principle of progress may extend to other worlds. Some of these are in a gaseous state, some condensed into fiery liquid globes, some covered with a crust of solidified volcanic matter, and some surrounded by a liquid, like water. Do not these facts justify the supposition, that the changes which our earth has undergone are merely a single example of a great principle in God's government of the natural world? If so, it presents the divine wisdom in an interesting aspect. We see the Deity employing the same matter for different purposes. Instead of creating it for one single economy of organic beings, he seems to have made it the theatre for the display of his benevolence through successive periods; but at the same time not losing sight of the highest use he intended to make of it, by the introduction of rational and immortal natures upon it. Human wisdom would have pronounced this impossible; but divine wisdom, prompted by divine benevolence, could accomplish it.

Finally, geology discloses to us chemical change as a great animating, controlling, and conservative principle of the material universe.

When Newton brought to light the principle of gravitation, and showed how it controls and keeps in harmonious movement the heavenly bodies, he developed the great mechanical power by which the universe is governed. And this power was supposed for a long time to be superior to all others. But geology has brought out a second great controlling and conservative agency, — the chemical power, — " the second right hand of the Creator," as Dr. McCulloch expressively calls it. Suppose matter under the control of gravity, and let it be balanced by a centrifugal force. You have, indeed, harmonious motions among the celestial bodies, and, if no disturbing cause come in, you have endless motion. But until you introduce chemical agencies, every thing in the individual worlds would be compacted by gravity into one dead mass of matter, destined to no resurrection. But let chemical agencies leaven that mass, let affinity and cohesion commence their segregating processes, and constant motion and change would follow, with a thousand new and splendid forms. Especially when the Deity had infused the living principle into portions of that matter, and put chemistry, and her handmaid electricity, under the control of the vital power, would these worlds teem with animation, and countless exhibitions of beauty.

And in all known worlds, these chemical changes are at work unceasingly. We know not whether those worlds are all inhabited, but we have evidence that all are undergoing the transmutations of chemistry ; not on their surface merely, but in their deep interior. The consequence is, universal change ; change often upon a vast scale ; change extending through thousands and millions of years, and through the entire mass of immense worlds. We have glanced, in these lectures, at the most important of those changes which this world has undergone, and we have seen it to be almost universal. We have found that the entire crust of the globe, many miles in thickness, and probably to its centre, has been dissolved by heat, and much of it also by water ; that a large part of it, at least, has, by the same chemistry, been made to constitute portions of the animal frame ; that, even now, much of its interior is held in igneous solution, and that probably the time was when its entire mass was a molten, self-luminous world. Indeed, the conjecture is not without some foundation, which carries back this chemical action one step farther, and makes the world originally a diffused mass of nebula.

At this point of the argument, geology appeals to astronomy, to show how widely this principle of chemical change has operated, and still operates, in the universe. We look first at the nebulæ; for here we probably find matter in its most chaotic and attenuated form, constituting self-luminous, diffused masses of vapor. In some of them, however, that matter has begun to condense, doubtless by the radiation of its heat. In the comets, we find probably similar matter, some of it still farther advanced in the process of condensation, so that perhaps a nearly solid nucleus may exist. In the sun and fixed stars, the condensation has gone on so far that cohesive attraction begins to operate, the latent heat of the vapor is extricated, and melted luminous worlds are the result. Around them, however, there probably still floats a wide atmosphere of the more elastic materials, which the heat dissipates, of which the zodiacal light, perhaps, furnishes us with an example. The nebulosity which surrounds the asteroids, Ceres, Pallas, Juno, Vesta, and Astrea, renders it probable that, though they have advanced so far in the process of refrigeration as to become opaque, they may still retain heat enough to dissipate much of their substance. Still farther advanced towards the condition of a habitable world is the moon; and yet volcanic desolation covers its surface. Not improbably Jupiter is nearly surrounded with a fluid like water, and Saturn by a fluid lighter than water — being still farther advanced towards the condition of the earth.

I acknowledge that these are but slight glimpses of the geology and chemistry of other worlds. And yet, taken in connection with the geological history of our own globe, do they not furnish us with some extremely probable examples of those changes to which our earth has been subject? They show us that worlds may exist in the form of vapor, and that some are actually at this time in the various conditions through which geology supposes this world to have passed. Do we not, in these examples, gather strong intimations of a great law of chemical change in the universe ? Gaseous matter, so far as we know, appears to have been the earliest state of the universe ; and then, by the agency of heat, it passes through the successive changes of liquid and solid, which have been described.

The chemical changes that take place on the earth, under our immediate cognizance, through the agency of water, usually proceed, under favorable circumstances, in a cycle ; that is, the substance, after passing through a series of changes, returns at length into the same condition from which it started. Thus aqueous vapor, by the loss of heat, is first converted into water, next into ice, and then, by the access of heat, into water again, and at last into vapor. The question naturally arises, whether those mutations, through which worlds are passing, may not form a similar cycle. We are able to trace them through several steps, from gaseous to liquid, and from the liquid to the solid ; and we are assured, on the testimony of Scripture, that the next change of the earth will be from solid to liquid. And in those stars which in past ages have suddenly broken forth with remarkable splendor, and then disappeared, may we not have examples of other worlds burnt up, — not annihilated, — but deluged by fire, and either dissipated or again cooled ? What changes, if any, will succeed the final conflgration of the globe, neither science nor revelation informs us.

Yet, if the laws of nature respecting heat are not entirely altered, other changes must follow ; and we have seen, in a former lecture, that those changes are perfectly consistent with our ideas of heaven, and that they may, in fact, enhance the happiness of heaven. They may go on forever ; in which

40

case, we can hardly doubt but they would form a cycle, though how wide the circuit we cannot conjecture; or they may, at least, reach an unchanging state. I confess, however, that the idea of perpetual change corresponds best with the analogies of the existing universe; and in eternity, as well as in time, it may form an essential element of happiness.

In this world, too, this unceasing change, though it presents at first view a strong tendency to ruin, is, in fact, the grand conservative principle of material things. In a world of life and motion like ours, it is impossible that bodies, especially organic bodies, should not be sometimes subject to violent disarrangements and destruction from the mechanical agencies which exist; and were no chemical changes possible, ultimate and irremediable ruin must be the result. But the chemical powers, inherent in matter, soon bring forth new forms of beauty from the ruins; and, in fact, throughout all nature, the process of renovation usually counterbalances that of destruction; and thus far, indeed, the former has done more than this; for every time nature has changed her dress in past ages, she has put on more lovely robes, and a fresher countenance. Can we doubt that this same principle of change, operating, as it does, on a stupendous scale through the universe, is one of the great means of its preservation? It seems, indeed, paradoxical to say that instability is the basis of stability. But I see not why it is not literally true; and I can hardly doubt but this principle is superior to the laws of gravity — superior to every other law, in fact, for giving permanence and security to the universe.

It is true that, in the case of man, connected as diminution and decay are with the curse denounced on sin, they assume, in his view, a melancholy aspect; and the perishable nature of all created things has ever been viewed by the sentimentalist with sad emotions.

> "What does not fade ? The tower that long had stood
> The crush of thunder, and the warring winds,
> Shook by the slow but sure destroyer Time,
> Now hangs in doubtful ruins o'er its base ;
> And flinty pyramids and walls of brass
> Descend ; the Babylonian spires are sunk ;
> Achaia, Rome, and Egypt moulder down.
> Time shakes the stable tyranny of thrones ;
> And tottering empires rush by their own weight.
> This huge rotundity we tread grows old,
> And all those worlds that roll around the sun.
> The sun himself shall die, and ancient night
> Again involve the desolate abyss." — *Akenside.*

If we turn now our thoughts away from man's dissolution, and think how speedily chemical power will raise nature out of her grave, in renovated and increased beauty, this universal tendency to decay puts on the aspect of a glorious transformation. We connect the changes around us with those which have taken place in the great bodies of the universe ; we see them all to be but parts of a far-reaching plan of the Deity, by which the stability of the world is maintained, and its progressive improvement secured. When we look forward, fancy kindles at the developments of divine power, wisdom, and benevolence which will in this manner be made in the round of eternal ages. We see that what our ignorance had mistaken for a defect in nature is, in fact, a great conservative principle of the universe, which Newton did not discover because geology had not yet unfolded her record.

Such are the developments of the divine character and plans unfolded to us by geology. Compare them now with the views which have hitherto prevailed. The common opinion has been, and still, indeed, is, that about six thousand years ago this earth, and, in fact, the whole material universe, were spoken into existence in a moment of time; and that, in a few thousand more, they will, by a similar fiat, be swept from existence, and be no more. On the other hand, geology places the time when the matter of the universe was created out of nothing at an epoch indefinitely but immensely remote. Since that epoch, this matter has passed through a multitude of changes, and been the seat of numerous systems of organic life, unlike one another, yet all linked together into one great system by a most perfect unity; each minor system being most beautifully adapted to its place in the great chain, and yet each successive link becoming more and more perfect. Nor does geology admit that any evidence exists of the future annihilation of the material universe; but rather of other changes, by which new and brighter displays of divine wisdom and benevolence shall be brought out, it may be in endless succession. Geology is not, indeed, insensible to the displays of the divine character which are exhibited on the present theatre of the world. Indeed, she distinctly recognizes the act which is now passing as the most perfect of all. Yet this scene of the great drama she regards as only one of the units of a similar series of changes that have gone by or will hereafter come; the chain stretching so far into the eternity that is past and the eternity that is to come, that the extremities are lost to mortal vision.

Do any shrink back from these immense conclusions, because they so much surpass the views they have been accustomed to entertain respecting the beginning and the end of the material universe? But why should they be unwilling to have geology liberalize their minds as much in respect to

THESE VIEWS CONSISTENT WITH REVELATION.   473

duration as astronomy has done in respect to space ? Perhaps
it is a lingering fear that the geological views conflict with
revelation.   Such fears formerly kept back many from giving
up their souls to the noble truths of astronomy.   But they
learnt, at length, that astronomy merely illustrates, and does
not oppose, revelation.   It showed men how to understand
certain passages of sacred writ respecting the earth and
heavenly bodies which they had before misinterpreted.   Just
so is it with geology.   There is no collision between its statements and revelation.   It only enables us more correctly to
interpret some portions of the Bible ; and then, when we
have admitted the new interpretation, it brings a flood of
light upon the plans and attributes of Jehovah.   Geology,
therefore, should be viewed, as it really is, the auxiliary both
of natural and revealed religion.   And when its religious
relations are fully understood, theology, I doubt not, will be
as anxious to cultivate its alliance as she has been fearful of
it in days past.

   " Shall it any longer be said," remarks Dr. Buckland, " that
a science which unfolds such abundant evidence of the being
and attributes of God, can reasonably be viewed in any other
light than as the efficient auxiliary and handmaid of religion ?
Some few there still may be whom timidity, or prejudice, or
want of opportunity, allow not to examine its evidence ; who
are alarmed by the novelty, or surprised by the magnitude
and extent, of the views which geology forces on their attention ; and who would rather have kept closed the volume of
witness which has been sealed up for ages beneath the surface of the earth than to impose on the student in natural
theology the duty of studying its contents — a duty in which,
for lack of experience, they may anticipate a hazardous c
laborious task, but which, by those engaged in it, is found to
                              40 *

be a rational, and righteous, and delightful exercise of the highest faculties in multiplying the evidence of the existence, and attributes, and providence of God. The alarm, however, which was excited by the novelty of its first discoveries, has well nigh passed away ; and those to whom it has been permitted to be the humble instruments of their promulgation, and who have steadily persevered, under the firm conviction that ' truth can never be opposed to truth,' and that the works of God, when rightly understood, and viewed in their true relations, and from a right position, would at length be found to be in perfect accordance with his word, are now receiving their high reward in finding difficulties vanish, objections gradually withdrawn, and in seeing the evidences of geology admitted into the list of witnesses to the truth of the great fundamental doctrines of theology." — *Bridgewater Treatise*, vol. i. p. 593.

Such, then, in conclusion of the subject, is the religion of geology. It has been described as a region divided between the barren mountains of scepticism and the putrid fens and quagmires of infidelity and atheism ; producing only a gloomy and a poisonous vegetation ; covered with fogs, and swept over by pestilential blasts. But this report was made by those who saw it at a distance. We have found it to be a land abounding in rich landscapes, warmed by a bright sun, blest with a balmy atmosphere, covered by noble forests and sweet flowers, with fruits savory and healthful. We have ascended its lofty mountains, and there have we been greeted with prospects of surpassing loveliness and overwhelming sublimity. In short, nowhere in the whole world of science do we find regions where more of the Deity is seen in his works. To him whose heart is warmed by true piety, and whose mind has broken the narrow shell of prejudice, and can grasp noble thoughts, these are delightful fields through which to wander. More and more they must become the favorite haunts of such hearts and such minds. For there do views open upon the soul, respecting the character and plans of the Deity, as large and refreshing as those which astronomy presents. Nay, in their practical bearing, these views are far more important. Mechanical philosophy introduces an unbending and unvarying law between the Creator and his works ; but geology unveils his providential hand, cutting asunder that law at intervals, and planting the seeds of a new economy upon a renovated world. We thus seem to be brought into near communion with the infinite mind. We are prepared to listen to his voice when it speaks in revelation. We recognize his guiding and sustaining agency at every step of our pilgrimage. And we await in confident hope and joyful anticipation those sublime manifestations of his character and plans, and those higher enjoyments which will greet the pure soul in the round of eternal ages.

LECTURE XIV.

SCIENTIFIC TRUTH, RIGHTLY UNDERSTOOD, IS RELIGIOUS TRUTH.

THE connection between science and religion has ever been a subject of deep interest to enlightened and reflecting minds. Too often, however, up to the present time, has the theologian, on the one hand, looked with jealousy upon science, fearful that its influence was hurtful to the cause of true religion; while, on the other hand, the philosopher, in the pride of a sceptical spirit, has scorned an alliance between science and theology, and even fancied many a discrepancy. Both these opinions are erroneous; and disastrously have they operated, as well upon science as upon religion. The position which I take, and which I shall endeavor to maintain, is, that *scientific truth, rightly understood, is religious truth.*

The proposition may be misunderstood at its first announcement, but I hope, ere its examination be finished, to satisfy you that it is true; and if so, that it ought to reconcile religion to science, and science to religion.

In arriving at correct conclusions concerning this statement, much will depend on the meaning which we attach to the phrase *religious truth.* Religion is properly defined to be piety towards God. This piety implies two things: first, a correct knowledge of God; and secondly, the exercise of proper affections in view of that knowledge. The former constitutes the theoretic part of religion, and is investigated solely by the understanding. The latter constitutes the practical part of religion, and depends much upon the will, the heart, or the moral powers of man. All truth, therefore, which illustrates the divine character or government, or which tends to produce right affections towards God, is properly denominated religious truth. If, then, I can show that all scientific truth, rightly understood, has one or both of these effects, it will follow that it is strictly religious truth.

Scientific truth is but another name for the laws of nature. And a law of nature is merely the uniform mode in which the Deity operates in the created universe. It follows, then, that science is only a history of the divine operations in matter and mind.

In order to avoid mistake, we must make a distinction between the principles of science, and the application of those principles to the useful arts of life. The principles themselves are an illustration of the divine wisdom and benevolence, but their application to the arts illustrates the ingenuity and wisdom of man. At the most, therefore, the latter only indirectly and remotely exhibits the character of the Deity, while the former directly shows forth his perfections.

I now proceed to establish my general proposition, by showing, in the first place, that *all scientific truth is adapted to prove the existence or to illustrate the perfections of the Deity.*

After all that has been written on the subject of natural theology, by such men as Newintyt, Ray, Derham, Wollaston, Clarke, Butler, Tucker, Paley, Chalmers, Crombie, Brown, Brougham, Harris, M'Cosh, and the authors of the Bridgewater Treatises, I need not surely go into details to prove that science in general is a great storehouse of facts to illustrate the divine perfections and government. It is, indeed, a vast repository, from which materials have been drawn on which to build the argument for the divine existence and character. Efforts have been made, it is true, in modern times, to show that the whole argument from design is inconclusive. It is said, that though the operations of nature seem to show design and contrivance, they need no higher powers than those that exist in nature itself. They do not prove the existence of an independent personal agent, separate from the material world. Animals, and even plants, possess an inherent power of adapting themselves to circumstances; and may not a higher exercise of this same power explain all the operations of nature without any other Deity?

This argument appears to me to be utterly set aside by the following considerations: In the first place, there is no power inherent in vegetable or animal natures which can properly be called the power of contrivance and design, except so far as it exists in their minds. All other examples show merely the operation of impulse, or instinct, and will not at all explain that wide-reaching contrivance and design which cause all the operations of nature to conspire to certain great results, and to constitute one, and only one, great system. In the second place, the operations of intellect furnish us with the only examples in nature of that kind of contrivance and design which must have arranged and adapted the parts of the universe. But in the third place, no intellect, within our knowledge, is capacious enough to have contrived and arranged the universe. Indeed, to the capacity of that mind which could have done this we can assign no limits, and, therefore, infer it to be infinite. In other words, we infer the existence of the Deity. In the fourth place, the whole force of this argument rests upon the supposed uniformity of nature. For no one imagines that there exists at present, in nature, any power of contrivance and design sufficient to work a miracle; in other

PROOF OF THE DIVINE EXISTENCE.

words, to introduce new races of animals and plants. " Could this uniformity once be broken up," says an ingenious expositor of this atheistic argument, " could this rigid order be once infringed for a good and manifest reason, it would change the whole face of the argument. Could we see the sun stand still in heaven, that the wicked might be overthrown, then should we be assured of a personal power with a distinct will, whose agents and ministers these laws were. Such an event would be a miracle. But if such events have happened, they are not a part of nature ; it is not nature that tells us of them, and it is only with her that we are at present concerned." — *President Hopkins*, *Quarterly Observer*, Oct. 1833, p. 309.

Geology, however, does reveal to us miracles of stupendous import, miracles of creation, which infinite power and wisdom alone could have produced. Hence, if the testimony of that science be admitted, this reasoning can no longer stand the test of examination, and it must be acknowledged that the argument for God's existence from design, which has ever been so satisfactory to every mind not clouded by metaphysics, is left standing on an immovable foundation.

To return to the point from which we started : it is not necessary, I say, to go into a detailed examination of each particular science, and show how its principles prove and illustrate the being and attributes of the Deity, for the work has already been done more ably and thoroughly than I can do it, and admitted by all, save the few who reject the argument from design altogether. There are a few sciences, however, which have been hitherto chiefly passed by, because they were not supposed capable of throwing any light of consequence upon theology. Let us see whether these sciences are as barren of religious interest as has been supposed.

Geology is a branch of knowledge, which, a few years ago,

would have been at once selected as not only destitute of any important religious applications, but as of a positively injurious tendency; and even now, such is the feeling probably of a majority of the religious world. True, it touches religion, natural and revealed, at many points; but so novel and startling are its conclusions, that they are thought to unsettle more minds than they confirm. They fall in with many of the views of scepticism, and especially confirm its doubts concerning the age of the world, and compel the religious man to give up long-cherished opinions upon this point, and on other collateral subjects. But we have gone into a careful examination of the religious applications of this science, and have we not found it most fertile in its illustrations both of natural and revealed religion? Let us just recapitulate the conclusions at which we have arrived.

In the first place, geology furnishes important illustrations of revealed religion. It confirms the statement that the present continents of our globe were once, and for an indefinite time, beneath the ocean, and that they were subsequently lifted above the waters by internal agencies. It agrees with revelation in making water and heat the two great agents of geological change upon and within the earth, and that the work of creation, after the production of matter, was progressive. It shows us equally with revelation, that the existing races of animals and plants on the globe were created at a comparatively recent epoch, and that man commenced his existence not more than six thousand years ago. It shows us, also, that the earth contains within itself the volcanic agency necessary for its future destruction by combustion, as described in the Bible.

But, perhaps, the most important illustration of revealed truth, which geology affords, is the light which it casts upon certain passages of the Bible relating to the creation. As those texts which represent the earth as immovable, and the heavenly bodies as moving diurnally around it, were not rightly understood, until astronomy had discovered the true theory of the solar system, so those passages which relate to the period of the creation of the universe, the introduction of death into the world, and the extent and operation of the deluge, were misinterpreted till geology disclosed their true meaning. It is still customary, indeed, to speak of geology and revelation as in collision with each other on these subjects ; but this is a false view of the case. Revelation is illustrated, not opposed, by geology. Who thinks, at this day, of any discrepancy between astronomy and revelation ? And yet, two hundred years ago, the evidence of such discrepancy was far more striking than any which can now be offered to show geology at variance with the Scriptures. We ought, therefore, to look upon that science as illustrating, instead of opposing, the Scriptures.

Having once admitted the conclusions of geology as to the great age of the world, and a flood of light is shed upon some of the most difficult points both of natural and revealed religion. It shows the occurrence of numerous changes on the globe which nothing but the power of God could have produced, and which in fact were most striking and stupendous miracles. Hence the arguments which have so long been employed to show that the world is eternal are rendered nugatory ; for if we can point to epochs when entire races of animals and plants began to exist on the globe, we prove the agency of a Deity quite as strikingly as if we could show the moment when the matter of the world was summoned into existence out of nothing. In the same manner, also, we silence the argument against the giving of a revelation from heaven, as well as the miracles by which it is substantiated, on the ground that we have no example of a special interference with the established course of nature. Here we have interpositions long anterior to man's existence, as well as by his creation, which take away all improbability from those which are implied in a revelation. We hence likewise establish the doctrine of a special providence over the world — a doctrine proved with great difficulty by any other reasoning of natural theology.

Still more abundant is the evidence derived from geology of the divine benevolence. And this evidence comes mostly from the operations and final effect of the most desolating agencies, heretofore regarded as a proof of malevolence, or, at least, of vindictive justice ; and we may reasonably infer, that could we look through the whole system of divine government, we should find that all evil is only a necessary means of the greatest good.

No one can examine existing nature without being convinced that all its parts and operations belong to one great system. Geology makes other economies of wide extent to pass before us, opening a vista indefinitely backward into the hoary past ; and it is gratifying to witness that same unity of design pervading all preceding periods of the world's history, linking the whole into one mighty scheme, worthy its infinite Contriver.

How much, also, does this science enlarge our conceptions of the plans and operations of Jehovah ! We had been accustomed to limit our views of the creative agency of God to the few thousand years of man's existence, and to anticipate the destruction of the material universe in a few thousand years more. But geology makes the period of man's existence on the globe only one short link of a chain of revolutions which preceded his existence, and which reaches forward immeasurably far into the future. We see the same matter in the hands of infinite wisdom, and by means of the great conservative principle of chemical change, passing through a multitude of stupendous revolutions, sustaining countless and varied forms of organic life, and presenting an almost illimitable panorama of the plans of an infinite God.

If such is the fruit which geology pours into the lap of religion, how misunderstood have been its principles ! In many a mind there is still an anxious fear lest its discoveries should prove unfavorable to religion ; and they would feel greatly relieved could they only be assured that no influence injurious to piety would emanate from that science. But we can give them far more than this assurance. We can draw from this science more to illustrate and confirm religion than from any other ; and we believe that the history of the past justifies the general conclusion, that those sciences whose early developments excited most apprehensions of a collision with religion, have ultimately furnished the most abundant illustrations of its principles.

Another science regarded as barren of religious applications, and even as sometimes positively injurious, is mathematics. Its principles are, indeed, of so abstruse a nature, that it is not easy to frame out of them a religious argument that is capable of popular illustration. But, in fact, mathematical laws form the basis of nearly all the operations of nature. They constitute, as it were, the very framework of the material world. When we look up to the heavenly bodies, we see them directed and controlled, along with the earth, by those laws, which vary not, by an iota, from century to century. The infinity of changes, which are going on in the constitution of bodies upon and within the earth, chemistry reduces to mathematical laws.   So far as organic operations depend upon chemical changes, — and this is very far, — mathematics is the controlling power.   I will not say, that life and intellect are in a strict sense under the guidance of mathematics; and yet I doubt not that their operations are limited and controlled by its principles.   Confident am I that atmospheric changes, apparently quite as anomalous and irregular as the movements of the vital and intellectual principles, rest on mathematics as certainly as do the revolutions of the heavenly bodies.

It seems, then, that this science forms the very foundation of all arguments for Theism, from the arrangements and operations of the material universe.   We do, indeed, neglect the foundation, and point only to the superstructure, when we state these arguments.   But suppose mathematical laws to be at once struck from existence, and what a hideous chaos would the universe present!   What then would become of the marks of design and unity in nature, and of the Theist's argument for the being of a God?

But mathematical principles furnish several interesting illustrations of truth, of no small importance.   In a former lecture, we have seen how the doctrine of miracles stands forth completely vindicated by an appeal to mathematical laws ; how, in fact, they might have formed a part of the original plan of the universe, when first it was conceived in the divine mind, and how their occurrence may be as much the result of a fixed law as the most common operations of nature ; so that in this way all improbability of their occurrence, on the ground that nature is constant, is removed.   These views are illustrated in that singular, yet original work of Professor Babbage, called the "Ninth Bridgewater Treatise," a work written, it is true, in part, under the influence of exasperated feelings, but yet full of original and ingenious suggestions. But these views have been so fully presented in the Lecture on Special and Miraculous Providence, and in that upon the Telegraphic System of the Universe, that they need not here be repeated.

Mathematics, also, aids our conceptions of truths of religion difficult or impossible, from their nature, of being understood by finite beings. All the attributes of the Deity, being infinite, are of this description. But it seems to me that the contemplation of a mathematical series, either increasing or decreasing, gives us the strongest apprehension of infinity which we can attain. It puts into our hands a thread by which we can find our way, as far as our powers will carry us, towards infinity. True, after we have followed the series till the mind stops exhausted, we are no nearer infinity than when we started; yet we do get most deeply impressed with the unfathomableness of the abyss that separates the finite from the infinite.

To many minds all statements of the biblical doctrine of the Trinity appear so absurd and contradictory as to be incapable of belief. Yet let it be stated to a man, for the first time, that two lines may approach each other forever without meeting, and it must appear equally absurd. But after you have demonstrated to him the properties of the hyperbola and its asymptote, the apparent absurdity vanishes. So, when the theologian has stated, that by the divine unity he means only a numerical unity, — in other words, that there is but one Supreme Being, and that the three persons of the Godhead are one in this sense, and three only in those respects not inconsistent with this unity, — every philosophical mind, whether it admits that the Scriptures teach this doctrine or not, must see that there is no absurdity or contradiction in it. And thus it may happen, that the solution of a man's difficulties on this

41 *

subject may come from a proposition of conic sections, as in fact we know to have been the case.

It is said, however, that mathematicians have been unusually prone to scepticism concerning religious truth. If it be so, it probably originates from the absurd attempt to apply mathematical reasoning to moral subjects ; or, rather, the devotees of this science often become so attached to its demonstrations, that they will not admit any evidence of a less certain character. They do not realize the total difference between moral and mathematical reasonings, and absurdly endeavor to stretch religion on the Procrustean bed of mathematics. No wonder they become sceptics. But the fault is in themselves, not in this science, whose natural tendencies, upon a pure and exalted mind, are favorable to religion, because its principles illustrate religion.

There are several other sciences, whose earlier developments were supposed for a time to be unfavorable to religion ; and hence has originated a ground of apprehension respecting science generally. When the Copernican system of astronomy was introduced, it was thought impossible ever to reconcile it to the plain declarations of Scripture ; and hence at least one venerable astronomer was obliged to recant that system upon his knees. Similar fears of collision between science and revelation were excited when chemistry announced that the main part of the earth has already been oxidized, and, therefore, could not hereafter be literally burnt. Because some physiologists have been materialists, it has been inferred that physiology was favorable to materialism. But it is now found that they were materialists in spite of physiology, rather than from a correct interpretation of its facts.

Strong apprehensions have also been excited respecting **phrenology** and mesmerism. And, indeed, in their present aspect, these sciences are probably made to exert a more un-friendly influence upon vital religion than any other. Those who profess to understand and teach them have been, for the most part, decided opponents of special providence and special grace, and many of them materialists. But this is not because there are any special grounds for such opinions in phrenology or mesmerism. The latter branch, indeed, affords such decided proofs of immaterialism, as to have led several able materialists to change their views. Nor does phrenology afford any stronger proof that law governs the natural world, than do the other sciences. But when a man who is sceptical becomes deeply interested in any branch of knowledge, and fancies himself to be an oracle respecting it, he will torture its principles till they are made to give testimony in favor of his previous sceptical views, although, in fact, the tones are as unnatural as those of ventriloquism, and as deceptive. When true philosophy shall at length determine what are the genuine principles of phrenology and mesmerism, we can judge of their bearing upon religion; but the history of other sciences shows us that we need have no fears of any collision, when the whole subject is brought fairly into the daylight.

Upon the whole, every part of science, which has been supposed, by the fears of friends or malice of foes, to conflict with religion, has been found, at length, when fully understood, to be in perfect harmony with its principles, and even to illustrate them. It is high time, therefore, for the friends of religion to cease fearing any injury to the cause of religion from science; and high time, also, for the enemies of religion to cease expecting any such collision.

In conclusion of this argument, we may safely challenge any one to point out a single principle of science which does

not in some way illustrate the perfections of the Deity ; and
if he cannot, scientific truth may be appropriately called religious truth, especially since such illustrations are the highest
use to which science can be applied.   It is no drawback on
the argument because so few make this use of science, nor
because some attempt to array science against religion ; for
this only shows how men may neglect the most important use
to which science can be applied, or how they can pervert the
richest gifts.

I derive a second argument in support of the general position, that scientific truth is religious truth, from the fact that
it will survive the present world, and its examination become
a part of the employments and enjoyments of heaven.

The Scriptures are, indeed, sparing in their details of the
specific employments of the heavenly world, except so far as
worship and praise are concerned.   But that worship will undoubtedly be the spontaneous impulse of the heart, (as it is in
this world when acceptable,) in view of some manifestations
of the divine character.   Accordingly, the first sentence of the
future song of Moses and the Lamb, as the saints stand with
the harps of God upon the sea of glass, is, *Great and marvel-*
lous are thy works, Lord God Almighty.   The works of God,
then, will be studied in the future world ; and what is that but
the study of the sciences ?   It is, indeed, said by the apostle,
that *whether there be tongues, they shall cease,* [that is, in a future world ;] *whether there be knowledge, it shall vanish away ;*
and hence it has sometimes been inferred that all the knowledge which we acquire in this world will disappear with this
world.   But this cannot be the meaning of the passage, for
in a variety of places the Bible represents both the righteous
and wicked in another world as conscious of what took place
on earth ; and, unless the nature of the mind be changed at

death, it is not possible to conceive that the knowledge we acquire here should be lost. This passage may refer to one of those gifts of inspiration peculiar to apostolic times, called by the sacred writer *the word of knowledge.* But more probably he meant to teach that, so much brighter and clearer will be the disclosures of another world, that most of our present knowledge will be eclipsed and forgotten. But this does not imply that our future knowledge will be essentially different in nature from that which we acquire on earth. The grand difference is, that now *we see through a glass darkly, but then face to face.*

We can, also, see why some branches of science cultivated on earth should be very much modified in a future world. There are several, for instance, dependent mainly upon the present organic constitution of nature; and of such branches only the general principles can survive the destruction of the existing framework of animals and plants. Take, for an example, anatomy and physiology. We believe, indeed, that the new earth, wherein dwelleth righteousness, will be material, and that the bodies of men will also be material. But even though these bodies should be organized, we learn from the Scriptures that this organization will be very different from our present bodies. *They,* says Christ, *who shall be accounted worthy to obtain that world, and the resurrection from the dead, neither marry nor are given in marriage, neither can they die any more; for they are equal unto the angels.* Paul's vivid description of the future spiritual body leaves the impression on the mind that it must be very dissimilar to our present bodies. He does not attempt to define the spiritual body, probably because we could not understand the definition, since it would be so unlike any thing on earth. He represents it as incorruptible, powerful, and glorious,

entirely in contrast with our present bodies, and declares
that it is not flesh and blood, and that it is not organized like
our present bodies.

It seems, then, that we have no certain evidence that the
future spiritual body will be organized; and in a former lecture we have seen that it is not necessary to suppose it endowed with organs. If not, it is obvious that the sciences of
anatomy and physiology can have no existence in a future
world, except in the memory. On the other hand, however,
there are some things in Paul's description of the future body
that make it quite probable that its organization will be much
more exquisite than any thing in existence on earth. He
represents it as springing from our present bodies as a germ
from a seed; and this would seem to imply organization;
though we must not infer too much from a mere rhetorical
similitude. But he also represents the spiritual body as far
transcending the natural body in glory and in power; and,
since the latter is fearfully and wonderfully made, we know
of nothing but the most exquisite organization that can give
the spiritual body such a superiority over the natural. Admitting that such will be its structure, and, although the
nomenclature of anatomy and physiology, which is adapted
to flesh and blood, shall pass away and be forgotten, yet
analogous sciences shall be substituted, based on facts and
principles far more interesting, and developing relations and
harmonies far more beautiful. It may be thought, indeed,
that, so different will be these sciences from any thing on
earth, that there can be no common principles and no link of
connection. But the longer a man studies the works of God,
the more inclined will he be to regard the universe, material
and immaterial, as founded on eternal principles; as, in fact,
a transcript of the divine nature; and that all the changes in

nature are only new developments of unchanging fundamental laws, not the introduction of new laws. Hence the philosopher would infer that in existing nature we have the prototype of new heavens and a new earth; and although a future condition of things may be as different from the present as the plant is from the seed out of which it springs, still, as the seed contains the embryo of a future plant, so the future world may, as it were, lie coiled up in the present. If in these suggestions there is any truth, there may be a germ in the anatomy and physiology of the present world, which shall survive the destruction of the present economy, and unfold, in far higher beauty and glory, in the more congenial climate of the new heavens and the new earth. If so, the great principles of these sciences which are acquired on earth, and which are so prolific in exhibitions of divine skill, may not prove to be lost knowledge. They shall be recognized as types of those far higher and richer developments of organization which the spiritual body shall exhibit.

It may be still more difficult to show that such a science as botany will have a place in the new earth; simply because we have no certain knowledge of the existence of vegetation there. We can infer nothing on this subject from the figurative representations of the new Jerusalem in Revelation, since the drapery is all derived from this world. But, on the general principle already stated, that the universe constitutes but one vast and harmonious system, and all the economies upon it, past, present, and future, are only different developments of eternal principles, this consideration, I say, should make us hesitate before we infer the annihilation of the vast vegetable kingdom upon the destruction of the present economy of the world. And it does give us an aspect of extreme barrenness and cheerlessness to think of the new earth entirely swept of every thing analogous to the existing foliage, flowers, and fruits. We have attempted to show, however, in another place, that the spiritual body may be of such a nature that it might exist in a temperature so high, or so low, as to prevent the existence of such organic natures as now exist. But how easy for the Deity to create such natures as are adapted to extremes of temperature as wide as we now are acquainted with ; and that, too, on the same type as existing nature ; so that the new earth, while yet an incandescent, glowing ocean, might teem with animals and plants, organized on the same general principles as those of the present earth ! But there is another supposition. I have endeavored to show that change ever has been, and probably ever will be, one of the grand means by which mind is introduced to higher spheres of enjoyment ; and even though the new earth at first should be destitute of organic natures, both animal and vegetable, they might be introduced in successive and more perfect economies, as a means of increased happiness, especially to rational natures. These are, indeed, only conjectures ; but the balance of probabilities seems to me to incline the mind to the belief that there may be a botany as well as zoöl-ogy in the future world, far transcending their prototypes on earth.

Among the things that we may be certain will pass away with the present world is the mode of communicating our ideas by language. This the apostle expressly declares when he says, *Whether there be tongues*, [that is, languages,] *they shall cease.* Now, the acquisition of languages, and the right use of language, or rhetoric and oratory, constitute a large part of what men call learning on earth. And the question is, whether there are any principles on which these branches of knowledge are based that will become the elements of new

and higher modes of communicating thought in a future
world. These branches are, indeed, rather to be regarded
as arts than sciences. Language is the drapery for clothing
our thoughts, and, unless we have thoughts to clothe, it becomes useless; and rhetoric and oratory merely show us how
to arrange that drapery in the most attractive and impressive
style. But there is such a thing as the philosophy of language
and the philosophy of rhetoric, whose principles are derived
chiefly from moral and intellectual philosophy. And these,
we have reason to believe, are eternal. Different as will be
the mode of communicating thoughts hereafter from the present, we shall find the same philosophical principles lying at its
foundation. Hence we may expect that there will be a celestial language, a celestial rhetoric, and a celestial oratory, in
whose beauty and splendor those of earth will be forgotten.

I now proceed briefly to consider those sciences which,
having little connection with material organization, we may
more confidently maintain will have an existence on the
new earth.

It will be hardly necessary to spend much time in proving
that intellectual philosophy will be one of the subjects of investigation in a future world. For it would be strange if the
noblest part of God's workmanship, for which materialism
was created, should cease to be an object of inquiry in that
world where alone it can be investigated with much success.
When we consider that the whole train of mental phenomena
is constantly passing under the mind's own observation, and
that a vast amount of time and talent has been devoted to
the subject ever since man began to philosophize, — that is,
for more than two thousand years, — it would seem as if
psychology ere this must have attained the precision and certainty of mathematics. But how different is the fact! I

speak not of a want of agreement in opinion on subordinate points, for these minor diversities must be expected in any science not strictly demonstrative. Even astronomy abounds with them. But metaphysical philosophers have not yet been able to settle fundamental principles. They are not yet agreed as to the existence of many of the most familiar and important intellectual powers and principles of action. The systems of Locke and Hume, constructed with great ability, were overthrown by Reid; Stewart differed much from Reid; and Dr. Thomas Brown has powerfully attacked the fabric erected by Stewart. And lastly, the phrenologists, with no mean ability, have endeavored to show that all these philosophers are heaven-wide of the truth, because they have so much neglected the influence of the material organs on the mental powers. Now, this diversity of result, arrived at by men of such profound abilities, shows that there are peculiar difficulties in the study of mind, originating, probably, in the fact that, in this world, we never see the operation of mind apart from a gross material organization. But in another state, where no organization will exist, or one far better adapted to mental operations, we may hope for such a clarification of the mental eye that the laws of mind will assume the precision and certainty of mathematics, and the relations between mind and matter, now so obscure, be fully developed. Then, I doubt not, the principles of mental science will furnish a more splendid illustration of the divine perfections than any which can now be derived from the material world.

Will any one believe that the principles of moral science and mathematics will be altered or annihilated by the conflagration of the globe? We believe them no more dependent upon the external universe than is the divine existence. God exists by a necessity of nature, and these principles have the same unchanging and eternal origin. If so, no changes in the material world can affect them. So far as we understand them here, we shall find them true hereafter; and we shall doubtless find that our present knowledge is but the mere twilight of that bright day which will there pour its full light upon these subjects. Mathematical and moral truths, which we now suppose to be general laws, we shall then find to be, in many cases, only the ramifications of principles far wider, which we cannot now discover, and which we could not comprehend were they open to inspection. And we shall also find that moral laws are as certain and demonstrable as those of mathematics; and that they form the adamantine chain which holds together the spiritual world, and gives it symmetry and beauty, as mathematics links together the material universe.

Among men who understand biblical interpretation, and also the principles of science, the belief in the annihilation of the material universe at the close of man's probationary state is fast disappearing, and the more scriptural, philosophical, and animating doctrine is embraced, that there will be only a change of form and condition of our earth and its atmosphere, and that the matter of the universe will survive, and successively assume new and more beautiful forms, it may be eternally. If so, all those physical sciences, which do not depend upon organic structure, will form subjects of investigation in the heavenly world. There will be the heavenly bodies, governed by the same laws as at present, and offering a noble field for examination. Nor will the heavenly inhabitants need, as on earth, visual organs and optical instruments, which, at best, afford us only glimpses of the material universe. For there, if we rightly conjecture, will they possess the power of learning, with almost intuitive certainty and intuitive rapidity, the character and movements of the most distant worlds. Nay, it may be that they can pass from world to world with the velocity of light, and thus become better acquainted with their more intimate condition. Thus will the astronomy of the celestial world surpass, beyond conception, that science which even now is regarded as unequalled for its sublimity.

We cannot be sure through what material medium the mind will act in a future world. But the manner in which we know heat, light, and electricity to be transmitted, makes it not impossible that the same or a similar medium may be the vehicle through which thought shall be hereafter transmitted. If so, we can easily understand how the mind will be able to penetrate into the most recondite nature of bodies, and learn the mode in which they act upon one another ; for the curious medium which conveys light and heat does penetrate all bodies, whether they be solid or gaseous, cold or hot. Hence we may learn at a glance, in a future world, more of the internal constitution of bodies, and of their mutual action, than a whole life on earth, spent in the study of chemistry, will unfold. Then, too, shall we doubtless find chemical laws operating on a scale of grandeur and extent, limited only by the material universe.

Universally diffused as light, heat, and electricity are, and diligently as their phenomena have been studied, yet what mystery hangs over their nature and operations ! They seem to be too subtile, and to approximate too nearly to immaterial substances, to be apprehended by our beclouded intellects. When, therefore, our means of perception shall be vastly improved, as we have reason to believe they will be in eternity, these will become noble themes for examination. For who can doubt that agents so ethereal in their nature, and apparently indestructible, and even unchanged by any means with which we are acquainted, will survive the final catastrophe of our world ? Probably, indeed, we are allowed to catch only glimpses of their nature and operations on earth, so that we may safely anticipate an immense expansion of the electricity and optics which will form a part of the science of heaven.

We have endeavored to show, in a former lecture, that the future residence of the righteous will be material; that it will, in fact, be the present earth, purified by the fires of the last day, and rising from the final ruin in renovated splendor. We have shown that this is the doctrine of Scripture, of philosophy, and of a majority of the Christian church. A solid world, then, will exist, whose geology can be studied by glorified minds far more accurately and successfully than the globe which we inhabit; for those minds will doubtless be able to penetrate the entire mass of the globe, and learn its whole structure. The final conflagration may, indeed, for the most part, obliterate the traces of present and past organic beings. But according to the doctrine of action and reaction in mechanics, in chemistry, in electricity, and in organization, every change that has ever passed over the earth has left traces of its occurrence which can never be blotted out; and it is not improbable that glorified minds will possess the power of discovering and reading these records of the past, if not on the principle just specified, yet in some other way ; so that the entire geological history of our planet will probably pass in clear light before them. Points which we see only through a glass darkly will then stand forth in full daylight; and from the glimpses we are able to obtain in this world of its present geological changes, what a mighty and interesting series will be seen by celestial minds ! If, even by the colored rays which come upon us through the twilight of this world, we are

able to see so many striking illustrations of the divine .aar-
acter engraven on the solid rocks, what a noble volu..ie of
religious truth shall be found written there, when the light of
heaven shall penetrate the earth's deep foundations! Those
foundations, figuratively described in revelation as so many
precious stones, bearing up a city of pure gold, clear as glass,
will then reflect a richer light than the costliest literal gems
which the rocks now yield. The geology of heaven will be
resplendent with divine glory.

We see, then, with a few probable exceptions, resulting
from a difference between the organism of heaven and earth,
that science will survive the ruin of this world, and in a nobler
form engage the minds, and interest the hearts, of heaven's
inhabitants. It will, indeed, form a vast storehouse, whence
pious minds can draw fuel to kindle into a purer and brighter
flame their love and their devotion; for thence will they derive new and higher developments of the divine character.
Shall we not, then, admit that to be religious truth on earth
which in heaven will form the food of perfectly holy minds?

The position which I laid down, at the outset, that scientific truth, rightly applied, is religious truth, seems to me most
clearly established. If admitted, there flow from it several
inferences of no small interest, which I am constrained to
present to your consideration.

*In the first place, I infer from this discussion that the prin-
ciples of science are a transcript of the Divine Character.*

I mean by this, that the laws of nature, which are synony-
mous with the principles of science, are not the result of any
arbitrary and special enactment on the part of the Deity, but
flow naturally from his perfections; so that, in fact, the varied
principles of science are but so many expressions of the perfections of Jehovah. If the universe had only a transient

existence, we might suppose the laws that govern it to be the result of a special ordination of the Deity, and destined to perish with the annihilation of matter. But since we have no evidence that matter will ever perish, and at least probable evidence that it will exist forever, the more rational supposition is, that its laws result from the nature of things, and are only a development of so many features of the divine character. If so, then the most important inquiry in the study of the sciences is to learn from them the phases in which they present the divine perfections.

In the second place, it does not follow from this subject that the most extensive acquisitions in science necessarily imply the possession of true piety.

Piety consists in the exercise of right affections of heart towards God, excited by religious truth. Now, I have attempted to show only, that the natural tendency of scientific truth is to excite such religious affections; but that tendency, like all other good influences, may be, and often is, resisted. Hence a man may reach the loftiest pinnacle of scientific glory whose heart has never heaved with one religious emotion. He may penetrate to the very holy of holies in nature's temple, and yet retain his atheism, in spite of the hallowed influences that surround him. Nothing is plainer in theory, and, alas! nothing has been more surely confirmed by experience, than that the possession of science is not the possession of religion.

In the third place, what a perversion of science it is to employ it against religion!

Rightly understood, and fairly interpreted, there is not a single scientific truth that does not harmoniously accord with revealed as well as natural religion; and yet, by superficial minds, almost every one of these principles has, at one time or another, been regarded as in collision with religion, and especially with revelation. One after another have these apparent discrepancies melted away before the clearer light of further examination. And yet, up to the present day, not a few, closing their eyes against the lessons of experience, still fancy that the responses of science are not in unison with those from revelation. But this is a sentiment which finds no place with the profound and unprejudiced philosopher; for he has seen too much of the harmony between the works and the word of God to doubt the identity of their origin. He knows it to be a sad perversion of scientific truth to use it for the discredit of religion. He knows that the inspiration of the Almighty breathed the same spirit into science as into religion; and if they utter discordant tones, it must be because one or the other has been forced to speak in an unnatural dialect.

In the fourth place, how entirely have the natural tendencies of science been misunderstood, when they have been represented as leading to religious scepticism!

I do not deny the fact that many scientific men have been sceptical. But I maintain that this has been in spite of science, rather than the result of its natural tendency; for we have shown that tendency in all cases to be favorable to piety. Other more powerful causes, therefore, must have operated to counteract the natural influence of scientific truth in those cases where men eminent for science have spurned away from them the authority of religion. Among these causes, the pride of knowledge is one of the most powerful; and before the mind has attained to very profound views of science, this pride does often exert a most disastrous influence upon a man's religious feelings.

He is looked up to as an oracle on other subjects, and why

should he not be equally wise concerning religion? It is natural for him to feel desirous, in such circumstances, of rising above all vulgar and superstitious views, and of convincing his fellow-men that he has made as great discoveries in religion as in science. He, therefore, calls in question the prevailing religious opinions. Having once taken his stand against the truth, pride does not allow him to recede, and he endeavors to convert scientific truth into weapons against religion. And this perversion produces the impression, with those not familiar with its natural tendency, that science fosters scepticism.

Another cause of this scepticism is a superficial acquaintance with the religious bearings of scientific truth. It is one thing to master the principles of science in an abstract form, and quite a different thing to understand their religious bearings. Moral reasoning is so different from physical and mathematical, that often a mind which is a prodigy for the latter, is a mere Lilliput in the former. And yet that mind may fancy itself as profound in the one as in the other, and may, therefore, be as tenacious of its errors in religion as of its demonstrated verities in science.

In the following extract it will be seen that Dr. Chalmers imputes the religious scepticism connected with science chiefly to a superficial acquaintance with science. His remarks may seem unreasonably severe and sweeping; nevertheless, they deserve consideration. And they accord with the idea of Lord Bacon, who says, " A smattering of philosophy leads to atheism; whereas a thorough acquaintance with it brings him back again to religion." " We have heard," Dr. Chalmers remarks, " that the study of natural science disposes to infidelity. But we feel persuaded that this is a danger associated only with a slight and partial, never with a

deep, and adequate, and comprehensive, view of its principles.   It is very possible that the conjunction between science
and scepticism may at present be more frequently realized
than in former days ; but this is only because, in spite of all
that is alleged about this our more enlightened day and more
enlightened public, our science is neither so deeply founded,
nor of such firm and thorough staple, as it was wont to be.
We have lost in depth what we have gained in diffusion ;
having neither the massive erudition, nor the gigantic schol-
arship, nor the profound and well-laid philosophy of a period
that has now gone by ; and it is to this that Infidelity stands
indebted for her triumphs among the scoffers and superficial-
ists of a half-learned generation." — *Chalmers's Works*, vol.
vii. p. 262.

Briefly, but nobly, has Sir John Herschel vindicated science
from the charge of sceptical tendencies.   " Nothing can be
more unfounded than the objection which has been taken *in
limine* by persons, well meaning, perhaps, certainly of narrow
minds, against the study of natural philosophy, and, indeed,
against all science, that it fosters in its cultivators an undue
and overweening self-conceit, leads them to doubt the immortality of the soul, and to scoff at revealed religion.   Its natural effect, we may confidently assert, on every well-consti-
tuted mind, is and must be the direct contrary.   No doubt the
testimony of natural reason, on whatever exercised, must, of
course, stop short of those truths which it is the object of
revelation to make known ; but while it places the existence
and principal attributes of a Deity on such grounds as to render doubt absurd, and atheism ridiculous, it unquestionably
opposes no natural or necessary obstacle to further progress ;
on the contrary, by cherishing as a vital principle an unbounded spirit of inquiry and ardency of expectation, it

unfetters the mind from prejudices of every kind, and leaves it open to every impression of a higher nature, which it is susceptible of receiving; guarding only against enthusiasm and self-deception by a habit of strict investigation, but encouraging, rather than suppressing, every thing that can offer a prospect or hope beyond the present obscure and unsatisfactory state. The character of the true philosopher is to hope all things not impossible, and to believe all things not unreasonable." — *Diss. on Study of Nat. Phil.*

In speaking of geology and revelation, Sir John says, " There cannot be two truths in contradiction to one another, and a man must have a mind fitted neither for scientific nor for religious truth, whose religion can be disturbed by geology, or whose geology can be distorted from its character of an inductive science by a determination to accommodate its results to preconceived interpretations of the Mosaic cosmogony." — *Dr. J. P. Smith's Lectures*, p. viii. 4th edition.

" We have often mourned," says M'Cosh, " over the attempts made to set the works of God against the word of God, and thereby excite, propagate, and perpetuate jealousies fitted to separate parties that ought to live in closest union. In particular, we have always regretted that endeavors should have been made to depreciate nature with a view of exalting revelation; it has always appeared to us to be nothing else than the degrading of one part of God's works in the hope thereby of exalting and recommending another." " Perilous as it is at all times for the friends of religion to set themselves against natural science, it is especially dangerous in an age like the present.

" It is no profane work that is engaged in by those who, in all humility, would endeavor to remove jealousies between

parties whom God has joined together, and whom man is not
at liberty to put asunder. We are not lowering the dignity
of science when we command it to do what all the objects
which it looks at and admires do — when we command it to
worship God. Nor are we detracting from the honor which
is due to religion when we press it to take science into its
service, and accept the homage which it is able to pay. We
are seeking to exalt both when we show how nature conducts
man to the threshold of religion, and when from this point we
bid him look abroad on the wide territories of nature. We
would aid at the same time both religion and science, by removing those prejudices against sacred truth which nature has
been employed to foster ; and we would accomplish this not
by casting aside and discarding nature, but by rightly interpreting it.

"Let not science and religion be reckoned as opposing
citadels, frowning defiance upon each other, and their troops
brandishing their armor in hostile attitude. They have too
many common foes, if they would but think of it, in ignorance
and prejudice, in passion and vice, under all their forms, to
admit of their lawfully wasting their strength in a useless
warfare with each other. Science has a foundation, and so
has religion; let them unite their foundations, and the basis
will be broader, and they will be two compartments of one
great fabric reared to the glory of God. Let the one be the
outer and the other the inner court. In the one, let all look,
and admire, and adore ; and in the other, let those who have
faith kneel, and pray, and praise. Let the one be the sanctuary where human learning may present its richest incense
as an offering to God, and the other the holiest of all, separated from it by a veil now rent in twain, and in which, on a

blood-sprinkled mercy-seat, we pour out the love of a reconciled heart, and hear the oracles of the living God."—*Method of the Divine Government*, p. 449, *et seq.*

In the fifth place, scientific men and religious men may learn from this subject to regard each other as engaged in a common cause.

If it be indeed true that scientific truth, rightly applied, is religious truth, then may the religious man be sure that every scientific discovery will ultimately contribute to the illustration of the character or government of the Deity ; and therefore should he encourage and rejoice in all such investigations, and bid God speed to the votaries of science. Even though he cannot see how the new discovery will illustrate religion, and though, when imperfectly developed, it may seem to have an unfavorable aspect, he need not fear to confide in the general principle that science and religion are alike of divine origin, and must be in harmony. On the other hand, the votary of science should remember that the state of society most favorable to his pursuits is one in which religion exerts the strongest influence. It is for his interest, therefore, merely as a lover of science, and much more as a moral and accountable agent, to have pure religion prevail. Scientific and religious men should, therefore, look upon each other as co-laborers in a most noble cause — in illustrating the divine character and government. All jealousy and narrow-minded exclusiveness should be banished, and side by side should they labor in warm-hearted and generous sympathy. Alas ! how different from this has been the history of the past ! and, to a great extent, how different it is at present ! " A study of the natural world," says Professor Sedgwick, " teaches not the truths of revealed religion, nor do the truths of religion inform us of the inductions of physical science. Hence it is that men,

43

whose studies are too much confined to one branch of knowledge, often learn to overrate themselves, and so become narrow minded.   Bigotry is a besetting sin of our nature.   Too
often has it been the attendant of religious zeal; but it is
perhaps the most bitter and unsparing when found among the
irreligious.   A philosopher, not understanding one atom of
their spirit, will sometimes scoff at the labors of religious
men ; and one who calls himself religious will, perhaps,
return a like harsh judgment, and thank God that he is not as
the philosophers ; forgetting, all the while, that man can
ascend to no knowledge except by faculties given to him by
his Creator's hand, and that all natural knowledge is but a
reflection of the will of God.   In harsh judgments, such as
these, there is not only much folly, but much sin.   True wisdom consists in seeing how all the faculties of the mind and
all parts of knowledge bear upon each other, so as to work
together to a common end ; ministering at once to the happiness of man and his Maker's glory." — *Discourse on the
Studies of the University*, 5th edition, p. 105, appendix.

*In the sixth place, the subject shows us what is the most im-
portant use to be derived from science.*

It does not consist, as men have been supposing, in its
application to the useful arts, whereby civilization and human
comfort and happiness are so greatly promoted ; although
men have thereby been raised from a state of barbarism and
advanced to a high point on the scale of refinement.   It is
not the application of science as a means of enlarging and
disciplining the mind ; although this would be a noble result
of scientific study.   But it is its application for the illustration of religion.   This, I say, is its most important use.   For
what higher or nobler purpose can any pursuit subserve than
in developing the character, government, and will of that

infinite Being, who is the sum and centre of all perfection and happiness? Other objects accomplished by science are important, and in the bustle of life they may seem to be its chief end. But in the calmness of mature years, when we begin to estimate things according to their real value, we shall see that the religious bearings of any pursuit far transcend in importance all its other relations; fo all its other tendencies and uses are limited to this world, ano will, therefore, be transient; but every thing which bears the stamp of religion is immortal, and every thing which concerns the Deity is infinite. It is true that but few who are engaged in scientific pursuits make much account of their bearings upon man's highest interests; but very different will it be in heaven. There, so far as we know, all the applications of science to the useful arts will be unknown, and the great object of its cultivation will be to gain new and clearer views of the perfections and plans of Jehovah, and thus to awaken towards him a deeper reverence and a warmer love. And such should be the richest fruit of scientific researches on earth.

In the seventh place, the subject shows us that those who are the most eminent in science ought to be the most eminent in piety.

I am far from maintaining that science is a sufficient guide in religion. On the other hand, if left to itself, as I fully admit, —

"It leads to bewilder, and dazzles to blind."

Nor do I maintain that scientific truth, even when properly appreciated, will compare at all, in its influence upon the human mind, with those peculiar and higher truths disclosed by revelation. All I contend for is, that scientific truth, illustrating as it does the divine character, p'ans, and government, ought to fan and feed the flame of true piety in the hearts of its cultivators. He, therefore, who knows the most of science ought most powerfully to feel this religious influence. He is not confined, like the great mass of men, to the outer court of nature's magnificent temple, but he is admitted to the interior, and allowed to trace its long halls, aisles, and galleries, and gaze upon its lofty domes and arches; nay, as a priest he enters the *penetralia,* the holy of holies, where sacred fire is always burning upon the altars, where hovers the glorious Schekinah, and where, from a full orchestra, the anthem of praise is ever ascending. Petrified, indeed, must be his heart, if it catches none of the inspiration of such a spot. He ought to go forth from it among his fellow-men with radiant glory on his face, like Moses from the holy mount. He who sees most of God in his works ought to show the stamp of divinity upon his character, and lead an eminently holy life.

Finally, the subject gives great interest and dignity to the study of science.

It is not strange that the religious man should sometimes find his ardor damped in the pursuit of some branches of knowledge, by the melancholy reflection that they can be of no use beyond this world, and will exist only as objects of memory in eternity. He may have devoted many a toilsome year to the details and manipulations of the arts; and, so far as this world is concerned, his labors have been eminently salutary and interesting. But all his labors and researches can be of no avail on the other side of the grave; and he cannot but feel sad that so much study and efforts should leave results no more permanent. Or he may have given his best days to loading his memory with those tongues which the Scriptures assure us shall cease; or to those details of material organization which can have no place or antitype in the future world. Interesting, therefore, as such pursuits have been on earth, nay, indispensable as they are to the well being and progress of human society, it is melancholy to realize that they form a part of that knowledge which will vanish away.

The mind delights in the prospect of again turning its attention to those branches of knowledge which have engrossed and interested it on earth, and of doing this under circumstances far more favorable to their investigation. And such an anticipation he may reasonably indulge, who devotes himself on earth to any branch of knowledge not dependent on arrangements and organizations peculiar to this world. He may be confident that he is investigating those principles which will form a part of the science of heaven. Should he ever reach that pure world, he knows that the clogs which now weigh down his mind will drop off, and the clouds that obscure his vision will clear away, and that a brighter sun will pour its radiance upon his path. He is filling his mind with principles that are immortal. He is engaged in pursuits to which glorified and angelic minds are devoting their lofty powers. Other branches of knowledge, highly esteemed among men, shall pass away with the destruction of this world. The baseless hypotheses of science, falsely so called, whether moral, intellectual, or physical, and the airy phantoms of a light and fictitious literature, shall all pass into the limbo of forgetfulness. But the principles of true science, constituting, as they do, the pillars of the universe, shall bear up that universe forever. How many questions of deep interest, respecting his favorite science, must the philosopher in this world leave unanswered, how many points unsettled! But when he stands upon the vantage-ground of another world, all these points shall be seen in the bright transparencies of heaven. In this world, the votaries of science may be

43 *

compared with the aborigines who dwell around some one of the principal sources of the River Amazon. They have been able, perhaps, to trace one or two, or it may be a dozen, of its tributaries, from their commencement in some mountain spring, and to follow them onwards as they enlarge by uniting, so as to bear along the frail canoes, in which, perhaps, they pass a few hundred miles towards the ocean. On the right and on the left, a multitude of other tributaries swell the stream which carries them onward, until it seems to them a mighty river. But they are ignorant of the hundred other tributaries which drain the vast eastern slope of the Andes, and sweep over the wide plains, till their united waters have formed the majestic Amazon. Of that river in its full glory, and especially of the immense ocean that lies beyond, the natives have no conception; unless, perhaps, some individual, more daring than the rest, has floated onward till his aston- ished eye could scarcely discern the shore on either hand, and before him he saw the illimitable Atlantic, whitened by the mariner's sail and the crested waves; and he may have gone back to tell his unbelieving countrymen the marvellous story. Just so is it with men of science. They are able to trace with clearness a few rills of truth from the fountain head, and to follow them onward till they unite in a great principle, which at first men fancy is the chief law of the uni- verse. But as they venture still farther onward, they find new tributary truths coming in on either side, to form a prin- ciple or law still more broad and comprehensive. Yet it is only a few gifted and adventurous minds that are able, from some advanced mountain top, to catch a glimpse of the entire stream of truth, formed by the harmonious union of all prin- ciples, and flowing on majestically into the boundless ocean of all knowledge, the Infinite Mind. But when the Christian philosopher shall be permitted to resume the study of science in a future world, with powers of investigation enlarged and clarified, and all obstacles removed, he will be able to trace onward the various ramifications of truth, till they unite into higher and higher principles, and become one in that centre of centres, the Divine Mind. That is the Ocean from which all truth originally sprang, and to which it ultimately returns. To trace out the shores of that shoreless Sea, to measure its measureless extent, and to fathom its unfathomable depths, will be the noble and the joyous work of eternal ages. And yet eternal ages may pass by and see the work only begun.